The Josephine Baker Story

Printed in the United Kingdom by MPG Books, Bodmin

Published by Sanctuary Publishing Limited, Sanctuary House,
45-53 Sinclair Road, London W14 0NS, United Kingdom

Web site: www.sanctuarypublishing.com

Copyright: Ean Wood, 2000

Photographs: © Pictorial Press, Redferns, Hulton Getty and the private
collection of Bryan Hammond

ISBN: 1-86074-286-6

The Josephine Baker Story

Ean Wood

Also available from Sanctuary Publishing by Ean Wood:

George Gershwin – His Life & Music
Born To Swing – The Story Of The Big Bands

Acknowledgements

In writing this book I have been helped by many people. Some have tracked down books and magazine articles, letters and photographs, recordings and videotapes. Others, who knew Joséphine or saw her perform, have provided me with stories and descriptions that have helped me understand the many facets of this multi-faceted woman.

I am grateful to the authors of three excellent earlier biographies of her. One by Lynn Haney; one by Phyllis Rose; one by Bryan Hammond and Patrick O'Connor.

My personal thanks go to Mike Crowley, Robert Fyson, Bernard Marlowe, Euan Pearson and Tom Vallance. Also to Alyn Shipton, of Bayou Press, for allowing me to quote from the as-yet-unpublished memoirs of the musician Rudolph Dunbar, who worked in Paris during much of the time when Joséphine appeared there; and to Peter Barrett, who was Joséphine's friend for some 16 years. And above all to Myra, for her encouragement, criticism, patience and love.

Ean Wood
London 2000

Contents

Prologue

In the revue *La Folie Du Jour*, at the famous Folies Bergère music hall in Paris, the curtains of the vast stage open to reveal a jungle clearing. Among tall trees with intertwining vines, a French explorer has set up camp. He lies down on a litter to sleep, surrounded by a dozen of his black porters, standing and sitting.

As he sleeps, to the sound of distant drumming music, a young native woman, Fatou, appears, high among the vines in the dim light of the jungle canopy. Crouching and creeping, like a cautious wild animal, she seems inquisitive about the scene below. Pausing in her approach, she sticks her thumbs in her ears and waggles her fingers mockingly. Whatever this strange new situation is, she is confident that she can deal with it.

Gleefully, Fatou runs across the vines to a tall tree at the side of the stage. She climbs swiftly down it and then erupts across the foreground, dropping into an animal crouch and looking alertly this way and that like a creature in unfamiliar surroundings. Above the waist she wears only a few long strings of beads. Her breasts are bare. On each arm are three bracelets – on the upper arm, at the elbow, and on the wrist. From her earlobes hang circular hoops of gold. On her fingers are many rings. Her hair is shaped in the fashionable bob of the day, but it is a heightened, stylised bob. Seeming almost varnished, it hugs her head like a shining black helmet, pointed at the nape of her neck. Not at all like a woman's soft flowing hair, it makes her appear not quite human – a spirit or an animal; a force of nature. On her feet are light sandals, and around her waist is an extraordinary girdle of golden bananas, each hinged loosely at one end to her waistband and otherwise swinging free.

As the whole audience knows, Fatou is the celebrated Joséphine Baker, the toast of Paris, the shocking, amazing "dark star" of the Folies. She is not the nominal star of the show, who is a middle-aged male comic called

Dorville, but such is her personality and impact that, compared to her, he almost fades into insignificance.

It is not simply that she is half naked; nudity has been one of the staple attractions of the Folies for 30 years. It is partly that she is brown-skinned, which to the audience makes her seem exotic, tempestuous and instinctive. Even more it is the speed, agility and strangeness of her dancing, which is unlike anything Paris has ever seen. And perhaps most of all it is the sensuous, witty sparkle of her personality, her being so at ease in her sexuality that she is able to mock it, and to mock her audience for being hypnotised by it. She is all joyous vitality – seductive, admirable and almost frightening.

Springing to her feet, she clasps her hands above her head and begins a fast, primitive dance, her feet hardly moving but her hips shaking rapidly and the bananas of her girdle pulsating. As she dances, she slowly rotates on the spot, turning completely around, and around again. Slender and long waisted, she is so lithe that even her bones seem supple.

Her arm movements become more frantic. Grabbing her right wrist with her left hand, still above her head, she flaps her right hand in a loose, derisive movement. She drops into a half split, her left leg bent, and then rises again, shimmying and dropping first one hand, then the other, to her hips. Facing the audience, she continues to shake her hips, gyrating her pelvis with wild abandon. The bananas flourish around her waist, quivering and jerking. The dance appears instinctive, unplanned. As she herself has said: "I listen to the music and do what it tells me."

Turning suddenly sideways, she freezes, hands on bent knees, head held proudly upright, her bum poked out cheekily towards the sleeping explorer. Her dance is over.

It is 1926, and this is Joséphine, aged 20, at the height of her early success. It was the writer Anita Loos, newly famous as the author of *Gentlemen Prefer Blondes*, who pointed out at the time that she had a cheeky bum.

A more typical member of the audience, at a performance of *La Folie Du Jour*, was a 22-year-old Liverpool University student, Cedric Fyson. On holiday in Paris, he went to the show with his girlfriend and her mother. Later, he wrote in his diary: "Sunday, August 22nd, 1926...took a taxi...to the Folies Bergère...A most extraordinary show, quite coming up to our expectations; a mixture of gorgeous clothing and none at all!! I have to admit that I enjoyed it thoroughly, however, despite the lewdness and vulgarity...Place was packed – indeed we only went on this Sunday afternoon, because the house was full for all the other performances. Of special note were the extraordinary & bizarre dances of a dusky, & very underclad, American girl, Josephine Baker, who appeared to be the star turn."

To the respectable – like young Mr Fyson, who had a strongly non-conformist Unitarian upbringing – she was a wicked excitement. To dancers and choreographers she was a revelation. To artists and photographers she was an exotic new image, a living example of the African art that intrigued them. To poets and café philosophers she was an emblem of instinct made flesh, in touch with the dark subconscious that respectable civilisation had suppressed. To journalists she was a gift. Her constant presence on the social scene, at clubs and restaurants and a thousand glittering occasions, gave rise to a flood of anecdotes and speculation.

And where had she sprung from, this spectacular talent? Well, there was no mystery about that. She was American, born in the southern city of St Louis, Missouri. But she'd come a long way from St Louis.

1 *Meet Me In St Louis*

Josephine was born on 3 June 1906. Her parents were a couple of young would-be entertainers, Carrie MacDonald and Eddie Carson, who had a small song-and-dance act. They were not married, but this was not unusual in the black community of that place and time, where being illegitimate was no great disgrace.

Eddie was a native of St Louis, but Carrie was from South Carolina, 1,000 miles to the south-east. She had come to St Louis two years before, when she was 19, like thousands of others, to find work at the famous World's Fair of 1904. This was the fair that was later featured at the end of the film *Meet Me In St Louis*, and indeed the song of that title was specially written to be the theme song of the fair. But downtown St Louis, where Carrie and Eddie lived and worked, was a lot different from the prosperous middle-class environment portrayed in the film. The run-down housing was grimy, and day and night over the narrow, cobbled, gas-lit streets wafted the stench of the slaughterhouses, tanneries and meat-packing factories, and the sooty grime from the railroads.

But St Louis was a city of character. It had been founded in 1794 as a trading post on a long bend of the Mississippi. In those days, Missouri, like much of the south-eastern USA, belonged to France, and as the town grew, this influenced its character. A French gentleman was judged by the refinement of his servants, so in the days of slavery it was a matter of pride for many owners to see that their slaves were educated. Many could read and write, and if a slave had ability as a craftsman, or sometimes even as an artist – a painter or sculptor – his skills would be encouraged. Some even achieved a broader education by attending their masters on trips to Europe. St Louis therefore became a leading centre of emerging black culture.

By 1803, when France sold its land in America to the United States (all 828,000 square miles of it) in what was known as the Louisiana Purchase, there were some 5,000 blacks in St Louis, comprising both slaves and some free men and women.

The trading post grew into a town, and then a city, and immigrants from other European countries as well as France began to flood into it. Many came from Germany, and others from Spain, Greece, Italy, Syria and the Ukraine. One reason why they chose St Louis was because it was a very desirable place to live. The ground around it was fertile, and it was well served for transport, having not only a growing number of railroads but also the Mississippi, part of that huge network of rivers whose boats linked it to other cities as far apart as Pennsylvania to the north and New Orleans to the south.

These European immigrants tended to have no prejudice against blacks, and indeed many held anti-slavery opinions. They also brought a strong musical tradition to the city. As a result, many blacks studied music formally, in the European tradition, and the standard of black musicianship in St Louis became as high as anywhere in America.

When the Civil War ended in 1865, and the slaves in the southern states were freed, a flood of them emigrated north from the places that had held so much unhappiness. One of the main centres they headed for was St Louis, which had the reputation in the South of much resembling the Promised Land.

Those blacks already living in St Louis before the Civil War tended to be the upper crust of black society there. They were the craftsmen, the best barbers, the best caterers, the most highly-paid servants. They settled on the South Side, living in substantial houses, and even though segregation was the rule in many areas of life in St Louis their children attended both public and parochial schools with the children of whites.

The freed slaves migrating north found less-skilled work as field hands, domestics, dockers and porters, and many of the men worked on building the rapidly-growing railroads, and the biggest railroad junction in America was, of course, St Louis. By 1900, when its famous Union Station was built, 42 railroads met there. Resembling a turreted mediaeval castle of stone, it covered three acres in the heart of downtown St Louis and served more passengers than any other station in the country.

The huge influx of blacks from the South meant that, by 1904, the time of the World's Fair, it was not quite the promised land that it had been. In particular, it was getting harder for unskilled men to find work. White labourers were beginning to resent so many blacks competing for jobs, and this was beginning to lead to tension between the races.

When Carrie MacDonald arrived from South Carolina, she was accompanied by her mother and her elder sister, Elvara. Elvara had lost her husband in the Spanish-American War of 1898, and thus received a small pension from the US Army. It was a very small pension, and they rented an apartment in the poorest part of town, on Lucas Street, in what can only be described as a disease-ridden slum. Its tenements were crammed between smoke-belching factories which made shoes and saddles, carpets and coffins, drugs and buggies, and one of St Louis' most famous exports: German beer.

The MacDonald family was of mixed race, part black and part Apalachee Indian, and Carrie was a good-looking young woman, tall and dark skinned, with high cheekbones, an aristocratic nose and a poised, graceful carriage (which she would pass on to her daughter). To a girl from the rural South, St Louis must have been a bewildering excitement, not to mention the fair, which was the biggest spectacle America had seen since the Chicago World Fair of 1893. Pretty 19-year-old Carrie soon found work as a waitress, and in her free time began to explore the city's exciting night life.

The popular music of the day was ragtime, and St Louis, with its strong musical tradition, had the best ragtime players in the world. Originally developed informally by itinerant Midwestern pianists, and later formalised by trained composer/pianists like Tom Turpin and Scott Joplin and eventually arranged for orchestras, during the 1890s ragtime became widely popular all over America.

St Louis was therefore alive with music, and in response to the music came dance, and Carrie was an exceptionally good amateur dancer.

The most popular dance of the day in the southern states was the cakewalk. This had a long history, part of its origin being the walk around, the traditional big finale of the minstrel show, in which couples would promenade and dance in a circle, competing to improvise fancy steps, and this in turn developed from the ring dance, the folk dance of the southern plantations, which was similarly competitive.

An important element of the cakewalk – which the walk around did not usually have – was its distinctive strutting step. This was said to have also developed on the southern plantations as a game of mocking the white folks in their grand ballrooms, dancing minuets or grand marches, although those same white folks, seeing such dancing, generally assumed that it was the way it was because blacks did not know how to dance properly, missing the mockery.

It was called the cakewalk because the prize for the best dancers would quite often be a cake, and one variation on it – also dating back to slave days – was known as the chalk-line walk, where dancers danced along a twisting chalked line with glasses of water on their heads. The couple that stayed the most erect and spilled the least water were declared the winners.

Carrie was a popular partner in this version of the cakewalk. She could dance along the line with a glass of water balanced on her head and never spill a drop, even once when she was seven months pregnant. Not only was she pretty and lively, and a good dancer, but she was also attracted to performing. Although she would never have the stage presence of a born performer, she took to acting in amateur theatricals, and it was at the Gaiety Theater, when both were cast as natives in "A Trip to Africa", that she met Eddie Carson.

Eddie, a fast-talking and sharply-dressed young man, was short, vivacious and olive skinned, and known locally as a "spinach" – a name which implied that he had some Spanish blood. A sparkling personality, he made a fair living as a musician, a drummer who played in street parades, at picnics and funerals, and in the saloons, brothels and vaudeville houses of St Louis' notorious Chestnut Valley, a red light district near Union Station. Chestnut Valley's main arteries were Chestnut Street and Market Street, and both were honeycombed with honky-tonks, with gambling halls featuring the simple games of faro and chuck-a-luck, and with barrel houses serving nickel shots of liquor.

The barrel house was the basic building of such districts, like New Orleans' Storyville, New York's Tenderloin and San Francisco's Barbary Coast. It was probably in San Francisco that they originated, during the Gold Rush of 1849. Starting out as simple shacks with a bar that was often just a plank of wood across two barrels, they soon developed a standard layout: a saloon with dancing downstairs and rooms for whores upstairs. In the saloon, hostesses would dance with the customers in order to get them into the mood to visit the other girls upstairs. (As well as bringing more conventional workers to St Louis, the steamboats coming north up the Mississippi brought a steady supply of whores and hostesses, many of them the sought-after light-skinned quadroons and octoroons.)

Eddie Carson enjoyed hanging out in pool halls and bars, but, despite his love of the sporting life, he never stopped trying to better himself. As well as having become a proficient drummer, once described as "the best parade drummer in St Louis", he also had ambitions to become a professional singer and dancer.

There was a dancing school in St Louis called Professor Julius Caesar Lucky's Dance Academy, which held a social every Friday night. Eddie agreed to play drums at these socials for nothing in return for free dancing lessons. He quickly became so proficient that Professor Lucky gave him work as a teacher, teaching the formal dances of the day: the grand square, the imperial, the parisian, the lancers, the waltz, the schottische and, of course, the cakewalk.

Carrie was swept off her feet by the exciting, handsome, dynamic Eddie, and it wasn't long before they decided to become a song-and-dance act, with routines devised by Eddie, and look for whatever work they could find in cheap and primitive vaudeville houses, bars, restaurants or wherever would employ them.

About a year after they met, along came Josephine – or, to give her her full name, Josephine Freda MacDonald. She was a plump baby, which caused Carrie to nickname her "Humpty Dumpty". This in time – possibly from Josephine's own childish mispronunciation – evolved into "Tumpie", a name which many of her St Louis contemporaries continued to use all through her childhood, and in some cases, when referring to her, all her life.

At this time Carrie was still living with her mother and her sister, Elvara, on Lucas Street. Naturally, she had to give up dancing towards the end of her pregnancy, and so Eddie took to working as the drummer in a trio. Restless and ambitious, and only a little older than Carrie herself, he wasn't yet ready to become a family man. He wanted Carrie to be free to continue their exciting night life. So although at first she often took her new baby to whatever wine room or vaudeville house at which the trio was working, just to be near her man, more and more often she took to leaving Josephine at home with her mother and her sister, Elvara.

After a while Carrie and Eddie resumed their song-and-dance act, playing wherever they could get work, and when Josephine was about a year old they began to carry her onstage occasionally during their finale.

In October 1907, when Josephine was 16 months old, Carrie produced a son, Richard. Eddie was again the father, but Richard's arrival was more than he was ready to take. He rapidly drifted away from Carrie. Their act folded, and poor Carrie lost at once her lover and her small career in entertainment. She didn't have the pep and drive – or, indeed, the real ambition – to make it on her own. Eddie had been her ticket into that glamorous world, and without him she was on the outside looking in.

She took it out on Josephine, not on the new baby, Richard. This was possibly because, much more than Richard, Josephine resembled her father. Her oval face, her prominent flashing teeth and her pert nose all came from Eddie. She also inherited his vivacious temperament and his talent for music. What she got from Carrie was resilience and courage, a capacity for hard work and a grim determination to survive.

Grim is the word for what Carrie became. Eddie's departure signalled the end of her youth. She became a demanding, disapproving mother, drudging to support her young family, cleaning and laundering and doing whatever menial job came her way. Although her carriage remained defiantly upright, her face became taut and unsmiling, certainly as far as Josephine was concerned. As Josephine said bitterly, much later in her life, "Richard was the child that was wanted."

On another occasion, she recalled: "Mama said things to me I'm sure she couldn't mean, that she hated me and wished I were dead." Such were among her earliest conscious memories: the feeling of unwantedness, the grinding poverty, and the missing father, because after Eddie drifted out of Carrie's life she would never again allow him to set foot in the house to see his children.

Josephine felt his absence keenly, and in books and interviews after she became famous she would invent fantasy fathers. At various times, she claimed that her father had been "a white boy who went to school with Mama", "a Spanish dancer", "a Jewish tailor", and "a Creole from New Orleans". Most often she chose to make him Jewish because, unable all her life to lose her feeling of being oppressed, she identified with the struggle of the Jews against oppression.

When Josephine was five, Carrie married Arthur Martin, a tall, hulking, dark-skinned man who was short tempered but not unkind. In her new life as Mrs Martin, Carrie moved out from Lucas Street with her two children to set up home with Arthur. However, they didn't have much in the way of a home. In their poverty they lived more or less like vagabonds, moving from one filthy hovel to another, sometimes being evicted for not paying their rent, and sometimes skipping out before that would happen. This rootlessness affected Josephine. The idea of home became important to her, and would remain so all her life. She came to view home as a fortress in a hostile world.

Part of the problem was that Arthur was an unskilled labourer. Work for unskilled men was not as plentiful as it had been a few years earlier, and the continuing flood of blacks coming from the South meant that there were more men seeking less work, and so Arthur was usually unemployed. Meanwhile, Carrie continued to take in laundry.

Arthur adopted Josephine and her brother, Richard, at least informally. What actually happened was that Carrie paid a few dollars to Sister Emma, a neighbour and friend who was a notary public, to stamp a piece of paper stipulating that Arthur was their father. Richard accepted him as such, but Josephine never did, although she liked him. He was not her father, and he was nothing like the sort of man she might have wished for a father.

He and Carrie soon produced two more children, both girls: Margaret and Willie Mae. Josephine became as intensely jealous of Margaret as she had been of Richard since his birth, but she loved Willie Mae. This was possibly because Willie Mae was a lot like herself. She was feisty, like Josephine, early to talk and quick to learn. When she was still quite young, the family dog clawed her, leaving her blind in one eye. This aroused all of Josephine's protective instincts, and her affection for Willie Mae grew even deeper.

Arthur Martin was darker than Eddie had been, and so his two children were darker than Josephine, as was Richard. This, coupled with her mother's stern disapproval, if not dislike, made her feel an outsider in the family.

Arthur continued to spend long hours queueing for work. At one time, things seemed to be looking up when he got a job in a foundry. However, although it was a regular job, it was far from ideal. The foundry was ten miles from their home and Arthur was put on a late shift, which meant that he often missed the last trolley and had to walk home. Unable to afford decent boots, when it was snowy on such nights he wrapped his shoes in newspapers, which he tied around his ankles. St Louis can be bitterly cold in winter, and indeed Josephine always remembered it as a cold city. She once claimed that the original reason why she started dancing was to keep warm.

The endless moving from house to house stopped when the family moved into a house on Gratiot Street, which they shared with another family. Gratiot Street, in the shadow of Union Station, was lined with brick

houses built by German immigrants, mostly in the 1850s. The simple, dignified façades, which were crumbling by the time Josephine lived there, still
had some of their original beauty, but the ricketty back porches were broken and ugly, and they overlooked filthy, foul-smelling courtyards strung
with the laundry of the poor.

The Martins had two rooms of the house in which to live. There was no
gas or electricity. In the evening, the rooms were lit by benzene lamps and
the room in which they lived was heated by a fire in a metal barrel. For
added insulation, and to cover up cracks, Arthur papered the walls with
newspaper. Water for cooking came from a communal tap in the hall. The
toilet was in the back yard, covered by a draughty shed. They bathed in a
laundry tub, and Josephine, as the eldest child, got the water last, after it
had been used by her mother, her stepfather, her brother and her half-sisters. Like all of the places in which they lived, the house was cold and full
of bugs, rats and smells. Arthur had a habit of putting his feet up on the
table, and when he did the smell was so bad that Josephine recalled that she
would have run from the room, except that it was usually freezing outside.

At least at Gratiot Street the children had a bed to themselves. In one
place in which they'd lived the whole family had had to sleep in one bed, the
children at the foot and Carrie and Arthur at the head with their feet in the
children's faces. Sometimes, to get away from the bedbugs and the smell of
her stepfather's feet, Josephine slept on the floor wrapped up in newspapers.

In Gratiot Street, however, Carrie and Arthur slept in one of their two
rooms, with the children in the other, but even here their thin and bumpy
mattress was alive with bugs. Twice a year Josephine and Richard used to
drag the bedsprings into the yard, soak them with oil and set them alight
to kill the bugs' eggs.

This didn't really do much good, but even worse than the bugs were the
rats. At night, their bed – even as infested as it was – was an island of safety. The wooden floors had holes through which that the rats came up.
Whenever they had an empty chili or tomato can they nailed it over one of
the holes, but the rats bit and clawed their way around the tins, invading
the bedroom and scampering across the floor, heading for the kitchen,
where they looked for food or poked around in closets, gathering papers
and rags for their nests. Richard, sitting up in bed, would try to pick them
off with a slingshot.

Then Arthur lost his job at the foundry. As Richard later explained,

"One time his boss underpaid him five cents. When he counted his money, and saw he'd been shortchanged, he ran back to the office and punched his boss. The police took him to jail. After his release, he was out of a job for a long time. Everybody said he was crazy for beatin' up his boss, but five cents could buy you a lot to eat in those days."

Thrown out of work, Arthur's fiery temper got worse for a while. On one occasion Carrie overcooked the hot dogs for his supper, and he grabbed up the whole lot and tried to cram them down her throat, choking her until she managed to wrestle free. But gradually he sank into a depression that, while worse for everybody, was at least less violent.

Not that Carrie couldn't be as violent as Arthur, albeit in a colder, sterner way. Once, when Richard took somebody's bicycle, she tied him up and beat him so fiercely that Josephine and Margaret begged her to stop. She said that she'd rather beat him herself, even risk killing him, than have him beaten and maybe killed by white men.

Happy to escape from Gratiot Street as much as she could, Josephine took to living for a lot of the time back on Lucas Street with her grandmother and her Aunt Elvara. Elvara was a formidable woman, as severe in her way as her sister Carrie had become. She was given to sudden, wild rages, and was fiercely proud of her Apalachee blood. Both Elvara and her mother, Josephine's grandmother, looked noticeably Indian, and Elvara looked down on Josephine's brother and half-sisters for being too black. (This was the opposite of her mother's feelings, that Josephine's skin was too light and too much like her father's.)

But even though she was her aunt's favourite, she was afraid of her aunt's rages. She felt closer to her grandmother, a plump, maternal woman with big, sad eyes. Almost all of the love that Josephine felt in her unhappy childhood came from her grandmother, who would bake cornbread, spread it with jelly and give it to Josephine, telling her stories. Her grandmother loved telling stories, and Josephine loved hearing them.

Perching the little girl on her lap, her grandmother would tell her of Little Red Riding Hood, of the Three Little Pigs, and of Snow White. She would tell her darker stories about the days of slavery, and of her own great-great-grandparents, who were brought against their will from their home in a faraway place. She sang songs and hymns which promised freedom after oppression, release after constraint, joy after grief, and told her stories from the Bible which carried the same message.

But the story which Josephine liked the best, the one which made the deepest impression, was that of Cinderella. The image of the young girl alone among the ashes seemed to reflect her own situation, and the message that Cinderella could achieve success and freedom through her own efforts, without even the help of Prince Charming, gave her real moral support. In a way, it seemed to make the same point as the Bible stories of Christ's crucifixion and resurrection, that pain, hard work and sacrifice will lead to triumph.

But somehow she found the Cinderella story more satisfying. Life in a palace with glamorous clothes, rich jewels and elaborate meals seemed more congenial to her than anything she had heard of heaven.

Josephine was always poorly dressed and hungry, and her playground became the yards of the great Union Station, looming above Gratiot Street. There, where everything was grimy from soot and cinders, she and her brother Richard would play among the wagons and watch the heavy, clanking freight trains and the great, gleaming expresses as they thundered through.

By the age of six, she was already street smart. Often before dawn, Arthur Martin would take her the two-mile walk to the Soulard Market, the city's great fruit and vegetable market, to scavenge for food. The market was in huge open-air sheds, covering half a city block, where every day farmers with horse-drawn wagons would bring their crops for sale. The sheds were crammed with stalls, and these would overflow with fresh vegetables: cabbages and potatoes, turnips and broccoli, squash and carrots.

Josephine loved the life and bustle of the market. Scrambling under the stalls she would scavenge for bruised and damaged fruit and vegetables. Soon she became well known to the stallholders, who were amused by her industry and beguiled by her charm. (She had already learned to use charm to get what she wanted.) They rewarded her with presents of fresh apples, oranges, apricots.

She and Richard also learned to earn pennies by picking up lumps of coal from the railway freight yards and selling them. It was common for poor families to send their children to do this, their theory being that the police would not prosecute children for minor offences. When she got a little older, Josephine improved on this by stealing coal from the wagons themselves. Daring and agile, she would climb up and throw down lumps of coal to Richard, Margaret and Willie Mae, who waited below.

When she was six, Carrie enrolled her at Lincoln School, where she started at first grade. It was only a short walk from Gratiot Street, because to get there Josephine could cut across a steel footbridge spanning the tracks out of Union Station. A squat brick building with overcrowded classrooms and a small playground, it catered to poor and middle-income blacks, and Josephine was among the poorest of the poor. At one time she wore the same clothes to school every day for a year, a blue middy dress trimmed in white. She often went barefoot, but at one time somebody gave the family a pair of cast-off high-heeled shoes. They must have belonged to someone with very small feet, because Arthur was able to cut off the heels and give them to Josephine to wear. The uneven soles gave her an unsteady gait, and with the heels cut off the toes stuck up, all of which made the other children laugh at her.

In defence, she took to mocking them (and herself) by pulling faces, sticking out her tongue or crossing her eyes or giving a big, goofy grin. Hating school, she became extremely disruptive. She missed the exciting life of the streets, and hated the discipline of the classroom. She said later: "I detested being told to do this and do that. I always preferred my liberty. And the teacher tried to get me to stop making faces. The face isn't meant for sleeping. Why not make faces?"

But school did have one or two small pleasures for her. In her history books, she found pictures of kings and queens in sumptuous costumes which mingled in her mind with the story of Cinderella and fed her imagination. Also, from time to time she saw her father, Eddie. Banned by Carrie from visiting his children at their home, when he heard that Josephine was at Lincoln School he took to hanging around outside the rusty wire fence of the playground and waiting for her to come out at recess. Josephine – who had hardly any memory of him – was wary, but of course accepted the sweets he took to slipping through the fence to her.

She also made a friend. The McDuffy's lived in a house behind the one in which the Martins lived. Joyce McDuffy was about the same age as Josephine, and they took to walking to and from school together over the iron footbridge and playing together during recess.

Joyce adored Josephine but found her company sometimes embarrassing. As she remembered, years later, "Tumpie was always needlin' people. She'd poke the kids and stick out her tongue at them. And Tumpie was dirty. I used to try to get her to clean herself up, but it didn't do no good.

She was much too fidgety. She'd wash half her face and forget to wash the other half." Many of the other girls would laugh at her because of her griminess, which may have stemmed from either low self-esteem or rebelliousness – or, more probably, both.

At around this time, when Joyce and Josephine were seven, a small black vaudeville house, the Booker T Washington, had recently opened in Chestnut Valley, on the corner of 23rd Street and Market Street. Its owner was Charlie Turpin, brother of the great ragtime pioneer Tom Turpin. Every week he ran a different show with a different theme – African, cowboy, Egyptian, and so on – and he managed to attract some of the best black talent of the time. Blues singers Ma Rainey and Ida Cox, the young Bessie Smith and the comedy team of Butterbeans And Susie all played there.

Joyce McDuffy had an elder brother, Robert, who was then aged twelve and was casting about for ideas to make some extra pocket money. With the excitement of the new vaudeville house in his mind, and with amazing enterprise, he hit on the idea of putting on shows for neighbourhood children in the family basement. He fitted out the basement with orange crates for seats, used candles in tin cans for lights, and constructed a multi-coloured curtain out of dozens of pieces of cast-off cloth. Meanwhile, every week he went to the Booker T Washington to spot professional routines that he could scale down for his amateur theatre. He called his productions "McDuffy's Pin And Penny Poppy Shows" because he charged either a penny or a pin (the pins being helpful in holding together his costumes) for admission. His chorus line boasted only two girls: his sister, Joyce, and Josephine.

Joyce remembered: "He was our flim-flam man. He was the big producer who put together the acts and collected the money. Tumpie and I didn't get nothin' for bein' in the show, but we loved it. We both kinda had it in our minds to grow up to be dancers."

At that time any thought of a full-time professional career in dancing would probably have been beyond Josephine's conception, even as an escape from her life of deprivation, but it is certainly true that she fell in love with the joy of dancing, and of performing. While appearing in the Pin And Penny shows she took to performing for the Martins in their own basement, making entrances down the cellar steps as if she were the star of a spectacular show – or, rather, making the same entrance again and again. Her brother Richard remarked rather grudgingly later in life: "She never changed her act."

St Louis in 1913 was a good place and time to decide to become a dancer. Even in the seven short years of Josephine's life, music and dance in St Louis had moved on and was continuing to move on fast, and a big influence on the music came from the riverboats. In the years before the Civil War, these had provided the main transportation for goods and passengers into and out of St Louis. However, the war put a stop to most of the Mississippi traffic for the five years it lasted, and after the war the growing railroads took away most of the trade. What goods there were on the river were now mostly towed in strings of barges behind tugs.

One of the main owners of the big riverboats was Captain Joseph Strekfus, who came from a German St Louis family. Seeing the decline in freight traffic, he decided to devote his boats to excursions, to turn them into showboats. Each of his boats had a resident band, mostly of black St Louis musicians, and in around 1910 he decided that he wanted not only musicians on his boats who could read music (as all respectable St Louis musicians, black and white, could do) but also those who had more life and rhythm in their playing. In particular he was looking towards New Orleans, at the mouth of the river, where he had heard that there was a music being developed that had a new drive and vitality. (It was not yet known as jazz.)

He appointed one of his bandleaders, Fate Marable, to be his chief talent spotter, and soon the boats of the Strekfus Line were bringing hot New Orleans musicians up the river to St Louis. Many famous names did spells in these bands, including clarinetist Johnny Dodds and his brother, the drummer Baby Dodds, bassist Pops Foster and, in 1919, Louis Armstrong. All of them learnt St Louis musical discipline from the disciplinarian Fate Marable, and St Louis musicians learnt to play with more fire and a looser, more complex rhythm.

This was reflected in the dances of the day, and by 1913, when Josephine was seven, America had gone dance crazy. In New York, tea dances had become the rage of high society, led by Vernon and Irene Castle, who virtually invented ballroom dancing. Such was the enthusiasm for dancing that it was estimated that, during the years from 1912 to 1914, over 100 new ballroom dances were invented.

But what the white patrons of New York's ballrooms mostly didn't realise was that most of these dances were smoothed-out versions of black vernacular dances from the southern and western USA, from cities like St Louis.

Dances came into town, or were invented right there, and were the rage for a moment before something new came along. Dancing anywhere she could find, in the streets or the yards or the houses around her, Josephine mastered step after step after step. Later in life she claimed that she learned to dance by watching the kangaroos in the St Louis Zoo, and this may have a grain of truth in it because many of the black dances of the day were based on imitating animal movements, such as the camel walk, the eagle rock, the turkey trot, the goose neck, the bunny hug, the crab step, the fish tail, the chicken scratch, the rooster strut, pecking, the kangaroo dip, the buzzard lope and the grizzly bear. ("It's a bear, it's a bear, it's a bear.") Such mimicking dances can be traced all the way back to Africa.

Other dances mimicked human movements – for instance the itch, break a leg, the pimp walk and through the trenches, which emerged after the Great War and imitated soldiers crouching to avoid sniper fire.

Some were frankly sexy, such as the shimmy, the snake hips, the black bottom, the grind and the mess around, and others were simply interesting or difficult or expressive or just good fun, with names that may or may not mean anything, including tack annie, trucking, the pasmala, the chugg, the slop and crossfire. Over the next few years, Josephine learned every dance that came her way, building up for herself a huge repertoire of practised steps.

It was a good job that she had (and would always have) a torrent of energy because her day-to-day life remained unremittingly hard. Her mother expected all of her children to contribute to the family's support, and always let Josephine know that, as the eldest, more was expected of her.

One day, when she was eight, Carrie announced that she had found her a job. She was to be a maid-of-all-work for a Mrs Keiser, a widow who lived alone. Josephine was to go and live at Mrs Keiser's house, and was terrified at being sent to live with a stranger. She wrote later: "I would have loved to run away but knew it was useless because I was too small."

At first Mrs Keiser seemed kind. She bought Josephine a dress and a pair of shoes. But that was as far as the kindness went. Josephine was made to sleep in the cellar with Mrs Keiser's dog, alongside piles of wood and coal, and every morning at five she was expected to get up and perform a succession of chores. She had to light the fire, peel the potatoes, empty the chamber pots, scrub the steps and sweep the rooms, and once a week she had to do the washing. Then she would set off for Lincoln School, because at the age of eight attending school was still a legal requirement.

What made everything worse was that Mrs Keiser was a bully. If Josephine made the slightest mistake she would be slapped around, and if she was late getting up Mrs Keiser would pull her out of bed by the ears and give her a beating. Losing her appetite from terror and depression, she took to giving half of her food to the dog and grew painfully thin. Gone was the chubby Tumpie of her babyhood.

Having already learned in life to be mistrustful of people, she had begun her lifelong habit of showering affection on animals, and the dog became her friend. What brought out her affection even more strongly was that he was crippled, having been hit by a car that permanently damaged his left hind leg. She named him "Three Legs".

Another creature in the house was a white rooster, who lived in a cage tucked under her work table. She named him Tiny Tim, and for months she fed and fattened him, talking to him as she worked, until one day Mrs Keiser told her: "Kill him. He's ready to be eaten." Josephine went numb with shock and distress. Obediently, she gripped her friend between her knees, stretching his neck downwards and cutting at it with a pair of scissors until the blood rushed out down her legs. She kept her grip on him until he stopped twitching, holding her breath so as not to smell the blood. Then she kissed him, plucked him, and handed him to Mrs Keiser.

At this horrible time, even school became a haven for her. She stared for longer than ever at the kings and queens in her history books, at the carriages in which they rode and the jewels they wore, the rubies and sapphires. She began to fantasise at school, and in her cellar bed at night, imagining queens (who were really herself) on thrones, issuing commands and dubbing knights. "All my queens were blonde," she wrote later. "I could see them walking step after step after step." It is interesting that she saw them endlessly walking because real queens would be going to some sort of place she did not know. All she could do was to let them go through a door and close it. She could not take the fantasy any further because she knew no further from her life.

Release from Mrs Keiser came suddenly and painfully. One day she let a pot boil over on the stove and Mrs Keiser took her hand and shoved it into the boiling water to punish her. Tearing herself free, Josephine rushed to the woman next door, howling with pain. The skin was already peeling from her hand, and when the neighbour took her in her arms she passed out from the pain. She woke up in a hospital bed to find her mother there with a doctor and a nurse. Carrie took her home, and that was the end of Mrs Keiser. But very soon she found another household that would give Josephine room and board in exchange for housework.

This time it was the home of a married couple, a Mr and Mrs Mason, and they were kind. Mrs Mason bought her clothes and fed her well enough so that she began to fatten up a little, and even made sure that she had time from her chores to play. Mr Mason was kind, too; in fact he became so fond of Josephine that Mrs Mason decided that it would be better if she were sent back home. Even in St Louis in 1914, eight was a little young. Not that anything untoward actually happened, but it was an early sign that Josephine was growing into an attractive young lady. This, too, she would learn to use, as well as to fear in a way.

After those two live-in jobs, Josephine set about hustling for jobs of her own choosing. She took to organising groups of children from her neighbourhood to go across town to where the rich white folks lived. There they would go from door to door offering to do anything that needed doing: washing floors, running errands, scrubbing stoops, minding babies, waxing furniture, shovelling snow – anything.

This went on for years, and she became adept at handling her problem, which was that she was so skinny and frail-looking that people were often reluctant to hire her. When that happened, she would flash her winning smile and say: "Oh, I know I'm small, but I'm really 15." Often it worked. On good days she reckoned that she could make 50 cents, of which she would contribute 45 to the Martin family budget. On bad days, when no work presented itself, she would lead the other children in scavenging in the rich folks' garbage.

Arthur Martin was by now becoming depressed at his inability to find work, and the more depressed he got the harder work was to find. He took to spending more and more time at home instead of out job hunting. Then he started spending most of his time in bed, and eventually he drifted off into a sort of madness. Fortunately, Carrie – toiling grimly to keep the household fed and housed – managed to land a steady job in a laundry run by Arthur's sister, and this allowed the family to move to a bigger house that even had a proper kitchen. It wasn't far away, at 2632 Bernard Street.

This was not lost on Josephine. Just as her father's absence had given her a mistrust of men, so did Arthur's inability to cope. In all of her life she never totally relied on any man. With her mother's example before her, she relied on herself.

One day in 1916, when she was ten, something happened that would influence her whole life. Down the cobbled streets of the neighbourhood came a travelling medicine man driving a brightly-coloured gypsy caravan. Such characters were common in the poorer parts of America at that time and earlier, when real medicines were expensive and many people were ill or had aches and pains. They were the sort of characters often played by WC Fields in his films, and indeed the great pianist/composer/bandleader Jelly Roll Morton once became one briefly in real life, selling a mixture of salt and Coca Cola that he and his companion swore would cure TB.

That was a small operation, but this medicine man visiting St Louis was something special. As well as his caravan, he had a portable stage which he set up not far from Bernard Street, and in order to attract customers for his "medicines" he organised an informal vaudeville show, at which local amateurs could appear, backed by a locally-recruited jug band, which was a novelty band common in black America in the early years of the century, using such cheap instruments as kazoos, harmonicas and maybe a guitar or fiddle, and with the bass notes provided by someone blowing into a jug.

As darkness fell that night, the medicine man lit kerosene torches to light his stage and announced that the show would now commence, and was entirely free. He was a white man, dressed as a typical southern gentleman, wearing a stetson hat, a pointed grey beard and a grave Prince Albert coat adorned with medals awarded to him "by the crowned heads of Europe, Asia, Africa and Australia".

Josephine, among the crowd, gazed at him, entranced. And she continued to be entranced as act followed rough-and-ready act. Then the medicine man announced that the next item on the bill would be a dance contest. Flooded with excitement, Josephine jumped up onto the stage and, as the jug band pumped out its crude country jazz, she threw her arms to the skies and kicked her legs in a succession of different dance steps, one after the other, exactly as the mood took her.

The audience laughed and cheered and slapped their thighs, and when the number finished they clapped and whistled, and the medicine man patted her on the head and awarded her a crisp new dollar bill.

This struck her with the force of a revelation. For the first time in her young life she had earned money for something that was not drudgery.

Racing home to Bernard Street, she cried out: "Mama! Mama! I won first prize for dancing!" After all, no matter how much her hard life had forced her to grow up, she was still only ten; and no matter how stern and even hostile Carrie had become, she was still Josephine's mother, and Josephine still yearned for her approval.

2 *"Just Look At That Child Shuffle!"*

In the same year that Josephine won her dollar for dancing, her Aunt Elvara died. As was the custom, her body was laid out in her coffin to be viewed by mourners, and Josephine later recalled being afraid to look at her, never having seen a dead person before. But her grandmother reassured her, and said: "There's more to fear from the living than from the dead, child."

If Josephine had ever doubted her grandmother's remark, it wasn't long before she would have dramatic confirmation of its truth, for in the very next year an event took place that coloured her life for ever, an event so shocking that in many of the accounts she gave of her life she began with it, as if all of her life dated from that moment. It was the East St Louis race riot of 1917.

East St Louis is sited opposite St Louis, on the Illinois bank of the Mississippi, the two towns linked by several bridges. In 1917, East St Louis was mostly a choking, industrial wasteland, grimy and smoke polluted, and sliced across by railroad lines. Much of the industry was meat related, with stockyards, slaughterhouses, packing plants and tanneries, but there were also aluminium smelters, breweries and chemical factories.

The housing was cramped and often poor. During the years since the turn of the century, East St Louis' black population had trebled, and so the poorer areas of the town were seriously overcrowded. Many blacks lived in wooden shacks or derelict boxcars, and they had begun to compete vigorously for the jobs available, just as they did in St Louis.

Attitudes were becoming aggressive and strained. Blacks were starting to campaign for their rights as free men, and whites – especially those among the labouring classes – were becoming increasingly fearful for their jobs and fearful that employers would take advantage of the situation to depress wages. The town was almost entirely segregated, and there was little social interaction between the two sides, who viewed each other from a distance with suspicion and growing hostility.

The usual rumours began to spread among the white population. Blacks were said to be arming themselves with guns and knives and invading white neighbourhoods intent on theft, rape and murder. These rumours were circulated during two election campaigns by not-always-truthful newspapers and by political agitators. Tension had been building up over months, if not years, and at the beginning of July 1917 the situation exploded in violence.

During the night of 1 July, mobs of armed whites invaded black districts, beating up the residents and smashing their homes. This was bad enough, but on the night of 2 July things grew much worse. There were more white mobs, many more homes were looted and whole neighbourhoods were set on fire. Fleeing blacks were not only savagely beaten but were in many cases shot or lynched. White children and young men and women stood by and cheered, often joining in the violence. In one case, a corpse was strung up on a telegraph pole by a group who shouted "Get hold and pull for East St Louis" as they hauled on the rope.

When it was all over, a Congressional Investigating Committee reported that "at least eight whites and 39 negroes were killed". (The black rights organisation the NAACP estimated the number at nearer 100). It was the worst race riot in American history.

Some blacks had tried to fight back, but many more fled. Fifteen hundred of them, pursued by their attackers, made their way across the Eads Bridge to St Louis. Mothers carried infants so that their men could use baby carriages to ferry the aged and infirm, and a few pitiful possessions, to safety. Children carried household pets.

Among the St Louis residents gathered at the west end of the bridge to watch the fleeing and panic-stricken hordes was the eleven-year-old Josephine, huddled with other children "behind the skirts of grown-ups, frightened to death". The riot so seared into her memory that she recounted it again and again over the rest of her life, her imagination heightening the story with incidents she had heard about and pictured so vividly that she came to believe that she had seen them.

For instance, 47 years later, when interviewed by Dotson Rader for *Esquire* magazine, she said: "East St Louis was a horrible place, yes, worse than the Deep South. I was a little girl, and all I remember is people. They ran across the bridge from East St Louis to escape the rednecks, the whites killing and beating them. I never forget my people screaming, a friend of my father's face shot off, a pregnant woman cut open. I see them running to get to the bridge. I have been running ever since."

Looking across the river, she saw the firelit smoke pouring up into the night sky from the burning buildings, and for ever afterwards she firmly believed that in it she saw a vision of God. She even heard a voice telling her "It's our Heavenly Father." (Seeing visions was not uncommon in the more enthusiastic black churches of the South, and although Josephine was raised as a Baptist she preferred from her childhood to go to the services of the Holy Rollers, which had more music and movement and were generally more ecstatic.)

To aid the fugitives, the Red Cross in St Louis set up a relief centre, providing food, clothing and shelter. It was at the Municipal Lodging House on South Twelfth Street, and because it was impossible for harassed officials to tell fugitives from St Louis residents many opportunists were able to stand in line and receive hand-outs. Josephine, of course, was among them.

The riot changed the feeling between the races in St Louis. Before it, in spite of the segregation, there had been a certain ease between blacks and whites. For years after it, however, blacks felt a perpetual undercurrent of dread, and on both sides there was an atmosphere of unease in which rumours flourished.

The riot reinforced Josephine's growing determination to escape. A sense of physical danger and a fear of homelessness was now added to all of her other insecurities. It was bad enough that her mother had twice sent her away from home to work; now it seemed that gangs of white racists could render you homeless by burning your home to the ground.

She was not sure at this point whether escape meant from her family or from St Louis, and she was not sure how. The one bright area in her life was her love of music and dancing. The city was still alive with music. New dance steps kept coming along for her to learn, and with a nationwide songwriting boom now in full swing there were always new songs, which she enjoyed singing. But as she approached her teens, she had no real hope that this would lead to anything in the way of a new life.

As she began growing from a little girl into a woman, her mother's attitude hardened further. Carrie's disappointment at the way her own life had turned out expressed itself in jealousy of her lively and likeable daughter. She began manipulating Josephine's craving for her approval by capriciously giving or withholding love, which drove her daughter into a state of needy dependence. Again and again she tried to win her mother's approval, by earning money for the household with odd jobs or by showing her a new dance step she had learned, and again and again Carrie was critical or dismissive. At the same time she let Josephine know that, as her oldest child, she must be the major breadwinner in the family after herself. And Josephine indeed worked hard, as she would at everything for all of her life. She was practical and warm hearted, and so her brother and half-sisters began turning to her for advice and support, even though at times they found her bossy.

It was Josephine, not Carrie, who made a Christmas for them. In the weeks running up to it, she would beg useful bits and pieces from the well-off white families for whom she worked – discarded dolls, bits of coloured chalk, lengths of rope that could be used for skipping – and begged pieces of used wrapping paper in which to wrap them.

Her own attitude was hardening, too, from the continual struggle and responsibility. It was during a pre-Christmas period that a woman whose floor she was scrubbing started telling her all about Santa Claus and his team of reindeer. "There is no Santa Claus," snapped Josephine. "I'm Santa Claus."

The tensions between her and her mother came to a head in the summer of 1919, when Josephine was 13. All of Carrie's children, including Josephine, were supposed to be home by nine o'clock every evening. It was impossible to miss this curfew because every evening at nine a nearby factory whistle was blown, and its sound could be heard for miles. There was never any excuse for being late.

On this particular evening, however, Josephine had had enough of this, and turned up home from wherever she had been a full hour late. Carrie started screaming at her. She threatened to have her sent to reform school, and when Josephine answered back she gripped hold of her, pulled down her pants and laid into her with a strap. As soon as she could get free, Josephine stormed out of the house and raced off down the street in tears, determined that she would never ever to go back. Getting a little way away, she slowed to a walk, still tearful. The night was warm, and the streets were still crowded with people. One was a man she knew, and who knew her, the owner of an ice cream parlour.

Seeing her distress, he spoke to her, asking what was the matter. She told him how unhappy she was at home, and that this was the last straw, and that she'd run away but had no idea where she was to go. He liked Josephine, and made her an offer: if she would come and work for him in his shop, she could live in his house.

Gratefully, she accepted. She did move into his house, and she did work for him, and all would have been plain sailing except that the man was in his fifties. She was a 13-year-old girl living alone in a house with a 50-year-old man who was no relation to her at all. This had to be immoral. Outraged neighbours whispered about it to each other, and soon a group of them visited Carrie and drew her attention to the shame her daughter was bringing on her. Carrie went to the ice cream parlour and rescued her daughter, but Josephine did not return home. Calmer now, she went to live with her grandmother, and got herself another job, as a waitress in a musicians' hangout on Pine Street, in Chestnut Valley. It was called the Old Chauffeur's Club.

Life then began to get a little better for Josephine. She was earning a regular wage, even if it was only a small one, and her grandmother also had some money coming in after Aunt Elvara's widow's pension had been transferred to her when she died. Also, life at the Old Chauffeur's Club was much to Josephine's liking. The best black entertainers in town frequented it and sometimes played there, and as she waited on tables she would kid around with them, imitating the way they sang and danced, amusing them by pulling the funny faces she had used as a mocking defence since her school days.

Next door to the club was the Pythian Hall, the clubhouse of the Pythian Society. It was in this society's marching band that her father, Eddie, played the snare drum, and while she was working at the club he was also drumming in the clubhouse band. Hearing that she was working in the Old Chauffeur's Club, Eddie took to dropping in to see her from time to time. Now in his mid 30s, he had married, taking on three stepchildren, and his career was doing well. Recently he had even played drums for a season with The Ringling Brothers' circus.

Seeing him as prosperous, Josephine often put the bite on him for money. He often gave her some, but when she asked him one time to buy her a watch he refused, saying that he couldn't run to that. Josephine was scornful. After all, he was supporting three stepchildren, and they were obviously getting money that was rightfully hers, she being his real daughter. (In actual fact, one of the three stepchildren remembered years later that Eddie didn't contribute all that much to his new family, but Josephine – then as so often in her life – had her own opinion and wasn't going to be told differently.)

No matter how much Josephine enjoyed working at the club, her favourite day of the week was Sunday, her day off. Every Sunday she would walk the short distance to the Booker T Washington Theater, pay her nickel admission and enter what to her was an enchanted world, a world of music and bright colours, of laughter and magic. To her this was true beauty. She envied the line of high-kicking chorus girls and their gossamer hair – so different from her own unruly bush of tight, wiry curls – and silky, light-coffee skin. In short, it was at this time that she became irrevocably stagestruck, aching for the approval of applause.

She started doing everything she could to improve her personal appearance. She would look in the mirror for hours, studying all the angles of her face, and she began attacking her difficult hair, combing it straight as best she could and giving herself kiss curls at her forehead and her temples, fixed in place with sugared water. She also watched closely the classy St Louis women who came to the Old Chauffeur's Club, wearing diamond rings and elegant clothes, and began to learn to carry herself more regally, as well as to realise the things which money can buy. She determined that one day, and as soon as possible, she would have that sort of money.

And of course there were also boys. After work she would often step out with one or other of the boys who hung around in the Valley, going dancing or to a show, and more and more she resented being poor, feeling that she looked like a ragamuffin. It was one of these boys, Willie Wells, who became the next big event in Josephine's eventful life. After she had been working for eight months at the club, and still aged only 13, she turned up one day at her mother's house and announced that she was quitting her job to get married to Willie Wells, who was only a few years older than she was herself.

Although the family knew nothing of Willie Wells, Carrie made no attempt to stop her or dissuade her. Possibly she felt that marriage would settle down her increasingly wayward daughter, or that Josephine, once married, would no longer be her responsibility. Or maybe she thought that, with Willie, there would at last be an earning man in the household, because Josephine's plan was that, once married, she and Willie would return home to live.

And Josephine? Obviously, in spite of being stagestruck, she was by no means yet committed to a showbiz career. Her need of home and emotional security, her desperate need to be taken care of, must have swamped all other feelings once Willie had asked her to be his wife.

The family somehow scraped together enough money for Willie and Josephine to have a traditional church wedding, with Josephine attending in a wedding gown and Willie in a suit, and after the ceremony the bride, groom and guests crammed into the Martin home for a solid meal of roast pork and baked macaroni.

Josephine flung herself whole-heartedly into the role of married lady. No longer working, she spent hours in the upstairs room that had become hers and Willie's, tidying it and cleaning it. Only a month or so after the wedding, without saying anything to the family, she started knitting baby clothes, stacking those that she completed neatly on her bureau. She even went out one day and came home with a wooden bassinet.

But Willie turned out to be a disappointment. He was no better a provider than her father or her stepfather, and Josephine took to berating him about his shortcomings. One evening, when they had been married for only a few months, Willie came bursting into the house like a thunderstorm. Whatever Josephine had been saying about him – or had been doing, or had bought – that he'd found out about nobody ever discovered, but he dashed past Carrie and Arthur, who were sitting in their livingroom, and hurtled up the stairs to his and Josephine's room, yelling: "Come out here! Lemme break your neck!"

The door slammed shut behind him, and Carrie and Arthur sat stunned, saying and doing nothing, until suddenly there was a loud smashing and banging and they ran together upstairs and into the room. Josephine stood grasping a broken bottle, and Willie, in shock, stood with blood pouring down his face from a deep cut just above one eye. Josephine, probably also shocked, seemed to Carrie and Arthur unnaturally calm. She simply said: "I was defendin' myself." Willie went off to the doctor to get his eye stitched and never came back, and that was the end of the marriage.

Josephine was desolated. For one of the few times in her life, all of the energy seemed to drain out of her. Her hopes for a steady, stable, loving life had vanished, as did the baby she seemed to have been expecting. Maybe the shock of her row with Willie and the break-up caused her to miscarry, or maybe (as her brother Richard believed) she went off somewhere and had a back-street abortion. Pulling herself together, she went back to waitressing at the Old Chauffeur's Club, and it wasn't long before her life took another turn.

Busking around the streets of Chestnut Valley was a ramshackle trio calling itself The Jones Family Band. Old man Jones, who led the trio, was a wizened, ill-favoured man who played a big brass horn. The other two members were his pretty common-law wife, who played the trumpet, and their daughter, Doll, who was also pretty, in her 20s, and who played the violin. They played in a ragtime style, performing outside bars or pool halls or anywhere they could find a good crowd, and then passed around a hat for money.

Somehow – possibly in the Old Chauffeur's Club – old Jones saw Josephine doing a bit of dancing and singing. At the age of 14 she was still quite small, and being a shrewd performer he realised that the perky, amusing young girl could be an asset in attracting crowds and money. He invited her to join The Jones Family Band. Josephine accepted his offer at once, quit her job at the club again, and began playing the streets. She sang catchy ragtime songs and danced. Mrs Jones, feeling that the instrument would suit her zany personality, taught her to play the trombone. She picked it up quickly, dancing fast and lively steps as she played, clowning and crossing her eyes. Among the crowds to whom they played, of course, were those queueing for admission to the Booker T Washington Theater. This ran four shows a day, cramming in five if the show that week was popular, and The Jones Family Band did its best to be there for every one.

This was a lucky break for Josephine because she started being noticed by the theatre manager, Red Bernett. Years later, he recalled: "She was a bitty thing, standin' there singin' to the people. She had a lovely voice, an' she kinda handled herself like Diana Ross. She was just that thrillin'." He made a mental note that, as soon as he got the chance, he would find her something to do in the theatre that would take her off the streets. It wasn't just that he could see that she had talent; it was also because he could see that she was shabbily dressed and ill fed, so it was obvious that she was poor, and this made him feel genuinely protective.

His opportunity came when the week's show at the theatre was being given by a touring troupe called The Dixie Steppers. Their producer, Bob Russell, was part owner of a company called Russell And Owen's Big Spectacular, which was based at Stile's Pekin Theater in Savannah,

Georgia. There he produced plays and musicals as well as revues, like this one, and often toured them. But arriving in St Louis he had a problem: as he explained to Red Bernett, his troupe was short of an act. During its previous week's booking in Kansas City, two hundred miles to the west, his husband-and-wife comedy team had fallen out with each other so badly that they'd split, personally and professionally, and gone their separate ways. Could Red Bernett come up with a substitute? Bernett at once thought of The Jones Family Band. He described them to Russell, who agreed that they might fit the bill. Old man Jones was sent for, and the whole family, including Josephine, was worked into the show. The band was scheduled to perform two spots, and during one of them Josephine would do a little comic dance.

Her dance was a great success. She later said: "Seeing everybody looking at me electrified me, as if I'd had a slug of gin." And as Red Bernett proudly recalled years later: "The minute she hit that stage, she arched her back just like an animal. She'd jut that ass up, like a rooster flipping his tail."

By now, at the age of 14, her huge repertoire of steps, her leggy goofiness and her face-pulling were beginning to develop into a style that was all her own. Never sticking to a set routine (because she didn't really know any set routines) but instead just going into whichever next step seemed right, she improvised in the spirit of the music like a jazz player.

Her family were proud of her success, but proudest of all was her younger half-sister, Willie Mae. Then aged nine, she rushed to the theatre every day straight from school and hung around backstage. She was a lot like Josephine in temperament, fast and clever and sassy. Red Bernett remembered: "That one-eyed girl had a whole lotta mouth. She wanted everybody to know she was Josephine's sister."

Josephine was in raptures. Here she was, a dancer at the Booker T Washington Theater, in the same show with a glamorous chorus line like those she had seen as a child. Except that she soon found out that, seen close up, it didn't look glamorous at all. She stood in the wings watching the dancers do their routines and all of their magic vanished.

Their ages ranged from about 18 to 35, and although their bodies were dancers' bodies, fit and muscular, even the youngest had eyes that were hard and faces that were blotched and worn from their hard life on the road. She wrote later: "The cheers, the lust of the men in the audience, the whistles, the laughs, the cries, never seemed to cross the footlights and reach them. They were only dancing because they didn't want to starve."

This is the difference between a star in the making and an ordinary performer. Josephine saw that the dancers of the chorus did not feel the audience, but she did, and always would, and would reach out to them. She saw at once that she was not like these dancers. Far from simply dancing not to starve, when performing she felt like a queen. And even if the glamour did vanish when seen close up, she knew that, for the public out there, it still existed.

Producer Bob Russell was amused by Josephine's dancing, and hired her and The Jones Family Band to stay with the troupe for the rest of its tour. She happily accepted, and her mother did nothing to discourage her. When told about the tour, she simply said: "If she's chosen her life, let her go."

In those late days of vaudeville, there were hundreds of acts touring theatres all over America. These were mostly booked by a few big agencies, assembling shows and sending them out on the road. The big white bookers were the United Booking Office, run by BF Keith and Edward Albee, and the William Morris Agency. Black performers had their own agency, the Theater Owners' Booking Association (known as TOBA), which functioned mostly in the South and Midwest, hiring blacks to play only to blacks. It was TOBA that was handling The Dixie Steppers' tour.

Some of the theatres at which white vaudevillians played were pretty terrible, but the places at which black performers played were often barely theatres at all. Many were rickety wooden shacks, often with leaking roofs or broken seats. Sometimes members of the audience had to sit on the floor.

The Dixie Steppers weren't playing the very worst theatres, but the ones they played were bad enough. The one real virtue they had was that black audiences were responsive. Often noisy and inattentive – running up and down the aisles, greeting friends, sometimes even fighting – if they did enjoy an act they would yell and applaud and stomp their feet on the floor and generally take the roof off. Their responses were so extreme that, when black performer Ethel Waters later succeeded in getting to play to white audiences, at first she thought that she was a flop because all they did if they liked you was clap.

The star of the show in which Josephine found herself was the singer Clara Smith, one of a string of fine vaudeville blues singers called Smith who were around at the time, none of whom were related. As well as Clara there were Mamie, Trixie and, of course, Bessie. Clara's voice was not unlike Bessie's; they even made several records duetting together. As well as singing the blues, Clara, like Bessie, also had a repertoire of saucy double-entendre songs that were a staple part of such shows, which were essentially composed of rough comedy, singing and dancing.

Josephine was getting nine dollars a week on the road, and although she was performing her dance there wasn't a lot else for her to do. She was too small and scrawny to join the chorus. Bob Russell tried her out in small parts in a couple of sketches. In one skit, called '20 Minutes In Hell', she played a prostitute and was chased around the stage by a man in devil's costume, yelling "Away with you, you little imp!" In another, a mock love scene, she was costumed as a cupid – naturally, a topless cupid – to be lowered down on a rope and fire an arrow at two young lovers sitting together. The rope jammed and she hung in mid-air in discomfort and some distress while the audience shrieked and whistled its delight.

All the same, she wasn't doing much for her nine dollars, and Bob Russell decided that she should also act as Clara Smith's dresser. Josephine was delighted. She idolised Clara, whose voice, she said later, gave you chills. Blues singers like Clara were the hot new thing in 1920, a nationwide craze kicked off by Mamie Smith's record 'Crazy Blues', which sold so many copies in Harlem that the record company sent a man there to make sure that somebody wasn't simply giving them away.

Clara, then aged 26, acted like a star. She had a big personality and knew that part of a star's job was to act glamorous both onstage and off. Although she was short and very fat, she did her best. To increase her height she wore high-heeled shoes, and as much as possible she wore the fashionable clothes of the day – a black evening cloak trimmed with white fur, for instance, worn over a hobble skirt. Sometimes she wore short, gauzy dresses over pink tights or a pink slip, and she loaded on the decorations: beaded headbands, heavy gold jewellery and ostrich feathers. Unfortunately, the effect was partly spoiled by her predilection for wearing a bright red wig and pale violet face powder, and by her offstage habit of clenching in her teeth (which were yellow) a corn-cob pipe. All the same, she knew the importance in showbusiness of glamour, and would explain it to Josephine, showing her pictures in magazines of more successfully-dressed stars.

Clara quickly acquired a real affection for Josephine. It helped that she came from South Carolina, as had Josephine's grandmother and mother.

Once, when she was kept to her bed with a bad attack of constipation, Josephine sat beside her for hours, telling her stories about life in Chestnut Valley. Josephine was a good story teller and a good mimic, and Clara was delighted. They took to spending their afternoons together, when Clara would help Josephine improve her reading and writing and would buy her little gifts of liquorice, peppermint sticks and sweet potato pie.

Another pleasure for Josephine was the fact that Clara always made sure that she had a good piano player to accompany her, and Josephine liked the one she had for this tour. At after-show parties he would play in a rolling, stomping manner that was reaching towards boogie-woogie, and he also had a huge repertoire of old songs from all over the South. Josephine would dance to his piano playing and sing the songs.

In spite of the excitement of touring in a show, in a company with flashy, larger-than-life performers and with constant movement from town to town, life on the road was tough. It was a grind even for white performers in the North, but for a black troupe touring the South it could come close to being a nightmare. It wasn't only the hot dusty roads and the grimy railroads with their lurching, racketty trains; those were also the worst days of segregation, worse even than just after emancipation. Hotels, movie houses and latrines could all be labelled "whites only". Even trying to buy a snack at a lunch counter might bring nothing but a hostile stare, and there was always the nervous knowledge that this was the home of the Ku Klux Klan.

The Klan was originally founded in 1866, after the Civil War, as a fairly harmless social club for young soldiers returning from the war, but it was always steeped in the notion of white supremacy, and after only a few years took to terrorism against blacks (and Northern carpetbaggers) and was disbanded by its then Imperial Wizard, General Nathan Bedford Forrest. However, it was refounded in 1915, only a few years before The Dixie Steppers' tour. This time it was vehemently against anything deemed "foreign", its principal targets being Catholics, Jews and blacks.

In the years just after the Great War, with the Kaiser defeated, young ex-soldiers were in desperate need of a new enemy, and for many the Klan helped them to find just that. All through the Twenties there would be a rash of beatings and burnings and lynchings, the last mostly committed against blacks, and so for The Steppers – and for Josephine, with her memories of the riot – there must have been many uneasy times.

And then there was the Jones family. On closer acquaintance they turned out to be an unsavoury bunch, if not downright weird. For a start, old man Jones believed in voodoo. This was not uncommon among uneducated black Americans, especially from the southern states, but Jones was a rather unpleasant example.

Much voodoo was based on long-remembered beliefs in African witchcraft, which continued for years to bubble along secretly underneath the prevalent outward Christianity, and even to mingle with it. Among Pa Jones' habits was that of making charms to ward off evil. He would, for instance, cut off locks of his wife's black hair, roll them around rusty tenpenny nails and tuck them under the edge of his mattress. Another habit was pricking his fingers until they bled and dripping the blood into his morning coffee. If it wasn't that in his coffee, it was crushed sow bugs (a variety of woodlouse).

On the tour, Josephine always had to share the lodgings rented by the Jones family. They cooked in the room in which they slept, and sometimes all four had to sleep in the same bed. Josephine, writing about this later, said that she found living like this degrading, which is rather a strong word when you consider that it was the way her family had lived for much of her life.

It has been suggested by someone who encountered The Jones Family Band at around this time that one or some or all of them molested her sexually. Certainly there was something sexually odd about the daughter, Doll, because when the tour reached New Orleans she fell for a Bourbon Street dwarf, who would frequently call around at their lodgings unannounced and give her an enjoyable whipping.

Whatever the case, in spite of her delight in performing, Josephine was finding life on the road lonely and bewildering. There were almost too many new experiences, many of them unpleasant. Ethel Waters, then also touring the TOBA circuit and ten years older than Josephine, ran into her and later said: "She was like an orphan."

But there was always Clara Smith. As her dresser, Josephine would wash and mend her costumes, and while they were in New Orleans Clara introduced her to the delights of creole cooking. And there was another pleasure in New Orleans: by this time (late 1920) jazz was beginning to hit its stride as a music even more exciting than ragtime, and New Orleans was full of it – clubs and bars and street parades and even funerals – because, to the black natives of New Orleans, music was part of the very fabric of life.

This was still true even though, in 1917, the US Navy had closed down Storyville, the city's red light district. (They were afraid of sailors on shore leave getting into fights or getting mugged.) This in turn closed a lot of joints and made work opportunities for musicians scarce, and within a few years many of the best had gone upriver to more open towns like Kansas City and Chicago, taking their music with them.

When the troupe left New Orleans, The Jones Family Band elected to stay behind. They were tired of travelling, and liked the city with its markets and waterfront and exciting music – and, of course, Doll was very much involved with her dwarf.

With Josephine even more alone (although glad to be so), the show continued its tour. At one point it even played St Louis again, and when visiting her family Josephine made a point to go there in a taxi, which caused a gratifying sensation.

They went on to Chicago, which by now had so many New Orleans musicians that it had become the hottest town on the jazz circuit. Its golden age was just beginning, and it would continue clear into the Thirties. Even the great Joe "King" Oliver was already there, leading the finest band in the country.

Most of this musical activity took place in the black district of Chicago, on the South Side. With dancers from the show, young Josephine made nightly tours of the South Side dance halls and illicit gin mills. (Prohibition had come about in the USA in 1919, banning alcoholic drinks, and the only places you could get a drink had to be illicit. In a mob-controlled city such as Chicago, with the cops duly bribed, such places were not hard to find. Nor were they anywhere else.)

Eventually, in April 1921, the troupe arrived at Philadelphia to play the last engagement of its tour at the Gibson Theater. It was here that Josephine at last succeeded in becoming a member of the chorus, filling in for a girl who had injured herself. However, she had to wear the other girl's costume, which was too big. The dress, which should have reached her knees, only reached her ankles, and the tights wrinkled on her skinny legs. She looked like a little girl playing dressing-up, and when she came on, at the end of the line, the audience howled with laughter. Happy with the laughter, which she had been deliberately provoking all her life, Josephine broke out of the line, improvising steps the way she had done with The Jones Family Band, and adding a few erotic bumps and grinds. The laughter and applause kept growing.

Then the tour was over. Fortunately for Josephine, who had no intention now of doing anything but performing and who certainly had no intention of going back home, another show was quickly put together by a performer called Sandy Burns, who had been on the tour. It was scheduled to play at the Standard Theater, and Josephine was to be in it, again as the odd one out on the end of the chorus line.

This was good, but now that her companions on the tour had mostly disappeared she became desperately lonely in that strange, big city. She had never been so far north before, and Philadelphians – both black and white – seemed colder than the people in St Louis. But, of course, there were still the house-rent parties.

House-rent parties were a feature of black big-city life all over the USA in those days. If a family couldn't scrape together the rent they would hire a pianist, and sometimes a drummer as well, and hold a party (for a small admission fee) for all comers, advertising it by word of mouth or by handing out slips of paper on the streets which gave the address and time. Neighbours would bring cheap drink and home-cooked food, and a rent party could go on for days.

It was at one of these that the lonely Josephine met a small, wiry, light-complexioned man in his mid 20s called Willie Baker. While not handsome, he had a warm, easy smile and a kind manner, and he danced well. Being an ex-jockey, he was fit, with good balance and reflexes. Retired from the track, he was at this time working for the railroad as a Pullman porter, and Josephine fell for him. With her need for affection and stability, he seemed to be just what she wanted. Because he was older and had a steady job, this offered her the security she needed. Willie, for his own part, also fell for her. She was young and amusing and full of life, and they both wanted to travel and find excitement, and so very quickly they decided to get married.

A problem with this was that Willie's parents took a poor view of their son hitching up with a chorus girl, and especially one so young. She wasn't legally under age, because she was now 15, but she was still ten years or so younger than he was. The simplest solution seemed to be for them to elope. (There might also have been some trouble in Philadelphia, with Josephine being only 15. States had different views of what was a marriageable age – after all, in Missouri she'd been allowed to marry Willie Wells when she was 13.)

Whatever the exact reason, when the show at the Standard Theatre finished its run the two of them headed for Camden, New Jersey, and were married in a short civil ceremony by a Justice Of The Peace, and so Josephine MacDonald became, and would remain, Josephine Baker.

Not that this marriage lasted much longer than her first one. Immediately after they were married she took her new husband south to St Louis and introduced him to her slightly-surprised family. Her brother Richard's later comment was: "He was a jolly guy, and seemed glad to meet us, but that was the only time we seen him."

Back in Philadelphia, they set up home in a theatrical boarding house, Moms Charleston's. Willie's father had a restaurant on South Street between 15th and 16th Streets, where the couple often ate, but there was always a subtle hostility from Willie's mother, who felt that Josephine was not only too young and in an unrespectable profession but also too dark skinned. As Josephine later told a friend, "If somebody came to the house, Willie's mother would find some excuse to keep me in the kitchen."

Most American blacks were sensitive about shades of skin until well into the 20th century. In general it was felt that, the lighter your skin was, the more high toned you were. However, there were many subtle variations, most of which Josephine encountered at one time or another, like her grandmother and aunt preferring her to her darker brother and half-sisters because, to them, she showed a touch of Apalachee in her skin colour and features, and like her mother finding her too pale skinned and reminding her of her father.

In this marriage, Josephine did not throw herself whole-heartedly into the role of wife and home-maker. She continued to pursue her career, and found occasional work singing and dancing at a well-regarded second-floor night spot called Vic Hamilton's Cabaret. The band there, Bobby Lee And His Cotton Pickers, were regarded as the best black band in the city, and other performers there were also pretty good. One of the dancers, Wilsa Caldwell, and her husband Eddie, a trombonist, told Josephine about a new black musical called *Shuffle Along* that was currently playing a short season in Philadelphia. It was currently playing at a series of try-outs around north-west USA, being polished up for an eventual hoped-for opening in New York, and the Caldwells had been hired to join it.

From the moment she heard about *Shuffle Along*, Josephine was unable to get it out of her mind. She had no intention of going back to St Louis, and had no intention of spending the rest of her life in Philadelphia. New York was obviously the place to be if you wanted to get anywhere in show-business, and *Shuffle Along* could get her there. Whatever happened, she was going to get herself in that show.

3 *Shuffle Along*

The showbusiness world that Josephine was working her way into was filled with excitement and newness. The Twenties was the decade of entertainment, and already by 1921 everything connected with showbusiness was changing fast. In the theatre, ragtime rhythms had shifted the musical from the style of a romantic Viennese operetta to something altogether more lively. That change had begun in around 1910, and with the arrival of composers like Jerome Kern on the scene the great years of the American musical were just beginning. Kern only ever wrote songs as part of his musicals, but there were also tens of thousands of songwriters hopefully turning out songs for the flourishing popular music industry known as Tin Pan Alley, whose undisputed king was Irving Berlin, a man who had made his name in 1911 with 'Alexander's Ragtime Band', a song which was not really much to do with ragtime, apart from being syncopated and lively.

Tin Pan Alley made its money from selling copies of sheet music, mostly for the piano, because in those days every respectable home had a piano. Also, because of the national craze for ballroom dancing, music publishers had started insisting that every song that was published had to be danceable. The music to which people were dancing was jazz, a music that arrived on the scene almost overnight when a group of young whites from New Orleans, calling themselves The Original Dixieland Jass Band, hit New York in 1917.

Vaudeville was still riding high, breeding innumerable singers, dancers, comedians, aerialists, ventriloquists, jugglers, acrobats and contortionists, although silent movies – spooling out an endless procession of long melodramas and short comedies – were already beginning to drive it out of business, a process that would be completed after radio arrived in 1923.

The record business was booming, too. In 1920, band leader Paul Whiteman (misleadingly billed as "The King Of Jazz") sold 3,500,000 copies of the song 'Three O'Clock In The Morning', one for every second phonograph in the country.

All of the people mentioned above were white. Whites had more money than blacks, and there were many more of them, and so the white entertainment world was much bigger and better paid than the world Josephine had entered with The Dixie Steppers. For this reason, ambitious black entertainers strove hard for a chance to play to white audiences, to get what the vaudeville world called "white time", and most especially to get to New York and play on Broadway.

But the two worlds were almost totally segregated. Even in the cheap white beer halls and honky-tonks where vaudeville grew up in the 1880s and 1890s, black performers had not been very welcome. Whites played to whites and blacks to blacks.

However, there were exceptions. Back in the 1890s there had been occasional black minstrel shows that played to white audiences. One, which came to New York in 1891 from Louisville, Kentucky, was called *The South Before The War*. It had in its cast the future king of tap dancing, Bill "Bojangles" Robinson, then aged twelve.

In 1896, Broadway saw another show with an all-black cast, *Oriental America*, organised by white producer John W Isham. This show was partly in the old minstrel-show format, but ended with a medley of operatic selections instead of the traditional cakewalk. White audiences had grown at least slightly used to the idea of blacks singing opera from the success in the 1890s of the black soprano Sissieretta Jones, known as Black Patti from the resemblance in her voice to the world-famous Adelina Patti, and who toured in a show called Black Patti's Troubadours.

On both sides of the turn of the century, a writer called Bob Cole produced three black shows in the operetta style, which indicates a problem that black entertainers were having in the early years of the century. Striving to integrate themselves into American society, writers and composers were trying to work in the prevailing white styles, and performers were fighting to get away from the clichéd images of blacks that had been established during the 50-year success of the minstrel shows (which were mostly performed by whites in blackface). The two most prevalent of these stereotypes were the idle, shiftless, superstitious plantation hand and the strutting, overdressed, big-city fashion-plate who misused big words.

The duo which had used these characterisations most subtly and successfully was the comedy team of Bert Williams and George Walker. In 1895, these men had been discovered performing in an Indiana hotel lobby by producer Thomas Canary, and were brought by him to New York to appear in Victor Herbert's *The Gold Bug* as a speciality act. The show flopped, but they were a huge success and continued together in vaudeville until 1909, when George Walker fell ill with paresis, dying two years later, aged only 39.

Bert Williams continued on his own, mostly in the Ziegfeld Follies, although when Ziegfeld first put him in the show, in 1910, and a part was written for him in a sketch with white performers, the whole cast threatened to walk out. All that Williams was allowed to do was his standard vaudeville act, alone. He was such a hit that, after the first night, the abandoned sketch was hurriedly restored to the programme. His act was a satirical mixture of songs, mime and monologues, delivered in an understated, rueful manner. He was shuffling and loose jointed, and many who saw him – including WC Fields and Buster Keaton – rated him among the very best. Some said that he was the equal of Charlie Chaplin.

In their double act, Williams had been the shuffling, slow one and Walker the dandy. In their private lives, Williams was quiet, gentlemanly and somewhat aloof, while Walker was truly a dandy, having an English tailor, wearing silk underwear and having his bedroom walls lined with pale blue satin. He was also seriously thoughtful about how blacks should present themselves onstage. In 1906, he said: "The one hope of the coloured performer must be in making a radical departure from the old 'darky' style of singing and dancing...There is an artistic side to the black race, and if it could be properly developed on the stage I believe that theatre-going public would profit much by it." It was this longing to be artistic, following European models, that would prove to be the wrong road.

Musicians had a similar problem. Established black composers, especially in New York, looked down on syncopated music as belonging to the despised minstrel shows, and reckoned blues (if they ever heard any) to be a low-down, no-account music played by primitive rustics. It's easy to be wise with hindsight, but they simply had no notion of the enormous store of rhythms, ideas and expression that were waiting to pour out of black America in the 20th century.

In the early years of the century, music was the one major area in which blacks performed for whites, mainly in big private houses or fashionable restaurants. This was a tradition that reached right back to the days of slavery. Many slave owners regarded music as a craft, and a slave with a useful craft was a more valuable property, so musical ability was encouraged. Later, after emancipation, the tradition continued because musicians were regarded in the respectable world as servants, and therefore music was deemed a suitable calling for blacks.

The first big success in this field was the remarkable James Reese Europe, a black New York bandleader who was one of the first to realise the power of syncopation and set out to swim against the tide of musical respectability. His band played for Vernon and Irene Castle, who in the 1910s more or less invented ballroom dancing. They did this by taking the kinds of steps danced by Josephine, which originated largely among blacks in the southern and south-western states, and smoothing them out into something more elegant and refined, which they then publicised as being not only a respectable but also a smart thing to do. However, a problem they ran into was that of finding a band that could play music suitable for the dances they were creating, but fortunately they heard The Jim Europe Orchestra in 1913 and demanded that only his music could be used for the dancing demonstrations they gave.

So by 1914 his was the most fashionable band in New York, and in 1917, when the USA entered the First World War, he enlisted in the army and, much like Glenn Miller in the Second World War, formed a fine army band that became so popular that, on its return to New York in 1919, was honoured with a ticker-tape parade down Fifth Avenue, led by its drum major, Bill Robinson. Unfortunately, in the same year he was knifed by one of his drummers, whom he had reprimanded, and died.

But as well as leading successful bands, Europe was also a great organiser. In 1910, when he was 29, he was a leading founder of an organisation called the Clef Club. This was partly a social club and partly a booking agency, formed to protect the interests of black musicians. Its headquarters were in New York, on West 53rd Street, and anyone who wanted to hire a band of black musicians, no matter how large or small, had to book through the club. Jim Europe saw to it that the musicians it sent out were dressed smartly and behaved professionally. Before the inception of the Clef Club, everything had been much more disorganised, and pianist/composer Eubie Blake once said gratefully that, before Jim Europe, black musicians had been no better off than wandering minstrels.

Eubie Blake, born in Baltimore in 1883, had been a member of Jim Europe's civilian band, Europe's Society Orchestra, as had his singer/lyricist partner, Noble Sissle, who was six years younger. Sissle and Blake were half of the team that were struggling to get *Shuffle Along* onto the New York stage.

Eubie Blake rejoined Europe's band after he was demobbed (Noble Sissle had stayed with him throughout), and after the band leader was killed they managed to get jobs as a piano/vocal duo with comedy backchat, singing their own songs on the prestigious white Keith/Albee circuit. They fiddled this by the simple expedient of blacking up like old-time minstrels. Both were fairly light skinned, and this gave audiences the impression that they were seeing white men blacked up. They got away with this so successfully that they even played the pinnacle of vaudeville: the Palace Theater in New York. (They weren't the only ones – Bert Williams always blacked up to appear in the Ziegfeld Follies, as did Bill Robinson, who by 1920 had also played the Palace.)

It was while on tour in vaudeville that Sissle and Blake first met the other half of the *Shuffle Along* team, the comedy duo of Flournoy Miller and Aubrey Lyles. Miller and Lyles had an act that was a mixture of snappy cross-talk and comic dancing fight routines. They wrote their own material and, like many comedy teams, one of them was tall (Miller) and one short (Lyles). In 1920, all four met up again in Philadelphia, at a benefit concert for the NAACP, and Miller said to his partner: "Sissle and Blake are the missing link."

Eubie felt indignant, thinking that they were being called apes, but Sissle, with a keener nose for business, said: "What do you mean?"

"Now we can do a show," Miller said. "We have the story. Your music is Broadway. Put the two together."

The story that Miller and Lyles planned for their show was based on two of their existing sketches, one called 'The Mayor Of Dixie' and the other 'Who's Stealin'?'. Put together, the plot told of a race between the two owners of a grocery store (Miller and Lyles), who both stand for the post of mayor of a small town called Jimtown, and who also suspect each other of stealing from the store's cash till. The plot is further complicated by the social ambitions of the candidates' two wives.

Ambitiously, they wanted *Shuffle Along* to be one of the rare all-black shows that played in white theatres to white audiences. To get booked into such a theatre meant interesting a white impresario in the show. Sissle and Blake were enthusiastic about the project, and said so, and then nothing happened for months. In fact nothing happened until the next year, when the two couples accidentally ran into each other again in Times Square, New York. Miller, as if he was simply carrying on the same conversation from Philadelphia, said: "John Cort is interested in the show, and he's got all those theatres."

This was not entirely accurate. So far all that had happened was that Miller and Lyles had approached a young promoter called Al Mayer, who had worked for the powerful Edward Albee and had booked them onto the Keith/Albee vaudeville circuit. Now struggling to establish himself as an independent producer, Mayer was interested in their idea for a show and had offered to approach Harry Cort, son of the well-known impresario John Cort.

The four went to see Mayer, who arranged a lunch for himself with Harry Cort. However, he was so little advanced in setting up his struggling business that Miller, Lyles, Sissle and Blake had to chip in $1.25 each so that he could pay the lunch bill. Miller also lent him a good-looking overcoat that he had recently bought. It was too big, and came down to Mayer's ankles, but it had the virtue of looking expensive.

The lunch paid off. Harry Cort liked the idea of the show and approached his father, John, who also liked it. Sissle and Blake, scared to death, were summoned to see him and performed the only song they'd so far written, 'Love Will Find A Way'. On the basis of that one song John Cort agreed that, if the show toured a short series of out-of-town try-outs and looked like being a success, he would find them a New York theatre in which to mount a run. The problem was that, while John Cort was well respected in the business, he'd been having a thin time of it and had no money to invest in the show. However, with his name behind them, the team set to work. Al Mayer managed to find some money from somewhere and invested it in the show, which gave them a little financial leeway.

They all set about assembling a cast, hiring performers from all over the country who were known to them, some from cabarets in San Francisco, New Orleans and Memphis, and a few from the Pekin Repertory Theater in Chicago, where Miller and Lyles had both written and acted. Harry Cort managed to dredge up second-hand costumes from two shows that had flopped: *Fay's Fables*, which had starred Irish-American comedian Frank Fay, and *Roly Poly Eyes*, which had starred comedian Eddie Leonard. They were worn and faded, with sweat stains under the arms and, worse, they bore little relation to the plot of the show.

When writing the songs, Sissle and Blake were forced to pen numbers justifying the costumes. For a set of oriental costumes from *Fay's Fables* they wrote 'Oriental Blues', and for a set of plantation costumes from *Roly Poly Eyes* they wrote 'Bandanna Days', the bandanna of the title referring to the headscarves worn by unsophisticated rustic women in the South. Both of these were good numbers, and in fact Sissle and Blake were coming up with a fine score. As well as 'Love Will Find A Way' there were others, including 'Gypsy Blues', 'He May Be Your Man But He Comes To See Me Sometimes', 'If You've Never Been Vamped By A Brownskin (You've Never Been Vamped At All)', 'In Honeysuckle Time', 'Baltimore Buzz', and the hit number of the show, 'I'm Just Wild About Harry'. This song was originally written in waltz time, and Eubie, a great admirer of Victor Herbert's European-style operetta songs, was aiming at a gentle romantic effect with it. Unfortunately, the singer who'd been cast as one of the two wives, Lottie Gee (who also happened to be Eubie's bit on the side), resolutely refused to sing it that way. Raised on the sort of minstrel-show and vaudeville songs that Sissle and Blake thought were old fashioned, she objected that people would laugh at a waltz in a black show, and she wasn't prepared to go through that.

Eubie was furious at possibly losing his beautiful tune, but Noble Sissle – always the more business-like of the pair – smoothed things over, and Eubie rewrote it (with some reluctance) in 4/4 time as a foxtrot. In due course, as a foxtrot it would stop the show, but Eubie brooded about the change for the rest of his long life, and on a piano album be recorded in 1969 (and on which Noble Sissle sang some numbers) he played it as the beautiful waltz it had been.

As well as Lottie Gee, the company hired a young singer and dancer, Gertrude Saunders, to play the other wife, along with two featured male dancers: Charlie Davis, who was a staggeringly fast tap dancer, and Tommy Woods, who did a slow-motion acrobatic dance. There was also a male chorus line of six and a female chorus line of 16.

Early in 1921, with the show assembled, they set off on their try-out tour, which was to begin with two nights in Trenton, New Jersey. To say that they still had no money would be putting it mildly – they were all stony broke. They didn't even have enough for the train fares even to Trenton, which is a very short hop from New York. The cast and crew of 78 stood around on New York's Pennsylvania Station, wondering what to do. The problem was solved by Al Mayer, who then and there sold his share in the show to a man called Gasthoffer, a quiet hanger-on who had attended many rehearsals and who was there to see them off.

So they reached Trenton, and from there went to Burlington, New Jersey, and then to Pottstown, Philadelphia. They were there for three weeks and went down well, but because nobody had heard of the show the audiences were small and they all made very little money. They also had to find lodgings with black families because hotels wouldn't accept blacks (and anyway they couldn't have afforded it), and they paid their rent with tickets for the show. Al Mayer bought his meals in the same way, slipping tickets to waitresses.

After Pottstown they had a last try-out at a theatre that was for blacks, not whites, but had the virtue of being one of the finest in the country, the Howard Theater in Washington, DC, where they were scheduled to play for two weeks – if they could get there. Again the cast and crew found themselves broke on a railway station, this time in Pottstown. It was a cold day, and they huddled in small, despondent groups on the platform. Al Mayer paced up and down, trying to think of something, when a man waiting for a train came up and asked him if he'd seen "that darky show".

"I'm the manager," said Mayer.

"Well," said the man, "you've got a gold mine."

Mayer said that that might be so but they had no money to get to their big opening in Washington. Needing 78 tickets, he doubted that he had money for five.

By an unbelievable stroke of good fortune, the man turned out to be the president of the railway. He took Mayer to the ticket office and said: "Give this man 78 full-fare tickets to Washington and charge it up to me." The stunned performers boarded the train (and the company did eventually pay the president for the tickets). This was something of a turning point. The two weeks in Washington made the company enough money for it to go on to another theatre, again one for blacks: the Dunbar Theater in Philadelphia.

But John Cort still hadn't found a New York theatre. While the show was playing in Philadelphia he came to see it with a friend, the great impresario Abe Erlanger. According to Noble Sissle, both men laughed themselves sick, but then Erlanger pointed out that in Philadelphia it had had a black audience, and that maybe whites wouldn't enjoy it. Cort still wanted to give it a go, however, and in order to keep the show alive he booked it a "graveyard tour" of three weeks of one-nighters in rural Pennsylvania.

Before they set off on that, while the show was still in Philadelphia, Wilsa Caldwell – who had already been hired to join the show – brought Josephine to the stage door of the Dunbar Theater and asked Sissle, Miller and Lyles if they would audition her for their chorus. Noble Sissle later remembered her as a nervous little girl "with big brown eyes like saucers. She stood shivering in the cold March rain that was coming in torrents outside." She danced for them, and they were impressed, but agreed together that she was too thin and too small, and also that she was too dark. It was the tradition for black shows to hire girls who were as light skinned as possible – quadroons or octoroons – because, in the black world of the day, light skin was considered more elegant and classy, and it was doubly important for a show aiming for a white audience.

But there was another thing. Flournoy Miller drew Sissle aside and said: "That kid looks awful young to me."

"I'm 15," Josephine interrupted. Of course, she was still only 14, but her fib did her no good. Noble Sissle patted her on the back and explained that New York law prohibited the use of chorus girls under 16.

Sissle was right, of course. There was even a child protection organisation called the Gerry Society, formed in the late 1890s, which saw to it that the law was rigidly enforced. But he was stunned by the effect that his explanation had on Josephine. "Big tears filled her eyes, and with drooping head looking like a wilted flower she slowly turned, half stumbling down the steps leading to the stage door exit. We stood there watching her as she walked down the alleyway leading to the street. We could hear her sobs, first faintly, then bursting forth in a flood of grief. As she stood at the gate, her lithe body seemed to falter slightly. Then, without even looking back, she disappeared into the rain."

It wasn't just not getting the part. What had upset her most was overhearing the words "too thin...too small...too dark". Too dark? She was being rejected by Willie Baker's mother and by *Shuffle Along* for being too dark, and by her own mother for being too light.

With no New York theatre yet found, the *Shuffle Along* company set off on its graveyard tour of one-nighters. These were even more of a financial disaster than the first part of the try-out tour had been. Not only had nobody heard of the show but by the time (usually enthusiastic) reviews appeared in the local papers the show had moved on. The company's inability to meet the wage bill also meant that from time to time they lost some of the cast. This was the reason why they had hired Wilsa and Eddie Caldwell in mid tour. By the time they returned to New York, the cast were owed $18,000 in back wages.

The good news was that at last John Cort had found a theatre. The bad news was that it was a broken-down old vaudeville house called the 63rd Street Music Hall. "It violated every city ordinance in the book," Eubie remembered. It was situated just north of Columbus Circle, which was rather an unfashionable area, but fortunately it was close to the farthest downtown end of Broadway. *Shuffle Along* opened there on 21 April 1921.

The theatre was close enough to fashionable Broadway for one of New York's leading theatre critics – Alan Dale, of *The New York American* – to attend its performances. He contrasted the vitality of the show with the tameness of white musicals, writing: "Every sinew in their bodies danced; every tendon in their frames responded to their extreme energy. They revelled in their work; they simply pulsed with it, and there was no let-up at all." His enthusiastic review drew the attention of other critics, who normally wouldn't have ventured that far downtown, and they came to the theatre too. Their reviews were admiring, if slightly confused. There was a general agreement that the music had something to do with jazz, although they disagreed on what. But they liked it, and when the dancing was added they found the combination irresistible.

Several commented on how well the chorus was drilled, although in fact it was anything but. However, what it did have was energy, rhythm and talent, and no previous chorus line had danced so much. Earlier shows had contented themselves with a line of pretty girls who paraded themselves and their costumes up and down, with just a little dancing. That was the show's major innovation.

Its other effect was to make black shows fashionable. All of that going to Harlem in ermine and pearls that society did in the Twenties started with *Shuffle Along*. As Eubie Blake said: "Society people felt that their guest tours were incomplete unless they brought their friends [to see the show]."

People enjoyed the comedy of Miller and Lyles as well. They alone in the show played in blackface, because audiences were used to seeing them so, and their outstanding routine was their dancing fight. This was always partly improvised, and could go on for 20 minutes. The future mayor of

New York, Fiorello La Guardia (then a congressman), liked it so much that he went to the show three times in one week. He especially liked the bit where tall Miller, dancing a time step, held his hand on the top of Lyles' head, with Lyles' short arms swinging punches that could not connect.

And as well as Miller and Lyles, the show had acquired another star. Somewhere along the way, Gertrude Saunders – who played one of the wives – left the show, hired away by the management team of Hurtig and Seamon, who ran a music hall on 125th Street which became Harlem's famous Apollo in the Thirties. Her place was taken by 26-year-old Florence Mills, who had been part of a singing trio with her sisters called The Three Dixie Songbirds. She was petite, pretty and light skinned, with a sweet, clear voice, and *Shuffle Along* made her a star overnight and the darling both of Harlem and of white society.

The poet James Weldon Johnson wrote: "As a pantomimist and a singing and dancing comedienne she had no superior in any place or race." She would go on to become an international star, appearing in Lew Leslie's *Blackbirds* in London, where it was reported that she socialised with royalty.

Shuffle Along became such a success that 63rd Street had to be made a one-way street to handle the traffic, and it became the benchmark for the flood of black musicals that followed in its wake. Trading on its name, a Harlem night spot opened in November 1921 calling itself the Shuffle Inn. It was later to be famous in the Twenties and Thirties as Connie's Inn.

Josephine remained keenly aware of *Shuffle Along*'s progress. Not only was it a show that she felt she could be in, and should be in, and one that could get her work in New York, but it was now also a smash hit. Turning 15, she took what little money she had, left Philadelphia (and Willie Baker) behind, and bought a one-way ticket to the big city. This was a brave and determined thing to do; the only people she knew in New York – and then not all that well – were Wilsa and Eddie Caldwell, and the only address she had for them was the 63rd Street Theater.

For a couple of nights she slept rough on a bench in Central Park, and then she found the theatre and Wilsa. Wilsa was pleased to see her, and was also encouraging. The show had been such a success that the management were assembling a second company to go on the road, and there was a chance that Josephine could get a job with that. Josephine borrowed some of Wilsa's lightest face powder and auditioned again, this time for Al Mayer. Asked how old she was, she told him that she was 17. He hired her, although with some misgivings about her being darker skinned than the rest of the line. Her wages were to be $30 a week.

It seems possible that she told the dance director how effective she had been as a comedy dancer on the end of the line because, when the road-show opened in Chicago, that was where she was. (The comedy end girl was a known role. According to Noble Sissle it started in around 1913 by a dancer called Ethel Williams in *Darktown Follies*, one of the few black shows to have played to white New York before *Shuffle Along*.) The opening scene of the show – played to its theme song, 'Shuffle Along' – featured a policeman directing traffic, with the chorus line coming on to back him up. From the beginning of the tour, stimulated as ever by having an audience, Josephine milked her role as end girl for all it was worth. She tripped over her own feet, she went knock-kneed, she crossed her eyes and she grinned her goofy grin, all the time dancing rhythmically and inventively around the music. Audiences loved her.

And of course the rest of the chorus line hated her. It's not quite true to say that she was scene-stealing, because that was what she had been hired to do, but certainly she was getting all of the attention. Some of the others took to tripping her up as she went onstage, but all that she did was incorporate her stumble into another improvised gag. They also despised her because she was darker skinned than they were, and nicknamed her "monkey", playing such tricks on her as taking all of her make-up and costumes out of their dressing room and dumping it in the corridor outside. Undeterred, she changed in the washroom.

But this sort of behaviour only served to mould Josephine's character further. In later years, no matter how much she socialised, and no matter how vivacious she was, she always remained a loner. Her own strong inner core was really all that she trusted – that and the love that came to her in waves from her audiences.

Because of her, the chorus numbers started getting encores. Reviewers singled her out for praise, and people started asking at the box office whether the cross-eyed girl on the end of the line was still in the show. When the touring company came to play a booking at a theatre in Brooklyn, word filtered across town to Noble Sissle and Eubie Blake that a phenomenon seemed to have emerged in it.

They were then too hard at work on a new musical – a racetrack comedy adventure called *In Bamville* – to go and see Josephine themselves, and so they sent an experienced old song-and-dance man from their office to check her out. Eubie always remembered how excited he was when he came back: "He came runnin' back to us. He said 'Get that girl. She's the greatest thing I've ever seen. Get her!'" Sissle and Blake soon did get to see her, and only then did Sissle realise that she was the girl who had come to audition in Philadelphia. It was decided that, when the number one company of *Shuffle Along* finished its run at the 63rd Street Theater and went on the road, Josephine would join it, billed as "that comedy chorus girl".

Its run finished in August 1922, after over 500 performances, and immediately set off – with Josephine – to play the Selwyn Theater in Boston. The way was further cleared for her success by the fact that Florence Mills had now left the show, hired away by white promoter Lew Leslie for his *Blackbirds* at three times the fee that *Shuffle Along* could afford to pay her. Josephine found herself the only new young star in the show.

It had been hard to get the Selwyn Theater booking because out-of-town theatre owners felt that it was a show that would really only work in New York, "a freak town that can take to a freak show". They managed to book the Selwyn for the last two weeks in August only because those two weeks were usually stiflingly hot and business was expected to be poor anyway. As things turned out, the show packed the theatre and stayed there for almost four months, leaving only because the show due to follow them – a play starring Julia Marlowe and the famous Shakespearean actor EH Sothern – sued the *Shuffle Along* company and forced them to move out.

Eubie Blake always conducted the orchestra for *Shuffle Along*, and he took Josephine under his wing. They became lovers, and remained so until she left America.

Oddly enough, sex never seemed all that important to Josephine, although she cheerfully enjoyed it. Raised when and where she was, alongside the brothels of Chestnut Valley, it was simply a natural function, without the guilt which the whites associated with it. This made it easy for her to mock her own sexy dancing, and her audiences for finding it sexy, by clowning. The clowning also helped her to keep men at a distance. Even in bed, as a later lover recalled, there was still a quality of remoteness in her.

What she most wanted in a relationship was warmth and security, and Eubie said years later: "She was a one-man-at-a-time girl." He also noticed a strongly-emerging trait in her, now that she was becoming successful, that when she wanted something she had to have it and to have it now, and to hell with the price. "One Sunday she was walking down Fifth Avenue with two other girls. They passed a candy store on 42nd and Fifth Avenue that had a big red box of chocolates in the shape of a heart in the window. It cost $35. Josephine bought it. That's exactly what she was making a week. $35." When he asked her why she hadn't bought a smaller box, she said "Because I wanted that box of candy." Then she asked him to advance her next week's salary to buy a coat she had seen. He refused, and so she went out and bought it on credit.

During her 15 year she had started to grow in height, and by this time she was 16 and no longer the shortest of the chorus. She was also proving to have a natural elegance and style in her offstage dress. In later years she would claim to have been the same sort of ragamuffin offstage that she portrayed on it, but the singer Elisabeth Welch, who joined the chorus of the number one company of *Shuffle Along* at the same time that Josephine did, later said: "Right from the beginning she was elegant. She had a black sealskin coat. I don't know whether it was real, but when she wore it, it looked real; she would take a piece of silk and wind it around her head, and even then she looked like some sort of oriental empress."

And she was having the time of her life. "She kept us in stitches all the time," Eubie remembered. "At rehearsal she used to stand behind me and mimic me when I was directin' the orchestra."

Her performance onstage was still mostly instinctive, and so Sissle and Blake gave her special coaching, trying to give her more professionalism. They tried to teach her how to give her act a structure, how to build up to her best effects and how to use tricks of showmanship. Sissle worked out a routine for her, and she would dutifully rehearse it, but once she was out there in front of an audience it would simply be forgotten in her excitement and she would improvise like she always did. Sissle was not pleased, but he ruefully admitted that her improvisations were usually wilder and funnier than anything they'd done in rehearsal. "She'd come offstage with the audience screaming and applauding and with her face lighted up with joy," he recalled. Once she came off to find him standing scowling in the wings. "Did I do the steps right that time?" she asked. He told her she hadn't done them at all, and she widened her eyes, put her hand over her mouth, giggled, and promised to do better next time.

After its four months at the Selwyn Theater, the show moved to Chicago. It was still having trouble finding theatres, and they only got into the Olympic – a run-down burlesque house – at the last minute. They stayed there for another four months, and then finagled their way into a good theatre, the Davidson in Milwaukee. They did this with the help of Abe Erlanger, who used his clout to pressure the assistant manager into booking the show while the manager, Mr Brown, was away. When Brown came back and found that a black show had been booked in his theatre, he announced that he was leaving town for the duration of the run, which he did. Hearing rumours of success, however, he sneaked back to have a look at the show from his private box, which turned out to have been sold for that performance, and so he had to stand at the rear to see it.

The show moved to Des Moines, to Indianapolis, and on to St Louis, where it played at the American Theater. Once again, Josephine took a taxi to visit her family at 2632 Bernard Street. Now dressing elegantly, she was appalled by the contrast between the world she had left and the one she now inhabited. The place seemed filthy to her – there were even dirty dishes under the bed. It was also as cold as ice, and the same old laundry tub in which she used to bathe was standing in the middle of the floor. She felt ashamed to have come from such a family. Carrie asked Josephine nothing about her new life and, as in the old days, Josephine felt guilty and rejected. Arthur asked nothing, either; deep in his depression, he lay on the couch in the living room, interested in nothing.

But Richard, Margaret and Willie Mae were interested in her life, and were proud, thinking her a great star, especially Willie Mae, Josephine's favourite, who was now eleven. As Josephine made to leave at the end of her visit, Willie Mae clung to her and begged to be taken along. Josephine reluctantly refused, torn (as she later admitted) between an urge to rescue her sister and a fear of being mocked by the rest of the chorus for dragging a one-eyed child around the country. She made some amends by promising to send Willie Mae money for clothes and to pay for her schooling, which she duly did. She also promised to come back for the following Christmas, which she didn't. She wouldn't see her family again after leaving St Louis for 14 years.

But in spite of her unsatisfactory visit home, her return to St Louis was mostly a triumph, and in their way all of her family were proud of her. They all came to see the show, even Arthur, as did the whole neighbourhood, with two notable exceptions: Red Bernett, who felt slighted because Josephine had never thanked him, in writing or otherwise, for pulling her in off the street and setting her on her way; and her childhood friend and dancing partner Joyce McDuffy, who resented the fact that Josephine made no effort to contact her.

During the St Louis booking, some local musicians clubbed together and sponsored a party for the cast at the Old Chauffeur's Club, and who should show up at the party but Josephine's father, Eddie Carson, bringing with him his wife and step-daughter. This meeting seemed to unnerve Josephine. Although she greeted them politely, she left the party soon after they arrived, and didn't come back. Eddie, however, made the most of the moment by asking Eubie Blake if he could be hired for *Shuffle Along* as a drummer, urging that he wanted to be near his daughter. "I'm sorry," Eubie had to explain, "I already got a drummer."

Shuffle Along went on to play Louisville, Lexington, Toledo, Grand Rapids, Detroit, Buffalo, Rochester, Atlantic City, Philadelphia, Cincinnati, Pittsburgh and even Peoria. In the summer of 1923 the company had a short layoff, and Miller and Lyles – who were to be no part of Sissle and Blake's next show, having failed to come up with a new story – left to star in a new musical called *Runnin' Wild*. They were replaced for the rest of the tour by comedians Johnny Hudgins and Lew Payton, who was writing the script for the new show with Noble Sissle.

By this time, *Shuffle Along* had become so famous that the resistance of theatre managers to booking it had evaporated completely, and by the time the tour ended, a few months after the summer layoff, according to Noble Sissle Josephine was at last beginning to learn some stagecraft: "She began to realise that a finished artist always knew what to do next and could weave a pattern of tricks and effects into an interesting sequence."

She was now a featured personality. *In Bamville* was now ready to go into rehearsal, and in it Josephine was to be one of the principals, in a part specially created for her. She was to get $125 a week, an amazing sum for those days, and she would be billed as "the highest-paid chorus girl in the world". Most of the time she was to wear bright, ragged cotton dresses and clown's oversized shoes, and would perform such routines as imitating the sound of the saxophone (in blackface) and parodying a dance that had been performed in Miller and Lyles' *Runnin' Wild* (not in blackface) and was now sweeping the country: the charleston. But in the scene she loved the most she was to wear a clinging white satin dress, slit up the side, and would parody a Twenties *femme fatale*, vamping the two comedians in the show, who were again Lew Payton and Johnny Hudgins.

The opening try-out concert was on 10 March 1924, at the Lyceum Theater, Rochester, New York. This show was much more lavish and spectacular than *Shuffle Along* had been, with a much bigger cast, rich costumes and three real horses, which engaged in a thrilling mock horse race. This time the chorus line were better drilled, dancing closely together, and Eubie Blake always thought that the show contained some of his best numbers, including 'Dixie Moon', 'Manda', 'Thinking Of Me', 'Jassamine Lane' and 'Fate Is A Slave Of Love', which he intended to be the follow-up to 'Love Will Find A Way'.

However, despite Eubie's songs and the spectacle, when it opened on Broadway in September 1924 (real Broadway this time, at the Colonial Theater), it didn't catch on. It played there for only three months before going on a short tour on the road. It had been cut down quite a lot during its try-outs, its title had been changed to *Chocolate Dandies*, and Josephine's billing had reverted to "the comedy chorus girl", but nothing seemed to help.

Payton's and Sissle's comedy dialogue was flat, quite frankly, which didn't help. However, the show's main problem was that it tried to imitate prestigious white shows – there was even an ill-judged scene in which the chorus girls wore hoopskirts and broad-brimmed hats, like southern belles, and swanned about romantically under trees hung with Spanish moss. This scene was set to the tune of 'Dixie Moon', sung by The Four Harmony Kings (who included the young Paul Robeson), but when the chorus entered the applause died. The problem was that white audiences expected black shows to be full of fast, exciting dancing and minstrel-type humour, and romantic numbers left them cold. It was useless for Sissle and Blake to protest that they could feel just as romantic as anybody else; they were seen as having succumbed to a fatal desire to imitate white Broadway shows.

The one exception to the general disappointment was, of course, Josephine. She was regarded as "the real coloured thing". One reviewer, who had slated the fatal white influence, went on to say that civilisation had spared "the comic little chorus girl, whose every gaze was syncopation and whose merest movement was a blues". And if Broadway thought that she'd been spared the deadening hand of civilisation, what would be thought of her in some city where blacks were a much less common sight – some foreign city like, for instance, Paris?

4 *La Revue Nègre*

After playing for three months on Broadway and five on the road, *Chocolate Dandies* folded in May 1925. By now Josephine was becoming well known and soon found work at a Broadway night club called the Plantation Theater Restaurant. This had been opened in 1922 by an entrepreneur called Sam Slavin for the express purpose of starring Florence Mills in an all-black revue. In 1925 Florence was still technically starring there, but when Josephine entered the show she happened to be away performing in the annual edition of Lew Leslie's *Blackbirds*. Appearing in her place was Ethel Waters.

The revue began each night at midnight, in order to catch the after-theatre crowd, and the club catered mainly to white "café society", that elegantly-dressed mixture of young socialites and Broadway show folk. Typical among the celebrities seen there were songwriter Irving Berlin, film star Norma Talmadge and theatre impresario David Belasco. The club also admitted the right sort of respectable blacks, although it did confine them to seats around the edges.

Josephine was again the dark one on the end of the chorus line, although she was also given a solo dance spot each night and was now enough of a star herself to be sharing a dressing room with Ethel Waters (and with another performer in the show, Bessie Buchanan, who would became a life-long friend and, equally ambitious and determined, would become the first black woman on the New York City legislature). In those days, Ethel Waters was not the matronly figure she became in later life. She was almost as skinny as Josephine, although ten years older, and for that reason was often billed as "sweet mama stringbean". Nor was she an actor in those days; she was a singer who danced a wicked shimmy and did a bit of comedy, and her current big number was 'Dinah', which she sang every night in the club.

Coming from Pennsylvania in the northern USA, and from as poor and dysfunctional a family as Josephine's, she had been more influenced in her singing by white performers like Nora Bayes and Fanny Brice than by singers of blues or spirituals. In fact, black singers of her type were known in the business as "cake-walking babies" to distinguish them from blues singers like Clara Smith. She was something of an innovator, and was one of the first performers to develop the wordless vocal style known as scat singing, which would later be made famous by artists such as Louis Armstrong, Cab Calloway and Ella Fitzgerald. Josephine would adopt it, too, because she was by now determined to become a singer. She enjoyed her dancing, and revelled in the success it was giving her, but more and more she yearned to be glamorous on the stage rather than a clown.

Always a hard worker, she practised singing during her afternoons, attempting to give weight to a voice that was light and a little shrill. One night she was given a small break when Ethel Waters turned up with laryngitis and Sam Slavin asked Josephine to sing in her place. She was petrified with nerves before going on, but got through 'Dinah' on sheer guts, and her bravery won her a stand-in's ovation. Furthermore, a member of the audience sent her a bunch of violets (the traditional non-romantic thank-you gift to a performer). She said later: "I didn't know men did such things for singers." This further strengthened her resolve to become one herself.

She received other, less welcome attention from some members of the audience. On one night a white New York actress invited four of the girls in the show, including Josephine, to an after-show supper in her suite at the Ritz-Carlton, promising to pay them for their time. Josephine was bowled over by her first sight of the Ritz. She felt like she was walking into a palace, and at supper she was dazzled by the actress's diamond bracelet. This was the way to live.

She noticed that the actress seemed a little tense during the meal, but thought nothing much about it. It certainly didn't prepare her for what happened after the meal was over, when the actress herded the four girls into her bathroom, handed each a lace negligée and told them to take off their clothes, put on the negligées and then come into the adjoining bedroom. The others obediently changed and trooped off out of the bathroom. Josephine, suspicious and increasingly apprehensive, took her time.

When she eventually did enter the bedroom, she found her three fellow performers laid out on the bed "like sardines", with the actress lying across them and working herself into a sexual frenzy as she caressed and kissed them. The unexpectedness of the scene shocked Josephine into uncertainty and fear, and she began to cry.

Then she got mad. She stomped back to the bathroom and put her clothes back on and headed for the door. But before reaching it, she had an idea. In a scene entirely typical of her later self, she marched right back into the bedroom and demanded her fee. It wasn't really all that surprising that "the woman kicked me out without giving me a cent".

It was undoubtedly the lesbian aspect of the scene that so unnerved her, because as far as men were concerned it was well understood at clubs such as the Plantation Theater Restaurant that the black girls in the show were more or less expected to make the male customers happy if requested. This was part of the white fascination with black life. Black women were supposed to be sexually freer than white women, more instinctive and adventurous. How much Josephine involved herself in this sort of activity is not recorded, however. It might have been frequently, because sex was something she took lightly, as not being all that important, or it may have been not at all, which would be consistent with her growing image of herself as a star.

As her weeks at the club stretched into months, she began to become restless. She had no clear idea where her career might take her next, or where she should try to direct it. But across the Atlantic, in Paris, events were already happening that would alter her life yet again.

André Daven was co-director of the Théâtre Des Champs-Elysées, along with Paul Achard. Opened in 1913, the first building in France to be made of reinforced concrete and claiming to be the first important theatre built in Paris for 40 years, its very first presentation was Sergei Diaghilev's Ballets Russes, the production in which Nijinsky danced Stravinsky's *Le Sacre Du Printemps* – not the 1909 version, where he scandalised Paris by dancing Ravel's *L'Après-Midi D'Un Faune*, but still adequately shocking.

The theatre closed during World War One, and Daven and Achard became its co-directors when it re-opened. They presented Anna Pavlova in *Swan Lake*, and with the help of the energetic intellectual and patron Rolf de Maré introduced to Paris the controversial Ballet Suédois, whose star and choreographer was Jean Borlin. De Maré was deeply involved with the whole avant-garde scene of his day. Among the many of those with whom he collaborated with were the Dadaist artist Picabia, composer Georges Auric, surrealist Man Ray, film-maker René Clair and the subversive artist Marcel Duchamp.

The Théâtre Des Champs-Elysées was huge, and was a difficult establishment to keep solvent in spite of its prestigious successes. It was de Maré who, in 1925, suggested to Daven and Achard that he bought the theatre, and that they turned it over to mounting high-class music-hall concerts, which both he and they did (rather to the disgust of its builder and previous owner, Gabriel Astruc). It was their announced intention to give music hall artistic respectability, rather as Edward Albee had tried to do in America and Sir Oswald Stoll and Sir Alfred Butt in London.

They opened their first such show, *Saison Opéra Music Hall*, on 3 April 1925, promising their audiences the greatest actors, actresses, singers and dancers, and an orchestra of the highest quality. It was fairly successful, but Paris was a city hungry for new sensations. All through the Twenties there was a great deal of money there, and it became the world's fashionable artistic centre. Painters, sculptors, dancers, poets and writers all flocked there, and so there was always some new thing to see – whether an art exhibition or a poetry-reading or a new ballet – and shows had to compete with hard-to-attract audiences. Producers constantly had to come up with productions that were not only new but were also exciting and different.

André Daven was friendly with the cubist painter Fernand Léger, who, like many of the artists and intellectuals of the time, had become fascinated with native African art. This interest in things African and Caribbean had been growing in Paris since the late 1880s, when, in the wake of France's colonial expansion, explorers had sent back many artefacts. These were exhibited in museums, and in 1874 many of them were gathered into a permanent collection, the Musée De L'Homme, in the Trocadéro Palace.

At first, such artefacts were considered by most people to be evidence of the primitiveness of African culture, but at some point in around 1906 artists such as Matisse, Modigliani, Dali and Picasso began looking at these objects with a new eye and started to build up collections of their own. They saw in African carvings and statues something simpler and more abstract than formal Western art, images that seemed to them to have a deeper and more instinctive reality.

When the Great War broke out, this interest acquired a further emphasis. If conventional reason and a rational belief in progress had brought about such horrors, perhaps the way to go was to trust man's deeper nature, his emotions and instincts. African art seemed to deal more directly with these. In Paris, in 1916, the Dadaists held African evenings at the Cabaret Voltaire, inspired by primitivistic masks made by Marcel Janco.

Nine years later, in mid 1925 there was an exhibition of African statuary at the Exposition Des Arts Décoratifs. Léger had just seen it, and was full of it, when André Daven told him of the problem he was having in coming up with a new idea for a show. "Give them negroes," said Léger. "Only negroes can excite Paris." Daven might have done nothing about this suggestion, but it planted the idea of a black show in his mind, so he was prepared to be receptive when, a short time later, American socialite Caroline Dudley swanned into his office and asked: "Would you be interested in presenting a show of authentic negro vaudeville?"

"Oui. Bien sûr," said Daven, although he admitted later that he had only the vaguest idea what she was talking about.

Caroline Dudley, then aged 35, was one of three remarkable sisters. All intelligent, lively and pretty, they had been raised in Chicago as the daughters of a successful physician. From girlhood they had devoured French art and literature, and so naturally they were among the many wealthy Americans who flooded Paris in the Twenties. It was pleasant for Caroline that her husband, Donald Reagan, who was an officer in the American Foreign Service, was shortly to be posted to Paris as commercial attaché to the American Embassy. Or, rather, it would have been pleasant, except that she happened to have lost interest in him. This rather left her feeling at a loose end and looking for something with which to fill her time. She was also aware that, of all of her family, she was the sister with no particular talent, just ideas and energy, and so she decided that a good way to make her name would be to set herself up as a producer, which she'd never been before, and bring a black show, such as maybe *Shuffle Along*, to Paris. She judged Paris to be ready for such a show, and her husband, hoping to keep her as his wife (vainly, as it later turned out), agreed to invest some money into the project.

Her father, a physician, was an active liberal who often invited blacks to his house for dinner. In fact, Caroline liked to boast (truthfully) that she "grew up on Booker T Washington's knee." As well as her interest in French art and literature, she also had a passionate interest in black music and dance, spending much of her time in New York as one of the members of café society attending black shows and cabarets.

With André Daven having already said *bien sûr*, there was little else they needed to discuss. "Go back to New York," he told her. "Cable me if you can find the performers for the show. I'll send you money to bring 30 people." And off she went.

By the time she got back to America she had decided that what Paris needed was not a repeat production of some existing show but something entirely new, and so, on reaching New York, she sought out the well-known composer Spencer Williams, asking him not only to write music for the new show but also to help put it together.

Spencer Williams was an important figure in early jazz. Born in New Orleans in 1889, he was raised in Birmingham, Alabama. However, he happened to be the nephew of one of the most famous New Orleans madams, Lulu White, a blue-eyed octoroon from the West Indies, and in his teens he returned there to play the piano in her famous brothel, Mahogany Hall, which had cost $40,000 to build and had five parlours and 15 bedrooms, each with an *en suite* bathroom. In celebration of this sumptuous establishment, Williams later wrote his famous composition, 'Mahogany Hall Stomp'.

Arriving in New York in 1916, he became active in the music business, and over a long career wrote or co-wrote hundreds of tunes, including 'I've Found A New Baby', 'I Ain't Got Nobody', 'Royal Garden Blues', 'Careless Love', 'Everybody Loves My Baby', and his biggest hit, 'Basin Street Blues', which – with lyrics added later by Jack Teagarden and Glenn Miller – eventually earned him $50,000.

With Spencer Williams' help, Caroline set about assembling her show. As her band's pianist and leader she hired 22-year-old Claude Hopkins, a bright young man who had studied Medicine and Music at Howard University (where both of his parents were on the faculty), and who had already led bands of his own around New York. As her leading male star and choreographer she hired the talented tap dancer Louis Douglas, who had already been to France and would eventually emigrate there permanently. As her set designer, she acquired the services of a rather amazing 21-year-old Mexican called Miguel Covarrubias, remembered by those who knew him in America as having the manner of Lucille Ball's husband, Desi Arnaz. A self-taught illustrator, Covarrubias had taught art in outdoor schools in Mexico before coming to the USA on a scholarship in 1923. Almost as soon as he arrived he was hired by the sophisticated magazine *Vanity Fair*, and the caricatures he drew for it influenced many other artists.

It was for the December 1924 issue of *Vanity Fair* that he produced a lively series of drawings of Harlem blacks that was called 'The New Negro, A Distinctive Type Recently Created By The Coloured Cabaret Belt In New

York', which, of course, was why Caroline Dudley had hired him. (After only a few years in America he would go back to Mexico and would so effectively develop his new-found passion for archaeology that a wing of the Archaeological Museum there now bears his name.)

Looking for a female star for the show, Caroline Dudley and Spencer Williams visited the Plantation Theater Restaurant. But it wasn't Josephine they were looking for – it was Ethel Waters.

After seeing the show, Caroline offered Ethel the job, and Ethel – nervous of going to a strange country where she wouldn't know the language – fended her off by asking for the ridiculous sum of $500 a week. This was way outside Caroline's budget, and so the offer collapsed then and there.

Caroline had seen and admired Josephine in *Shuffle Along*, but had no idea what had become of her since, or that she was appearing at the club, and she was delighted to come across her again, saying "She stood out [on the end of the line] like an exclamation point!" With sudden inspiration, and knowing that she would still have to find a singing star, she asked Josephine if she would join the show as a dancer. Learning that Josephine's salary at the club was $125 a week, she offered her $150.

Josephine, while not as nervous as Ethel about going to France, was still pretty nervous. First, she impulsively said that yes, she'd go, but then she began to have misgivings. After all, nobody in the business had ever heard of Caroline Dudley; she'd never produced a show in her life, and so was an unknown quantity. Was it a good move to go across the ocean to a strange land to work in a show that might turn out to be a total flop?

She later told Caroline that she'd changed her mind and wouldn't go. Caroline offered to raise her salary to $200 a week. Wanting to be a glamorous singer rather than simply a clown, she asked Caroline if she could have the role in the show that Ethel might have had, but Caroline, aware of Josephine's rather high and thin voice, said no, giving as a reason that she needed a comic, and Josephine was the best comic she could get. She would dance and she would act in a sketch. Josephine said that she'd think it over.

There were a number of reasons why she felt that she really should take up Caroline's offer. First, she was always bold, and willing to take a chance, as she had done in leaving St Louis to tour with The Dixie Steppers, and as she had done when leaving Willie Baker to go to New York. Second, she had discovered that she loved to travel and see new places, and she had heard that France was a good place for blacks, where they were treated equally.

Also, she had liked the few French people she had met in New York (who were mostly waiters). Paris seemed to offer her freedom and dignity. Third, and the reverse side of the coin, she had come to dislike the way blacks were treated all over America. Even in a sophisticated and cosmopolitan city like New York, there was racial prejudice. A black woman wasn't allowed to try on a bra or a slip in many Harlem shops, or a hat in a Fifth-Avenue store, and in as late as 1938 the singer Billie Holiday – appearing with Artie Shaw's white band at the Hotel Lincoln on Eighth Avenue – was asked by the manager to use the freight elevator so that customers wouldn't get the idea that there were blacks staying there.

A fourth reason was that she was impressed by Caroline Dudley as a role model, by her elegance and style. But still, understandably, she dithered. What did she know about how French people behaved? Spencer Williams urged her to go, assuring her that in Paris she would be a sensational success. Caroline Dudley raised her offer to $250 a week, and at last Josephine took a deep breath and accepted.

As well as considering Ethel Waters as her female singing star, Caroline Dudley had been considering Gertrude Saunders, who had also been in *Shuffle Along*, but eventually she hired Maud de Forrest, a good vaudeville blues singer with a strong voice in the mezzo-soprano range (and a disconcerting tendency, after a few gins, to sing solemn spirituals).

The cast and band were now almost complete, the band acquiring at the last minute the splendid New Orleans clarinetist Sidney Bechet, who would also spend much of his later life in France. A powerful and passionate improviser with a ravishing tone and driving rhythm, Bechet was comparable only to Louis Armstrong as a jazz originator. Born in 1897, he had already toured Europe (including France) in 1919 as part of The Southern Syncopated Orchestra, a black outfit playing mostly concert music with set arrangements and led by the former classical violinist Will Marion Cook. Bechet, who could not read music, was featured in blues specialities, and it was during this tour that he was famously praised by the Swiss composer Ernst Ansermet as being "an extraordinary clarinet virtuoso" and an "artist of genius".

The band for Caroline Dudley's show, led by Claude Hopkins, eventually became a fairly standard eight-piece group, comprising trumpet, trombone, clarinet, alto sax, piano, guitar, bass and drums. With a cast of 16, plus Spencer Williams, the company thus totalled 25, slightly less than the 30 for which André Daven had offered to pay passage.

The plan was that they would appear as the second half of what would otherwise be a conventional Parisian music-hall bill. It was fashionable in Paris for many of the audience to miss most of the early part of the show, turning up just before the interval to hear the singing star, who traditionally closed the first half. In this case this slot was performed by the singer and impersonator Saint-Granier, mostly remembered today for having had a huge hit with his recording of the French version of the song 'Ramona'. As they were to be only half of the show, the company's performance was to last just 45 minutes, and before they left New York they had a few preliminary rehearsals, where they chose songs, worked out dances and ran through the dialogue for sketches. It was Caroline's intention to present a loosely-structured show, with room for the cast and band to improvise their songs and steps, like jazz musicians.

Claude Hopkins, as the bandleader, was delighted with the way Josephine performed in rehearsal. As he said in an interview with Warren Vache, Sr, in 1986, "She was very beautiful, with an outgoing and friendly personality, and she did everything well, singing, dancing and fitting into the comedy skits without any effort or strain. It was easily apparent that she had exceptional stage presence."

Caroline Dudley, too, was increasingly impressed by the maturing of Josephine's talent. As well as producing her show, she began to see herself as having a further mission: to see that Josephine fulfilled her talent as an exceptional comedienne. She took Josephine under her wing, and Josephine – never one to miss an opportunity – announced one day that she would need an evening gown to wear on the boat. Caroline obligingly took her to the showroom of a Seventh Avenue designer, and as the models paraded expensive creations for their approval she was surprised at how at home Josephine appeared in this unfamiliar situation. It was as if she'd been choosing designer clothes all her life. "No, no," she would say, or "That won't do." Then a model appeared in a simple scarlet gown, slashed low in the front. "That's it," said Josephine.

Josephine's growing excitement at the forthcoming trip and her growing confidence of success began to make her skittish. Because she was just 19, and thus technically still a minor, Caroline had to go with her her to the passport office in Lower Manhattan, acting as her guardian. Filling in the forms, the clerk asked her: "Single?"

"Yes and no," said Josephine.

"Married?"

"Yes and no."

"Divorced?"

"Yes and no."

At this point, the man lost his patience and snapped: "Which is it?"

Josephine simply shrugged and flashed him a radiant smile. But somehow the forms were filled in, and Josephine and the whole troupe sailed for France on the evening of 15 September 1925 on the *SS Berengaria*.

As the liner steamed down the Hudson and out through Upper New York Bay into the broad Atlantic, Josephine stood at the rail near the bow and looked back at the disappearing city. As she wrote later, "My life passed in review before me. I saw Bernard Street and my raggedy playmates...When the Statue Of Liberty disappeared over the horizon, I knew I was free."

This is most likely coloured by hindsight. In spite of the reassurances of Caroline Dudley, and of the two members of the show who had already been to Paris, Sidney Bechet and Louis Douglas, the world outside America was still an unknown quantity to her. It would probably be truer to say that she felt more free, and hoped that she was free.

But certainly she had come to detest America. In spite of her success in *Shuffle Along* and *Chocolate Dandies*, in later life she rarely spoke of those days, saying in one of her rare comments: "America was evil then."

Even aboard the *Berengaria* the evil was still present. Taken from the Germans in 1918 as part of war reparations, she was now American owned and as rigidly segregated as any hotel in the USA. Thus, although the first-class section teemed with the rich and socially prominent, Caroline Dudley and her troupe were travelling in steerage.

They did, however, have one moment of contact with the first-class passengers. To help recoup something towards the cost of their passage, Caroline arranged to put on a show in the first-class lounge, not using the material they were going to present in Paris but instead cobbling together a string of acts for the occasion. This naturally demanded a certain amount of rehearsing, but Josephine refused to participate in this, and nor was she going to dance. She was going to sing. She was going to sing like Ethel Waters. So all she did was choose a song and work out with Claude Hopkins the key and tempo in which she would sing it. The song she chose was a fairly chirpy, medium-tempo number called 'Brown Eyes (Why Are

You Blue?)', and she appeared onstage to sing it wearing the elegant, low-cut scarlet gown that Caroline had bought for her on Seventh Avenue.

It was a disaster. The acoustics of the lounge were poor – it was bigger than the Plantation Theater Restaurant – and Josephine had not yet learned to project her voice. The band swamped her.

"She was a flop," recalled Caroline Dudley. "A dead duck. I knew she would be, but I let her go ahead. I wanted her to realise that her forte was comedy."

Josephine was furious. She had a formidable temper, which was partly a determined attempt to get what she wanted – backed by her full histrionic talent – and partly a scream of rage at life for being unfair. She turned this on Caroline, accusing her of deliberately humiliating her. Accosting her outside the lounge, she shouted (among other things) "You're fixin' t'kill me! I'm finished! I'm leavin' tomorrow."

Caroline, like the poised socialite she was, said politely: "Do just as you like, but you can't leave tomorrow. We're in the middle of the ocean."

By the next morning, Josephine had calmed down, but all of the insecurities that had caused her outburst remained. Subdued and scared, she went to Caroline's cabin and knocked softly on the door. Caroline opened it. "Miz Dudley," said Josephine, "why you choose me? Why you want me to come?"

One thing to be said about Josephine's sudden changes of mood is that, in her life, she was not so much devious and manipulative as impulsive and honest. Whatever she felt at the moment – sad, excited, envious, angry, playful or afraid – she expressed. It was her lightning changes of mood, so strongly demonstrated, that made her unpredictable and, to some, unnerving. But in her way she was always straightforward. When she came so contritely to Caroline's cabin, Caroline put an arm around her and smiled. "Because you are beautiful and chic and you can dance," she said, which was supportive but not entirely true, because, like Josephine herself, Caroline had never thought of her as a beauty.

After almost a week at sea, the *Berengaria* docked at Le Havre early in the morning of 22 September 1925, and the whole troupe boarded the waiting boat-train for the 100-mile journey to Paris. Once on their way, they all headed for the refreshment car for a breakfast of coffee and croissants. For the band – except Sidney Bechet and Louis Douglas – this was their first experience of a truly non-segregated atmosphere. They were not only immediately accepted as customers but they were also greeted with welcoming smiles. Even though they had been told that they could expect this, the unfamiliarity of it was almost unnerving.

Louis Douglas assured them that in France they would find this sort of civilised treatment everywhere, and that if they went to the theatre they would even be allowed to sit in the stalls. Bechet told them, not for the first time, that this was one of the main reasons why he had wanted to come back.

At about ten o'clock in the morning the train pulled into the Gare St Lazare, where André Daven was waiting to meet them. He was feeling a little uneasy because he still had no clear idea what sort of a show he might expect, and it was due to open at his theatre in only ten days' time.

The day was dark and rainy, and the station was chilly, which proved the perfect contrasting backdrop for the sight that soon greeted him. Out of the carriages, he recalled, "spilled a little world. Rocking, boisterous, multi-coloured, carrying bizarre musical instruments, all talking loudly, some roaring with laughter. Red, green, yellow shirts, strawberry denims, dresses in polkadots and checks. Incredible hats – cream coloured, orange and poppy – surmounted 30 ebony faces, wild and joyous eyes." Josephine, wearing black-and-white overalls, rushed up to him. Throwing her arms in the air in excitement, she exclaimed: "So this is Paris!"

Daven had hired a tour bus to transport them to the Théâtre Des Champs-Elysées. His anxieties had been somewhat relieved by the colourful energy of the troupe, but he would not feel easy in his mind until he had seen them perform. For this reason he had scheduled a rehearsal for that very afternoon.

As the bus drove through the eighth arrondissement, the business centre of Paris, Josephine stood on its observation platform, staring through the rain at the grey office buildings, the arcades and the shops, and at the smartly-dressed Parisians. She was very happy. During her 19 years she had amassed an armoury of superstitions to guide her. (She had with her, for instance, a lucky rabbit's foot given to her in New York by an old black man.) One of these was that it was lucky to arrive anywhere for the first time in the rain.

The bus arrived at Avenue Montaigne, where the theatre was situated. As a welcome to the troupe, André Daven had floodlit its front façade, but the troupe were not that interested. As soon as they had alighted they headed straight for a small café called Le Bar Du Théâtre. They wanted more coffee and croissants.

Standing in front of the theatre, waiting to welcome them, was an up-and-coming artist called Paul Colin, then aged 33, who would turn out to be an important influence on Josephine. A short, outgoing man, he had been born in Nancy, 180 miles east of Paris, in 1892. His father had a secure (if modest) job in a government office, and hoped that his son would take up a similar post, but Paul was drawn to art, and at the age of 15 made a move in that direction by getting himself apprenticed to a printer. Three years later he enrolled at the local École Des Beaux Arts, and in obedience to the urgings of his concerned father he joined the architecture school. It didn't take long for the professor there to see his talent for drawing and have him transferred to the painting school.

In 1912, after two years at the école, he moved to Paris to try and make it as an artist. He had starved, and would have gone on starving for longer if the Great War hadn't intervened in 1914. Called up, he served the full four years it lasted, emerging with a Croix De Guerre for distinguished service and the rank of sergeant-major.

Resuming his artistic career in Paris, he at once began to do better. He made a modest living by making illustrations for several small publications, and through a friend he won a commission to paint a mural. This earned him enough to rent a studio where he could work. In 1922, he sent 25 paintings to an exhibition being held in his home town of Nancy, and all 25 were sold, which was an encouraging sign of better things to come. In the previous year, on a Parisian street, he ran into an old friend from his army days: André Daven.

Daven, by hiring him as a poster artist, brought him into contact with the world of entertainment, with which he'd never previously had anything to do, and it proved to be the perfect inspiration for him. He had an outstanding ability to create a distilled essence of a performer's face and posture in a strong, simple image that was instantly recognisable.

At this time, in 1925, he had been commissioned by Daven to draw the poster for Caroline Dudley's show, which, it had been decided, would be called *La Revue Nègre*. Paul's immediate problem was that, with the opening so close, he had only 24 hours to get his design to the printers, and so he too was anxious for the rehearsal to begin.

Entering the theatre with coffee cups and croissants in their hands, and chattering excitedly, the cast found the stage brightly lit. Crossing the darkened auditorium, they set about preparing. Josephine ducked into the shadows behind a flat and changed out of her black-and-white boiler suit into her first costume.

The band tuned up, and suddenly the rehearsal was on. They roared into an up-tempo nonsense song written especially for the show by Spencer Williams, 'Boodle-am Shake'. A tall, long-legged man danced and began tapping and singing, and a line of chorus girls danced behind him, singing: "Boodle-am, boodle-am, boodle-am now/Skoodle-am, skoodle-am, skoodle-am now/Gag-a-lag, gag-a-lag, gag-a-lag too/Skag-a-lag, skag-a-lag, skag-a-lag do."

The number finished, the male dancer made his exit, and Maud de Forrest entered and began to sing in her strong vaudeville voice a slow version of the spiritual 'Sometimes I Feel Like a Motherless Child'. The chorus, still there behind her, incongruously shook and shimmied.

As the rehearsal continued, André Daven became more and more appalled, as did Rolf de Maré, who was with him. The show was too noisy and too scrappy. There was also too much tap dancing, and Parisians weren't all that keen on tap dancing. Maud de Forrest's slow spirituals and blues they found depressing, and perhaps worst of all there was nothing much in the show that was very sexy. Parisians – used to the semi-nudity of their leading music hall, the Folies Bergère – would never stand for something so erotically bland.

Nor would they stand for the ridiculous costumes. In one scene, the women wore high-button green shoes with red laces and hats over-decorated with flowers and fruit. This might have been Harlem's idea of a stunning colour scheme but it certainly wouldn't do for Paris. The whole show (which was also too long) would have to be completely redesigned.

Paul Colin, sitting sketching in the stalls, had been concerned as well. He wanted to catch what he thought of as "the soul of Harlem" in his poster – a new, exciting, sensuous, lively soul. And how was he to do that by using the image of the show's star? Maud de Forrest was short and slightly plump, and using her shape to create that feeling would be difficult.

Then on came Josephine to do her speciality dance, and he saw at once that this was what he was looking for. "Her face seemed ordinary," he wrote later, "but her body was beautiful. And I never saw anybody move the way she did. She was part kangaroo and part prizefighter. A woman made of rubber, a female Tarzan. She had the perfect figure for a poster."

But how to get all that down in the short time he had? How to capture her essence? When she came offstage he beckoned her over to him. She gave a radiant smile and came to where he sat. He spoke no English and she spoke no French, but he showed her what he was doing, making a few rough sketches of her. She took his pencil and added a few doodles herself, and he saw that she was intelligent, "perhaps too intelligent". He decided that the best way to capture her for his poster would be to get her to come to his studio, away from the distracting hurly-burly of the theatre. Finding somebody to interpret for him, he explained what he wanted and told her the address: "Place De La République. Entendu?"

"Yes. Yes," she said.

He had asked her to come at ten that evening, but he had doubts about whether she would arrive. After less than half a day in a strange city, without knowing the language, would she be prepared to set off for an address that was clear across town? But he didn't know Josephine's boldness, her determination, and the sheer delight that was buoying her up on her first day in Paris. She was there on the dot, wearing what Paul later described as "an unbelievable get-up – red dress, green shoes, aigrettes on her head". Elisabeth Welch might have praised Josephine's natural elegance at the time of *Shuffle Along*, but taste in 1925 was still Harlem rather than Paris, and Paul was something of a clothes snob.

Using sketches and gestures he explained to her that he wanted her to undress. She was reluctant at first, unsure of the situation in which she found herself, but she undressed down to her underclothes and posed for him. Not a single static pose, but a succession of them – dancing a step or two, arching her back, striking an attitude – and as he sketched, she relaxed. A new feeling grew in her. Here was a man looking at her intently and making no attempt to come on to her. Yet from the light in his eyes it was obvious that he liked what he saw. She felt safe with him, and very soon took off all of her clothes. For the first time in her life she began to feel that she was truly beautiful.

Paul certainly felt so, observing that she had the natural grace of movement of an animal. But he did notice two things about her that told of her hard early life: her feet were calloused from years of walking hard pavements and wearing ill-fitting shoes, and her forehead was already becoming faintly lined.

The poster with which Paul Colin showed up at the theatre on the following day, which became the poster for *La Revue Nègre*, is – while striking and effective as a poster – in truth one of the poorest drawings he ever did of Josephine. To capture all of her vitality and movement and the unique sensuous line of her body in a drawing was no easy task, and besides he had observed few blacks – a few African and West Indian immigrant workers, that was all. The poster is in bold, simple colours – black, white and red – and shows two large male faces in the foreground, one a chubby oval with thick lips and round bright eyes and the other with a wide, toothy grin and rakishly tilted derby, and is very much the standard black vaudeville image of the time. Behind them is a three-quarter-length picture of what purports to be Josephine in her slip, but which in fact is a near copy – even down to the pose – of one of Miguel Covarrubias's drawings from *Vanity Fair* from the previous year called 'Jazz Baby'.

Paul explained to André Daven why he had chosen Josephine to be on the poster rather than Maud de Forrest, and said that it was a pity that the show itself didn't star Josephine.

"We'll see," said André. He was happy with the poster but much more pre-occupied with the show, which he was beginning to feel might never open at all. He was still trying to pull it into some sort of shape. The band was fine, but the other performers were ragged and undisciplined, and were creating nothing like the smooth routines he was used to seeing at the Moulin Rouge or the Folies Bergère. Calling his frustrating rehearsal to a halt, he stormed out of the theatre and took a taxi to the office of Jacques Charles, the resident producer at the Casino De Paris and generally regarded as the city's most talented choreographer for shows. André asked Charles to take over the production of the *La Revue Nègre*, and the choreographer accepted the offer.

They immediately went back to the Théâtre Des Champs-Elysées and Jacques Charles watched another run-through. Gradually, he began to smile. A few years previously, Irving Berlin had taken him on a conducted tour of Harlem night spots, and what he saw here reminded him of the excitement of that time. He felt that the show had possibilities, but that the cast needed pulling into line. Through an interpreter, he told them "You must let me shape this show or you'll have to go back on the boat. I want total obedience. This will be your only chance."

But what was he to do? Covarrubias's sets were already built (with a little help from two of Caroline Dudley's sisters, Katharine and Dorothy, both of whom were artists and lived in Paris), and so the big, full-company set pieces would have to be left pretty much alone.

Well, first of all there was the chorus line. The shows he had seen in Harlem a few years earlier were rather freer and more ragged than this one was trying to be. It was trying to be *Chocolate Dandies* rather than *Shuffle Along*. He had the (slightly wrong) impression that this lot were trying to put on airs to impress the French, and he found it pretentious. Everyone knew that the great thing about blacks was their natural instinctive rhythm. Obviously the thing to do was to make more use of Josephine. For a start he would adopt André Daven's suggestion and feature her performing the dance that was all the rage in America, the charleston.

At least the problem of the over-gaudy costumes was being dealt with. André had sent Katherine and Dorothy Dudley out to the flea market Le Marché Aux Puces at Place Cligancourt to gather all the ragged colourful old clothes that seemed suitable, and as rehearsals began again they marched in with armfuls of material. Later, Jacques Charles would mix them incongruously to compose crazy dreamlike costumes: "I put Louis XIV tricorned hats with overalls and straw hats with fur coats."

When his first rehearsal was finished, Jacques Charles knew that there was still something missing. It was the sense of wildness and exoticism. Paris' idea of blacks was basically that of Africans, of wild, primitive, sexy jungle dancing. That was what people expected to see. To add this missing spice to the show he would create for Josephine an authentic black *pas de deux*, and he would call it *danse sauvage*. For her partner, he knew just the man: his name was Joe Alex, he was from somewhere like Martinique, and he could often be found at a black club in Montmartre called Le Grand Duc. Joe Alex was summoned.

Jacques Charles further felt that, for maximum effect, both dancers should be almost naked, dressed only in a few feathers between the legs and around the ankles, like true Africans. This would be a first in another way: female nudity above the waist was commonplace in Paris shows, at the Folies Bergère and elsewhere, but always among the showgirls and dancers, not with the stars. Josephine would be the first star to sing and dance and also appear half naked.

When he told Josephine this idea, she was appalled. This wasn't the glamorous image she was aiming for, to appear bare-breasted in front of God knew how many thousand Parisians! What about the queenly silks and satins of which she had dreamed for so long, all the way back in her days on Bernard Street? In floods of tears she demanded to be taken back to the boat. However, Jacques Charles was tougher minded than she expected. He told her firmly that he would take her back only after the opening night. She gave in and obediently agreed to work on his dance.

With Jacques Charles moulding the talent that Caroline Dudley had assembled, the show began to burst into life. André Daven and Rolf de Maré were soon so confident of its success that they arranged a preview performance of two of the numbers from it, in front of 50 invited celebrities, after only three more days' rehearsal. This was almost a full week before the show was due to open, and their idea was to get the whole town talking. Among those who came were artists like Fernand Léger, the art dealer and lover of African art; Paul Guillaume; fashionable people such as the Princess Murat and Baron Biedermann; actresses and cabaret performers; and Mistinguett, the greatest star of the Paris music hall – and, of course, journalists.

The two numbers Daven and de Maré chose to present were a levée scene called 'Mississippi Steam Boat Race' which featured the whole cast, including Maud de Forrest singing, Louis Douglas tap-dancing and Josephine dancing the charleston. The second was the *danse sauvage*, which turned out to be both deeply erotic and slightly comic.

The audience was ecstatic, and the publicity generated by the event gave Paris to understand that what was about to happen would be an "event", like the Ballets Russes had been in 1909 or the African evenings at the Cabaret Voltaire had been in 1916, one of those moments when some aspect of French culture would be sent racing off in a different direction.

After the preview the whole audience and cast were given an elaborate supper party right there on the stage, organised by Rolf de Maré. Josephine entered on the arm of Paul Colin, wearing a dress designed by Paul Poiret, whose fashion ideas – involving the discarding of petticoats and corsets – did much to liberate women from the stifling decorum of the 19th century. In fact, it was Paul Colin who had advised Josephine to buy the dress. Since his first attempt at drawing her in his studio, she had been there again and again to be drawn. She had relaxed more and more in his company, and he took to showing her around Paris. He enjoyed her company and her delight in the city.

The only problem was that he wasn't happy with her dress sense. One outfit in particular he later remembered, a bright red-and-white checked shirt and blouse with green shoes, yellow socks, and a hat trimmed with poppies, sunflowers and daisies. Chic Parisian women stared at her, which rather embarrassed him, but it didn't bother Josephine at all. "She wanted people to look at her," he recalled. "She was a born exhibitionist."

She was also intoxicated by the rich possibilities she sensed for herself in Paris, and was rapidly coming to terms with her new image. No longer the plain-looking comic one, she realised that Paul Colin wasn't the only one who thought that she was beautiful, who thought that her whole body was beautiful. She was beginning to realise that her planned onstage nudity was itself a form of glamour, and that in Paris it was thought to be nowhere near as shocking as it would have been in America. In fact, she was beginning to enjoy the idea. Upset as she had been when Jacques Charles suggested it, now that she had agreed to appear semi nude she would go on appearing so for years.

At the after-preview supper the cast mingled with the audience and drank champagne. Up until that moment, André Daven and Rolf de Maré had exerted every effort to keep them away from alcohol, their somewhat confused idea being that, as America was in the grip of Prohibition, none of the troupe would be used to it and thus would be unable to handle it (although Louis Douglas had managed to sneak Josephine a solitary glass of anisette).

The supper and the publicity were both a roaring success. Rehearsals continued, and on 2 October 1925, at 9.30pm after the intermission, *La Revue Nègre* opened. The lights dimmed, the audience fell silent and the curtains parted to reveal the band, wearing red jackets, sitting on the right-hand side of the stage in front of a Covarrubias backcloth depicting a black man dancing on a bold black-and-white checked floor. They began to play, at first with just the snare drum playing softly, then with the bass coming in, then the piano, and eventually the whole band, gradually getting louder and hotter until the trumpet led them out with an exciting crescendo.

Then the backdrop was raised to reveal the tree-lined levée scene of the 'Mississippi Steam Boat Race'. All of the cast strolled about in bright costumes, the women wearing headscarves. Maud de Forrest sang, Louis Douglas danced, and at the climax of the scene Josephine erupted onto the stage on all fours, stiff legged and with buttocks high in the air, to the tune of 'Boodle-am Shake'. Whirling around, she beat time on the ground with the palms of her hands. She was wearing plaid dungarees with one leg cut to hip length and one to knee length. Her hair, which for so long had been a trial to her, was now cut extremely short, into the stylish bob of the day, a helmet of tight black waves. Standing erect, stomach sucked in and bottom jutting out, she began writhing and shimmying and dancing the charleston, bowing her legs and crossing her eyes and all the time emitting what Paul Colin described as "a strange high-pitched noise", but which in fact was scatting as she had heard Ethel Waters do.

This was dancing like Paris had never seen. She slapped her bottom in time with the music, spun and bent and twisted, linking together different steps from her huge repertoire. Like Paul Colin, writers trying to describe her resorted to animal terms: she was a kangaroo, a snake, a giraffe, a panther, a monkey, a tropical bird. At one point, unrehearsed she leapt for a nearby tree and pretended to try and scramble up it, clawing and slipping.

Some of the audience, unused to such exuberance, feared that Paris was prey to some sort of barbarian invasion. One woman yelled: "Stop it! Stop it! We didn't come to see such ugliness." Others whistled their disapproval. But they were far outnumbered by the wildly approving crowd. Ending her spot, Josephine performed a somersault and skipped offstage.

Other scenes followed. Against a backdrop showing a stylised Manhattan skyline, Sidney Bechet entered pushing a handcart and pretending to be a peanut vendor. Stopping, he played a slow and moving blues on his clarinet. (Josephine always felt that he was the finest artist in the show, and enjoyed his playing enormously.) To his playing, Louis Douglas and Marion Cook walked on portraying a pair of lovers, danced to his music, and walked off.

Next was the sketch 'Louisiana Camp Meeting', in which Josephine and Maud de Forrest played two brides competing for the same man. They fought, and the man – Louis Douglas again – was left alone, dancing around his top hat. Douglas would receive almost as much praise as Josephine. He was a fine tap dancer who could shower the stage with rapid taps without seeming to move anything but his feet. As the eminent dance critic André Levinson wrote, "To see him beating time with one foot, whilst the other slides, or hangs loose, numbed, one is seized by an irresistible gaiety, then, using unexpected side-steps and sham falls saved at the last minute, he fluidly breaks up the uniform rhythm of the 'step'...[He] is one of the most inventive dancers I know."

At last came the finale, called 'Charleston Cabaret', set in a night club and featuring the *danse sauvage*. After some singing, one-stepping and tapping, Joe Alex and Josephine entered. The young Indianapolis writer Janet Flanner, who as Genêt had just begun writing a "Paris Letter" for the newly-founded *New Yorker* (as she would go on doing for over 50 years), recalled them much later in her book *Paris Was Yesterday*. She wrote: "[Josephine] made her entry entirely nude except for a pink flamingo feather between her limbs; she was being carried upside down and doing the split[s] on the shoulder of a black giant. Midstage he paused and, with his long fingers holding her basket-wise around the waist, swung her in a slow cartwheel to the stage floor, where she stood, in a moment of complete silence. A scream of salutation spread through the theatre."

Josephine – who in fact also wore feathers around her ankles and neck, as Joe Alex wore strings of beads – began their "primitive mating dance". Joe was tall and dark and muscular, and she twined her way around him and away from him and back to him, flowing over him like liquid as she caressed him. Her breasts were small and round and firm, and her skin seemed to glow. She involved herself totally in the dance, as if her passion was beyond her control. Unlike her charleston, which was a dance of the legs and arms, this was a dance of the belly and the rear end, made up of appropriate steps from St Louis and New York: the shake, the shimmy, the mess around.

For a while, Louis Douglas – playing a waiter – came on and tap-danced around them. Other dancers danced together in the scene as night club customers. But it was Josephine that everybody watched.

At last Joe Alex again took her narrow waist in both hands and raised her high in the air, holding her aloft while her body quivered in orgasm and stilled.

For a moment the audience sat stunned, and then rose to their feet, some hissing and booing, but most applauding and cheering. A number broke from their seats and made a rush towards the stage. Josephine was so frightened that she fled into the wings. But she had conquered Paris, and would find that a new world was hers.

5 *From Paris To Berlin*

La Revue Nègre was just the sensation that André Daven and Rolf de Maré had hoped it would be. Fashionable Paris found it shocking and exciting (especially Josephine), and argued ferociously about whether this was a good thing or a descent into savagery that imperilled the whole of civilised life. The debate raged in the press and the cafés. No one had ever seen such unbridled sexuality on the stage. Articles were studded with words like "instinct", "exotic", "primitive" and "savage".

One reviewer castigated the show as "the triumph of lubricity, a return to the manners of the childhood of man", but a well-known portrait painter, Émile Blanche – who had been to see the African statues at the Exposition Des Arts Décoratifs, hoping to find in them a "manifestation of the modern spirit" – felt that he had found a great deal more of that in *La Revue Nègre*.

Reviewers confused colony with colony, mingling the Congo with the South Seas. They referred proudly back to famous French explorers like Bougainville and La Pérose, and poured out references to the jungles of the Congo and the palms of the Pacific. After all, these were all faraway places of which people knew very little, apart from their names and the blackness of their inhabitants. The only black community they mostly failed to mention was the one from which the show had truly come, the one in America. Josephine, to them, was an African – it could be seen from the way she bent her knees and jutted out her bum that she was just like one of those African statuettes.

One reviewer who did see the show as American was Robert de Flers, writing in *Le Figaro*. As a member of the Académie Française, he thought it a "lamentable |example of| transatlantic exhibitionism which makes us revert to the ape in less time than it took us to descend from it". Harking back to the 18-century philosopher Rousseau, with his romantic image of Tahitian "noble savages", de Flers protested that these performers were no such thing, that they were poor and uneducated people from the dregs of modern civilisation. Another writer, who agreed with him, felt that, if the gates were opened to black culture, France might as well burn all of her books and libraries: "All masterworks of the human spirit will be thrown onto a huge bonfire, around which savages will dance naked."

Caroline Dudley, aiming to show that her performers were truly civilised, attempted to counteract such charges of savagery by arranging for the troupe to perform a benefit on the prestigious stage of the Opera House for those wounded, widowed or orphaned in the war.

Art dealer Paul Guillaume, a passionate crusader for primitivism in art, weighed in against de Flers in particular. Listing all of the painters and writers he knew who had been influenced by African art, he declared: "We who have a soul will blush at the poverty of our spiritual state before the supremacy of blacks, who have four souls: one in the head, one in the nose and throat, the shadow, and one in the blood."

The dance critic André Levinson believed that Josephine "had the compelling potency of the greatest examples of negro sculpture". In the show, "the plastic sense of a race of sculptors came to life and the frenzy of African Eros swept over the audience. It was no longer a grotesque dancing girl who stood before them but the black Venus that haunted Baudelaire." So Josephine's initial success in Paris arose as much from her embodying a somewhat imaginary black ideal as it did from her dancing. However, her dancing attracted the same mixture of shock and delight as her black nakedness did. It was like nothing most Parisians in those days had ever seen.

Even more than jazz, black American dance owed a debt to Africa. African dance, unlike European ballets and social dances, tends to be flat-footed. Europeans tend to move each part of the body in a single rhythm; African dance at its most complex uses different rhythms in different parts of the body – arms, legs, head, torso, buttocks – all at the same time, and each of these African features was present in the way Josephine danced.

Furthermore, she brought a spontaneity to her dancing that was all her own. When she danced the charleston, she gave it the sense of release that it was meant to possess, flinging her arms out in abandon. It was a dance that was harder to do well than it looked, and Josephine did it extremely well. Her years of learning – beginning when she danced for her own amusement in childhood – were paying off now more than ever.

Now grown to her adult height, but still not all that tall, she neverthe-less looked tall onstage, partly because of her long-waisted slenderness and partly because of her confidence and vivid personality. Even her legs, which were not all that long and not all that slender, looked so when she danced.

After the first night there was, of course, a party. Writer Henri Jeanson, a fervent admirer and defender of Josephine, saw her on her way there and noticed that, in contrast to the fiery performer she was onstage, she looked chic and elegant, "wearing a diadem, like Cécile Sorel, a lamé cloak – like Spinelli", and he observed that perhaps at heart she was well and truly Parisian.

Yes, she was. She adopted the French spelling of her name, with the accent, becoming Joséphine, and in quite a short time her performances would come to owe as much to the Paris music hall as they did to Harlem or St Louis. Meanwhile, she set about enjoying life as she had never enjoyed it before. She devoured the world around her – light hearted, greedy and irresponsible. At last she was having the childhood denied her as a child.

Paul Colin, of course, escorted her to the first-night party. He was con-tinuing to draw her again and again, and was delighted to educate her in the ways of Paris. For a while they even became lovers. Under his guidance she learned to dress in the style of Paris rather than that of Harlem. At the party, as well as the diadem and the lamé cloak, she wore an ice-blue dress cut on the bias, chosen by Paul from a Paris design house.

But she kept something of her own style, too. On the next morning, tak-ing an autobus to morning rehearsal, she found the other passengers amused by her wearing baggy knickerbockers and a sweater. Knickerbockers, to them, were for English schoolboys. She was happy that they laughed. Shrewdly, she reasoned: "If I'm going to be a success I must be scandalous. I must amuse people."

Paul Colin wasn't the only artist to portray her. At that morning's rehearsal – which took place on the roof of the theatre, the day being sunny – the American surrealist Man Ray arrived to photograph the cast, although it should be mentioned that this sort of work was simply his way of making a living, not part of his true output. At the end of the session he singled out Joséphine to photograph her on her own, posing her against the railings at the edge of the roof. She strutted and posed and mugged, and when Man Ray was finished she was delighted to discover that she had attracted an audience. "Since it was so warm, everybody had their windows open. The secretaries and maids and elevator operators in the adjoining buildings all applauded."

"Paris is the dance," she said later, "and I am the dancer." In love with the city, and with herself in it, she set out to explore it. Somewhat to her surprise, it was smaller than New York, which made it feel more intimate. Full of joy and energy, she walked it from end to end, taking in the gardens, the open-air art galleries, the shops, the markets and the people on the streets. To make things even better, these were Les Années Folles, the French equivalent of the Roaring Twenties. France, like America and most of the rest of the world, was enjoying a decade of release, joy and experiment, emerging not only from the horrors of the Great War but also from a century of moral earnestness.

Among the many men who clustered around the stage door of the Théâtre Des Champs-Elysées, avid to meet her, was a 22-year-old Belgian journalist from Liège, George Sims, who would later become a successful author under the name of Simenon. He remembered Joséphine giving him $75 to send to her mother in St Louis because she was unable to cope with filling in the forms in the post office.

With Paul Colin she went to the Salon De L'Automne art exhibition at the Grand Palais and to tea dances at Jean Cocteau's restaurant, Le Boeuf Sur Le Toit, where a small jazz band played. Cocteau loved jazz, finding it "a better intoxicant...than alcohol". He came to see *La Revue Nègre* six times.

All over the city she went to parties, dressed in the height of chic and making sure never to stray too far from the food, because old habits die hard. Still insecure under all the flash and fire, it took her a while to realise that the famous and fashionable of the city, *le beau monde*, adored her. French waiters in New York had told her that the way to win Paris was to be chic and amusing, and she set out determinedly to be both.

For a time she and Maud de Forrest shared an apartment, and sometimes while she was there she would stand in front of a mirror looking at her body, the body that had been found too short, too skinny, too light and too dark. She was becoming used to the miraculous idea that people found her beautiful, not just amusing, and her confidence in her beauty was growing.

Among those who found her beautiful was the famous designer and *bon vivant* Paul Poiret. Before the war, the Ballets Russes had inspired a fashion for harem pants, which he had developed and elaborated on. Now that *La Revue Nègre* was a similar sensation, he latched onto Joséphine as a model. Her electric vitality and streamlined body were perfectly suited to his wish to liberate the female body from the restricting fashions of earlier years. "It was for me that Poiret created the Zouave pants," she said proudly, years later, but he created many other designs for her as well. One morning dress, described by him as "un rien" (a trifle), cost the trifling sum of 9,000F. Other couturiers, such as Madame Vionnet, did similar, showering her with outfits. Some billed her for them, like Poiret, but many gave them to her for free, regarding her as a walking advertisement.

She avidly collected press clippings about the show for her scrapbook, hunting among the unfamiliar foreign words for the familiar names of the cast, and in the process used the clippings to teach herself French.

Not that there was a shortage in Paris of English-speaking Americans. In the Twenties, in the aftermath of the Great War, rich and even mildly-rich Americans flocked to Paris. There was an atmosphere of leisure and graciousness there far removed from the prevalent American ethic of hard work and progress. Also, it was possible to drink legally, and the exchange rate was very favourable.

American artists and writers went, too, stimulated by a culture in which the arts were appreciated. Man Ray was only one – Scott and Zelda Fitzgerald also went there, as did Ernest Hemingway, Dorothy Parker, Robert Benchley, John Dos Passos, Gertrude Stein and Alice B Toklas.

There was a considerable community of American blacks as well. Several of James Reese Europe's band stayed or returned there after the war, and some musicians had even settled there before the war, including the drummers Buddy Gilmore and Louis Mitchell, who had gone there on a tour with Vernon and Irene Castle. Mitchell saved up and bought himself a little night club in Montmartre, which was where most of the black entertainers lived.

A more famous black night club owner was Gene Bullard. In 1914, when the war began, he had wanted to become a pilot. Having no hope of learning to fly in America, he headed for France and joined the Foreign Legion. Eventually he became a member of the famous Lafayette Escadrille, the squadron formed by the French in 1916 and composed entirely of expatriate Americans. He won 15 medals, and during the years after the war he came to Montmartre to run the minute club named Le Grand Duc, owned by a Mr and Mrs George Jamerson. It had only six tables, with room for maybe half a dozen more customers at the bar. (It was to Le Grand Duc that producer Jacques Charles had sent someone to find Joe Alex.)

In early 1924, Bullard hired from America the first black female entertainer to appear in Paris, the singer Florence Embry. Pretty and lively and somewhat arrogant, she not only sang but also acted as the club's hostess, chatting with the customers and making them feel welcome. She wore stylish clothes with style and the fashionable Parisians adored her, and so Le Grand Duc quickly became a great success, filling with celebrities night after night.

For a while the black poet Langston Hughes, then in his early 20s, worked there as a dishwasher, a relief cook and sometimes as a waiter. He was there in the kitchen in May 1925 when he heard a woman enter the club, say something to Gene Bullard and then break down in tears. He knew that Florence Embry had decided to move to Louis Mitchell's club, which would be renamed Chez Florence in her honour, and Langston Hughes guessed from her voice that this woman must be Florence's replacement. She was. Her name was Ada Smith, and she had been hired by Gene Bullard from America on the advice of Florence's husband, Palmer Jones, at $75 a week. Jones had told Bullard that she couldn't sing all that well (although she'd once been in a trio with Florence Mills), but that, as hostess at Le Grand Duc, her personality would be irresistible.

She was crying for two reasons. One was that she had been seasick for the whole eleven days of the crossing from New York, and the other was that she couldn't believe that the club was so tiny. Had she crossed the miserable ocean just for this?

Gene Bullard was at a loss to know how to comfort her, but Langston Hughes, sensitive gay poet that he was, hurried out to her from the kitchen and said "You need something to eat." He took Ada into the kitchen, fed her, and reassured her that she would come to love the club and Paris, and would be a great success, all of which she did. Adopting the name "Bricktop" because of the reddish tinge to her hair, she was Paris' favourite night club hostess by the time Joséphine arrived, a year and four months later.

Pale skinned, witty, short and slightly plump, she once described herself as "100 per cent negro with a trigger Irish temper". Bursting with joy and vitality, in time she took to turning cartwheels down the Rue Blanche, showing off legs that one reporter described as "more beautiful than Mistinguett's", which from a Parisian was high praise.

Even more than Florence Embry before her, she attracted the rich and famous to the club. It was she who introduced the charleston to Paris (although Joséphine, when she arrived, did it much better), and in the course of time she gave charleston lessons to Scott and Zelda Fitzgerald, Ernest Hemingway, Cole Porter and his wife Linda, and the Prince Of Wales (in a private back room, because he was shy). Cole Porter was so taken with her that he wrote 'Miss Otis Regrets' especially for her to perform.

But as well as her performing and hostessing ability, she had a warm, down-to-earth personality, and was stable and practical. People would come to her for help and advice, which she readily gave. One such was Joséphine, and soon they became fast friends.

Bricktop was ten years older than Joséphine, and the dancer, who was sometimes confused by the intensity of her new stardom and the unfamiliarity of her new world, would turn to her for advice. "She wouldn't go around the corner without asking my advice," Bricktop remembered later, exaggerating slightly.

Among the things that Bricktop tried to teach her was not to adopt the habits of the rich people with which she was now socialising, to remain true to herself and her roots. Remember, she said, "there's nothing in this world like a pork-chop sandwich".

The advice didn't entirely take root. Sometimes even Bricktop found Joséphine's airy acceptance of stardom slightly unnerving. Once she visited her at her apartment and found the floor casually strewn with expensive designer clothes. She suggested that it might be a good idea to have someone hang them up. "Oh no, Brickie," said Joséphine. "They are going to take them away tomorrow and send me another pile."

Indirectly, Bricktop also helped Joséphine in her attempts to develop her singing. Appearing at Le Grand Duc as Bricktop's support was the half-black English singer Mabel Mercer. Gentle and rather shy, Mabel was a subtle singer with a beautiful rich mezzo-soprano voice. While entertaining the clientèle she could drift from talking into singing with hardly a break, bringing out all the subtlety and feeling of such songs as 'Bye Bye, Blackbird'. She would go on performing until she was in her 70s, moving to America and influencing such singers as Frank Sinatra. Joséphine not only adopted something of Mabel's intimate delivery but she also learned from watching Bricktop coaching Mabel, helping her to perfect her performing style. "Stop waving your arms around. Cup them in your lap, like a lady."

She also observed the fact that, as hostess of an intimate club (or, as such places were familiarly known, a *boîte*), Bricktop had considerable prestige. One night when she was there, the designer Elsa Schiaparelli, who had put money into the club, was there with a large party and asked Bricktop to charge their bill to their account. Bricktop was able to insist that she paid then and there. This was obviously a good situation to get yourself into.

Another club host whom Joséphine met was the Jamaican Jocelyn Augustus Bingham, who went under the name of Frisco. (He had been a longshoreman in San Francisco for a while.) Having enlisted during the Great War, he was one of those who decided to settle in Paris after it had ended. He was tall, dark and handsome, and a man of considerable talents. He could speak nine languages, including not only Portuguese but also such exotic tongues as Arabic and Magyar. At his club, Frisco's, he played the piano and danced. As Bricktop became for Joséphine a sort of surrogate mother, similarly Frisco became a sort of father.

She had met him at the Hotel Fournet, where black musicians often met to chat and jam and have informal parties, and Frisco noticed that, at such get-togethers, Joséphine would sometimes suddenly leave, going off to the quiet solitude of her suite. She had a lot to get used to, and needed to be alone at times. Occasionally Frisco would follow her there, and sit talking with her quietly, reassuring her that she was on the right road and would go far. Years later he remembered how very young she could look at that time, younger even than the 19 she was. "She was such a baby then," he said. "She had the sweetest eyes."

Baby or not, she was alert and witty. Like so many writers, Fernand Devoire produced a rhapsodic praise of her, which followed thus: "Josephine Baker, our lives on the banks of the Seine were weary and depressing before you came along. In the eyes of Paris, you are the virgin forest. You bring to us a savage rejuvenation." Joséphine, having this passage translated to her, turned it around to express her own delight in her new life. "To me," she said, "Paris is the virgin forest."

La Revue Nègre continued its triumphal run, although some of the more severe critics – including Janet Flanner – felt that its performances began to become somewhat sloppy. This may have arisen from a growing arrogance in the cast, who were conscious of their huge success, and also from friction between them and André Daven, who continued to regard them rather as unruly, child-like creatures who needed constant watching if they were not to fall prey to spending too much time and money in the Montmartre night spots drinking too much alcohol, because he was sure that they were unused to drinking.

He even instructed his theatre doorman to keep an eye on them at their hotel. There wasn't actually a lot that he could do to control their comings and goings, but nonetheless they resented his presence, and in the third week of the show's run decided to move some way away, to the Hotel Fournet, which stood on the Boulevard Des Batignolles, at the foot of Montmartre. Joséphine decided to join them there and, determined to continue enjoying her success, she rented a suite. It had two bedrooms and a living room, and Paul Colin – a practical Frenchman – was disapproving, feeling that she was being extravagant and heedless.

As much she cared. Enthusiastically, she set about decorating it. From the store Galéries Lafayette she bought a *cretonne* bedspread patterned with bright blue flowers, she bought dolls in multi-coloured frilly dresses to place on her pillow, and she bought a set of antique portable steps to place at the foot of the bed. "Just like Napoleon probably had," she said.

She was proving to have a natural affinity with the famous and powerful, feeling quite at home as a celebrity among celebrities. The kings and queens of her childhood imaginings no longer seemed quite so remote.

Shortly after moving into her suite she indulged her love of animals by buying a parakeet, a parrot, two baby rabbits, a snake and a pink baby pig. She named the piglet Albert, after Albert Tartaglia, the hotel's doorman. Bewitched by Joséphine, he was delighted not only by the pig but by all of her other creatures. Paul Colin, however, was less so – none of them were house trained, and her suite rapidly acquired the atmosphere of a farmyard. He even had trouble finding somewhere clean to sit down.

After *La Revue Nègre* had been running for a month, the first half of the bill at the Théâtre Des Champs-Elysées changed. Its star was no longer Saint-Granier but the singer Damia. Damia was known as "la tragedienne de la chanson", and at that time she was performing a rather moody song by Jules Jouy entitled 'La Veuve' ('The Widow', France's historic nickname for the guillotine). For this, the climax of her act, the stage was bathed in blood-red light, with a backdrop depicting the guillotine in lowering silhouette against the dawn sky.

Damia was a pioneer in the field of stage lighting, using dramatic spotlights and changing colours, a technique that she had learned from the

American ballet dancer Loie Fuller, of whose troupe she had been a member. It was also Damia who invented the customary costume of the Parisian chanteuse: a simple, short-sleeved black dress, which was later imitated by such stars as Edith Piaf and Juliette Greco. She wore one in this show, standing bare armed in the shadows to sing in her grainy, soulful voice.

Joséphine, alert to learning the performing traditions of France, watched her performance eagerly every night, sitting in the wings on a fireman's stool. Damia later recalled: "Extraordinary, that little girl...each night, between two scene supports, Joséphine, who did not then know a word of French, would watch me with her big eyes, with a grave, attentive expression, not missing a word." Damia, too, would become an influence on her singing style as it took form.

Soon Joséphine was not only performing in *La Revue Nègre*; she and the band from the show were also hired to appear late each night at the famous Moulin Rouge music hall. She started to follow a pattern that was common in both America and Paris, of performers appearing in a show and then going on to appear again at another venue, or sometimes several venues. She would go on doing this for years.

The run of *La Revue Nègre* was extended twice at the Théâtre Des Champs-Elysées, but eventually the pressure of other bookings there forced it to close, on 19 November 1925. It had played for seven weeks.

And it went on playing. It moved at once to the smaller Théâtre De L'Étoile, on the Avenue Des Champs-Elysées, where it continued well into December. The whole cast would have happily stayed in Paris for ever, but Caroline Dudley wanted to capitalise on its success by taking it on tour. For a start, she had booked it to appear for six weeks as the last act on the bill at the Cirque Royale in Brussels. After that it was to play six weeks at the Nelson Theatre in Berlin, followed by a further six in Moscow.

This presented Joséphine with a small problem. Paul Derval, the director of the Folies Bergère, had naturally come to see *La Revue Nègre*. Impressed by Joséphine, "whose explosive personality seemed to set the very stage afire", he had returned on the following night and, after the show, introduced himself to her and asked if she would star at the Folies in his next show. Joséphine in turn went to see his current show, which was called *Un Soir De Folie* (all Folies shows contained the word "folie" in their titles, and each title was, for luck, exactly 13 letters long).

The Folies Bergère was, of course, the most famous and lavish music hall in the world. The most famous stars in Paris appeared there, prominent among them in the years between the wars being Maurice Chevalier and Mistinguett. Its vast stage and stunning productions impressed Joséphine enormously. Guardedly, she mentioned to Caroline Dudley that it had been suggested that she might one day appear there. Caroline advised her against doing any such thing, saying that the Folies would turn her into nothing more than a feathered mannequin. "Josephine," she said, "you will hurt your soul," to which Joséphine replied "Missus, I'm feeling fine." She returned to Paul Derval and agreed to star in his next show, to be called *La Folie Du Jour*. Derval produced a contract, and she signed it.

Of course, he knew that she was going off to tour in *La Revue Nègre*, but she did not tell Caroline Dudley about the contract. In any case, she would always retain a naïve suspicion of contracts; to her, raised an underdog, they were simply a means by which the rich and educated and powerful could keep simple ordinary folk in their places, to manipulate them and cheat them.

After Paris, Brussels was relatively uneventful. Their time at the Cirque Royal was exhausting for the troupe, because they were expected to present their show three times a day. They were relieved when their six weeks was up. But again the show had been a massive hit, and again Joséphine was singled out for acclaim by critics and public alike. One show was even attended by King Albert of Belgium and his family, which was another first for Joséphine – her first royal performance.

Then it was on to Berlin. In many ways Joséphine liked Berlin even more than Paris. As a stream of taxis drove the troupe through the evening from the Potsdammer railway station to the Hotel Bristol, situated on the famous Unter Den Linden, she stared in delight at the sea of white electric bulbs that ornamented the city's theatres, dives and cabarets. The bright, brash nightlife of the city felt more like the America she was used to than Paris did, more like the nightlife of Harlem and of Chestnut Alley back in St Louis, but at the same time it was very different.

In those years of the Weimar Republic, between the end of the Great War in 1918 and the rise of Nazism in 1933, Berlin had had a hectic, almost despairing quality. The worst years of inflation – when money became almost valueless and people's savings vanished overnight – were over, but they had left many people with the feeling that it was useless to save, and that the smartest thing to do with money was spend it while you had it, and so, although there was still desperate poverty to be seen on the streets, in the night spots money flowed freely.

Decadence was fashionable, too, with acts taking sexual images and attitudes straight out of Freudian psychology. (Many influential early sexologists, such as Hirschfeld and Krafft-Ebing, were either German or German-speaking Austrians.) In the Berlin night world, exploring exciting new variations in sexuality – fetishism, transvestism, sado-masochism – (or at least dressing as if you might) became quite the thing. It was another variation on hunting wildly for sensation and throwing away the dead proprieties that had led to the disaster of the Great War. In a way, these attitudes were stronger and more desperate in Germany, which had not only suffered through such a war but had also lost it.

The atmosphere of Berlin suited Joséphine at this time because her own mood was hectic. She was ready to enjoy such high living as she had never known, and was dazzled by the endless parade of wealth and fame and talent among which she now moved, still slightly unsure of her own place in the world and fearful that if she stopped chasing her success she might sink back into the life of poverty and despair from which she seemed to have escaped. She lived an incessant round of partying and performing, diverting herself from her underlying fears.

La Revue Nègre was almost as great a success in Berlin as it had been in Paris, and Joséphine was again a sensation. Her slim, small-breasted body was sufficiently boyish to appeal to the gender-bending sophisticates, as was her hair, now straightened to death and cut shorter than ever into a schoolboy-influenced "Eton crop", with a fringe of short curls covering the left half of her forehead.

At that time, the Germans, like the French, were prone to idealise the "noble savage" as representing a healthier ideal of living than that which the increasingly mechanised modern world seemed to offer. Again, Joséphine was seen to embody this, although it was not an attitude that she much understood. When somebody praised her as an embodiment of German primitivism, she became indignant, taking this as an American-style slur on blacks as savages. "What are you trying to say?" she replied. "I was born in 1906, in the 20th century."

Her onstage near-nakedness also appealed to the vigorous and growing German *nacktkultur* (nudist) movement, in which members of all strata of society united in throwing off their clothes in their homes and health clubs, believing that air on the body was more natural and health-giving, and that this freer life would help release people from the neuroses arising from the pressures of modern society.

However, opposed to both the cabaret-goers and the nudists there was a strongly-emerging right-wing movement which was bent on purging decadence in any form from German society, aiming thus to bring into being a nation that was healthy, fit and strong. This was, of course, the infant Nazi movement, and to them Joséphine – being not only decadent but also racially impure – was anathema. The Brownshirts, as the party members were then known, issued pamphlets which condemned her, but fortunately they were still then regarded as only a lunatic fringe and Joséphine was able to shrug them off, saying "I'm not immoral. I'm only natural."

In the night-club world, where she spent much of her time, she was regarded as a star. "In the dance halls," she recalled proudly, "when I walked in, the musicians stopped playing. They stood up and saluted me." Of course they would; jazz came to Berlin later than it did to Paris, but an important recent event there had been the appearance in May 1925 of a show from New York called *Chocolate Kiddies*, with music by the black band of Sam Wooding. Not only was this show received rapturously by a large section of the public but it also influenced young composers such as Kurt Weill (who would later compose many jazz-influenced scores) and Ernst Krenek, who, a couple of years later, would turn out one of the first-ever jazz operas, *Jonny Spielt Auf*, whose composer hero was, in Krenek's words, a "ponderous, inhibited Central European intellectual". In contrast to him was Jonny, a black jazz violinist, seen by Krenek as "a child of nature, totally free of inhibitions, acting on the spur of the moment".

Jazz, of course, came from America, and so to German dance band musicians the uninhibited Joséphine seemed its embodiment. As in Paris, she was celebrated as much for what she symbolised as for her performing. She began to cultivate her image shrewdly and deliberately, setting out to present herself as the person people wanted her to be. In Berlin she posed in studio sessions for several photographers, appearing more naked than she ever had or would again, and frequently crouching in a deliberately animalistic manner. If the people of Berlin wanted a wild and free jungle nudist, she would give it them.

She was invited to all of the smart cafés and clubs and dances and parties, and of course she went to them, still engaged in her hectic chase after sensation and diversion. At this time, she also seems to have engaged in a hectic sex life. It's hard to say how much truth – if any – there is in the many stories of her sexual rapacity in Berlin, which state that men were seen queueing outside her hotel room door, and that she worked in a high-class brothel during her nights.

Undoubtedly, much of this was untrue gossip, generated by her onstage image as the personification of unbridled sexuality, but she certainly had a number of affairs and one night stands at this time, but her remoteness remained. One of her lovers reported: "She didn't need conversation. Sex was like champagne to her. It would last 20 minutes, perhaps one hour, but it was body to body the whole time. She was a free spirit 'way back. Just because a man spent an hour with Josephine, he could never feel that he owned her."

Claude Hopkins, who had a brief fling with her during their time in Berlin, saw her more romantically, describing her later as "a sweetheart", warm and charming. Meanwhile, her old Paris friend and mentor, Frisco, who happened to be appearing at a Berlin club while she was there, commented on how happy she was if a man told her that he loved her. Maybe, given her childhood around the red light district of Chestnut Alley, she simply found it difficult to associate sex with love.

As well as the partying and performing, she had quieter moments as well. Two of the places she enjoyed the most in Berlin, as in almost every major city she would ever visit, were the zoo and the shopping centre, which in Berlin was known as the *vaterland*, a huge area of restaurants and shops selling items from all over the world. Joséphine bought tourist souvenirs by the cartload. She could never have enough of the companionship of animals (which are simpler to deal with than people), and she could never have too many material possessions (which are reassuring).

The fashionable and famous continued to flock to the show. Members of the Krupp family, the wealthy industrialists, came to it almost every night. On one night, Joséphine was told that the most famous German theatrical director, Max Reinhardt, was in the house. Originally Viennese, he had come to Berlin in 1894 when he was 21, and by 1925 he was running four theatres there, including the prestigious Deutsches Theater, where he mounted elaborate and innovative productions of Shakespeare.

Joséphine was unimpressed, having been told too many times over the past weeks that so-and-so was "the greatest", "the most eminent" or "the finest". As she said, "Perhaps this was sometimes the case, but in my ignorance how was I to know?"

Nonetheless, when Reinhardt came around to her dressing room, as she was wiping off her make-up after the show, something about him impressed her. His intense personality and the articulate way in which he discussed her performance, when he seemed to understand exactly what she was about, made her realise that he was indeed something special. Almost at once he asked her if she would become his pupil at the Deutsches Theater. If she would, he told her, he would turn her into a great actress.

His reason for seeking her out was that, back in New York in 1924, he had attended a performance of *Shuffle Along* (which then didn't include Josephine), and had become convinced that the expressive body language of black performers could do much to inject new life into European theatre. As he told Joséphine, "The expressive control of the whole body, the spontaneity of motion, the rhythm, the bright emotional colour – these are your treasures. No, not yours only – these are American treasures. With such control of the body, such pantomime, I believe I could portray emotion as it has never been portrayed." However, in spite of his wonderful way with words, Joséphine, deeply suspicious from childhood, did not at first take this offer seriously. But she responded to his intelligence and power, and began spending much of her spare time with him and his friends.

One of these was the playwright Karl Gustav Vollmoeller, author of *Achtes Wunder Der Jungfrau Maria* (later translated and published as *The Miracle*), which Reinhardt had famously directed. His young mistress, Fräulein Landshoff, was known for her fondness for wearing male attire, and he was known for giving lively informal parties, at which he mixed guests from the whole spectrum of bohemian life: dancers, choreographers, writers, publishers, people who were simply habitués of recherché cafés, boy prostitutes from the "daisy bars", and "just-discovered" actresses.

Another was Count Harry Kessler, nicknamed "the Red Count" for his mildly left-wing views. His father had received his title for making a huge fortune as a banker, and to say that he was well connected would be putting it mildly. He knew everyone who was anyone in anything. He knew Einstein. He knew the Kaiser, then well into his long exile in Holland. By profession he was a diplomat, but he was also an art collector, a publisher and a biographer, and he kept an observant diary that gives a vivid picture of Berlin between the wars. In it he writes of the night in February 1926 when Max Reinhardt phoned him at one in the morning, just as he had finished showing out the last of that evening's dinner guests, and asked him to come over to the party Vollmoeller was giving to meet Joséphine Baker.

Kessler had seen *La Revue Nègre*, of course, and needed no urging. Quickly he got himself to the party, where he found Vollmoeller surrounded by near-naked women. One of these was Joséphine, who was wearing only a pink muslin apron and was doing what he described as an intricate series of improvisations on a basic pattern. He was told that she frequently did this for hours, apparently tirelessly, as happy as a child at play, and it does seem that, by this time in her life, such private dancing had become almost a sort of meditation for Joséphine, a quiet communion with herself that she found relaxing and spiritually rewarding.

Kessler also observed that, whereas he found her dancing bewitching to watch, it was surprisingly unerotic: "Watching her inspires as little sexual excitement as does the sight of a beautiful beast of prey." He began to imagine her as an ancient Egyptian dancing girl reincarnated, and himself as Solomon or Tutankhamen watching her.

By the time this fantasy had begun to establish itself in his mind, Joséphine had started dancing with Fräulein Landshoff, who on this occasion was wearing only a man's tuxedo. This inspired Kessler with the idea of turning his fantasy into reality by planning a ballet or pantomime, in which Fräulein Landshoff would be Solomon, wearing a tuxedo, and Joséphine, dressed in an ancient style, would be his dancing girl – or, as Kessler put it to himself, his Shulamite (although nobody is at all sure what the word Shulamite – which is applied to the bride in 'The Song Of Solomon' – actually means). The music, he thought, should be a cross between jazz and oriental, and might be composed by Richard Strauss, with whom he had already collaborated as co-librettist on the composer's ballet *Josefs-Legende*.

Being a man of action, he set about developing this idea, and ten days later invited Joséphine to a party at his home to discuss it further. She was picked up from the Nelson Theatre after that night's performance by Fräulein Landshoff and a gentleman friend, and was and taken to the party. Kessler's home was a far cry from Vollmoeller's bohemian digs; it was large and splendid, with paintings and sculptures and *objéts d'art*, and the party was being held in his library. The guests were a rather formal collection, mostly of men, but there were a few women. Joséphine was unnerved by the magnificence and formality of the place and the guests, and by the fact that Kessler was a nobleman. As she usually did when faced with such a situation, she withdrew into her shell.

Kessler had expected her to dance for his guests, as she had at Vollmoeller's party. To give her room, he had even cleared his library of furniture and sculptures (except for his current favourite piece, a large nude by Maillol called 'Crouching Woman'), but Joséphine declared that she would be embarrassed to dance nude in front of the women present. She sat in a corner and withdrew into herself.

Kessler made the best of the situation by beginning to outline the ballet he had imagined. Over the previous ten days his concept had become more ambitious. He was now thinking of casting the great dancer Serge Lifar as Solomon. Joséphine was still to be the Shulamite, and Solomon was to shower her with gifts. The more he gave her, the more she would become elusive to him. Continuing to give, he would become more and more naked while she, in her elusiveness, became ever harder to see, until at last she would disappear inside a tulip-shaped golden cloud composed of the jewels and rich fabrics which he has showered on her.

Joséphine listened to this story, entranced. She loved fairy tales, and this, with its image of a woman being given more and more while a king lost everything for love of her, suited her down to the ground. As soon as it was over, her cheerfulness restored, she got up, undressed, and began to dance. It wasn't until she had got into the rhythm of her dancing that she noticed the sculpture 'Crouching Woman'. Dancing over to it, she began structuring her whole dance around it, oblivious of the watching guests. She copied its pose, then parodied it. She pretended that it was an idol and danced in worship of it. Then she began to frolic before it, parodying herself as priestess and it as goddess.

Kessler was entranced, not only by her dancing and imagination but by the fact that his sculpture seemed more real and interesting to her than his assembled guests. This, to him, seemed only right: it was a case of genius – "for she is a genius in the matter of grotesque movement" – speaking directly to genius.

Nothing, however, was to come of his ballet, which was never performed by anyone. Neither did Joséphine's temptation to take up Max Reinhardt on his offer of working with him at the Deutsches Theater come to fruition. Everything began to change when, at a party one night, she found herself in conversation with a Parisian visitor who said how much he was looking forward to seeing her at the Folies Bergère. "Don't count on it," she said.

Unknown to her, the man was a friend of Paul Derval's. Returning to Paris, he told Derval that there seemed to be some danger that he might no longer have a star. Derval was horrified. His writer and producer, Louis Lemarchand, already had preparations for *La Folie Du Jour* well in hand, and the staging of a Folies Bergère production was as expensive and elaborate an exercise as that of a Hollywood musical, involving months of work and hundreds of performers, designers, dressmakers, musicians, technicians, scene painters, songwriters and publicists. He hastily sent his agent, Monsieur Lorett, to Berlin to impress on Joséphine the necessity of honouring the contract she had signed. Lorett took the first train he could and headed for the Nelson Theater.

After waiting for two hours in the biting cold outside the stage door for the evening's performance of *La Revue Nègre* to finish, he was finally admitted to Joséphine's dressing room. Suddenly confronted with the necessity of making a difficult decision, she became defiant. Quite apart from the exciting offers she was receiving from Reinhardt and Kessler, she liked Berlin. Devoted as she was to Paris, she found Berliners more easygoing and informal; in Germany there wasn't the same pressure to dress in the approved style and eat with correct manners. It was true that she and the troupe were shortly to move on to Moscow, but after that she could go wherever she liked.

And then there would be the problem of confronting Caroline Dudley to tell her that she was quitting the tour to appear at the Folies Bergère, which would naturally cause the tour to collapse.

Monsieur Lorett continued to impress on her the vast amount of work that had already been put into the show. It would need 1,200 costumes, which were already being designed and made. And did she realise that songs to suit her had been commissioned from both Spencer Williams and Irving Berlin?

Later in life she would claim that it was the mention of these names that inspired her to return to Paris and star at the Folies. She felt more at home dancing to the American music she knew than she would if she allowed herself to become some foreign thing created by Harry Kessler or Max Reinhardt.

But she refused to allow the Folies to turn her into a "feathered man-nequin". No matter how they presented her, she would remain defiantly herself: Joséphine. As impulsive as ever, she told Monsieur Lorett that she would consider starring in *La Folie Du Jour*, but only on the condition that she was paid 400F more per performance than had been agreed.

Later in life she was candid about her greed (which is always a disarm-ing trick if you can pull it off), saying that she felt that, if he needed her that much, he might as well pay for it. She never forgot how it felt to be wretchedly poor, and no matter how much money she made she never felt that she had enough.

When Lorett told him of her demand, Paul Derval realised that he had no option. "What could I do?" he said later. "The show was too far advanced for us to cancel it, and there would have been no point in taking her to court. I surrendered."

It was necessary for Joséphine to return to Paris almost at once, and so she was then faced with the unpleasant problem of telling Caroline Dudley that she was leaving *La Revue Nègre*. This she solved by delegating the chore to Sidney Bechet. He duly delivered the news, and Caroline Dudley announced to the troupe that the rest of the tour would have to be can-celled. The disappointed performers, afraid of Joséphine's temper, instead turned their anger onto Caroline. "I'm gonna have two men guard you," Bechet told her. "Somebody might cut your throat."

Caroline paid the boat fares back to New York for those who wanted to go, and when all of the bills were paid she discovered that overall *La Revue Nègre* had left her $10,000 in the red. Later she tried to sue Joséphine for this amount, but the case never came to court. Nonetheless, Caroline was understanding about the matter. "How could I blame her?" she said. "She was a bastard off the floor. She was kicked around all her life."

6 La Folie Du Jour

Joséphine returned to Paris in March 1926. Now that she was to star at the Folies Bergère, and longed to be accepted by respectable Paris, she chose not to live in the cheerful and bohemian quarter of Montmartre, even though that was where she would spend most of her time, both working and socialising. Instead she chose the up-market district of L'Étoile, renting a two-room apartment on the Rue Beaujon, a quiet street near the Parc Monceau, where she would sometimes walk and relax. Not that she had much time for relaxing, because almost at once she began six weeks of hard rehearsal at the Folies Bergère.

A large theatre, seating 920, it had begun life more modestly in 1868 as France's earliest music hall, built in imitation of the music halls that had sprung up in London after the Canterbury opened in Lambeth in 1849. That had been the first building in the world to be specifically designed and used as a music hall, and in it – as in the early Folies Bergère – the audience sat at tables to eat and drink while watching the performance.

The Folies presented songs and sketches, circus-type acts like acrobats and jugglers, mimes, and even mini operettas. The French grew to love the tradition of the music hall, and although it had started later there than in London it continued to flourish as a major entertainment right into the Thirties, long after the tradition was dying in Britain and America.

Over the years many stars appeared at the theatre, among them Yvette Guilbert, Yvonne Printemps, Edith Piaf, Georges Brassens, Grock and Arletty. But in spite of such headliners, by 1926 it was the spectacle of the show that predominated, the elaborate décor and costumes, the lighting and the music – and, of course, the nudes.

Nude (or, to be accurate, bare-breasted) girls had first appeared at the Folies in 1894. At that time, like many top music halls, such as the Empire in London's Leicester Square, the theatre was still rather disreputable. Both were places where prostitutes cruised the lobbies looking for business.

It was the Great War that spelled the end of this trade. Respectable public opinion was appalled that so many young officers on leave from the trenches seemed unable to resist temptation. In London, bowing to public agitation, the Empire's owner, Sir Alfred Butt, closed its famous promenade in 1916, and three years later it was Paul Derval himself who banned *les dames de trottoir* from the Folies when he took over the running of it in 1919.

A former stage hand and vaudeville actor, then aged 39, he also changed the nature of the shows considerably, lifting the Folies to the international fame that it came to enjoy. He did this by featuring much more nudity, but also by sanitising it, by treating the female body as an aesthetic spectacle rather than an erotic one. This made his shows available to the respectable bourgeoisie who wanted to feel daring. His tableaux of stately showgirls, more elegant than sexy, became his theatre's biggest box-office draw, although there was also a strong feeling among many Parisians that the acts of the music hall were – and should be – the Folies' major attraction, and that the nudes were an irrelevant intrusion.

It was generally agreed, however, that Derval's shows were splendidly spectacular. Joséphine now found herself at the centre of a vast enterprise, with a cast of over 40 and a crew of literally hundreds. For the costumes of such a show more than 500 kilometres of fabric were required, and a single feathered costume could take four dressmakers a whole week to make.

Among the composers whose music was used in *La Folie Du Jour* were Irving Berlin, Spencer Williams (who had also returned to Paris), and Vincent Scotto, who, in a career of writing over 4,000 songs and a dozen operettas, would provide several that became a permanent part of Joséphine's later repertoire. Among the impressive list of names who designed the décor and costumes were Brunelleschi, José de Zamora, Georges Barbier and Erté, the great exponent of art deco.

But the most famous costume in the show, and one of the most famous in showbusiness history, was created by none of these. This was Joséphine's famous girdle of bananas. In later life, she claimed that an English friend, a Miss Crompton, visited her at her apartment one day for "le five o'clock". Joséphine was sewing, and wondering what to wear for a new dance, and Miss Crompton suggested that a good idea would be a skirt cut out to represent bananas.

This account sounds dubious. It was in *La Folie Du Jour* that Joséphine wore the bananas for the first time, and with the amazing wealth of expertise available at the Folies Bergère it's unlikely that she would have been expected to come up with her own idea for a costume. A more believable story is that it was designed by Paul Colin, possibly originating as a fanciful drawing that Paul Derval saw and liked. Whatever the reason, it was such a success that Joséphine went on wearing versions of it in different shows for some years.

Her starring at the Folies began a change in Joséphine's performance. Before she had left for Berlin, while she was still appearing in *La Revue Nègre*, the writer Paul Brach had written in an article: "Josephine Baker, will you be serious for one night? Wear a becoming hairdo with giant plumes, like the white stars in our shows. Have a long train carried by twelve black pages. Make a majestic entrance and sing a soft sentimental song of your country." Whether or not this particular piece influenced her (and there were others similar), it accorded perfectly with her own inner wishes. Being a dancing clown had brought her success in America, and being a daring and shocking dancing clown had brought her even greater success in Paris. For all of her life she would never give up touches of clowning, but in her heart she wanted to be graceful and beautiful – or, rather, to exhibit the grace and beauty for which she had always yearned and which Paris had taught her that she truly did possess.

She didn't have top billing in *La Folie Du Jour*. That honour went to the popular comedian Dorville, a stout, middle-aged man who sang innuendo-laden songs in a broad Parisian argot. Successful in his day, in 1933 he would appear as Sancho Panza in GW Pabst's film *Don Quichotte*, which starred the great Chaliapin. Nonetheless, as with *La Revue Nègre*, most of the artwork publicising the show was built around the image of Joséphine. At the entrance to the Folies, Paul Derval erected immense illuminated colour photographs of her, and above the marquee, for the first time, her name appeared in lights.

Within the show, Derval had cast only blonde and red-haired fair-skinned showgirls to accentuate her darkness. Her own hair had by now undergone a further change, and the short Eton crop she had worn in Berlin was now smoothed down flat around her head, shining with egg-white as if varnished.

During the six weeks of rehearsal she was a torrent of enthusiasm, involving herself in all aspects of production. She took an interest in the sets, the lighting, the costumes and the stage machinery, and this enthusiasm spread to everyone involved in the production. Part of this sprang from her feeling that the whole show was there as a glittering setting for herself, and so everything must be just right, but part of it also came from her exuberant joy in her success.

Not that she couldn't also be self-indulgent and temperamental. Her moods swung from radiant cheerfulness to screaming ill temper, sobbing despair, and then back again.

She had never worked with such a disciplined company before, and to them her approach sometimes appeared cavalier. Often she arrived late, at least once wearing only a nightgown under her fur coat. Sometimes, when being fitted for a costume, she would grow bored and fretful and would wander away, saying to herself (as she later admitted) "I don't have the calling to be a pincushion." These displays of temperament unsettled some of her co-workers, who tended to tiptoe around her, unsure of her moods. To some extent these mood swings arose from her own sense of uncertainty. In her high excitement, she was still trying to come to terms with her new life and her developing public persona.

In an attempt to keep some sort of contact with her roots, to keep her feet somehow on the ground, she wrote to her mother describing the preparations for the show, and even to her husband, Willie Baker, asking him to join her in Paris. Willie, still working as a Pullman porter in Chicago, sensibly refused. He still loved her, but realised that her new world was not his, and he could have no real place in it. He told her that he wouldn't go unless he had a job, that he wouldn't "ride on the coattails of no woman".

La Folie Du Jour opened with a 40-minute showpiece in which eight showgirls, representing Americans visiting France, saw unfolding before them a series of tableaux representing Parisian shop windows, laden with luxurious clothes and accessories. In a witty reversal of the striptease, the girls began almost naked and ended the scene fully clothed.

After that came Joséphine, as Fatou, in her banana-skirted jungle dance. The American poet ee cummings, writing that September for the readers of *Vanity Fair*, performed the difficult task of capturing her dancing in words as well as anybody: "She enters through a dense electric twilight, walking backwards on hands and feet, legs and arms stiff, down a huge jungle tree – as a creature neither infrahuman nor superhuman but somehow both: a mysterious unkillable something, equally nonprimitive and uncivilised, or beyond time in the sense that emotion is beyond arithmetic."

Indeed, the whole show was cleverly designed by Louis Lemarchand to make use of exactly the contrasts mentioned by cummings, interweaving scenes of civilised Paris and primitive Joséphine throughout. This provided a perfect setting for her.

Her next appearance was her biggest production number. A huge, glittering, golden, egg-shaped cage, entwined with roses, was slowly lowered into sight from the flies. This was *la boule des fleurs*. As it descended, the top half slowly hinged open to reveal Joséphine, reclining on a mirror and wearing a short skirt of silk fringes, reminiscent of a grass skirt, and with feathers around her neck. When it reached the stage floor, she jumped up and, dancing on the mirror, went into her famous charleston to the music of the original James P Johnson tune. The theatre spotlights, reflecting from the mirror, threw dozens of wildly dancing shadows onto the scenery. This was, to many, the highlight of the show. Once her dance was over, the eggshell closed again and slowly it ascended back out of sight.

Her third main appearance in the show was during a production number based on the image of the fan called 'Les Plus Beaux Éventails Du Monde'. This contained the parodic song 'Tous Pour Joséphine', which was written by Jacques Frey to words by Louis Lemarchand and Georges Henri, and was performed by Dorville, but mostly the act consisted of another series of tableaux, this time showing girls dressed as fans – of ivory, of lace, of feathers, of fire.

Joséphine wore the feathers, a forest of long ragged plumes, as a short skirt, with more of the same as a bustle on her witty rear end and with nothing above the waist but strings of bead necklaces, with matching earrings. Her character was billed as "Le Chasse-Mouche" (The Fly-Whisk), and here she did an acrobatic dance with handstands and cartwheels to a tune called 'Let Me Linger Longer In Your Arms'.

The finale of the show, 'Le Roué Vers L'Or', featured gold heavily. (Chaplin's silent comedy *The Gold Rush* had been the smash-hit film of the previous year.) It opened with a new song by Vincent Scotto, 'Alaska', and presented the girls in a parade of gold lace, feathers, ribbons and flowers, all set against a background of craggy golden rocks and imitation fountains of gold. When the principals entered – clowns, comedians, acrobats, singers and solo dancers – all were dressed in shining gold, although

Joséphine's costume was restricted to a golden version of her banana skirt, this time studded with rhinestones and with the bananas curved cheekily upward at the ends instead of hanging like a bunch. In this act, she led the entire company in dancing the charleston.

The reviews for the show were not totally admiring. One criticism was that this edition of the Folies had too much spectacle and nudity and too little dialogue. This was seen as a continuing attempt by the Folies to appeal to rich visitors (mainly Americans) rather than to the music hall lovers of Paris, and it brought to the surface an increasing feeling that the city was being overrun by tourists. This in turn was seen as being caused by the devaluation of the franc, another cause of popular resentment.

The reviews for Joséphine herself, however, were universally ecstatic. People adored her new, more glamorous, image. ee cummings, in his *Vanity Fair* piece, underlined the change. Remembering her from way back in *Chocolate Dandies* as a "tall, vital incomparably fluid nightmare which crossed its eyes and warped its limbs in a purely unearthly manner", he observed how preposterous it seemed that this nightmare could become the most beautiful star of the Parisian stage. "Yet such is the case."

One of the few dissenting voices from the unisonant dithyrhambus was that of Paul Colin, who began to see her rather less often. "As soon as she started sticking feathers in her ass and trying to imitate Mistinguett," he said later, "I lost interest in her."

Another dissenting voice was, naturally enough, that of Mistinguett herself, another child of the slums. Born in 1873 under the name Jeanne Bourgeois, she was raised in the red light district of Ménilmontant and first performed in café concerts at around the middle of the 1890s. In those days there was a vogue in Paris for English music hall performers. The famous Little Tich was one favourite, as was Harry Fragson, "the Entente Cordiale singer", who was shot dead by his aged father in Paris at the end of 1913. So young Jeanne adopted the (to her) English-sounding name "Miss Tinguette", later running the two words together and dropping the final *e*.

Never a great singer or dancer, she nevertheless had a captivating stage personality. Her frequent co-star and some-time lover Maurice Chevalier once said: "Mistinguett was Paris – the symbol of gaiety and good humour and courage and heart." She could perform wistful, sad numbers or she could play comedy, and over the years she had developed three different, but related, characterisations.

The first was as a raggedly-dressed gamine wearing a cloth cap or a headscarf and broken shoes, singing tough but sentimental songs about the hard life of the Paris streets.

In around 1908, she developed this into something sexier: the Paris streetwalker, clad in a black satin skirt slit to the thigh, a closely-fitting white top, a beret, a band of red velvet fixed around her throat and criss-crossed ribbons on her calves. In this outfit she would dance the classic Apache Dance, "Apaches" being the Parisian slang of the day for young, knife-wielding toughs whose special target was the police. These, as portrayed onstage, wore striped undershirts, red spotted neckerchiefs, bell-bottomed trousers and peaked caps, and the dance itself was a mixture of sensuous caress and violence.

Her third character was the showgirl, as seen at the Folies Bergère but without the naked breasts. Her costumes and head-dresses were of flowers and plumes, jewels and sequins, silks and satins and cloth of gold. They were shining and fantastic and elaborate, and in them she showed off her famously magnificent legs, notably while descending the high (and notoriously steep) grand staircase at the rear of the stage at the Casino De Paris. This establishment was the second most famous music hall in Paris, and it might almost be said that Mistinguett had created it. She wasn't the star of its opening show (that honour fell to Gaby Deslys), but her triumphant appearance there soon afterwards established it firmly.

Having been the queen of Paris music hall for years, Mistinguett naturally looked on Joséphine as a dangerous competitor. She was also famous for being a bitch (although the great clown Grock claimed that he always found a hint of humour in her bitchiness), and became more so as she got older. After Joséphine opened in *La Folie Du Jour* and all of Paris was talking about her, Mistinguett was dismissive of her success. At one dinner party, for instance, she turned to Michael Gyarmaty, a young Jewish-Hungarian artist who would later become the creative director of the Folies, and asked: "What's the name of that *petite nègre* who dances in bananas?"

Not so the general public. By mid 1926, Joséphine's celebrity in Paris was astounding. Photographs of her were selling everywhere. Indeed, she was believed at the time to be the most photographed woman in the world. Dolls of her dressed in her banana skirt were bought by the thousand, and cocktails and bathing suits and hairdressing products were named after her.

Her glowing, coffee-coloured skin entranced people, and she was paid by the company making Valaze Water Lily beauty cream to let them feature her in their advertising. A shop window on the Place De L'Opéra contained a giant moving doll of her, alongside a sign saying "You can have a body like Joséphine Baker if you use Valaze cream."

This was unintentionally ironic. Still fretting from childhood about her skin colour, at the same time that this campaign was running she was spending an hour a day in her dressing room at the Folies rubbing herself all over with lemons in the hope that the juice would whiten her. This was part of her growing sense of her body being a commodity, of being her capital. It was to her what an instrument is to a musician, and she began taking good care of it, as she had seen Sidney Bechet take care of his clarinet.

To many young women she became a symbol of liberation. For a start, there was the charleston; although she was not the first to dance it in Paris, she was identified with it, and it affected *couture*. Smart dresses became dancing dresses, and in order for their wearers to be able to dance the charleston the skirts needed to be short – hence the Twenties' short skirt, which also suited the craving for freedom in female dress encouraged by Paul Poiret and others.

More directly, she was a symbol of sexual liberation. The equivalent French word for the "flapper" of the Twenties was "*une garçonne*". This came from a novel by Victor Marguérite, *La Garçonne*, published in 1923, whose heroine, Monique Lerbier, a student at the Sorbonne, cuts her hair short, wears a man's jacket, joins in orgies, has a child out of wedlock and flirts with lesbianism. Monique became a role model for the bright young things of Paris, and Joséphine – at least as far as her public reputation went – had enough in common with her to become another.

Artists continued to portray her. One was Picasso, who a little earlier had scandalised the city by announcing that an African sculpture of a nude Hottentot woman was lovelier than the Venus De Milo. Joséphine claimed to have posed for him many times, saying years later "He did not see the outside, but saw inside. He was very intense and very strong. He pulled you to him." In the ignorance of her youth, she was not so sure about him, saying in one interview "A little while ago a lady showed me a tiny little painting which had been very expensive. Didn't I think it was absolutely lovely? It was made by Penaszo. What was his name? I posed for him. Ah yes, Picasso. It was just a couple of stupid streaks. Awful."

Sculptor Alexander Calder made a caricature of her in wire in 1926. This was a protoype of his most famous invention, the mobile. Designed to be suspended, the movement of air made it quiver with life. Later he would create several more sculptures of her.

She also posed for Van Dongen and Foujita – and Picasso – at the Salon Des Beaux Arts, and the cubist Henri Laurens depicted her dancing the charleston. "Sem" (George Goursat), the famous caricaturist of the social scene, drew a wicked cartoon that astutely observed the hopelessness of her desire to be accepted in society which showed her dancing, in profile, elegantly clad and bejewelled, but with a monkey's tail swishing from her cheeky behind.

Writers referred to her in their works as an important image of the time and place. F Scott Fitzgerald, in *Babylon Revisited*, referred to her "going through her chocolate arabesques", while Erich Maria Remarque, author of *All Quiet On The Western Front*, said that she was "une grande actrice". Paul Morand wrote the novella *Baton Rouge*, in which the central character, a black American entertainer named Sophie Taylor, was quite evidently Joséphine.

Alice B Toklas, meanwhile, created a sweet in her honour called "custard Joséphine Baker" (the main ingredient being bananas), and Ernest Hemingway claimed to have danced the night away with her on one occasion, naked under a fur coat. This is possible, although Hemingway's memoirs are not always to be trusted.

Certainly she danced away many nights. She was always on the go. After the show each evening she would move on to at least three Montmartre cabarets, such as L'Impérial, Milonga and Le Grand Duc, usually contributing a free guest performance. Spencer Williams wrote a new song for her, 'I Love Dancing', to celebrate the fact that she seemed to dance all over the city.

In her afternoons, she took to dancing at the tea dances at Les Acacias, a elegant club off L'Étoile which was then run by a short, stout social climber from San Francisco called Elsa Maxwell. People of fashion took advantage of Joséphine's presence there to get her to coach them in the charleston. With all of this outside activity, on top of her rehearsals and performances at the Folies, she is said to have frequently danced for up to twelve hours in a day. Even for Joséphine this must be an exaggeration, but to onlookers it certainly felt like that.

Then there were the lovers. There was a long-established tradition in Paris that the girls in Folies shows were available – at a price. Paris had plenty of whores, but to spend a night with a Folies girl had glamour. They were in a way the heirs to the tradition of the *grandes horizontales*, the high-priced courtesans of the late 19th century. Indeed, one of these, La Belle Otéro, had appeared at the Folies as a sensuous Spanish dancer. Joséphine became part of this tradition, although she liked to give her public the impression that men showered gifts on her out of admiration for her "art". She did this partly for money and gifts (more and more she was finding herself reassured by material possessions) and partly out of a morbid fear of being alone, even in bed at night. For all of her life she slept badly, suffering from insomnia and nightmares so much that she was rarely able to sleep a whole night through.

In her memoirs, she generally portrays the rich men she slept with – or who wanted to sleep with her – with contempt. Often, too, she treated them with contempt. She consented to spend the evening with one, a rich industrialist, only on condition that he paid her a hefty sum in advance, and in addition gave her a nice present – a diamond, say. He came to the stage door on the appointed night bringing a stone "as big as a frog's egg". They dined at a small, crowded restaurant with a blind pianist and an Argentinian atmosphere, where Joséphine "ate like an ogre", drank champagne, "danced like a fool", laughed and generally amused herself.

However, when they left in a taxi and the man gave the address of his apartment to the driver, she not only refused to go there but raised such a fuss that the frustrated man lost his temper with her. Immediately she appealed to the driver, throwing herself on his mercy and explaining that she was Joséphine Bakaire of the Folies Bergère, and was there no chivalry left in Paris? She was amused to recall that the driver ejected the man from his cab and drove her to her own home.

Another, more humble admirer was a young architectural student with whom she had become friendly when she was still appearing in *La Revue Nègre*. He helped her learn French, and together they would laugh at her mispronunciations. Becoming smitten with her, he took to sending her flowers every day, even though his only income was an allowance from his father.

One day they had been dining together in the Restaurant Calvini on the Rue Pigalle. He took out his wallet to pay the bill and Joséphine, spotting a 1,000F note in it, reached out, took it and put it in her purse. The student protested that that was his whole allowance for the month, and if she took that then he would have nothing to live on. "If you go out with artists you must pay," said Joséphine, and kept it.

Years later she explained this as an act of racial revenge, a repayment for the oppression imposed on her race by his, and this attitude also partly explained her increasing wilfulness while in *La Folie Du Jour*, a determination to show who now held the whip hand.

It showed, for instance, in her habitual late arrivals at the theatre. Waiting for Joséphine became a nerve-wracking ritual. While the stage director stood out on the street corner waiting for her car, the orchestra would sometimes have to play extra interludes. Sometimes the management even had to alter the order of the acts. At the very last minute, and often later than that, the stage door would bang open and she would burst in. Paul Derval recalled such an entrance: "A hat went flying, a fur coat was flung to the floor. Leaving a trail of clothes, shoes and underwear, Joséphine Baker tore past me *en route* to her dressing room."

Even when she reached her dressing room this didn't mean that all was now plain sailing. On one evening, when she was due onstage, the stage manager, coming to give her her call, found her door locked. Getting no reply from within, in desperation he kicked open the door. Joséphine was sitting naked on the floor eating a lobster with her fingers. Rebuked for holding up the show, she simply got into her costume (of which fortunately there was not much) and made her dignified way to the stage, still chewing.

And then there were the animals. Even her dressing room acquired its own menagerie. Paul Derval was driven to stretch his tolerance to the limit, saying later "[She] considered every animal in creation her friend. She had rabbits nesting in the wardrobes, white mice in the drawers, and cats, dogs and birds more or less everywhere. A baby tiger and a boa constrictor were among the more exotic of her acquaintances. One day I put my foot down when Josephine befriended a young goat. There was a scene, of course, but by then I was used to her scenes." The situation got so bad that at one point he was driven to take her to court to make her leave her creatures at her apartment. She eventually agreed to this, but only after a considerable amount of haggling.

Her desperate need of pets arose from her deep feeling that they would never let her down in the way that people had always done, and at this time, the autumn of 1926, there was one man who let her down badly.

Referred to in her memoirs simply as "Marcel", he was the owner of a large automobile company. Unlike her usual parade of casual lovers, she took him seriously, letting herself fall in love with him and allowing him to rent her a lavish apartment on the Champs-Elysées. He even had a marble swimming bath installed in it for her, and showered her with presents, including, of course, more creatures: mice, parrots and a small monkey.

Hoping that at last he represented a full entrée into French society, and craving security, she hinted at marriage, telling him "I'd like to have a baby." (She diplomatically omitted to tell him she was still married to Willie Baker.)

Marcel's reaction was swift and to the point. Not only was she totally beneath him in society but she was also black. There was not, and never had been, any question of their getting married. With outward dignity, Joséphine moved back at once to her apartment on the Rue Beaujon, but inside she was devastated. To make things worse, she also caught bronchial pneumonia. This could be fatal in the days before antibiotics, and for three weeks she was confined to bed, shaking with fever. Even she, with her torrent of energy, felt drained and listless, and in spite of the fact that her apartment was constantly full of visitors, loneliness crowded in on her.

Her mistake with Marcel had been to misunderstand the rigid nature of respectable French society. Yes, in a way she had conquered Paris, but only as an exotic entertainer or an entertaining companion. As far as her yearning to be accepted by conventional society was concerned, she was doomed always to be on the outside looking in.

As she recovered from her pneumonia her energy returned, and on 25 October 1926 she went into a studio to make her first record. Singing in English, she recorded seven American pop songs of the day, among them such still-remembered songs as 'Who?', 'That Certain Feeling', 'Dinah' and 'Sleepy-Time Gal'. She even recorded the minstrel-type number 'Bam Bam Bamy Shore', although it would not be long before she refused ever again to sing what she referred to as "mammy songs".

The seven-piece band accompanying her was the standard jazz line-up of trumpet, trombone, clarinet, alto saxophone, piano, banjo and drums, and they are believed by French discographers to be members of a band called Olivier's Jazz Boys. The music they played was not really jazz; it was instead more a sort of jazz-flavoured vaudeville style, and was slightly old fashioned even for the time. Their rhythms are mostly ragtime rhythms, reminiscent of the James Reese Europe band that had stunned Paris in 1919 but with the characteristic double beat of the fashionable charleston frequently added. All of the numbers were cheerful, up-tempo songs, and Joséphine sang surprisingly well for someone who so far had done little singing onstage. Although her voice was still rather thin, especially in the upper register, her diction was excellent, and even today her lively personality comes across strongly.

From her school days she had been a talented mimic, and echoes of many of the vaudeville singers she had heard, such as Ethel Waters, can be heard. On 'Dinah', the song she had once sung as Ethel's stand-in, she even attempts a couple of improvised scat choruses, using Ethel's rhythmic style but with a sense of harmony that seems to be all her own. It comes off well, although considering her childhood in swinging St Louis she has – and always would have – surprisingly little feeling for jazz. Her rhythms have the more simple and energetic drive of music hall.

She never really enjoyed recording much. Her great delight in performing was the response of her audience, and in a recording studio – with its forest of cables, stands and screens, and a crew too intent on technical problems to react warmly to her singing – she tended to feel as if she were doing all of the giving and getting nothing back.

Her energy at this time was astonishing. She wasn't just a workaholic, she was a lifeaholic. On top of rehearsing and starring in *La Folie Du Jour*, and dancing elsewhere during her afternoons and nights, and posing for artists, and having love affairs, and collecting and looking after beasts and birds, she had somehow found the time to learn to play the ukulele. A few days later, in early November, she was back in the recording studio recording three more songs, accompanied only by her own playing. On this session she boldly attempted the song that had been such a disaster for her on the boat coming to Europe, 'Brown Eyes (Why Are You Blue?)'. With only her ukulele as backing, and not having to make herself heard over the likes of Sidney Bechet, she sang it confidently and well.

Her recording became prolific. A few days later, still in November, she was back in the studio again recording four more songs, accompanied only by a jazzy violinist and a pianist. Interestingly, the last of the four was her first recorded attempt at a slow number, Irving Berlin's famous 'Always', and in singing it she modelled her voice on the Parisian singers she had heard, such as Damia, complete with a touch of Gallic tremolo. Such was her ability as a mimic that she almost sounds like a different person, and although her performance foreshadows the style that she would adopt successfully in later life, here she was attempting to sing in a lower register than that which she was used to, and her pitch is somewhat uncertain. In January 1927 she would be back in the recording studio twice more, but before then a number of other events occurred in her life.

One of these was that *La Folie Du Jour* was filmed, more or less in its entirety, albeit silently. The director of the film was Mario Nalpas, and the fragments of it that survive show Joséphine performing her Fatou routine and, against the same scenery (no doubt for reasons of economy), her charleston from 'La Boule Des Fleurs'.

Another was that, in October 1926, she was invited to perform each night at a *boîte* called L'Impérial, which was on the Rue Pigalle, as was Le Grand Duc, where Bricktop reigned. This was a shrewd move on the part of the proprietors of L'Impérial because Le Grand Duc was notoriously tiny, and they figured that any overflow from it would be lured across the street to see Joséphine. They even changed the name of the place to Joséphine Baker's Impérial to make sure that people knew she was there. "They didn't pay me," she recalled, "but how I was fed. I was introduced to soufflés...Oh! là là...how I ate them...with cheese, mushrooms or sweet with vanilla, chocolate or liqueurs. They gave me indigestion, but I didn't care." She once said of herself that she ate herself fat and danced herself thin, but with so much rich eating it is hardly surprising that she wasn't all that thin by today's standards. Nor was she any longer the skinny kid of her teens; in late 1926 she weighed 135 pounds.

It was also at around this time that Paul Colin, hoping to take advantage of Paris's continuing infatuation with all things black, decided to publish a book of his lithographs of black entertainers, including Joe Alex and Adelaide Hall, and famous Parisians who were presumably caught up in the craze, such as Maurice Chevalier, Damia and Suzanne Lenglen. It also included – as revenge for Sem's caricature of Joséphine – a drawing of Sem himself as a rather ratty, long-limbed, pot-bellied monkey attempting to dance. (Sem himself was notoriously neat and elegant.) Paul decided to call his book *Le Tumulte Noir*, which was then the fashionable Paris expression for the black domination of the art and entertainment worlds. Eventually published in January 1927, it turned out to be probably the most important work of his career.

Naturally he had made many more lithographs of Joséphine than of anyone else, so he asked her whether she would lend her name to the book by contributing a short foreword. She agreed. Published in the book in the form of a facsimile, in a single page of her own ill-formed handwriting, it is a cheerful and headlong series of thoughts, jokes and images on the two themes of blackness and the charleston. Entitled "Topic Of The Day", it begins: "When the rage was in New York of colored people, Monsieur Siegfied of Ziegfied Follies said its getting darker and darker on old broadway. Since the *La Revue Nagri* came to Gai Parée I'll say its getting darker and darker in Paris. In a little while it shall be so dark untill one shall light a match then light another to see if the first is lit ore not."

As part of the publicity for *Le Tumulte Noir*, Paul Colin arranged for her to be interviewed by Marcel Sauvage, a journalist for *L'Intransigeant* and a pacifist writer who had won the Prix Gringoire for his book *Le Premier Homme Que J'ai Tué*. Marcel, who spoke no English, arrived at Joséphine's apartment one day at noon to conduct the interview. As she usually didn't rise until four in the afternoon, he found her still in bed, asleep, but cheerfully she got up and threw on a rose-coloured bathrobe, not bothering to fasten it very securely, and Turkish slippers to match. Her hair was her then-customary shiny helmet and her fingernails were silver. As she spoke little French (although possibly more than she admitted), Marcel had arranged for an interpreter to be present. As it happened, he arrived late, and while they waited for him Joséphine put a record on her gramophone and clip-clopped round the apartment in her slippers. The phone, which was on an extra-long cord so that she could wander around and use it at the same time, rang incessantly. When she answered it, she frequently became vexed, unable to understand what her callers were saying.

The apartment itself was an untidy clutter. Clothes and records and stacks of letters from fans were strewn untidily about, and among the possessions Marcel noticed that she had assembled were a bust of Louis XIV, a bowl of 100F notes, an Empire cabinet, a cardboard doll thumbing its nose and a huge French dictionary, which she told him that she never opened.

And, of course there were the animals. At around this time, Eubie Blake, who was passing through Paris, paid her a visit. As he later recalled, his astonishment at her meteoric rise to fame was not as great as his nervousness about her animal companions, the "boa constrictors, cheetahs and monkeys that she kept in her apartment". He remembered not venturing too close to the area of the apartment where they were kept, although he was invited to do so by Joséphine.

As well as her other animals, Marcel noted that there was a parrot, who added considerably to the noise, and, alongside Louis XIV, two parakeets in a cage. "Pauvre oiseau," she said to one of them, which was one of the few French phrases he heard her utter. At one point she showed him a copy of a children's book of French fairy stories, indicating that she was trying to use it to learn the language.

When the interpreter arrived, the interview began. It went well. Joséphine talked at top speed (with occasional French interjections like "merveilleux!" and "formidable!"), and soon Marcel was struck with an inspiration. He asked her whether she had ever thought of writing her memoirs. Joséphine burst out laughing. "Write my memoirs? Oh, là là," she said, going on to explain that writing her one-page introduction to *Le Tumulte Noir* had taken her 25 whole minutes and that she wasn't going to put herself through anything like that again. "You don't know what it's like to write," she assured the journalist/poet. "I dance. That's what I do. I love that, and I love only that. I will dance my whole life."

Nonetheless, Marcel persevered, explaining that he would do the actual writing down. All that she would have to do would be to talk to him about her life. Gradually the idea began to appeal to her. It was agreed that they would work together on a book of her memoirs, and almost at once they began. Marcel, working on *L'Intransigeant* during the day, would come to Joséphine's apartment near Le Parc Monceau in the middle of the night, after she finished work at L'Impérial. He was obviously less easily unnerved than Eubie Blake. Night after night in the apartment, sometimes with his wife Paulette there as well, Joséphine would tell him about her 20 years of life in her fractured French, and he would write it down for later polishing.

Being Joséphine, much of what she told him was romantically embellished or romantically simplified, and she was always keenly aware of presenting a public image. But even so, Marcel, working so closely with her, saw glimpses of her private self. For instance, he noted that, while she was quite definitely and cheerfully "une fille de joie" during her Folies years, her pride meant that she wanted no one to think of her as just a call girl, and that, while she undoubtedly obtained pleasure from sleeping with men, what really satisfied her was amassing expensive possessions. With child-like pleasure, she listed for him some of the loot that she had acquired: "I got sparkling rings as big as eggs, 150-year-old earrings that once belonged to a duchess, pearls like buck teeth, flower baskets from Italy, six lacquered Chinese chairs, toys that run on electricity, Russian ivory elephants cut by the poor people of Siberia, lots of stuffed animals – a bear, a duck, a rabbit, a cat – peaches…great big strawberries, perfume in a glass horse, a pair of gold shoes, four fur coats, and bracelets with red stones for my arms and legs." For her 20th birthday, in June 1926, one lover had even given her a car, a brown Voisin convertible upholstered in snakeskin. Unable to drive, she hired a chauffeur, outfitting him in a beige uniform with gold buttons.

For a while, Marcel even became a sort of unpaid unofficial secretary to her, mainly by helping her deal with the untidy stacks of fan letters that continued to pile up. There were simple letters of adoration, there were requests for assignations, there were begging letters, and there were so many that contained proposals of marriage that Marcel composed for her a form letter of polite refusal.

Then one day another young journalist appeared at the apartment, and Joséphine told Marcel that he was also going to help with her letters and press cuttings. It was the young Belgian journalist who had introduced himself to her at the Théâtre Des Champs-Elysées in 1925, the future Georges Simenon. Now married, he and his wife, Régine, had frequently socialised with Joséphine in Parisian clubs. They had become friendly, and it was as a friend, not as an employee, that he had agreed to help her out with her paperwork. Marcel already knew Simenon and, both working for Joséphine, they became firm friends. Both also found it considerably embarrassing, Marcel recalled, "trying to answer letters while Joséphine walked round her apartment completely nude."

Embarrassed or not, Simenon was sufficiently self-assured to rise to the occasion when it became obvious that Joséphine had become seriously smitten by him. Sexually voracious himself, married or not, he was just the physical type that appealed to her, said Marcel, "tall and handsome, with broad shoulders and clear skin."

Simenon also found in Joséphine, he later claimed, the must uninhibited woman he had ever met. They had a passionate affair, coupling anywhere and everywhere on the spur of the moment, but unfortunately all of the love came from one side. For Simenon it was just another brief fling among thousands of others, and after a few months he quit both helping with the paperwork and her.

He and Joséphine remained friendly, but with the memory of "Marcel" still fresh in her mind she was again devastated. She began having bouts of severe depression, interspersed with periods of almost hysterical activity. Marcel Sauvage's wife, Paulette, remembered many nights she spent with him at Joséphine's apartment, waiting for her to return. She would come home completely exhausted from frantic dancing, wash the eggwhite out of her hair, and fall into bed. On these occasions she would often call out, in the little-girl voice she tended to use when feeling vulnerable but safe. "Madame Sauvage," she would call. "Venez! Venez!" And Paulette, going to her bedside, would sit by her and hold her hand and tell her fairy stories, the same stories over and over, about birds and animals and kings and queens, and Joséphine, the highest-paid entertainer in Europe, would lie there listening, wide eyed like a little child.

Late in 1926, the poet Langston Hughes, who had returned to America after working at Le Grand Duc in 1925 and published there his first volume of poems, *Weary Blues*, returned to visit Paris. He waited at the stage door of the Folies for Joséphine to arrive. Her Voisin pulled up, her chauffeur held the door open for her, she greeted Langston warmly and he followed her into the theatre, with maids attending her all the way to take her cloak, gloves and purse, to place a make-up towel around her neck, and to remove her shoes. "Here indeed was a star," Langston wrote years later, "treated as no star I have ever seen, white, black, green, grizzly or grey, treated in America." Yet as she talked to him he sensed her incredible loneliness. All that she would talk about were the people they both knew in Harlem, and the clubs – the Cotton Club, Small's Paradise, Connie's Inn. His impression was that she desperately wanted to come home, but that was only partly true. It was more likely that meeting him, fresh from New York, had brought the part of her that felt homesick to the surface. And then, only a few days later, an event took place that would drive any homesickness away, or at least into the back of her mind.

In Montmartre, high up on Rue Florentine diagonally across from Bricktop's, was a somewhat raffish club called Zelli's. Its premises were basically a large room with a bar and a dance floor where partners could be hired, hostesses for the men and sleek-haired gigolos for the women. The club catered mainly to slightly elderly Americans. Joe Zelli himself was an Italian-American, loved and respected for his generosity toward down-

and-out expatriates. He would help regular customers with their rent, and if any of them died broke he would give them a funeral on the house.

Joséphine often went there because she had become friendly with an Italian caricaturist who worked there, making sketches of the clientele. His name was Zito, and she liked to turn up at around the time he was quitting work so that they could tour the joints together. Bricktop didn't really think that Zito was much of a date but observed that by now Joséphine was so famous that many men were afraid to ask her out, taking it for granted that she must have somebody rich and famous protecting her.

On one evening she turned up to find that Zito had a cold and wanted to go home, but so that she wouldn't be left alone he introduced her to a cousin of his who was from Rome and was working at Zelli's as a gigolo, although he preferred the title "dance instructor". His name was Giuseppe Abatino, and although he was not originally from Rome – he was from Palermo, where he had been a stonemason (or possibly a bricklayer) by trade – he had frequently visited Paris, and Zelli's, on previous occasions. Whenever he did so he took to going under the name of Count Pepito De Abatino. He felt that it had more class.

Certainly he had an air of self-possession that went well with a title, and Joséphine was much taken with him. He was of middle height, with swept-back dark hair, a small moustache and dark, deep-set eyes. Elegantly dressed, he sported a monocle, a cigarette holder and spats, and carried a walking cane, and although at 37 he was a little old to be a dance instructor he made a success of it by being handsome and suave. Like Joséphine, he was given to re-inventing his past to suit his current role, claiming to have been an outstanding equestrian, a lieutenant in a crack cavalry regiment and a diplomat who had grown bored with paperwork and the endless round of official cocktail parties.

Joséphine had never heard his cousin Zito claim any noble connections, and so, shrewd as she was, she must have realised that he was a phoney. But it was a case of like calling to like. Once, when one of her own assertions about her life was called into question, she snapped "I don't lie. I improve on life."

She and Pepito spent that night visiting club after club, dancing and talking. He told her how much he had admired her in *La Folie Du Jour*. She had been unlike anything he had ever seen.

At the end of the night, as the dawn was breaking, they entered

Bricktop's, just as the band was packing up to go home. Bricktop, still in those days concerned with Joséphine's welfare, soon drew her to one side. "Josephine," she said, "what are you doing with this bum? He can't even buy a glass of beer."

Joséphine shrugged and answered simply: "Zito has a cold."

During the following days, Pepito determinedly set out to win her, using all of his Italian charm. He sent her love notes. He met her each evening after her performance at the Folies and squired her on her tour of the clubs, opening doors and helping her on with her coat and holding her chairs out for her to sit. All of this, and his charming flattery in conversation, made her feel like a queen.

Soon they were lovers. He spent a lot of time at her apartment, which discouraged other suitors, and she cheerfully became much less promiscuous than she had been. Pepito turned out to be not simply a sponger. He genuinely fell in love with her and set out to become accepted as her manager, allaying her fears that all of her success might evaporate by promising to turn her into a more polished performer and, even more disarmingly, into a lady. He would arrange for her to have singing lessons and proper dancing lessons and French lessons, and he would show her how to comport herself in society, how to handle cutlery and how to make small-talk. It wasn't long before he achieved his aim, and was not only her manager and her lover but also her impresario.

Once accepted as such by Joséphine, he didn't waste any time. One of the first things he did was fulfil her desire to have a *boîte* of her own, like Bricktop's. The money to rent it was provided by a doctor, Gaston Prieire, who had been one of her "protectors" and was actually something of a crook. He made his money by running three clinics that were supposed to treat workers suffering from illness or accident. In fact, what happened was that every day hundreds of workers suffering from nothing at all would check into his clinics, Dr Prieire would pay them a small sum for doing so, and he would then collect larger sums from their insurance companies for treating them.

Although Pepito was turning out to have a ferocious streak of Sicilian jealousy (which, on the whole, Joséphine found flattering), he always managed to control it when one of her admirers was to part with money, and he diplomatically stayed well in the background until the good doctor signed the lease. Then she left her well-fed job at Joséphine Baker's

Impérial, and Chez Joséphine opened on the Rue Fontane in Montmartre on 14 December 1926.

It was another tiny club like Le Grand Duc, and its prices were outrageous – 45F for a dozen oysters, for instance. But those who could afford it (and probably many who couldn't) cheerfully forked out for the chance of seeing Joséphine close up and maybe exchanging a few words with her. It was an immediate success. Pepito, with his ability to organise, took on the role of manager, and they hired as cook an ebullient black American woman called Freddie.

Joséphine also loved to cook, and she suggested to Freddie many of the club's specialties. Mostly these were dishes from her childhood, and the menu became an odd mixture of *cordon bleu* and soul food. Such dishes as duck à l'orange and shrimp pâté shared equal billing with chitterlings, rooster combs, greens and black-eyed peas. The clientèle found this entrancing. Her own favourites to eat at her *boîte*, incidentally, were beef tartare, plovers' eggs and, above all – as it would be all of her life – spaghetti and red peppers.

At around this point, she had also somehow found time to involve herself in charity work. Always exquisitely dressed, she visited foundling homes and was photographed kissing the babies there. She distributed dolls to poor children and soup to the aged, and she performed without pay at many charity benefits.

At Christmas 1926, at her suggestion, the Folies mounted a free charity matinée for the children of the traffic police of Paris. Dressed as Santa Claus, she danced the charleston (joined onstage by a pantomime horse, "the elastic Pegasus of the Folies Bergères") and presented a magician. She gave each child a toy and gave everyone in the audience cake, and the whole thing was an enormous success. The only thing that bothered people was why she had chosen such an unexpected group to receive her charity. "Oh," she said, when somebody finally raised this question, "it's because they're blacks," which in her vocabulary meant that she felt that the traffic police were badly paid, overworked and under esteemed.

In January 1927 the film of *La Folie Du Jour* was released, which meant that Paul Derval would now have to mount a new show at the Folies itself. It was decided that this would be called *Un Vent De Folie*, and that Joséphine would be the star.

7 *Un Vent De Folie*

Un Vent De Folie was created by very much the same team who had worked on *La Folie Du Jour*, including writer and producer Louis Lemarchand. Ambitious to improve the Folies presentation, this time he eliminated out-and-out comedy routines entirely. In his opinion they were vulgar. Instead he designed a show that concentrated entirely on spectacle, carefully planning the tempo of each scene in succession so that it would be all of a piece. It would also contain an innovation: the use of film. As Joséphine danced the black bottom, a filmed image of her dancing the same routine would be projected behind her. Such early experiments in mixed media were very much in the air among the theatrical avant garde of 1927.

To help overcome the reactions of those who thought that the Folies already had too much spectacle and too little music hall, Paul Derval decided to bill the new show as a "hyper-revue", as if it were something so new that it should only be judged in its own terms.

It had been intended that Joséphine would be the sole star, but things didn't quite work out that way. Derval and Lemarchand also wanted the white performer Pépa Bonafé to appear in the show. She consented to appear, but only on that condition that she would have star billing. This presented Derval with a problem. He ingeniously solved it by billing Joséphine as the black star of the Folies and Pépa as the white star, which seemed to satisfy everybody.

In January 1927, while these preliminary discussions were going on, Joséphine made two return visits to the recording studio. On the first occasion she recorded five tracks, accompanied by her own band from Chez Joséphine. This was a lively seven-piece outfit that had been assembled for her by trumpeter Léon Jacobs, who had previously been working in the band at the Moulin Rouge. Mainly consisting of Belgian musicians, it was called Le Jacobs' Jazz, naturally enough, and on the released records Joséphine was given her new title: "L'Étoile Noire Des Folies Bergères".

For her last number on the session she chose 'Bye Bye, Blackbird', which she had heard Mabel Mercer sing at Bricktop's, and again she sounds like a different person. There are faint echoes in her singing of Mabel's conversational style, as well as a Parisian night-club tremolo. But her performance is more confident here, her voice is growing stronger, and gradually all of her influences are beginning to build into a style that is all her own.

Her own band was also with her for the next session, which took place later in January, although at this she also recorded two songs accompanied by a piano duet. One of these was 'Lonesome Lovesick Blues', composed by Spencer Williams for *Un Vent De Folie*, on which she is credited as having co-written the lyric with him.

Un Vent De Folie opened in April 1927. Joséphine's costumes were even more elaborate than they were the year before. For one number she wore a sort of skeleton one-piece bathing suit of coral and pearl beads with a fan of dark orange feathers sprouting from each side of her behind. It revealed not only her breasts but so much more of her that, in as late as 1986, when a colour photograph of her in it was reproduced in the colour supplement of *The Observer*, a lady reader objected that she had been embarrassed at having to carry it to church.

For the finale, 'Paris En Folie', Joséphine wore an extraordinary costume vaguely reminiscent of a harlequin: delicately-patterned spangled tights decorated with pom-poms, red gloves with little balls on the fingertips, a sort of feather duster swinging from each hip, and a larger one sticking straight up from a small conical cap on her head. Audiences found it sensational.

Nonetheless, the show received mixed reviews, and a large part of the problem was Joséphine. She was beginning to repeat herself. Although she performed dance in a scene depicting 'Un Hostellerie Sous Louis XIII', where a co-dancer was Lila Nicolska, former prima ballerina at the National Theatre in Prague, she also performed the black bottom – a close relation of the charleston – in a skirt of red marabou feathers, as well as another dance in the banana skirt (albeit now more bespangled and more spiky). She even reprised the ragamuffin costume she had worn in *La Revue Nègre*, dancing a number called 'Plantation', accompanied by a band of black musicians in southern field-hand costumes that called itself Le Thompson Jazz Orchestra.

There was beginning to be just a hint in the air that Paris felt that it had seen pretty much all there was to Joséphine, and that it was ready for something new. There were even mutterings to the effect that she wasn't really all that black, after all, which could have come about because she had taken to always powdering her face a lighter shade. The dance critic Arnold Haskell wrote that she "always seems to be playing up to what the public wants the negro to be", and another reviewer commented that it would take more than "un vent"; it would take a cyclone to stop her wriggling in the same old way.

She was lucky to have Pepito, and she knew it. Seventeen years older than she was, he was part lover and part father, and all hustler. Some people saw him as a fraud and a sponger – Bricktop, for instance, would refer to him as the "no-account count" and claim that, seen alongside Joséphine's elegance, he looked like the stonemason he was. However, Bricktop was biased; before Pepito came along, she had regarded herself as Joséphine's mentor and guide, but after he arrived she no longer was. The fact is that, in all of his dealings with Joséphine, he was scrupulously honest and did much to advance her career.

To keep her prominently in the public eye, he arranged for her name to be used to publicise even more products, one of which was Pernod. He also ran into an Argentinian chemist who had patented a hair-straightening pomade. The chemist was planning to use the well-known Corsican singer Tino Rossi to publicise it, but Pepito exercised his persuasive charm and he agreed that the product would sell even better if he used Joséphine. He even renamed it Bakerfix, and it became by far the most successful of her endorsements, going on to sell for over 30 years.

In the spring of 1927 she took driving lessons. Although she was somewhat impetuous as a driver, her excellent co-ordination and swift reactions soon enabled her to pass the test, and when she so did Pepito arranged for the driving school to take out a full-page advert featuring her portrait.

He also encouraged her to carry on working with Marcel Sauvage on her memoirs, and he continued to manage Chez Joséphine, where she was proving to be even more popular as a hostess than she had been as a dancer. Every night, at around one am, she would make her entrance there, sweeping in accompanied by her maid, her chauffeur, whatever hangers-on had attached themselves to her at the Folies and a selection of animals, and at once the place would come to life.

Several of Joséphine's animals had actually taken up residence at the club. One was the goat that Paul Derval had banned from her dressing room, whom she had named Toutoute, and another was her pig, Albert, whom it was her habit to douse with the Worth perfume Je Reviens. Albert lived in the kitchen, and eventually became so fat from the scraps on which he fed that he had difficulty cramming himself in under the boiler where he slept. In fact, in doing so he once broke some of the boiler pipes, and part of the kitchen doorway had to be broken down to get him out. "Pauvre cochon," said Joséphine.

On her arrival at the club she would pass among the tables, greeting and joking with the customers, and it became clearer than ever that her real asset in life was her personality. Never a top-rank dancer or singer, it was her bubbling vitality that turned out to be her greatest talent. Her presence made the world a more enjoyable place, and in the close confines of her club she was almost unbelievably dazzling. She would dance with her customers to the music of Le Jacobs' Jazz, and would dance by herself in performance, improvising steps endlessly, as usual. If she felt that things were getting a little dull she would organise a dance competition, awarding a potted plant to the winner. People who had heard her records began asking her to sing as well, and it was here that her long career as a night club singer got under way.

Describing her nights at her *boîte*, Joséphine said: "I never amused myself more. I made jokes. I caressed the skin on the heads of bald-headed messieurs; they never laughed harder before. Everybody did the charleston, the boys, the maîtres d'hôtel, the cook, the cashier, the errand boys, the goat and the pig...and me, I dance, I dance, I laugh, I burst out laughing, I pull the nose the nearest to me, the hair, the beard, and all in the midst of streamers, balls and all night the lights keep changing."

Pepito himself was a considerable asset as the club's manager. Using all of his Latin charm, he played up to the American tourists that he rightly judged were the club's best source of income, giving them the pleasure of socialising with a real count. To prevent them from becoming bored, he introduced amusing diversions such as playing "tennis" with paper racquets and balls, and to give them a souvenir of their evening he sold them vast numbers of foot-high Joséphine dolls.

Of all of the famous people who sought out Joséphine at her *boîte*, the one who gave her the most enduring pleasure to know was Colette, then in her mid 50s. At first flattered by being sought out by the most famous French woman writer of the day (although at the time of their meeting she had probably not read a word of Colette), Joséphine soon found that they had a lot in common. For a start, Colette had also been in music hall. After divorcing her first husband, Willy, whom she had married young and who had been her mentor and impresario in encouraging her to write, she had become a performer mainly in order to make a living. Like Joséphine, she had delighted in being shocking. She too had appeared topless and even in lesbian scenes, and when she first visited the *boîte* she brought Joséphine a copy of her novel based on her experiences, *L'Envers Du Music Hall*, as a gift.

She endeared herself to Joséphine by asking whether there was an English chorus girl at the Folies who spent every spare moment knitting for her baby.

"Oui," said Joséphine. "Do you know her?"

"There always is one," Colette replied.

For her part, she was charmed by Joséphine, calling her "little brown daughter" and once inscribing a book to her, writing "To the most beautiful panther, the most charming woman, with my friendship." It was a friendship that would last for years.

The number of Americans visiting Paris was continuing to increase, and this was increasingly affecting the atmosphere of the city. Not only were clubs like Bricktop's and Joséphine's thronged with Americans, and music halls like the Folies and the Casino De Paris subtly adjusting their programmes for American appreciation, but such un-French things as cocktail bars were beginning to appear and American attitudes were being heard expressed everywhere.

One night, Joséphine ran into an upsetting example. It was the night of 21 May 1927, and Joséphine, to her intense pride and pleasure, was given the job of announcing to the Folies audience the news that the 27-year-old American Charles Lindbergh had successfully completed his solo flight across the Atlantic, and that he had safely landed at Le Bourget airfield in his plane *Spirit Of St Louis*. To the Americans, this was the most amazing and newsworthy stunt of a stunt-crazy decade. Gertrude Ederle's swimming the English channel, Shipwreck Kelly's flagpole-sitting, Mary "Hercules" Promitis' marathon-dancing – none gave the American public of the Twenties more excitement than Lindbergh's transatlantic flight.

When he landed in Paris, the French also went wild. Many, never having heard of Joséphine's home town, assumed that his plane was given its name to honour Louis IX, the sainted king of whom Lindbergh had probably never heard.

"Bonnes nouvelles! Ladies and gentlemen," Joséphine announced, "Charles Lindbergh has arrived." The news caused such joyful pandemonium among the audience at the Folies that it almost stopped the show. But somehow it managed to continue, and afterwards Joséphine was invited by some friends to celebrate at a chic restaurant called L'Abbaye De Thélème, hedonistically named after the abbey built by Rabelais' Gargantua, who gave it the motto "Do what you will". It was filled with the noise of cheerful celebration, and all was joy and jollity, until an American, sitting with his wife at a table alongside Joséphine's, summoned a waiter and loudly announced "At home a nigger woman belongs in the kitchen."

A hush fell on the room. The manager hurried to the table to find out the cause of the disturbance, and the American repeated his complaint. "You are in France," the manager told him firmly but politely, "and here we treat all races the same." Gradually the room went back to celebrating, but Joséphine was mortified. "I felt that if the floor could open up and swallow me, it would be a blessing."

It was a brutal reminder that even in France she was not completely free. This was brought home to her further when the management of a hotel on the Right Bank refused to let a suite to her and Pepito, telling them apologetically that admitting a coloured guest might harm their American trade.

Fortunately, though, such events were rare, and for the most part her life was filled with pleasurable excitements.

Early in 1927, soon after *Un Vent De Folie* opened, Paul Derval again arranged for Mario Nalpas to make a film – not of the whole revue, this time, but of selected scenes based on it. The film, again silent, was called *La Revue Des Revues*, and Joséphine's section of it, entitled 'An Excursion To Paris', was simply a series of shots of her dancing the charleston on a mirror with a cubist representation of American skyscrapers as a background.

A few weeks after the film opened, Mario Nalpas sent a representative to Joséphine's dressing room at the Folies to ask whether she would star in a feature film that he and Henri Etiévant were planning to make. She needed little urging. Although she had found the process of filming uncomfortable under the hot, bright lights, she had been delighted to see herself on the screen. "Pepito! Look at me!" she had said. "Look at me! Aren't I wonderful?"

The film was to be based on a novel by the popular author Maurice Dekobra, who shortly after the war had had considerable success with a potboiler called *La Madone Des Sleepings*, which was the story of a woman driven mad by passion. His novel on which the film was to be based was mostly set in the South Seas, and was called *La Sirène Des Tropiques*. The film was to have the same title, and Joséphine's role in it was to be tailored to suit her character. (She was never really able to play any character other than Joséphine.) Dekobra wrote the screenplay, and Pepito collaborated with him to some extent, making suggestions and seeing to it that the image of Joséphine it presented matched her public persona.

It certainly did. The film is the story of an innocent native girl from the Antilles, named Papitou, who leaves her island to go to Paris and there is transformed by elegant clothes into a beautiful woman. (Joséphine played Papitou, of course.) Near the beginning of the film she is pursued by a lecherous white trader. Fleeing from him, she falls into a flour bin and turns white. She goes to a pond to wash off the flour and he follows her there, and she is only saved from being raped by the intervention of the handsome hero, played by Pierre Batcheff. To exact his revenge, the villain lures Batcheff onto a weakened rope ladder. It breaks and Batcheff falls into a ravine, but Papitou rescues him. They fall in love, and we see her in a circle of members of her tribe, all happily dancing a native dance that suspiciously resembles the charleston.

Desperate to get to Paris, about which she has heard so much, and having no money, only beads, she stows away on a ship. This leads to a succession of comic situations, ending with her being found naked in his bath by the captain.

Having reached Paris, she attends a party with a jungle theme. Elegantly clad and fêted, she is, of course, again dancing the charleston. Soon she marries a rich aristocrat, her husband, played by none other than Pepito. However, Batcheff also turns up in Paris and becomes involved in a duel, but Papitou rather unsportingly climbs a tree and shoots his opponent. Although still in love with him, she renounces her love in order to spare the feelings of his fiancée, who is so touched that she gives Papitou a Bible inscribed with the message: "Sacrifice is the purest form of joy on Earth."

The film was shot during the late spring and early summer of 1927.

Much of the early part of the story was filmed in the forest of Fontainbleu, just outside Paris, which gave a not-very-convincing impression of the Antilles, and the Parisian interiors were shot at Studio Éclair in the northern suburb of Épinay. For the duration of the shoot, Joséphine spent her time filming during the day, dancing at the Folies in the evening and being the hostess of Chez Joséphine at night.

She did not enjoy the filming. Acting in a drama was different from simply being filmed dancing. She had little success in learning to shrink her gestures and reactions from the grandiose ones she was used to making in the theatre, and she found that having to hit precise marks chalked on the floor in order that she would remain properly in focus, made her feel confined. Furthermore, she found the studio lights even hotter and more blinding than she remembered. In those days film was so insensitive that a huge amount of light was needed for a good exposure, to the extent that technicians often wore dark glasses to protect their eyes, which of course the actors could not do. Worst of all, she felt that she had been used. She felt that Nalpas, Etiévant and Dekobra (even with Pepito's help) had failed to study or use her true nature. She found playing the role assigned to her undignified.

Furthermore, at around this time she had bad news from home. Her favourite sister, Willie Mae, had got herself pregnant, had attempted to induce an abortion, and had bled to death. She was 17. With all of this weighing on her mind, during the filming Joséphine often became difficult and temperamental. At one point, according to Pierre Batcheff's wife, she demanded to be given a fur coat before she would continue filming.

Another blow-up came when the film's composer, the jazz-influenced writer Alain Romains, suggested that Bricktop – with whom he was friendly – be hired to play in a night club scene. Joséphine hit the roof and stormed off the set. This was her film, and she wasn't having any black female competitor in it. She won her point.

It so happened that one of the assistants working on the film was the future great director Luis Buñuel, who was then at the very beginning of his career. He was impressed by neither the script nor Joséphine's behaviour. As he recalled in his autobiography, *My Last Breath*, "I must confess it wasn't one my my nicer memories; the whims of the star appalled and disgusted me. Expected to be ready and on the set at nine in the morning, she'd arrive at five in the afternoon, storm into her dressing room, slam the door, and begin smashing makeup bottles against the wall. When someone dared to ask what the matter was, he was told that her dog was sick."

While shooting was still in progress, the plot of the film gave Pepito and Joséphine an idea. In mid June 1927, they gave a press conference to announce that they were now husband and wife, having been secretly married on 6 June, Joséphine's 21st birthday. This was a shrewd announcement to make for several reasons. One was that it gave them respectability as a couple without the bothersome necessity of arranging a divorce from Willie Baker. Another was that it was splendid publicity for Joséphine and the film, as well as for the Folies. Paul Derval wasted no time in having a sticker pasted onto every poster advertising *Un Vent De Folie*. The posters showed Joséphine in her banana skirt, and the sticker read: "Countess Pepito De Abatino".

Papers reported their marriage all over the world, but most especially in France and the USA. On 20 June they gave another press conference, this time for the American press only. Because it was conducted in English, of which Pepito knew only a few words, this time Joséphine was completely in charge. "I'm just as happy as I can be," she told the reporters. "I didn't have any idea that getting married was so exciting. I feel like I'm sitting on pins and needles. I am so thrilled."

She also held up for their inspection a 16-carat diamond wedding ring that she claimed Pepito had given her, explaining that she wouldn't be wearing it all the time because it was too heavy. (Could this possibly have been the ring that the rich industrialist gave her, with its stone "as big as a frog's egg"?) "That ain't all he gave me, either," she told them. "I got all the jewels and heirlooms that have been in the Abatino family for generations."

The journalists had naturally researched Pepito's background as soon as the story broke. They could find no Abatino family in any reference book relating to European nobility, and at the register of foreigners in the Paris Prefecture Of Police Pepito's occupation was given as "plasterer". But knowing they had a good story anyway, for the most part they did not press the point. When one reporter did ask directly about Pepito's lineage, Joséphine handled the question expertly. "Sure he's a count," she said. "There ain't no fake about that title. I had it looked up and verified by a private detective in Rome before I signed on the dotted line. He's got a great big family there and lots of coats of arms and everything. I understand they live in a big swell château, and as soon as my contract with the Folies Bergère is finished I am going down to visit them…You know, Pepito had a good job before he met me, with the Italian government, but he couldn't work and make love to me at the same time, so he had to give it up."

To Americans, and especially the black communities, it was a fairy tale come true: poor black girl marries European nobility. As the black supper-club singer and pianist Bobby Short recalled, women at teas and parlour socials in America discussed her endlessly, saying: "My god! She's conquered France and now she's married this count." She gave young black American girls a new and higher mark at which to aim. In the Thirties, scores of them scraped up enough money to head for Paris, hoping to emulate her success.

The only trouble with Pepito and Joséphine telling their wonderful story turned out to be that they weren't very good at remembering its details. At various times they claimed that the marriage had taken place in Italy, at the Italian consulate in Paris, at the American consulate in Paris, and at a town hall in one of the Paris arrondissements, but they couldn't remember which.

Of course, as the story cooled, the press started seriously questioning the validity of Pepito's title. Joséphine laughed the whole matter off. When asked by a reporter if she was really a countess, she said: "Yes, at least in Maurice Dekobra's film, in which my manager, Pepito Abatino, also has a part. You know him, don't you? A guy with a dark moustache who looks like Adolphe Menjou? That's him, my husband. My husband in the film, right? Well, since it was amusing to be married, I let it out around town that I was. My, how quickly false news spreads! What I told a few friends as a joke, everyone took me seriously. It was nice. It's fun to be called 'madame' and to get telegrams from everywhere on Earth congratulating me."

But when stories started circulating that the marriage was a publicity stunt, and that Pepito's title was a sham, members of the black press were inclined to treat these as racially-motivated slurs, and the impression remained with many of their readers that the original story had been the true one. Nonetheless, Joséphine quietly dropped her title, saying when questioned that it hadn't been what she'd married him for anyway.

The one person who knew definitely that she couldn't be legally married, but who kept his mouth shut, was Willie Baker, who read the story with some surprise in *The Chicago Defender*.

Black America at this time received another shock. The darling of black entertainment, the girl that *Shuffle Along* had made into a star, Florence Mills, died. A month after returning from a successful London season, and welcomed home rapturously by press and public, she suddenly died of peritonitis after a routine appendectomy, aged only 32. Thousands of mourners, both black and white, turned out for her funeral procession along Seventh Avenue in Harlem. Chorus girls from her show, *Blackbirds*, marched behind the coffin dressed in grey, and a plane flying overhead released flocks of blackbirds as it passed.

Joséphine, eleven years younger, had of course remained aware of Florence's success, which in London had almost paralleled her own in Paris, although had been based less on scandal and eccentricity. Learning of Florence's death, she briefly wondered whether it had opened a place for her in New York, because Florence had also been a pixyish dancer with a high, light voice. But she was painfully aware that Florence was a far better all-round dancer and a more accomplished singer than she had yet become. The critic James Agate, for instance, reviewing *Blackbirds* in London, had written: "Miss Florence Mills is a superb artist, whether she is imitating the epileptic frenzy of a witch dance or indulging her native melancholy. The notes she warbles are real wood notes, and you would say that her voice is untrained. Untrained because of its astonishing facility. This singer has taken her high C and come down again while more ponderous prima donnas are still debating the ascent." So in spite of the small part of her that yearned to return to America, Joséphine feared that comparisons with Florence would not be to her advantage, and she had no intention now of appearing anywhere as anything but a major star.

She felt the same way about American films. Now embarked on a possible career in the movies, she had received tentative approaches from Hollywood (which in interviews she invariably inflated into firm offers), but these alarmed her more than they attracted her. She was having enough trouble in Paris struggling out of her typecast role as an eccentric dancer, so how she likely to be typecast in a Hollywood film? As a domestic servant, perhaps, or as a slave or a whore.

Pepito felt that she should respond to some of these advances, aware of the healthy state of the dollar, but Joséphine refused to budge, saying: "They'll make me sing mammy songs."

In July 1927, three weeks after she and Pepito had announced that they were married, Joséphine's book *Les Mémoires De Joséphine Baker, Recuillis Et Adaptés Par Marcel Sauvage* was published, illustrated with drawings by Paul Colin. It would be the first of five autobiographical books which she co-authored during the course of her life, and in many ways it is the best. Later ones were more elaborate and calculated, but this is fresh and endearing. While less than faithful to the facts of her life, it gives a true picture of her tastes and her vivid personality, flicking from idea to idea and emotion to emotion.

In it she chatters on about her hard childhood, her rules for life, her pets, the gifts she has received, her favourite meals, her likes and dislikes, and she comes across vividly as warmhearted, humorous and, in an odd way, realistic. Her beauty advice is to dance a lot and sweat a lot, which makes you sleep, which is good for the eyes. Also, the best toilet water is rainwater, which keeps indefinitely. "Bathe in the milk of violet petals. Moisturisers made from bananas fight wrinkles. Rub strawberries on your cheeks to give them colour."

She tells how she prays before going onstage and before going to bed, and attributes her success to the lucky rabbit's foot she was given by the old black man in New York. She loves animals and thinks that we have a lot to learn from them, and swims every day because land animals are never as elegant as fish. She quotes spirituals, love letters she has been sent, and snatches of poems dedicated to her. She also gives recipes for corned beef hash and hot cakes, although her favourite dish is spaghetti.

She loves the cinema but hates the telephone. (What a pain to hear a person's voice and not see him! Better to see him and not hear his voice.) She hates ballet dancing and can't abide Pavlova (who couldn't abide her, either). When it comes to women's future, or even their present, she has no idea, but hates lace and loves liberty.

Above all, she loves to dance. She wants to dance her whole life through and die breathless, exhausted, at the end of a dance, but not in a music hall. She is tired of that artificial life, of being spurred on by the footlights. "The work of being a star disgusts me now. Everything she must do, everything she must put up with at every moment, that star, disgusts me. Bad choices, sad choices...I want to work three or four more years and I'll then quit the stage. I'll go live in Italy or the south of France. I am going to buy land on the Riviera...I will get married, as simply as possible. I will have children, and many animals. But if one day one of my children wants to go onstage in the music hall, I will strangle it with my own two hands, that I swear to you."

This feeling of revulsion for the stage sounds somewhat unexpected from someone who would always relate more easily to audiences than to individuals, and who fed avidly on the reassurance of applause, but it is an early expression of a conflict that would bedevil Joséphine for the rest of her life. As well as her craving for applause, she had a deep need to put down roots, and to have a settled home and a family. She would never successfully manage to reconcile the two.

Her desire at times to escape from the Folies was genuine. At around the time she was writing the book, she attempted to break her contract with Paul Derval on the grounds that she had signed it when she was under age. Derval shrewdly told her that if she wanted to leave the show then of course she was perfectly free to go – hearing which, of course she stayed.

When the book was published, a book-signing session was arranged at Les Acacias for her and Marcel Sauvage. Champagne was served to the attendant poets and critics, and Joséphine took the occasion seriously, wearing for the role of authoress, a sober dark silk dress, and signing the books laboriously in a careful schoolgirl hand.

The book was a great success, but it did have one unfortunate repercussion. In devoting so much care to her own body, as an instrument to be kept in perfect condition, Joséphine had conceived an abhorrence of any sort of physical deformity, and this had led her in the book to make an off-hand comment about disabled ex-soldiers. "I've heard a lot about the war," she said. "What a funny story! I swear I don't understand it at all, but it disgusts me. I have such a horror of men with only one arm, one leg, one eye. I sympathise with them with all my heart, but I have a physical repulsion from everything unhealthy." Ex-servicemen's organisations were incensed, both at her attitude to mutilation and to her calling the war "a funny story". They took to demonstrating outside Chez Joséphine. Then things escalated: the French Association Of Mutilated War Veterans threatened to sue her.

Joséphine hastily issued a statement saying that it was all Marcel Sauvage's fault, that he had put words in her mouth, and that she in turn would sue him if he didn't see that the offending words were removed from the book in future editions.

Marcel retorted that of course she had said those things, and that if she did sue him he would tell the world what their conversations had really been like. "Believe me," he said, "it would be pretty picturesque." He suggested further that thinking was not her strong suit, and that while he had not shown her the proofs of the book, which she would have had difficulty reading, he had shown them to several of her French-speaking entourage, including Pepito.

Eventually the whole matter blew over, and she even remained on good enough terms with Marcel to work with him on another book about herself a few years later, but litigation would turn out to be a perpetual feature of Joséphine's life. In fact, by 1927, she had already been involved in two lawsuits that actually did come to court. The first originated from couturier Paul Poiret, who sued her for the 5,000F that she had owed him since October 1926. This action was possibly an attempt by Poiret to advertise his connection with Joséphine but, whatever the reason, he asked the courts to authorise him to seize back clothing to that value from her dressing room.

Unfortunately for Poiret, it emerged in court that, over the years, he had sold Joséphine frocks, coats and furs to the value of 285,000F, of which she had paid him 280,000F. The judge ruled that he was being somewhat unreasonable in taking such drastic action in pursuit of the last 5,000F and dismissed the case. Naturally, Joséphine also dismissed Poiret, and transferred her main custom to Jean Patou.

The second lawsuit came from the proprietors of L'Impérial, who claimed that she was still under contract to appear at their establishment, and that by not only leaving them after appearing there for only a month, but also by taking with her to Chez Joséphine some of their staff and most of their clientèle, she had caused them loss of income amounting to 300,000F.

At this point, Pepito astutely persuaded her to put all of her money and assets in his name, so that technically she was penniless. It says much for the trust she had in him, and the security she felt that their relationship possessed, that she agreed. L'Impérial's case against her came to nothing, and she and Pepito were now bound together more firmly than ever.

As part of his plan to widen her appeal, he suggested that she should make appearances in countries other than France. This would not only introduce her to a wider audience but it would allow her to return to France refreshed. Joséphine, with her appetite for travel whetted, gladly agreed.

Pepito set about planning a long tour, which would take them through 25 countries in both Europe and South America, and would occupy almost two years. Joséphine would make theatre appearances, and in several cities Pepito also arranged for a local night club to be taken over and renamed Chez Joséphine for the duration of her stay. By making dual appearances she would be able to earn twice as much money, although her earnings would be substantial anyway. At this time she was earning 1F million a year from her appearances at the Folies, and Pepito demanded that the venues that booked her for the tour paid her at an equivalent level.

She had little difficulty collecting such sums. One venue that had offered to book her was London's Embassy Club, and before leaving Paris she proudly showed around a signed contract they had sent to her with the space for her fee left blank, to be filled in with whatever figure she desired. For some reason, however, this never came to anything; Britain was one of the few European countries that their tour would leave unvisited.

They were to leave early in February 1928, and Pepito arranged that, at the end of January, Joséphine would give a grand farewell concert at the Salle Pleyel. The other performers on the bill would be the most famous jazz piano duo in Paris, Jean Wiener and Clement Doucet, who were normally resident at Jean Cocteau's club, Le Boeuf Sur Le Toit.

Of course her own club, Chez Joséphine, would have to be closed. Doctor Prieire, who owned the lease, offered several other dancers the opportunity to take it over but found no taker, and so when Joséphine left he closed it down.

The film was finished, *Un Vent De Folie* came to the end of its run, and Pepito and Joséphine began organising themselves to leave Paris. Joséphine was in two minds about leaving, especially about leaving Montmartre, where she had so many friends, like Bricktop and Frisco and Sidney Bechet, and which in many ways reminded her of Chestnut Alley from her St Louis childhood.

For her farewell concert, *Les Adieux De Joséphine À Paris*, the Salle Pleyel was packed. It took place on Sunday 28 January 1928, and all of fashionable Paris seemed to be there, along with almost every American in the city. Pepito, with his usual shrewdness, had planned that the concert would give a tantalising hint that there was a new Joséphine about to be born. For her first appearance she wore her old ragamuffin costume and danced a loose-limbed charleston. The audience was polite but slightly bored. They had been seeing this Joséphine now for two years.

She went off and re-appeared wearing a tight-fitting cloche hat, glinting with rhinestones, and an elegant, well-cut dress. She had been wearing such dresses for nightclub appearances ever since she had come to Paris, but this was the first time she had appeared in one onstage. Then, perching herself on the piano, she sang, and for the first time ever in public sang in French, the slow, sentimental song 'Mon Coeur Blessé'. After that, still in French, she made a hesitant little speech: "Je voulais...remercier le public...qui a été si gentil...J'étais une pauvre toute petite fille...et il a fait de moi une grande...grande...chose."

The whole presentation was inspired. Here was this immensely popular star showing just how much she had allowed Paris to bring her from her backward nativeness to the elegance of civilisation, how well she had learned her lesson, and how grateful she was to have had the privilege and good fortune to be given it. The audience were enchanted and enthusiastic, and to drive the point home Joséphine began to invite up to the stage many of the people who had contributed to civilising her: Monsieur Perugia, who made her shoes; Madame Agnès, her hairdresser; her couturier; her furrier; and her lingerie maker.

Unfortunately, by this point her sense of production had deserted her, and her list went on and on. The audience started to become bored and restless, and she made things worse during the intermission that followed by beginning to auction off programmes autographed by herself and by Wiener and Doucet for charity. By the time she had embarked on her third auction, the audience was becoming positively hostile, and there were cat-calls. She won them back, though; facing them regally, she admonished them: "Je croyais, pourtant, être en France" (I though I was still in France).

Her aplomb won her renewed applause, and her singing and dancing for the rest of the evening were received well, although not ecstatically. The whole evening gave her a further illustration of how fickle the public could be, and how they could turn against her in a moment.

8 On The Road

Joséphine and Pepito had several objects in mind when they planned her tour. One was to get her away from Paris while she was still a huge star and before the public's small dissatisfaction with the sameness of her performances could grow any greater. Their hope was that her absence would make their hearts grow fonder. In addition, the tour would give her an opportunity to create a new Joséphine, to develop an image that was nearer to what she wanted to be: more *soigné* than eccentric, more glamorous than amusing, and as much a singer as a dancer. As part of developing this new image, Pepito would continue to educate her in acting like a lady while on tour. He would hire tutors to teach her French and Spanish and German, and he would constantly work on polishing her table manners. "Hold your fork this way, *chérie*. Chew with your mouth closed, *chérie*. Don't speak in such a loud tone of voice, *chérie*."

No other performers would travel with them; instead local singers, dancers and musicians would be hired wherever they were performing. This inevitably led to somewhat variable standards of performance, and it put a great deal of pressure on Joséphine to carry her shows. Quite early in the tour, her weight had dropped from around 135 pounds to 115. Fortunately for her health, though, the tour would not be absolutely continuous. There would be gaps in it, and from time to time they would even manage to make trips back to Paris, although not to perform.

The first city on their itinerary was Vienna, and unknown to Joséphine and Pepito, as they made their way there, they were entering a fraught situation. Austria, like most of Europe in the aftermath of the Great War, was in a somewhat unstable state. Cut off from its former territories in the Austro-Hungarian Empire by the terms of the Armistice, it was now a relatively small country struggling to support not only itself but its sizeable capital, Vienna.

This gave rise to discontent and political ferment. The old empire had been overburdened with nobility, who had ruled over their great estates like mediaeval barons, and now that it had collapsed there was a great move towards socialism, towards creating a better world for the common man. There was also a move towards conservatism, because in times of great change there is a natural movement by many of the public towards old certainties, and in Austria one of these old certainties was Catholicism. The country therefore had many conservatives and many Catholics, and these were two groups to whom Joséphine was anathema.

Not that most of the population knew all that much about her, or even about the kinds of shows in which she appeared, for in Austria there was no tradition of music hall. But to herald her arrival, the city had been plastered with posters showing her wearing only pearls and an ostrich feather. Never had such posters been seen in Vienna. The newspapers investigating this phenomenon had published lurid tales of her riotous and debauched life in Paris. She was seen to embody licence and licentiousness. Furthermore, she was black.

Most of the population of Austria was Germanic, and rising out of its political unrest was a growing racist movement, encompassing both socialists and conservatives, that believed that Nordics, such as Saxons and Scandinavians, were the most superior race of man. The conservatives believed this out of a pride in their country's past, such as their history of producing great music and architecture, while the socialists believed it out of envy and resentment towards the country's Jewish minority, who owned many of its most profitable and successful businesses and who held many of its highest academic positions. Out of a fusion of these was growing the Nazi movement, who called themselves National Socialists but were in fact deeply conservative.

Joséphine, being black, was even further beyond the racial pale than the Jews, and by the time she and Pepito had arrived in Vienna at the beginning of February 1928 the city's small group of young proto-Nazis had declared loudly that they would see to it that she did not perform. Some of the most ardent had even used the word *negersmach*, meaning the insult it would be to the white population if she did.

Part of their hatred of black performers grew out of a belief that jazz was the natural enemy of great Viennese music, of Haydn, Mozart and Schubert, not to mention the waltzes of the Strausses. This feeling had been focused and inflamed by the recent performance in the city of the first attempt at a jazz opera, *Jonny Spielt Auf*, written by the young composer Ernst Krenek, who was himself Viennese, although living and working in Berlin, where he had seen and been influenced by not only the Sam Wooding band but also by *La Revue Nègre*. What was even worse than the decadent negroid music of *Jonny Spielt Auf* was the fact that Jonny, the black jazz violinist in it, boasted openly of his sexual power over white women. Joséphine obviously had an equivalent power over white men, and she would have to be stopped. For a start they would mount a demonstration.

The Catholic authorities felt much the same. One church, St Pauls', announced that it would start ringing its bells the moment her train arrived, warning good churchgoers to stay off the streets so that they didn't inadvertently catch sight of this "demon of immorality" and be contaminated. Several other churches announced that they would do likewise.

Another grievance held against her by a substantial section of the public was financial. Austria being poverty stricken, there was anger at the large amounts of money that people would be paying to see her, which it was felt would be better paid to an Austrian and then not leave the country. There was anger at the well-publicised price of some of her costumes, which cost up to 25,000F apiece.

Joséphine later that said she sympathised with those who campaigned against her on these grounds; she had known poverty, and understood how high-priced and seemingly frivolous things like clothes and theatre tickets seemed to mock the poor. What she found horrible was to be faced with people who regarded her as the devil incarnate or a demon of immorality without ever having seen her.

Nonetheless, there were still vast numbers of people in the city who were not only happy but agog to see her, and when her train pulled into the station she was greeted by cheering crowds – as well as a police escort, because the city was quite naturally nervous of public unrest.

In a horse-drawn carriage, she and Pepito were driven from the station along the grand and beautiful Ringstrasse to their hotel, the Grand Hotel. The streets were snow covered and the church bells rang, and Joséphine was delighted. She loved the excitement and the drama. But as it soon began to dawn on her how strong the feelings of some Viennese against her were, she began to feel a little unnerved. There was an uncomfortable similarity between some of the mobs she encountered and those she had seen in her childhood during the East St Louis race riot. Outside the Grand

Hotel, members of the anti-Joséphine movement were making their protest. As she and Pepito made her way towards the front door, a pamphlet was thrust into her hand. It bore the headline: "Can She Be Punished As She Deserves?"

In their suite, reporters came to interview her and she received them smilingly and professionally, allowing herself to be photographed surrounded by her luggage – 15 trunks, 196 pairs of shoes, 137 stage costumes, assorted furs, innumerable dresses, and 64 kilos of face powder. She also had two dogs with her: a Brabançon, whom she had named Fifi, and a Pekinese, Bébé.

Joséphine might have had misgivings, but Pepito was delighted with the commotion, seeing it as excellent publicity. Soon, however, he received a setback. Conservative groups had lobbied the Vienna City Council to such good effect that, two days after their arrival, it withdrew permission for Joséphine to appear in the Ronacher Theater, into which he had booked her. It did this on a small technicality, some formal concession that the theatre manager had failed to obtain.

Fortunately, the fact that it had blocked them in this way, and not by ruling on Joséphine and her possible demoralising effect on the susceptible, left the way open for her and Pepito to find another theatre, and by good fortune they quickly found one: the Johann Strauss. It wasn't as big as the Ronacher, and it wouldn't be available for four weeks, but at least it was a theatre.

The ensuing four weeks, however, gave the conservatives time to mobilise their forces. This time they lobbied the Austrian Parliament itself. A deputation from the Nationalist party brought a petition to the minister of the interior, Herr Hartleb, requesting that her "pornographic exhibition" be banned. They claimed that the party was receiving thousands of letters every day protesting against Joséphine's "brazen-faced heathen dances", and warned him that her appearance onstage would elicit riots and possibly bloodshed.

The controversy was now becoming so heated that the parliament decided that there was only one thing to do: they had to debate the question of whether Joséphine actually did represent a threat to public morals.

While waiting for this debate to be held, Joséphine set out to explore this new city and its surroundings. She and Pepito even went to the alpine resort of Semmering for a few days, some fifty miles south-east of Vienna, and there she learned to ski.

In spite of Austria's poverty, and the grimness of some of the more polit-ically-minded citizens, Vienna itself was still a cheerful and civilised city. Joséphine enjoyed the raffish, bohemian world of the coffee houses, and it was in one of those that she had the good fortune to run into the man who would champion her.

A member of parliament, his name was Count Adalbert Sternberg, although he was better known socially by his nickname, Monschi. A warm, genial, hard-drinking man who made friends easily, he was oddly enough a real-life Bohemian. He was a member of one of the oldest and wealthiest families in the kingdom of Bohemia, in what had been the Austro-Hungarian Empire. His family was so ancient that it was recorded in Czech history as far back as 1100AD. His visiting card proudly boasted that he was descended from Charlemagne, and it was believed that one of his even more distant ancestors was Gaspard – that Gaspard who, with Melchior and Balthasar, brought gifts to the newborn Jesus. For this reason, the fam-ily coat of arms was the star of Bethlehem.

Naturally the Sternberg family – including Monschi – were Catholics, but his religion was so deep rooted and so much a part of him that he was able to wear it as lightly as he did his life. He saw no reason for the uproar against Joséphine and decided that he would enjoy defending her.

The debate was opened by Dr Jerzabezh, a Viennese physician of some 25 years' standing and a prominent member of the Clerical party. Passionately, he laid into Joséphine, claiming that she would corrupt the citizens of Vienna by appearing in public "dressed only in a postage stamp". He was considerably upset by the poster that had appeared on the streets, showing her wearing nothing but feathers and pearls, "like a Congo savage". He did go out of his way, however, to stress that it was her nudity to which he objected, not the colour of her skin.

Speakers who followed him were less generous. They made unfavourable comments not only about Joséphine's colour but also about her figure, and described her acting as "perverse", an emotive term in a city where Dr Freud was still actively in practise.

Then Monschi got up to speak. He described Joséphine as a force of nature, saying that, through her dancing, she highlighted the anaemic qual-ity from which modern civilisation was suffering, through having lost touch with its primitive roots. "Whites don't know how to dance," he explained. "Only blacks conserve in dancing its human and sacred quality."

Enlarging on the religious theme of his argument, he went on: "The highest ideal of human art is always the female nude, and that part of the unclothed human female which strikes fear into the heart of Deputy Jerzabezh is always represented without dread in real art. Besides, he who combats nudism blasphemes God, who created man naked." He told his colleagues that they would do well to visit St Peter's in Rome and have a look at the pictures in the dome, saying: "The most daring nudes are there in the house of the Pope. Therefore, what is the meaning of this campaign of poorly-educated priests against Joséphine?"

In his allusions to nudity, Monschi was appealing in part to the nudist movement which, from the Twenties onwards, attracted many followers in Germany and, to a lesser extent, in Austria. German nudists took their nudity with a high-minded seriousness that was a world away from Joséphine's cheerful exuberance, but Monschi's mentioning this respectable and growing movement helped his argument, and the house voted in his favour. Joséphine would be permitted to appear at the Johann Strauss Theatre.

Unfortunately, in spite of the force of Monschi's religious arguments, opposition to her from the Catholic clergy remained strong. It so happened that St Paul's Church – the church that had instigated the ringing of the bells – was situated right next door to the Johann Strauss Theatre, and its priests announced that if she opened there they would hold three days of services, "in atonement for outrages on morality committed by Josephine Baker and other performers".

They were as good as their word. On the morning of 1 March, the day her act was to open, Father Fey, a Jesuit priest, offered up a special mass for her endangered soul in front of a packed church. His sermon, depicting her as the embodiment of decadence, was so vivid and compelling that after the service many of the congregation rushed hot-foot next door to buy tickets.

The show, a revue, was to be called *Schwartz Auf Weiss*. In it, among the recruited local talent, was the Viennese comic Albin Berg, and in spite of continued grumblings from the anti-Joséphine organisations it was received enthusiastically by press and public.

Apart from her farewell concert in Paris, this show was the first in which Joséphine sang onstage. With Pepito, she had worked out a disarming first appearance for herself. Instead of opening with one of her dazzling shockers, she entered wearing a beautiful but demure long cream dress and sang (in

English) 'Pretty Little Baby', a simple cheerful love song written in America a couple of years before, and that she had recorded in January 1927.

She wanted to show people that she was genial and unthreatening, and her voice during that first song was a little uncertain due to her fear of how she would be received. She wanted the audience to relate to her as a person, not as a demon of immorality, nor as a curiosity, nor yet as a symbol of anything – not of decadence, luxury nor even (in spite of Monschi's successful arguments) as a standard bearer for nudism.

The show played for three weeks to packed houses, and in addition she went on to appear every night at a temporary Chez Joséphine, a fashionable night club called the Wolf Pavilion.

On one night – this being Vienna – a group of psychoanalysts came to see her there. Analysts were one of the social groups who generally approved of Joséphine. After all, one of the tenets of their science was that society had created neuroses by inhibiting instinctual behaviour, and who was a healthier example of a lack of inhibitions than she was? This group had come directly from a meeting at which a paper had been presented by one of their number, Sándor Ferenczi. After performing a dance, Joséphine came among the audience to chat. She homed in on Ferenczi and sat herself firmly on his lap. He was bald, and she ran her hand over her own shiny helmet of hair and then across his baldness. "There," she said. "Now it will grow." The psychoanalysts were charmed.

As an interesting post script to Joséphine's short season in Vienna, and an indication of how much she appealed to many Viennese, ten years later, when Hitler's Germany annexed Austria and the young National Socialists who had protested against her had gained political control, Hitler himself came to Vienna. He commandeered the elegant Weinzinger Hotel for his entourage and the hotel owner's suite for himself. Getting into bed that night he was not best pleased to find a photograph of her looking down at him from the wall.

From Vienna, Pepito and Joséphine, along with Fifi and Bébé, went next to Budapest, Hungary, and there again she found herself the centre of controversy. This time it wasn't because the people felt that she represented a moral danger. (She had been officially cleared of that accusation after performing a sample of her charleston for the Hungarian minister of the interior and a committee of censors. They granted her permission to appear, and her show duly opened at the Royal Orpheum Theatre on the

Boulevard Elizabeth.) The problem turned out to be her luxurious lifestyle, her high earnings and her foreignness. Hungary, like Austria, was poor, and as in Vienna student activists resented so much money going to an outsider. During one performance, while she was onstage dancing, a group of them threw ammonia bombs onto the stage, shouting: "Go back to Africa!" She kept on dancing, but admitted afterwards that the protest had shaken her.

Pepito, far from shielding her from the unpredictable public, repeatedly exposed her to it in attempts to wring as much publicity from her notoriety as he could. For instance, he had her drive through downtown Budapest in a small buggy exotically drawn by an ostrich.

His schemes to generate publicity were endless. As in Vienna, he had arranged for Joséphine to appear in a night club after her show each night. There she was seen by a handsome Hungarian cavalry officer, André Czlovoydi. In fact he came there to see her repeatedly, and developed such an infatuation for her that he began to write love poems to her in school-boy French. In one he called her "la soleil noire de la cité de la lumière".

Pepito, being Sicilian, was ferociously jealous of Joséphine's admirers, but he frequently managed to hide the fact. In this instance he turned it brilliantly to his advantage by slapping the officer across the face and challenging him to a duel. Seconds were appointed. They selected swords as weapons, and agreed on St Stephen's cemetery the following day at dawn for the place and time. Pepito then hurriedly sent a message to Czlovoydi, explaining that this was to be only a publicity stunt and not to be taken seriously. Czlovoydi cheerfully agreed to go along with it. There would be no real danger of him getting hurt, and to fight a duel over the famous Joséphine Baker would make him a hero among his fellow officers.

The whole thing went off perfectly. Pepito had arranged for a squad of reporters to attend, and once the duel had begun he wielded his foil with the flair of Douglas Fairbanks, while Joséphine looked on and screamed so continuously and dramatically that it was almost unnerving. Nor did she ever make it clear which of the combatants she favoured. Eventually, Pepito received a scratch on the shoulder, which was solemnly inspected by the seconds. Honour was declared to be satisfied, and everybody went happily off to breakfast.

With such publicity, and in spite of the continuing background of student protest, Joséphine's show at the Royal Orpheum Theatre was a great success. In it she made a further experiment in enlarging her repertoire: she acted in a short sketch that had been written for her before she left Paris by Maurice Debroka, the writer of *La Sirène Des Tropiques*.

As usual, she also gleefully explored the city, taking a steamer trip along the Danube, among other things, which she found was wide and powerful enough to remind her of the Mississippi. However, the unrest and controversy she found she was stirring up made her uneasy. It brought home to her how welcome she had been in Paris, and this in turn made her set herself more determinedly than ever before to learn to speak French well.

Fortunately, the subsequent cities that she and Pepito visited were in general less unnerving. It is true that at a show in Zagreb, a month after Budapest, student members of Yugoslavia's Clerical Party rioted during one of her performances, shouting "Long live Croatian culture! Down with vulgarity!", and at another a young Croatian actually managed to bring the show to a halt by yelling "Get out! The people of Zagreb are starving and you are paid a fortune!", but in general she aroused more enthusiasm than hostility.

It was also in Zagreb that she received another dramatic protestation of love. André Czlovoydi hadn't been the only Hungarian who had fallen for her madly; another was a 21-year-old draughtsman named Alexius Groth. He too had fallen in love with her in Budapest, and had followed her to Zagreb, bombarding her with flowers and love letters. Finding her unresponsive, he presented himself before her as she was leaving a night club and dramatically stabbed himself, falling at her feet. *The New York Times*, reporting the incident, observed: "He wounded himself severely but may recover."

When she and Pepito arrived in jazz-loving Prague, their train was besieged by fervent admirers. They pressed so excitedly around her, as she made her way out of the station, that she was forced to climb onto the roof of her waiting limousine to get out of their reach. A minor riot developed. Several station windows were smashed and several fans were injured badly enough to have to be taken to hospital. There were serious fears for her safety, and only when a horde of policemen surrounded her car was it able to proceed slowly, with Joséphine still perched on its roof. Even so, the fans would not allow it to drive to her hotel until it had made a tour of the city, with Joséphine – her composure quickly recovered – waving to the cheering crowds like royalty.

So familiar were the Czechs with her life that they seemed to know all about her. They knew about her lucky charm, for instance, and at the end of every performance she gave in Prague they showered the stage with rabbits' feet.

It was amazing how much her fame had spread during 1928. She was constantly in the news all over the world, but especially in Europe. Photographs of her and interviews constantly appeared in newspapers and magazines. Her three silent films – *La Sirène Des Tropiques* and the two showing her dancing – were distributed widely. Likewise her records. Her memoirs had also been translated into German, Spanish and Italian. It seemed as if her fans couldn't get enough of her.

She was adored in Bucharest, although she was amazed at how primitive Romanian conditions were. At her hotel, for instance, there were fleas in the bed and cows in the lobby, and she reacted to the backwardness of the place by walking the streets barefoot, causing some locals to think that she had to be a gypsy.

One of her shows there was presented at an open-air theatre. The day was hot, it was threatening to rain, and the manager had crammed 3,000 people into an auditorium designed to hold 1,700. Furthermore, if rain caused the performance to be cancelled before it reached its halfway point, he was legally required to refund all of their money. As the band began to play the opening number, the rain began to fall in big, splashy drops. As it got heavier, the musicians began to miss notes. Hurrying to reach the halfway point, performers began muscling acts offstage as soon as they had finished, and then racing through their material. Many of the audience left, but others came in to take their seats.

By the time it was Joséphine's turn to appear, the rain was pelting down. As a born trouper, this was just the sort of situation to which she always rose magnificently. She danced on, holding up an umbrella (as many of the audience were doing) and wearing her banana costume.

Soon she found the umbrella useless and threw it away, dancing passionately in the warm rain. Her make-up ran and her costume began to disintegrate, and still she danced. Even when the manager shouted from the wings that the half-way point had been reached and the show could be stopped, she danced – and the drenched audience adored her. "What an audience," she later wrote. "What enthusiasm. What a storm. What a bath. So much for Rumania."

The tour continued all over Europe, moving on to Italy and to Switzerland, where, in Basle, having received six curtain calls, she sang an encore in excellent German, and where in Lucerne the orchestra leader set such a fast tempo for one of her dances that at the end of it she fainted from exhaustion.

In Berlin, in view of her success there in 1926, she was booked to appear at the Theater Des Westens for six months, opening in October 1928. Reunited with her in the show was an old colleague from *La Revue Nègre*, the dancer Louis Douglas, who had now settled in Germany. She also planned to open a Chez Joséphine for the duration of her visit.

Jazz had become even more popular in Germany than at the time of her previous visit. Berlin radio stations in the late Twenties and early Thirties were famous for the amount of jazz they played. Two years previously, the most popular shows in Berlin had been the operettas of Franz Léhar. Now the hottest ticket in town was Kurt Weill and Bertolt Brecht's jazz-influenced *Threepenny Opera*. To celebrate Joséphine's return, Weill wrote about her in his weekly column for Berlin's radio journal, writing how pleased he would be to write songs for her.

In the autumn of 1927, the Hoch Conservatory in Frankfurt had announced that it would begin giving courses in performing jazz at the beginning of the following year. This announcement naturally caused howls of protest from the conservative music press, who considered jazz to be anti-German and degenerate.

But musical conservatives were not the worst antagonists Joséphine had to face. The Nazi movement had also grown and strengthened during the past two years, and although it was still only a shadow of what it would become it was still making its presence felt, and so, in spite of he happy memories of Berlin and her optimism at being back there, things were to turn out badly for Joséphine.

Part of the problem facing the show was that its producers were Jewish. There were two of them, both surnamed Rotter. Well liked and successful, they owned three theatres and presented shows of all kinds: plays, revues and operettas.

The *soubrette* in the show was the blonde singer and actress Lea Seidl, who later recalled her memories of the time to author Patrick O'Connor. On the first night of Joséphine's show, Lea was onstage with fellow performer Paul Heidlemann when a large group of Nazi sympathisers in the audience began to hoot and whistle. Paul whispered to her: "This is terrible. Oh God, they will kill us!"

As it happened, they did little but hoot and whistle. Their anger wasn't really aimed at Lea and Paul, who were not Jewish, but at the Rotters – and, of course, at Joséphine. After the first night, a Nazi critic wrote: "How dare they put our beautiful blonde Lea Seidl with a negress on the stage."

Joséphine and Lea, who had adjoining dressing rooms, became friendly, but the incessant barracking from Nazis in the audience night after night and the vilification in the right-wing press went on, and for Joséphine it all became too much. About three weeks into the run, Lea was onstage performing when she noticed Joséphine standing in the wings. She had on her street coat – an elegant chinchilla – and was carrying a big sack over her shoulder. To Lea it looked like a sack of potatoes, but most likely it was simply her belongings. Joséphine whispered: "Don't say anything. I disappear. I run away." Then she left. She and Pepito fled back to Paris and the show was forced to close.

They arrived back in Paris in time to learn that Gaston Prieire, the doctor who been one of her causal lovers and had backed Chez Joséphine, had finally been nailed by the law for his insurance swindles and was even then on trial. Joséphine went to court to visit him, and was photographed by the press standing in the halls of justice with Dr Prieire's lawyer, Maître Pinganaud. Wearing a lavish fox fur coat, in the photograph she looks somewhat apprehensive, as well she might, because Dr Prieire was sentenced to two years in prison.

Having now a substantial hole in her schedule, she and Pepito decided to continue their tour by heading north into Scandinavia. But she was not yet finished with Germany, being contracted to appear at theatres in both Munich and Hamburg, and so, with some misgivings, she set off with Pepito for Munich.

But she never appeared there. Learning of her impending performance, the Munich press, which was by this time largely controlled by the Nazis, demanded that she be deported as an undesirable alien. It further suggested that she would place an unfair burden on the local police, who would undoubtedly have to protect her from a hostile mob if she did appear. The police accordingly banned her from performing in the city. She was, however, able to make her appearance in Hamburg, where the Nazi party had at that time obtained less control.

After Germany, Scandinavia came as a relief. The first city she visited was Copenhagen, and from the start she was captivated by it. It would remain one of her favourite cities for the rest of her life. After all, this was the home of one of her favourite writers, Hans Christian Andersen.

On her arrival at the Palace Hotel, she held her usual press conference and entranced the gathered reporters by reciting to them 'The Emperor's New Clothes' in French, as if they were little children. As one reporter wrote: "I didn't think the good French language could be so beautiful. It is quite an event to hear Joséphine Baker talk with such a lovely voice."

The effort she was putting into polishing her French was certainly bearing fruit. Indeed, from this point on in her life French became her favourite language to speak. There was a curious reason for this. Her English, as she was only too well aware, was full of grammatical mistakes and mispronunciations. So was her French, but if she spoke English she sounded poorly educated, whereas if she spoke French her mistakes were forgiven as natural errors from someone not speaking her native tongue.

One of the reasons she liked Copenhagen was its cleanliness. As she was later to say of her Scandinavian tour: "It's crazy how clean everything is in those countries. You can lean anywhere."

She liked the Danes, too. Compared to the excitable middle Europeans, whether for her or against her, they were polite and rather gentle and tended to view her as a work of art rather than as a curiosity – apart from the fact that blacks were a much rarer sight in Scandinavia than in other countries she had visited.

It is true that, while she was in Copenhagen, there was one little hiccup. A Danish pastor, learning of her impending arrival and alarmed by what he had heard, started a campaign against her because of her immorality. As it happened, he was eventually persuaded to attend one of her performances, and was so converted by what he saw that he applauded enthusiastically.

From Copenhagen, she then went to Stockholm, Sweden. Again there was some debate as to whether she was a danger to morals, but again it swiftly dissipated, helped by the fact that the Swedish royal family attended one of her shows. Among them was the Crown Prince Gustav. In 1960 Joséphine gave Stephen Papich (who staged shows for her during an American tour) a long and detailed account of a torrid affair she claimed to have had with him. As Gustav was well into his 40s in 1928 and looking it, and even though he was in fairly good physical shape, some doubt has been cast on her assertions. But the fact is that he was royalty and, given Joséphine's romantic notions about kings and queens, if he had shown any evidence at all of being attracted to her there is little doubt that she would have responded.

In his book *Remembering Josephine*, Papich retells her account of an enchanted evening which she claimed to have spent with Gustav in the royal carriage of a train speeding through the heart of Sweden. "I'll never forget that bed," she told him. "It was like something out of a Hollywood movie. It was like a dream. It was a bed shaped like a swan...I just dropped my dress. I didn't have anything on. I was ready for anything...I looked like a little boy with my slicked down hair and my hard little dancer's body."

Leaving Sweden for Norway, Joséphine found herself presented with a small yet unexpected problem. On entering Sweden, she had required special permission from the customs officials to bring in her two dogs. As it happened, during her stay in the country one of them (it's not recorded which) had produced two pups. On passing through customs on her way out, she was asked by an official if the dogs had been declared on the way in. "Yes," said Joséphine.

"How many?"

"Two," said Joséphine.

The official pointed to the puppies. "And those?" he asked. "Aren't they dogs?"

"No," said Joséphine, "they're just samples, and you wouldn't want me to put them back where they came from, would you?" She and her dogs were allowed to proceed.

In Oslo, the audiences again received her with enthusiasm, and the whole Scandinavian section of her tour did much to repair the damage that had been done to her confidence in the Catholic and racist countries further south. It says much for her strength of character and her sense of self that she was able to cope successfully with being told vehemently that she was both a wonderful "force of nature" and "a demon of immorality" at one and the same time.

En route back to Paris for a break, Pepito had booked her to appear in Amsterdam, where ecstatic crowds awaiting her arrival jammed the city's traffic system for two hours. During the show she danced the charleston in Dutch clogs, and was such a success that her show was booked to play for twice as long.

Joséphine and Pepito arrived back in Paris in April 1929, and almost at once they made the rounds of the newspaper offices to announce her presence, as Pepito had taught her to do everywhere they had been. She also wanted them to hear how well she could now speak French, and to tell them something about the new Joséphine they could expect when she returned permanently. "I don't want to live without Paris," she assured them. "It's my country. The charleston, the bananas – finished. Understand? I have to be worthy of Paris. I want to become an artist."

"I want to show a wholly new Joséphine Baker," Pepito put in. "She's no longer a curiosity. She's an artist now. She sings beautifully and she's a good comic actress. She'll be a great French star."

"But I am French," said Joséphine. "I'm black, but I'm French. And I love Paris. I adore Paris. I will have that written on the roof of the house I just bought. Yours is the only country where a person can live in peace."

The house that had been bought by Joséphine – and by Pepito, their finances now being inextricably entwined – was in fact a 30-room mansion in the leafy Paris suburb of Le Vésinet, on the west bank of the Seine, about ten miles west of the city centre. Situated at 26 Avenue Clemenceau, it was named Le Beau-Chêne (The Beautiful Oak) because of the ancient oak trees which lined the long white gravel driveway that led from the high gates to the front door. The house had been built in around 1900, of red and grey brick. It was also stone clad, and looked almost like a fairy-tale castle, with pointed turrets and ornate dormer windows, its façade decorated with mock mediaeval shields. It also had a terrace, a formal garden, a greenhouse, several ponds and extensive grounds, providing plenty of room for all of the creatures she had acquired – and would continue to acquire – over the years. At last Joséphine had a proper permanent home, and she would continue to live there for years.

A little over 15 miles from the centre of Paris, Le Beau-Chêne was far enough outside the city to feel as if it was in the country. At the centre of Le Vésinet – which has an un-Parisian atmosphere all of its own – was a flourishing fruit and vegetable market. To Joséphine it resembled the market in her childhood in St Louis.

When she bought the house, its interior was somewhat gloomily decorated and poorly lit, and Joséphine, cheerfully referring to it as her "shanty", enthusiastically set about planning its redecoration. There was to be no overall plan. Each room was to be decorated individually. There was to be a Louis XVI room, ornate with gilt; an East Indian room, complete with temple bells; a billiard room; a room in which for Joséphine to rehearse; little salons; big salons; an office for Pepito, decorated in chrome and robin's-egg blue; and an extravagant bathroom for Joséphine, with mirrors for walls and a chrome-encased bath. When the redecoration was complete, the house magnificently reflected her vivid and stylish personality.

Before the work could be carried out, however, there was the tour to complete, and the next leg was to take her back across the Atlantic to South America.

When she and Pepito landed in Buenos Aires, she was shocked and disconcerted to discover that here, too, she was the subject of controversy. As she later wrote bitterly: "The old Catholic parties hounded me with a Christian hatred from station to station, city to city, one stage to another." One newspaper, *Calle*, held to the Catholic view, and its campaign against her received a strong boost when Argentina's president, Hipólito Irigoyen, weighed in on its side, attacking Joséphine as an object of scandal and, again, as a demon of immorality.

This caused the anti-government paper *Critica* to adopt her as a symbol in their ongoing political battle, and vehemently campaign in her support. At her performances there were frequently loud shouts from the audience: "Down with Irigoyen!"

At her 50th Buenos Aires performance, things reached a climax when members of both factions in her audience mounted demonstrations. They hurled abuse at each other and threw firecrackers. Joséphine stood hidden behind the stage curtains listening to the orchestra play tango after tango while the management waited for the disturbance to subside.

She was sufficiently discomposed by this to write an angry open letter home to the Paris newspapers, announcing that she was going to give up dancing, "which practised by a white woman is moral and by a black one transgresses." She began to realise that racism, which she had at first believed to be peculiarly American, was in fact a world-wide problem, and this realisation would affect her future attitude. It would reinforce her already firm stance against racism, and she would militantly campaign for people of every colour and country to be regarded as equal.

After Buenos Aires, still remaining in Argentina, she would give performances in Córdoba and Mendoza before returning to Buenos Aires again in September 1929. There a fête was given in her honour by an organisa-

tion for expatriate Frenchmen. They presented her with three baby croco-
diles, and Joséphine, delighted, responded by singing three tangos in
Spanish: 'Mama Yo Quiero', 'Garufa' and 'Haragan'.

It was while she was making this second visit to Buenos Aires that her
film *La Sirène Des Tropiques* had its American première, at the Lafayette
Theater in Harlem. The première was attended by New York's mayor, the
affable Jimmy Walker, and it was the first time that a mayor of New York
had ever attended a Harlem theatre. The whole thing was made into quite
an occasion. After all, this was the first time that a black American girl had
ever been the star of a feature-length movie. After the showing, a special
stage show was mounted in celebration, featuring such black stars of the
day as singer/comedienne Edith Wilson, acrobatic dancers The Berry
Brothers and tap dancer Bill "Bojangles" Robinson. The celebration went
on into the early hours of the morning.

Joséphine, learning of all this, felt encouraged about possible future success in America, but some of her pleasure was taken away by an item in a
Buenos Aires newspaper, reprinting a protest about her film performance
from one of the black American papers. It accused her of "indecent performance, imitating the French...if she were to give a free performance for
coloured people, you can tell her from me, the theatre would be empty".
This was a criticism from which Joséphine would increasingly suffer. In
achieving success with white audiences, and especially with white European
audiences, she would increasingly be felt by the black American community to be no longer one of them or of their entertainment tradition.

From Buenos Aires, Joséphine and Pepito went to Uruguay and then to
Chile. She experienced no problems in either country, and was received
well. It was the same in Brazil when they moved on there, although in Rio
De Janeiro she was again obliged to perform first in private before a committee, this time composed of police and this time wearing her banana
skirt, so that they could be sure that it was a fit and proper costume to be
seen in their city.

Travelling around South America involved covering long distances and
spending endless time on trains and planes. Joséphine liked planes, however (she once said that a plane felt like a cradle with wings), but she found
it tiresome to sit still for so long. It was not something she was good at.

To pass the time she took to telling Pepito the experiences of her early
life, delving deeply into her childhood memories, explaining the climate

of racial discrimination in America, her dismay at finding it again in Central Europe, her realisation that in fact such attitudes were worldwide, and her desire to do something about it. Pepito suggested that a way to do that might be for them to collaborate on a novel, basing it on her memories of her youth. She agreed, and during subsequent journeys they set to work making notes.

Early in December 1929, they set off from Rio back to Europe, sailing on the French liner *Lutetia*. Joséphine later recalled that she boarded it feeling some apprehension, knowing that she was on her way to present Paris with the new Joséphine, a Paris that had not seen her perform for two years.

Fortunately, almost as soon as she boarded, she met a Parisian who adored her. He was Charles-Édouard Jeanneret, better known to the world at large as the architect and town planner Le Corbusier. Then in his early 40s, he had been in Brazil and Uruguay lecturing on his advanced theories of design and advising on building projects. A keen student of jazz, he came to see Joséphine when she gave a performance in the ship's salon, dancing and singing and playing the guitar, and afterwards he invited her back to his cabin. She brought her guitar with her and sang some more for him, including Florence Mills's famous number 'I'm A Little Black Bird Looking For A Blue Bird'.

The two of them got on like a house on fire. On subsequent days he sketched and painted her, writing in his journal: "She glides over the roughness of life. She has a good little heart. She is an admirable artist when she sings, and out of this world when she dances."

They became lovers, of course, and when a committee was formed among the first-class passengers to organise a costume ball they decided to attend it together, and Le Corbusier seriously set to work designing costumes for them both. After he had made several preliminary sketches, he settled on wearing blackface (which looked satisfyingly odd with his thick owlish glasses), convict's striped trousers and an Indian army guard's vermilion coat. Joséphine dressed as a clown, appearing in whiteface and with her eyes ringed in black. The effect their appearance had on their fellow revellers was gratifyingly stunning.

In spite of their instant closeness, after the voyage they cheerfully went their separate ways, Le Corbusier to marry within a few weeks Yvonne Gallis, a gypsy Monegasque whom he later described as "a slender brunette with dark eyes who did not mince words and had an emphatic way of expressing herself". Joséphine, of course, went happily off with Pepito to their new home. But although they were setting up house together, the incident with Le Corbusier underlines a slight shift that had taken place in their relationship. More and more Joséphine was beginning to regard him as a business partner, and even as an employee. She rarely even bothered to introduce him as her husband any more.

This hurt Pepito deeply. He knew about her affairs, and was upset by them, and frequently his jealously flared into anger, but he came to realise that there was nothing he could do to change her nature, and gradually learned that she would never be able to commit herself completely to one man, nor ever to totally trust in anyone but herself.

Returning to Paris after two years on the road, Joséphine had definitely changed. She was more assured, if still given to bouts of insecurity. She was softer spoken and less frenetic, and she was now a poised singer and comedienne as well as an elastic dancer. To a Paris journalist, she said: "The *danse sauvage* is finished. I was 16 when I danced the charleston almost nude. Now I am a woman. You have to grow and change all the time. When you no longer have anything new to do or say you disappear." Woman or not, at 25 there was still something of the child in her. To the journalist she resembled a little girl trying to be well behaved and please her parents, and this he found touching.

One of the first things Pepito did on their return was to hire the writer Félix De La Camara to work with him in turning the notes that he and Joséphine had written into a novel. The book that quickly emerged was entitled *Mon Sang Dans Tes Veines* (My Blood In Your Veins). Published in 1930, it is pretty terrible. Few copies were printed, it was harshly reviewed, and it did nothing to advance Joséphine's career. Nonetheless, because of her very inadequacy as a writer, she has no art to conceal herself, so its simple honesty provides a surprisingly clear insight into her barely-formed ideas.

The plot, set in America, begins with Ira Cushman Barkley, a successful and wealthy chewing-gum manufacturer, building himself an estate called The Oaks at a location an hour west of Boston. (Oddly for New England, it much resembles a southern plantation.) He dies shortly after doing so, leaving his wife and an eight-month-old son, Fred. When Fred is ten, his mother's black maid has a daughter, Joan. Fred and Joan, growing up together in the household, become close friends.

As the years go by (and here there is a short digression making the point that ancient civilisations valued dark skin more than light), Fred leaves to fight in the Great War and returns to devote himself to running the family chewing-gum business. He and Joan are now in love, but he finds himself forced to renounce her love because of her black skin. Soon his business affairs leave him little time for Joan, and she misses him deeply.

One day, while wandering lonely in the woods of the estate, she happens on a small neglected chapel and is amazed to find inside it a painting of a black madonna. She asks Fred about it, and he explains that it is a copy of a Polish icon from Krakow. Joan thinks how nice Europeans must be if they worship a black madonna. This leads her to ponder the injustice of racial discrimination for many pages. The household dogs, Topsy and Pat, are black and white, and they happily eat from the same bowl. Why, then, not the people who visit the household?

Barred from participating (like Cinderella), she watches Fred and his rich young friends enjoying themselves on the estate. Prominent among them is a pretty flapper from New Orleans, Clarence Clifton. Pleasure seeking and selfish, Clarence sits smoking while Fred's mother sits knitting sweaters for poor children.

Being from the south, Clarence is also a racist. She hates Joan, frequently expresses her contempt for blacks in general, and dislikes seeing the old family snapshots of Fred and Joan together as children. Nonetheless, to please his mother, and against his instincts (being still secretly in love with Joan), Fred becomes engaged to her. But before they can marry, Fred has a riding accident in the woods. Unconscious and badly injured, he is carried to a nearby hut, where a doctor happens to live.

The doctor explains that Fred urgently needs a blood transfusion, which must come from somebody young. Joan, being the youngest there, offers to give hers. "A black giving blood to a white?" somebody questions.

"Scientifically," says the doctor, "there is no reason not to." (At this point there is a long discussion about blood, its nature and its symbolism: how the blood of various races mingled on the mud of the battlefields of France; how, in Egyptian legend, Isis cried over the bloody body of Osiris; and how Christ's blood redeemed mankind.)

Radiant with joy, Joan sees the transfusion tubes set up between herself and the unconscious Fred, and as the transfusion takes place she begs the doctor never to reveal to him whose blood saved him.

After having given several pints, Joan is so weakened that she falls into a decline and dies. Fred, recovered and intent on finding out who his donor was, breaks into the doctor's files. He is amazed to learn that he now has black blood in his veins, and dashes off to tell Clarence that their marriage cannot be. She agrees, telling him: "You've become a black white man."

Blood as a theme was much in the air at the time that Joséphine wrote this. Transfusion as a technique was very much in its infancy, and there was much popular debate about its possible effects. Racists believed that blood held substances that made each race what it was, superior or inferior, and that adulterating the blood of the superior race would lead to the decline of its civilisation. Joséphine's book does its best to make a case against such ideas, but she has a further blood image as well: Joan's blood sacrifice is done out of love for all mankind.

To drive her point home, the title page of the book carries an illustration showing three black men kneeling at the foot of Christ's cross, raising their hands to Him in supplication. Only the lower half of His body is visible, and it is clear that His legs bear a strong resemblance to those of a certain Mademoiselle Bakaire.

TOP LEFT: Joséphine's mother, Carrie (seated), and her sister, Margaret (standing), with the wife of her nephew, Richard, holding one of the Rainbow Tribe at Les Milandes in the Fifties. TOP RIGHT: Joséphine in blackface performing in *Chocolate Dandies* on Broadway in 1925. ABOVE LEFT: Studio portrait of Joséphine in Berlin in 1925. ABOVE RIGHT: The "Danse Sauvage". Joséphine and Joe Alex, appearing in *La Revue Nègre* in Paris in 1925.

TOP LEFT: Joséphine's costume for the finale of *Un Vent De Folie* at the Folies Bergère in 1927. TOP RIGHT: Joséphine photographed in 1927 by Madame d'Ora, wearing a cap designed by Aques. ABOVE LEFT: Joséphine, costumed by Georges Barbier for *Un Vent De Folie* at the Folies Bergère in 1927. ABOVE RIGHT: Joséphine in her famous banana girdle. This version is the one which Joséphine wore in the finale of *La Folie Du Jour* in 1926.

ABOVE: Joséphine, as "Le Chasse-Mouche", in *La Folie Du Jour*, in 1926.

TOP LEFT: Joséphine, Pepito and an ostrich in Budapest, taken during their 25-country tour in 1928. TOP RIGHT: Joséphine and Pepito. ABOVE LEFT: Joséphine with Chiquita at the time of *Paris Qui Remue* in 1930. ABOVE RIGHT: Joséphine in her bandleader's costume for *La Joie De Paris* at the Casino De Paris in 1932.

TOP: Joséphine onstage with a soldier during one of her wartime shows. MIDDLE: Le Beau-Chêne. ABOVE LEFT: Joséphine at the opening night of her New York "Chez Joséphine" in February 1936, with celebrity guests. ABOVE RIGHT: Joséphine sailing to New York in 1935 to appear in the Ziegfeld Follies.

TOP LEFT: Joséphine back in Paris after the Liberation, wearing her uniform of the Women's Auxiliary of the Free French Air Force. TOP RIGHT: Joséphine and Jo Bouillon by their pool at Les Milandes. ABOVE: Joséphine and husband Jo Bouillon with their daughter Marianne.

TOP: Joséphine introducing her tenth child, Mara, to the other members of the Rainbow Tribe at Les Milandes in 1959. MIDDLE: Joséphine's château at Les Milandes. ABOVE LEFT: Joséphine and the Rainbow Tribe in Monaco in 1969. ABOVE RIGHT: Joséphine rehearsing with her rhinestone microphone at the London Palladium for the *Royal Variety Show* of 1974.

ABOVE: Joséphine evicted from her château on 12 March 1969.

9 *Le Beau-Chêne*

Arriving back in Paris in December 1929, Joséphine and Pepito found the theatre world in a state of near panic. The cause of this was not the Wall Street Crash, which had occurred on 24 October and the effects of which would not be deeply felt in either America or the rest of the world for some months, signalling the end of the carefree Twenties; what was depressing theatre owners was the arrival of the talkies, the new sensation that was enticing away their audiences.

Nonetheless, the theatres were doing their best to fight back, and after some negotiation Pepito managed to get Joséphine engaged to star in a revue at the Casino De Paris, the Paris music hall regarded by the general public as second only to the Folies Bergère and by many music hall aficionados as its superior, with more and better singing and dancing and fewer parading nudes. This revue, to be called *Paris Qui Remue* (roughly translated "Paris Stirs Things Up"), was not to begin rehearsals until the autumn, so in the meantime the two of them began to settle into Le Beau-Chêne, and Pepito set about organising for Joséphine to make a prolonged tour of Spain. This tour began early in April 1930, and the first Spanish city in which Joséphine appeared was Seville. She was there during Holy Week, and the sight of hooded penitents in a religious procession reminded her uneasily of the Ku Klux Klan.

From Seville they toured Pamplona, Valencia, Grenada, Córdoba, Madrid, Valladolid, Malaga and Barcelona, where La Macarona, the famous gypsy dancer, gave Joséphine lessons in dancing the flamenco. In later years she would often dance it as part of her night club act. Spanish audiences, while fascinated by her dancing, were also slightly bewildered by it. Apart from the flamenco, the dances with which they were most familiar were the ballets performed in operettas. These, like the flamenco, were relatively formal, and that word could hardly be applied to Joséphine, even in her new, more stately incarnation.

When they returned to Paris, and to Le Beau-Chêne, Joséphine went shopping for antiques with which to furnish it. Among them in time she would buy a 15th-century suit of armour to decorate the entrance hall and a huge 18th-century bed which Pepito tried to convince the press had once belonged to Marie Antoinette. In a room alongside the master bedroom, Joséphine installed cages for her monkeys, and outside, in a recess on the north wall of the house, she fitted a large, round aviary for her parrots, parakeets, macaws, cockatiels and cockatoos. Roaming the grounds were her domestic birds – the ducks, chickens, geese, pheasants and turkeys – and her dogs, cats, rabbits, piglets and tortoises.

It turned out that she was also a talented and enthusiastic gardener. In her greenhouse she raised orchids, and behind the house she had something she'd long desired: a vegetable garden. She took to doing some work in it almost every day, dressed simply, as she always was at Le Beau-Chêne, and not afraid to get her beautifully-manicured hands caked with earth.

To help her with the gardens in the rest of the estate, she hired three gardeners. One of the first jobs she gave them was to plant gaudy red-and-yellow-leaved coleus plants along her terrace, proudly spelling out "JOSÉPHINE BAKER".

On the eastern edge of the estate, more than a quarter of a mile away from the house, across the front lawn and half hidden among shrubs and oak trees, was a large marble pool filled with goldfish and water lilies. This secret area she turned into what she called her Temple Of Love. Around the pool she placed a semi-circle of Corinthian columns, also of marble, with a statue on each of some classical beauty – Diana was there, and Venus, and Circe, the bewitcher of men. It became Joséphine's pleasure on warm afternoons to bathe naked in the pool, uncaring that the bushes bordering the grounds didn't completely hide her from the street outside.

If she was uncaring, so too were the inhabitants of Le Vésinet. They were delighted by her, and proud that she lived among them. She became a visible part of the community, frequently shopping at the local stores and the market, adept at the French art of haggling.

She became a benefactor to the poor of the community, too. One store, owned by Madame Henriette Levoisier, provided coal. Joséphine would frequently ask Madame Levoisier to give her a list of poor families who were having difficulty paying their fuel bills, and would then settle them herself. Also, at each Christmas, she arranged for such families to receive twice the coal they paid for.

Near Madame Levoisier's store was a electrical shop selling lamps and light fittings. It was owned by electrician George Guignery, and Joséphine and he became friendly a year or so later, when she hired him to rewire Le Beau-Chêne. She had originally hired the Paris department store Galeries Lafayette to redesign its dim lighting, but the lamps that they fitted she felt were insufficiently theatrical, and so she asked Georges Guignery to have a go. Naturally he was proud and flattered to be asked, and drew on all of his resources of skill and his equipment to do a good job. He trained giant spotlights onto the statues in the Temple Of Love, and threaded strings of small lights through the filigree bars of her aviary. With an array of white bulbs he lit the coleus plants spelling her name. At night, the gardens of Le Beau-Chêne came to resemble an illuminated pleasure garden.

Joséphine was so proud of her house that she had cards printed with a map of Le Vésinet and an arrow pointing to it. She gave out these cards by the hundred, to friends and fellow workers and often even strangers, inviting all and sundry to drop by and visit it.

Meanwhile, *Paris Qui Remue* approached. A year earlier, the Casino De Paris had been bought by the partnership of Henri Varna and Oscar Dufresne from its previous owner, Léon Volterra. It had cost them 9F million. Dufresne was a former music hall comic, while Varna had started out playing bit parts at the Théâtre De Belleville, had appeared in vaudeville and opera, and had then gone on to become a notable producer. It was he who had realised that Joséphine had developed sufficiently as a performer to be capable of starring in a Casino De Paris revue. For their first annual show, that of 1929-30, Varna and Dufresne's star had of course been Mistinguett, who was closely identified with the Casino by Parisians. As a tribute to her, the show had been called *Paris Miss*.

One of their reasons for choosing Joséphine for their 1930-31 season was that, in 1931, Paris was to hold a vast Colonial Exposition. To coincide with this, the theme of their show was to be the colonies of France, and so Joséphine, because of her colour, was the natural choice.

A second reason was that they planned to feature Joséphine and Mistinguett as their future stars in alternate years – the queen of the Paris music hall and her only possible competitor – and so build publicity out of the rivalry between them, which was anything but imaginary.

Joséphine was not all that bothered by Mistinguett, who was in any case more than 30 years older than she was, but Mistinguett was considerably bothered by Joséphine. On one evening, when Joséphine and Pepito had arrived at a film première at the Cinéma Apollo and were standing in the foyer, Mistinguett made an entrance, squired by two elegant young men. At once fans flocked around her, begging for her autograph. From the middle of this throng, spotting Joséphine, she called out: "Well, Pickaninny, why don't you come up and salute me?" At once the old Joséphine resurfaced. Grace and elegance forgotten, she thrust her way through the swarm of fans, dug her nails into Mistinguett's arm and spat in her face. Mistinguett, from a similar background, spat back.

Another problem for Joséphine, when she began rehearsals at the Casino, was her dressing room. Naturally it was the star's dressing room, and equally naturally it was regarded by the company – most of whom had been in *Paris Miss* – as belonging to Mistinguett, who did not help matters by letting it be known that she did not want "that little black girl" using it. When word of this reached Joséphine, she cleverly defused the situation by moving out of it and changing in a sort of tent rigged up in one of the backstage corridors until the fuss had died down and she was able quietly to move back in.

It did not help her, either, that one of the choreographers for *Paris Qui Remue* was Earl Leslie. An American, he had not only worked on some choreography for *Paris Miss* but he was also Mistinguett's dance partner and current lover.

Many members of the chorus, both male and female, were distinctly unsure of Joséphine's ability to sing well enough or dance in a suitable manner to star at the Casino. Earl Leslie worked hard to reinforce this uncertainty, letting it be known clearly that he felt Joséphine to be inadequate. At one point, he approached Henri Varna with the query: "You are not going to have her walk down the same stairway as Miss?"

"Pourquoi pas?" asked Varna calmly. Of course Joséphine would make her entrance down the Casino's grand staircase.

Varna knew exactly what he was doing. He knew that, even if Joséphine was not yet quite polished enough to be his star, she very soon would be. He took over the task of grooming her, and in Joséphine's life quite firmly and definitely took over from Pepito as her mentor. After all, Pepito, with his natural grace and his ability to imitate the manners of the titled and wealthy, had only his native wit to help him, while Varna was an experienced professional producer. He had Joséphine practice descending the staircase again and again, first with two books balanced on her head, then with three, with four, with five, and eventually with six, improving even further the natural carriage and balance inherited from her mother, who in years gone by had danced the chalk-line walk with a glass of water on her head, not spilling a drop.

He also taught her to take stately bows – not as an eager young girl grateful for the applause, but regally, as if it was her due tribute from her loyal subjects. He also gave her a young cheetah which he bought from the famous animal farm in Hamburg, Hagenbeck's, to keep and parade around Paris. It would complement her image perfectly: part half wild creature of the jungle, part elegant sophisticated woman.

The cheetah – described by many writers (including, possibly, the Casino's publicity department) as a leopard – enchanted Joséphine. She named the animal Chiquita, ignoring the fact that he was male, and bought him a magnificent choker studded with square diamonds. Chiquita, of course, would also appear in the show (Henry Varna was no fool), and would be featured on the cover of its programme, drawn by the illustrator Zig, sitting up on his hind legs to offer a lavishly beribboned bouquet to a befeathered Joséphine.

Joséphine began to take Chiquita almost everywhere. He naturally became the most favoured animal at Le Beau-Chêne, and took due advantage of this by spending much time catching and eating the ducks that lived around the ornamental ponds.

Joséphine appeared on magazine covers with him, and took to parading him down the Avenue Des Champs-Elysées, attracting hundreds of onlookers. "You couldn't get within blocks of her," Bricktop remembered. "Everything stopped cold. The Frenchmen and the women too would come running up to her. 'Joséphine! Belle Joséphine! Bravo, Joséphine!'" Parisians joked that it was impossible to tell which end of the leash held the wild animal.

During the summer, she and Pepito took Chiquita on holiday to Deauville, causing a sensation on the seafront and in the casinos. That August, back in Paris, she took him to the theatre to a performance of *La Bohème*, seating him on her lap. Unfortunately for Madame Ritter-Ciampi, the famous operatic soprano, it was while she was performing Mimi's tragic death scene that Chiquita somehow got free of his leash, jumped off Joséphine's lap, raced up the aisle and leapt into the orchestra pit, with Joséphine in hot pursuit. The amount of resulting publicity, in newspapers as far afield as America, was highly gratifying.

Pepito, however, was not all that charmed with the animal. He was unhappy about him sharing their bed, and Chiquita, for his part, was unhappy about Pepito's driving, which tended to be fast and slightly erratic, with much unsettling rapid braking. Joséphine began to take him to engagements by taxi and meeting Pepito at the venues.

The items in *Paris Qui Remue* were all in some way related to the forthcoming exposition. There were references to the colonies of Martinique, Algeria, Indochina, Equatorial Africa and Madagascar. As one critic remarked, if the French don't know geography it's because they don't attend the music hall. One sketch, 'Noblesse D'Auto', with sets designed by Paul Colin, depicted a series of high-class limousines setting off – a Voisin, a Bugatti, a Mercedes, a Rolls Royce, a Chrysler, a Delage (Joséphine, as it happened, had recently bought herself a Delage) – bearing the cream of fashion to the exposition.

Her first entrance in the show was magnificent. Representing a wonderful white-plumed forest bird, she was resplendently swathed in huge swan-feather wings. She elegantly descended the great golden staircase, bathed in flickering light patterns from eleven projectors. Coached by Henry Varna, she had now perfected another of her trademarks, the stately but fluid Joséphine Baker strut, often (and rightly) described as "panther like". A line of chorus boys descended behind, presenting her to the audience. Reaching the front of the stage, she stopped, surveyed the house, and winked. Inside the new Joséphine was still a lot of the old Joséphine.

The set behind her was of stylised palm trees and lianas in pale greens and pinks, set against a midnight blue background. In this setting she danced a number called 'L'Oiseau Des Forêts', which had been choreographed by her old dancing partner Joe Alex.

The first song she sang in the show was 'La Petite Tonkinoise', written by Vincent Scotto as far back as 1906 for the music hall artist Polin, and in fact the song that had first brought him fame. It is the cheerful sentimental song of a little Vietnamese girl who is the mistress of a French colonist. She sings of how charming and lively she is, like a little bird, how she is his "petite bourgeoise", his Tonkinoise, and that, although other girls may make eyes at him, he loves her the best. Revived for *Paris Qui Remue* in a sketch purporting to reflect the music of the colonies, its basically ragtime rhythm was embellished with Madagascan drums, Indian bells and Algerian tambourines. Joséphine sang it well, her voice now increasingly strong and confident, and it would be a song that she would sing again and again.

It was another of Scotto's songs in *Paris Qui Remue*, however, that would become the most important to Joséphine. This time written specially for her, it was called 'J'ai Deux Amours', and told of how she had two loves: her country and Paris. During the preparing of the show, Scotto had told Henri Varna that he had been struck with the idea for the song while walking down the Rue Chaussée D'Antin, on his way to the Casino, and had been so taken by it that he had immediately stepped into a doorway and written it down.

It was helpful to Varna that Scotto had been struck by such a splendidly appropriate idea because at that time he was having a difference of opinion with his partner, Oscar Dufresne, who thought Joséphine's voice to be neither strong enough nor interesting enough for a Casino show, and who was urging that she shouldn't be allowed to sing at all but should be restricted to dancing. 'J'ai Deux Amours' changed that. When Joséphine sang it in the show, the audiences loved it, and so did she. She would sing it at every performance she gave for the rest of her life.

Of course, everybody – including Joséphine – understood "her country" to mean America, but in fact in *Paris Qui Remue* she was playing another colonial girl in love with a French colonist, this time an African. The sketch was called 'Ounawa', it was (of course) set in the jungle, it featured a dramatic hurricane (from which she was rescued by a gorilla), and it was here that Chiquita made his appearance.

Playing another beauty from yet another colony, this time Martinique, she sang the seductive song 'Voulez-Vous De La Canne À Sucre?' (How'd You Like Some Sugar Cane?). For this she wore a long, full-skirted dress based on West Indian styles, with heavy bead earrings and necklace, and the chorus girls were dressed in wearing headscarves and brightly-patterned hooped dresses, which were supposed to represent candy.

Another sketch, which this time took place in a forest, featured Joséphine's favourite costumes from the show, designed for her by set designer Georges Barbier. Again it gave her wings, this time diaphanous and rather like those of a dragonfly. Wearing it, she descended a steel ramp into a forest scene, where she was pursued by savage hunters. She pleaded with them, and managed briefly to escape from them, but eventually they surrounded her and brutally ripped off her wings, leaving her huddled in despair.

One song celebrated Joséphine herself, which she sang with a chorus of young men in evening dress, wearing a simple but elegant close-fitting dress herself. Entitled 'Dis-Nous, Joséphine', and based on her two years of touring Europe and South America, it almost takes the form of a press conference, with the chorus asking her if she feels that Paris has changed while she was away. She replies that she is charmed by all of the cities of the world, but reassures them that "there's only one Paris".

The new Joséphine delighted press and public alike. "Joséphine Baker, *quelle surprise, quelle stupéfaction,*" wrote Pierre Varenne in *Paris Soir.* "We said goodbye to a perky and amusing but primitive little black girl. An artist, a great artist, comes back to us."

Jean-Paul Sartre and Simone de Beauvoir saw the show and admired her as not simply a sex symbol but as an artist who embodied the spirit of theatrical anarchy. Many compared her to Mistinguett, and generally concluded that she was now at least Mistinguett's equal.

One critic who had a slight reservation was *The New Yorker*'s Paris correspondent, Janet Flanner. She was enthralled by the show as a whole, with its "British dancing choruses of both sexes, a complete Russian ballet, trained pigeons, a live cheetah, roller skaters...the four best Can-Can dancers in captivity...and an aerial ballet of heavy Italian ladies caroming about on wires," but she had regrets about the new Joséphine, writing: "She has, alas, almost become a little lady. Her caramel-colored body, which overnight became a legend in Europe, is still magnificent, but it has become thinned, trained, almost civilised...There is a rumour that she wants to sing refined ballads; one is surprised that she doesn't want to play Othello. On that lovely animal visage lies now a sad look, not of captivity, but of dawning intelligence."

Of course, in a way, Flanner – being an American – regrets that Joséphine's persona now owes more to Paris than to Harlem, and naturally that didn't bother her Parisian audiences at all. They were enchanted that in 'J'ai Deux Amours' she had at last sung a conventional French song, and not something "exotique", like the songs of Spencer Williams and Irving Berlin.

Paris Qui Remue ran successfully for a year, for 481 performances, and it was calculated that overall Joséphine drew larger houses than Mistinguett had in *Paris Miss*. She had conquered Paris all over again.

On 12 July 1930, at around the time at which *Paris Qui Remue* opened, Joséphine went back into a recording studio for the first time in two and a half years and recorded six songs. She was accompanied by musicians from the show, and four of the numbers she recorded came from it: 'La Petite Tonkinoise', 'Voulez-Vous De La Canne À Sucre?', 'Dis-Moi, Joséphine' and, of course, 'J'ai Deux Amours'. On this last she is joined by singer Adrien Lemy, who sang it with her in 'Oumawa'. As in the show, he comes in to sing the words the second time the chorus comes around, and over his singing Joséphine improvises a confident and fluent yet wordless vocal, soaring up near the top of her range.

The other two songs she recorded that day were 'Suppose!', a song she had picked up during her tour of Spain, and 'Pretty Little Baby', which she had already recorded early in 1927, and with which she had opened her tour in Vienna.

Paris Qui Remue continued its run. Her old colleague Noble Sissle came to see it and to ask her if she would come back to America to appear in a show that he was devising: a new version of *Shuffle Along*. Joséphine, as ever, was attracted by the idea of becoming a success in the States, but at the same time she was nervous. She was nervous about how she might be received there, but also because Noble's show was to have an all-black cast, and Joséphine – with her now-increasing social conscience – felt that she might be of more use in helping her race gain acceptance if she stayed in white shows, as she could in Paris. Feeling defensive about explaining such a high-flown attitude, she simply told Noble that she couldn't be in his show because she preferred to stay in Paris. Naturally, he assumed that this was because of her success there, and because she wanted to be with Pepito.

Several royals, who might have felt that the Folies Bergère an unsuitable theatre at which to be seen, were happy to come and see her at the Casino De Paris. The king of Sweden came, and the ex-king of Spain and the entire royal family of Denmark, and from farther afield came the king of Siam, who was so impressed by Joséphine that he offered her an elephant. To everyone's surprise, she politely refused it.

From the other end of the social scale, and quite out of the blue, she received a short letter from Mrs Jones, who had taught her to play the trombone in her days with The Jones Family Band. "I think of you," it said.

"Your success has given me pleasure." With it she enclosed a typically Jones Family piece of voodoo: a bent and rusty nail with a lock of her hair wrapped around it. Joséphine gave it as a good-luck charm to Henri Varna, telling him: "I am this nail and you have hammered me into shape."

Varna continued expertly to exploit her publicity value. One night during the show, ending a number with an over-enthusiastic splits, Joséphine tore a ligament, and Varna had the personal physiotherapist of George V's wife, Queen Mary of Teck, flown in from London to treat her.

In November 1930, Joséphine was invited to be guest of honour at one of a series of lunches celebrating successful books to be held at the Lido Des Champs-Elysées. In this case, the book was *Les Mémoires De Joséphine Baker, Recuillis Et Adaptés Par Marcel Sauvage*. Normally at these lunches authors read passages from their books, but in Joséphine's case the organisers took the opportunity to arrange something more lavish. The singer Adrien Lemy, four of the hoop-skirted chorus girls from *Paris Qui Remue* and ten members of its orchestra were invited there to join her in a performance of 'Voulez-Vous De La Canne À Sucre?' Joséphine didn't wear her West Indian costume from the number but instead wore a simple, dark evening gown with a pleated skirt.

Her book of memoirs wasn't the only book about her life that was around at this time. Marcel Sauvage was updating the memoirs themselves, writing a book which covered her two years of touring. He would call it *Voyages Et Aventures De Joséphine Baker*.

Pepito was at work on another. Using Joséphine's scrapbooks, he was compiling an anthology of all of her best reviews since she first came to Paris, the vast majority being of her performance in *Paris Qui Remue*. It would be published in 1931 under the title *Joséphine Baker Vue Par La Presse Française* and would be illustrated with many of the caricatures of herself that she liked to collect. As well as the reviews and the caricatures, the book contained a short prose poem by Joséphine herself:

> "At the age of eight I was already working to calm the hunger of my
>   family
> I have suffered: hunger, cold –
> I have a family
> They said I was homely
> That I danced like an ape

Then I was less homely – Cosmetics
I was hooted
Then I was applauded – The crowd
I continued to dance – I loved jazz
I continued to sing – I loved sadness; my soul is sick
I had an opportunity – Destiny
I had a mascot – a panther – Ancestral superstition –
I made a tour of the world – In third class and in Pullman
I am moral
They said I was the reverse
I do not smoke – I have white teeth
I do not drink – I am an American
I have a religion
I adore children
I love flowers
I aid the poor – I have suffered much
I love the animals – they are the sincerest
I sing and dance still – Perseverance
I earn much money – I do not love money
I save my money – for the time when I am no longer an attraction."

One thing in this is untrue: she was not saving money. Quite apart from her natural tendency towards extravagance, by 1931 she was supporting (or at least helping to support) a vast army of people. Quite apart from those in her actual employ, like maids and gardeners, there were also hairdressers, couturiers, vets, voice coaches and make-up artists – and of course Pepito.

In March 1931 the Colonial Exposition was to open, and the organisers asked Joséphine if she would be their "Queen Of The Colonies". She was delighted to be chosen; she felt that she was at last being accepted by conventional French society.

However, this turned out not to be the case. When the news that she was to be the the exposition's queen appeared in the papers, it caused a furore. Letters of protest were sent, not only to the papers but also to the general commander of the exposition, Henri Olivier, to France's minister of the colonies, Paul Reynaud, and even to the president of France, Gaston Doumergue. The protests were based on the facts that she was not French (she came from Harlem, which was not even a French colony) and that she did not speak good French or the language of any of France's colonies.

One objection that hurt her considerably was the rather illogical one that African women marry and have children very young, even at twelve or 13, and that therefore by her age, almost 25, she should rightly be a grandmother by now, and so she was obviously too old for the position. This hurt her in two ways. One was that she was already worrying that, as a performer, she might be getting old and *passé*. The other was that it touched on her growing desire to have children.

From America came another, familiar objection: that she had removed herself from the black community, and had become a sort of ersatz white. *The New York World-Telegram* focused on the way she had straightened her curly hair, running the headline: "Queen, Where Is Yo' Kink?"

Reluctantly, the committee had to withdraw its offer, but once the exposition had opened she toured it as an honoured guest, escorted by Henri Varna. She was delighted by the whole thing, and told him that he had never provided her with better backdrops.

Joséphine's life at this time began to divide in two. On one hand there was the glamorous creature of the Casino De Paris, the public figure opening fêtes, modelling expensive dresses and riding in the Bois De Boulogne, while on the other there was the simply-dressed inhabitant of Le Beau-Chêne, where she gardened, cooked, walked her dogs, played with her cats and napped with Chiquita. There was a childlike simplicity about her life there that she felt was real when her stage existence was phoney, which in a way was true; but even on the stage, no matter how glamourised she was, that same childlike simplicity always showed through. It was a large part of her charm.

Visitors came to Le Beau-Chêne in droves, work colleagues of every sort, including designers, writers, dancers, musicians, directors and secretaries, along with casually-met strangers and the rich and famous. Jean Cocteau was frequently there, and Cécile Sorel, senior leading lady of the Comédie Française. On occasion, even Frisco and Bricktop turned up.

Bricktop, as usual, was slightly dismissive. "Josephine had to have been here before as a queen or something," she once said. "She traipsed around her château just like she always lived that way. I think she thought she was Napoleon's Josephine."

For a while the famous Italian dramatist, Pirandello, spent much time there. He told Joséphine that he was planning to write a play about her, and so needed to study her. Unfortunately, he never managed to make it work, and eventually stopped appearing.

Another visitor who felt that Joséphine would appeal as a character in fiction was the actress and singer Libby Holman. She first visited Le Beau-Chêne in 1931 with her husband-to-be, Zachary Reynolds, heir to the Reynolds tobacco fortune. When he was murdered on 5 July 1932, after they had been married for only a few months, Libby was accused of being the murderer. Although she was acquitted, the case made her a celebrity.

Her real name was Elizabeth Holtzman, and she had been born in Stamford, Connecticut, exactly eleven days before Joséphine. A handsome, olive-skinned Sephardic Jew, fascinated by Harlem and its night life, she was famous for frequently wearing a man's suit and a bowler hat, and was attracted to both sexes. Among her parade of lovers were reputed to be Jeanne Eagels, Tallulah Bankhead and Montgomery Clift, and also – according to her biographer, Milt Machlin – Joséphine Baker.

Some years after her first visit to Le Beau-Chêne, Libby decided that a play based on Joséphine's life story would make an ideal vehicle for herself as the dramatic actress she yearned to be. She travelled to London, hired writer Noel Pierce to be the playwright, and brought him to meet Joséphine. The play, when it was completed, bore the title *Dusk*, but unfortunately for Libby (and Joséphine) it failed to attract backers.

Simple and domestic as Joséphine's life at Le Beau-Chêne may have been, one trait that she had displayed in her high-pressure theatre life she retained when there: her mercurial temperament. She could be playing on the carpet with her dogs, or working happily in her garden, when a chance word or a disturbing gesture would send her without warning into a paroxysm of rage. As one of her former servants, Josette Reboux, recalled: "She was always in a crisis. I never knew what started them. Sometimes there would be one per day; other times two per day or only one per week. Sometimes a crisis would last a week. They were like seizures that took hold of her." It was a good thing for Pepito that he was temperamentally able to live with such outbursts. He didn't enjoy them, but being emotional himself he was able to understand them and sometimes even to calm her down.

Another feature of their life at Le Beau-Chêne was Joséphine's lessons. Pepito found teachers to coach her in singing, in dancing, in acting. Her most influential singing teacher was Madame Paravinci, known to her pupils as "Para", who had only one real claim to fame before she started to coach Joséphine, although it was a considerable one: at some point in around 1910 she had introduced herself backstage to the young Yvonne Printemps, told her that she was using her voice abominably and in two years would find herself unable to sing a note, and began to give her free lessons.

The voices of Yvonne Printemps and Joséphine were similar in that both were instinctive, self-taught singers with a natural sense of music, and both had developed a style of their own. The best thing that a teacher could do for such a singer, and which Para did for Joséphine, was to teach her how to breathe effectively and how to sing strongly while using the minimum breath.

During 1931, for dancing lessons Pepito secured for her the services of the Russian-born tutor George Balanchine, then in his late 20s and already having been choreographer for the Diaghilev Ballet. Pepito's idea was that Joséphine should learn some of the techniques of ballet. With Balanchine, for the first time she began to practice dancing in blocked ballet shoes rather than the light, flat shoes she had always used in the past. She didn't much like either the ballet shoes (if given the choice she would have danced barefoot), or the practising, but Pepito kept her at it, insisting that she did 45 minutes a day, wherever they were. On occasion he would lock her in her room until she had finished.

For Pepito, doing his utmost to help her career was the best way that he could figure out to keep her his. He kept reassuring her that she was a great artist, but at the same time he let her know that the price of being a great artist was continual dedication and hard work. Although Joséphine saw that in a way he was right to keep drumming this into her, his attitude did nothing to help their crumbling relationship. Now that he had been mostly supplanted as her mentor by Henri Varna, Pepito was beginning to appear to her more as a sort of policeman, keeping her under surveillance.

She continued to be a part of the life of Le Vésinet. Given her growing desire for a family of her own, and her fondness for children, it was only natural that she should involve herself with the St Charles Orphanage, situated a few blocks from Le Beau-Chêne. She was introduced to it by the local electrician Georges Guignery, who had designed her lighting.

The orphanage had been founded after the Franco-Prussian War of 1870-1, originally for the children of soldiers killed in it. Every year it organised a benefit called *Les Gosses À La Mer*, which gave disadvantaged children a trip to the seaside. In 1931 Joséphine worked on the committee for this, helping to raise funds by donating clothes, furs, jewellery and *bric-à-brac* to be auctioned off at a bazaar. Soon after, she announced that she would henceforth be godmother to every one of the 50 or so orphans that the orphanage housed. She had a playground built in the grounds of Le Beau-Chêne, with swings and slides, and allowed the children who came there to play with her animals.

The children, of course, were delighted. During their visits Joséphine almost became one of them. She would happily watch them chase her monkeys round the house, careless that the monkeys, climbing her blue satin curtains to escape, became loose bowelled from fear and rage. "Joséphine was a wonderful playmate to the children of St Charles," remembered Hélène Guignery, Georges' wife, "but she never disciplined them. If a child did something she didn't like, she told one of the servants to speak to him."

In the autumn of 1931, *Paris Qui Remue* closed. As Mistinguett was to be the star of the Casino's next revue, Joséphine employed herself by setting off on tour with a band of jazz musicians. She named them "The 16 Baker Boys". Their leader was tenor saxophonist Romeo Silva, and among them were trumpeter Léon Jacobs, who had been her bandleader at Chez Joséphine, alto saxophonist Joe Hayman, who had come with her to Paris as part of the Claude Hopkins band for *La Revue Nègre*, and the Argentinian guitarist and composer Oscar Aleman.

Aleman was one of the most talented musicians with whom she would ever work. He had only arrived in Paris in that year (1931) and would stay until the advent of war in 1939, becoming as highly regarded in the French world of "le jazz hot" as the Belgian gypsy Django Reinhardt. Indeed, the two became good friends.

The tour went well. In Marseilles, after she had appeared triumphantly at the Pathé Palace, a reviewer wrote: "She is not just a dancer, or just a singer with a beautiful voice. She belongs now to that great race of artists with overwhelming personalities that the public take to their hearts."

In spite of her recurrent uncertainties about the durability of her success, or about herself as a woman, Joséphine's indomitability and courage were getting even stronger. On 12 September 1931 she was aboard the *Orient Express*, having just left Budapest on her way back to Paris, when a bomb went off under it as it crossed a viaduct. This was later said to have been the work of Communist terrorists, protesting against the poor conditions suffered by railroad workers. The engine and nine carriages plunged 100 feet down off the viaduct into the ravine beneath. Twenty were killed and over a hundred were badly injured. Joséphine's was not one of the carriages that fell, but the passengers in it were badly shaken. As they sat frozen with fear, Joséphine did the best thing she could to calm them: she sang.

Back in Paris, there was more friction between herself and Pepito. As a lover she had long found him inadequate. He was, after all, 17 years older than her, and not all that robust. She began looking for someone else, not as a casual lover but as the man in her life, and her eye fell on a young singer and dancer who had been in the chorus of *Paris Qui Remue*.

His name was Jacques Pills. He was more or less the same age as she was, elegant, handsome and fiercely ambitious, although he hid his ambition behind a winning smile and a pleasing personality. Born René Victor Eugène Ducos in a small town in the Les Landes region of south-western France, he had trained as a pharmacist, and indeed had become one, until the prospect of spending his whole life as a provincial chemist appalled him and he headed for the bright lights of Paris and got his job in Henry Varna's chorus. Although he was Joséphine's age, he was a mere beginner in show-business, and this was one of the things about him that appealed to her. She liked the idea of having a protégé of her own.

Pepito was even more hurt than usual about this relationship, simply because it was obvious that Joséphine had really fallen for Jacques. It was clear to her from the start that he had no intention of marrying her, partly because he sensed how dangerous was her combination of extreme attractiveness and demanding self-centredness, and partly because his main concern in life was to further his career.

Joséphine felt that this was a pity, because of her growing desire to raise a family, but otherwise she adored him. There was even a rumour around Paris at one time that he had changed his mind and asked her to marry him, and that she had moved out of Le Beau-Chêne and in with him. But whatever the truth was, it was soon obvious that she was still living in her own house with Pepito.

In February 1932 she performed in Italy for the first time. She had not managed to do so before because she had been forbidden to appear there by the country's Fascist prime minister, Benito Mussolini. For some reason he had relented, and she made her Italian début in Milan, where she was praised as "una Yvette Guilbert danzante". She was even introduced to him, and reacted to his strength of personality and air of authority almost like a gushing fan, saying afterwards that she felt that his and her destinies must be linked.

At around this time, continuing to involve herself in good works, she went to Bordeaux to give a charity performance in aid of a new children's wing at L'Hopital De St André. After the show, to her delight, she was asked by a group of medical students to go drinking with them. ("I do not drink – I am an American.") After she had phoned Pepito to assure him that the show had gone well and that she was now going straight to bed, she and the students headed off to a café in the student quarter. In its back room they ate and drank and laughed and chatted, and eventually Joséphine, accompanied on the piano by one of the students, sung then almost her complete repertoire. After she had sung 'La Petite Tonkinoise', the students, being medical students, sang her a dirty version of the same song. "Oh!" she said with a delighted laugh, "how filthy!", and immediately learned the words: "Veux-tu baiser en levrette...sur le plumard..." Later she gave each of them a charleston lesson.

On the next morning the students called on her at her hotel to thank her and wish her goodbye, and to their surprise, after such an hilarious evening, found her quiet and subdued. It turned out that she wanted desperately to visit the maternity ward of the hospital and see the newborn babies, and was afraid that she would not be able to arrange it. Nothing easier, said the students, and took her there. The young nun in charge of the ward accompanied her as she moved from crib to crib, occasionally patting a baby, or kissing it, or feeling to see if it was wet. Then, to everyone's surprise, she suddenly turned to the young nun and, in a voice that was a howl of despair, said "I can't have a baby!"

Was this so? Had she perhaps recently had herself examined to find out why she had never conceived? One possible explanation for her lifelong barrenness might be that, as her brother Richard believed, she had had a back-street abortion after separating from her first husband, Willie Wells, and was damaged internally.

Soon the time was approaching for her to start preparing for her next revue at the Casino De Paris. It was to be called *La Joie De Paris*, and was to open in December 1932. In it, profiting from her lessons with Balanchine, she would perform a number in ballet shoes. Between them they had devised a way in which the jerky and angular movements of black vernacular dance could be merged with the line and posture of a ballerina in a hybrid style unkindly described by the dance critic Sally Banes as "trucking on point".

Her two most successful songs in the show were a slow, sad number called 'Sans Amour' and a strange number which made fun of the growing fad for sunbathing, pointing out that she was now lighter skinned than a lot of tanned Parisian girls. It was called 'Si J'étais Blanche', and for it she wore a platinum wig of marcelled ringlets.

This did not go down well with some of her old admirers, such as bohemian socialite Nancy Cunard, who adored everything black. She castigated the French critics for failing to understand what was best in Joséphine, and for encouraging her producers to Frenchify her, trying to bring her into line with "the revolting standard of so-called 'national taste'".

In the show Joséphine also sang her theme song, 'J'ai Deux Amours', wearing a long, red satin dress, and for her first-act finale she performed a splendidly up-beat number called 'The Soul Of Jazz', for which she was dressed elegantly in top hat, white tie and tails, and played the part of a bandleader, leading her "22 coloured boys of jazz".

On one evening during the run of the show, the director of the Pernod company – for whom Joséphine had done some publicity work – came backstage with a friend of his, Bernard Tamisier. Introducing him, he explained that Tamisier's wife, Henriette, was about to have a baby, and in fact had gone into labour that day. "I'll be its godmother," said Joséphine at once. On the next day, hearing that the baby had been born and was a boy, she set off hot-foot to the hospital, greeted Tamisier and his wife, and announced to them: "The baby must be called Richard after my brother Richard who lives in St Louis. I love him very much."

What could the Tamisiers say but "d'accord"?

Later, in a note to Henriette Tamisier, she again referred to her own inability to bear children. "It isn't anything physical," she wrote. "It's because God doesn't want me to have a child."

She wasn't just Richard Tamisier's godmother in name; she also took a keen interest in his welfare, and the Tamisiers, who lived in a small village outside Paris, would frequently bring him to her dressing room in the Casino, where she would hold him and talk to him. On one occasion, when she was holding him on the lap of her red satin dress, he thoroughly wet himself. Instead of changing into another, she went out to sing 'J'ai Deux

Amours', proudly drawing the audience's attention to the big wet stain and telling them: "My son did this."

In July 1933, the Paris jazz world was bowled over by the arrival of Duke Ellington And His Famous Orchestra (as it was always billed in those days). Fresh from a short but triumphal tour of Britain, where the dance music paper *Melody Maker* carried the headline "Embarrassing Success Of Duke Ellington's Band", Duke was to play two concerts at the Salle Pleyel, on succeeding Saturdays.

Bricktop gave a party in his honour at her *boîte*, and invited Joséphine to attend. Knowing Bricktop's jealous loathing of Pepito, Joséphine arrived escorted by Spencer Williams. Bricktop later wrote: "She was wearing an organdy dress and an organdy hat and looked absolutely beautiful." She was seated next to Duke (with Franklin D Roosevelt, Jr, on his other side), and naturally invited him out to Le Beau-Chêne, offering to send her Rolls Royce to collect him. Duke was charmed by the simplicity and warmth he found in her, and by her "honest-to-goodness hospitality" at Le Beau-Chêne, saying that she "heaped goodies on me as though I were really somebody."

La Joie De Paris finished its run in September 1933. The Casino's next show was not to star Joséphine or Mistinguett; Henri Varna and Oscar Dufresne had decided to experiment by hiring Cécile Sorel, the famous actress from the Comédie Française, who was anxious to try her hand at music hall. She was to appear in a patriotic revue, *Vive Paris!*, written by the famous actor and playwright Sacha Guitry.

Joséphine, as was usual between shows, immediately set off on tour. This one, organised of course by Pepito, was to last for 18 months. (One of Pepito's reasons for this, as well as to show her in as many countries as possible, was to keep her away from Jacques Pills.) Before setting off, Joséphine had one sad duty to perform. Chiquita the cheetah had been becoming increasingly difficult to control as he grew to full maturity. He would claw at women's legs, and one night had even managed to escape over the wrought-iron fence that surrounded Le Beau-Chêne and crawl in through the open bedroom window of a neighbouring old lady. Panicked out of her wits, the old lady had called the police, who arrived with sirens screaming.

Everyone knew that the beast was Joséphine's, and although she did her best to charm the police, promising that such a thing would never happen again, it was obvious that something had to be done, and the sad decision was taken to send Chiquita to a zoo. The chosen zoo was a small one in the Bois De Boulogne, the Jardin D'Acclimatation, and Joséphine duly took him there before setting off on her tour. Over subsequent years she would visit him there less and less frequently.

The tour – for which Pepito and Joséphine had assembled a small company, including musicians – was to present a selection of numbers from her two revues at the Casino, always ending with Joséphine, in top hat and tails, leading the band in a stirring version of 'The Soul Of Jazz'. Their first stop, in October 1933, was to be London. It would be her first visit to Britain, and she was to open at the Prince Edward Theatre for a four-week booking. As everywhere on the tour, her troupe would not provide the whole evening's entertainment; there would also be supporting acts. Supporting her in the London show were Toni Birkmayer's dance troupe, Les Ballets Viennois.

This London appearance was not a great success. For a start, to Londoners she looked old fashioned. They viewed her as a relic of the Roaring Twenties, of the charleston craze and of Le Tumulte Noir, which had now run its course in Paris. Nor was Joséphine at ease with her show. After the elaborate sets of the Casino and the Folies, such scanty scenery and props as she was able to take on the road seemed dowdy and inadequate.

Nonetheless she worked hard at rehearsals, pouring energy into the company, and at the end of its four weeks it had made a modest profit. She had even been encouraged by the discovery that, even if they were lukewarm about your performance, English audiences clapped much more enthusiastically than the coolly restrained French.

While in London she also achieved another first. She went to a studio at 16 Portland Place and made an appearance on John Logie Baird's experimental new medium: television.

This tour, like the one which began in 1928, took her all over Europe, and even briefly into Asia and Africa. After London she went on to Holland, Denmark, Finland, Italy, Greece, Turkey and Egypt. In Greece she appeared in the Acropolis, and in Rome the entire Italian royal family turned up to see her. While on tour, her thoughts often strayed back to the Casino De Paris. She knew where she was with Mistinguett, but Cécile Sorel was an unknown quantity. Would she bring something so new to music hall that Joséphine would seem outdated? In Brussels, a Parisian friend, Paul

Bringuier, came to see Joséphine, and she asked him nervously, not wishing to mention Cécile by name, "Alors, vous êtes allé la voir, l'autre?"

She needn't have worried. The Paris to which she and Pepito returned in the spring of 1934 was in a state of turmoil. Not only was the Depression at its worst but France had also been rocked by a financial panic caused by what became known as the Stavisky scandal.

The financier Alexandre Stavisky, born in Russia but a naturalised Frenchman, had floated millions of francs' worth of bogus bonds, using the municipal credit establishment of the seaport of Bayonne. When the fraud was uncovered, it almost caused the economy of France to collapse. Stavisky, arrested, either shot himself or was shot by the police – it was never established which. There were riots on the streets of Paris, a general strike, and two governments fell.

More directly affecting Joséphine, the Casino De Paris had also suffered a tragedy. Henry Varna's partner, Oscar Dufresne, had been found murdered in his office – another crime which remained unsolved. With that, and the strikes and riots, Cécile Sorel's revue had been forced to close.

Overall, Joséphine's tour had been a fair success, but Pepito was still ambitious for her. In particular, more than anything he still wanted her to become a movie star, and determinedly he set about making her one.

Back in 1928, he and Joséphine had made the acquaintance of a wealthy Tunisian casino owner named Aris Nissotti, and even as the tour progressed Pepito engaged in discussions with him to organise the production of a film starring Joséphine and tailored to her personality and talents. The plan was that she and Pepito would also invest money in the film, thus giving them a certain amount of control over how Joséphine was presented. The film was to be called *Zou-Zou*, and the basic idea of the script had been suggested to Pepito by his brother. Writer Carlo Rim was hired to write the screenplay, and the director was to be Marc Allegret, who had been making films since 1927 (and would go on doing so until 1970) and who was the adopted nephew of André Gide.

While the film was in preparation, Joséphine embarked on yet another book of her memoirs. This time her co-author was the journalist André Rivollet, and the book was to be called *Une Vie De Toutes Les Couleurs*.

Meanwhile, Marc Allegret continued his preparations. For Joséphine's co-star he cast a 30-year-old actor who until 1931 had been a chorus boy in music hall, even appearing at the Folies. He had sensibly shortened his real name (Jean-Alexis Gabin Moncorgé) to Jean Gabin, and he would go on to be one of France's greatest-ever film stars.

The script that Carlo Rim came up with tells the story of how Jean and Joséphine, although unrelated, have been adopted and raised together as brother and sister in the Mediterranean seaport of Toulon. Jean goes off to sea as a sailor and Joséphine, who has fallen desperately in love with him, moves to Paris and becomes a laundress. Jean, visiting her in Paris while on leave, falls in love with one of her fellow laundresses, played by the blonde actress Yvette Leban. Among the lingerie that Joséphine and Yvette launder is some belonging to a temperamental star of the music hall, played by Edith Méra. This cunning twist in the plot enables the film to move to the music hall, and gives Joséphine the chance to improvise a dance on the empty stage, while Jean operates a spotlight, throwing her magnified shadow upwards onto the backdrop behind her.

Jean is arrested for a crime that he hasn't committed, and to raise money for his defence Joséphine consents to replace Edith in the show, as the star has conveniently run off with a lover, leaving the management in the lurch. Joséphine is of course an overnight sensation, and we see several scenes of her performing. She dances almost nude in a bird cage, in which, dressed as a bird, she sings the song 'Haiti', which was written by Vincent Scotto and tells of how she misses her island home. She also sings a torch song, 'C'est Lui', for which she wears a magnificent evening gown. These are her only two songs in the film.

Jean is acquitted, and Joséphine, going to meet him on his release from prison, happens on him tenderly embracing Yvette. Her heart is broken.

Joséphine was happy during the shooting. "The film enchants me," she was reported as saying. "Everyone seems so happy with what I do that even I am getting optimistic about it. Everything seems easy, because I feel the story very strongly. It all seems so real, so true, that I sometimes think it's my own life being played out on the sets."

When the film was released, audiences were happy, too, and it became a considerable popular success, although many of the critics were less than happy with the trite plot. Although the strongest thing in the film is Joséphine's assured and radiant personality when performing her numbers, she also turns out to be a more-than-competent actress. Appearing completely spontaneously, she shows her ability to express a wide range of emotions, from gaiety to tenderness and sorrow, although her stage-created tendency to use exaggerated gestures often plays somewhat uneasily against Gabin's already magnificent underplaying. (Incidentally, he also has a fine musical number in the film, waltzing with Yvette Lebon as he sings the number 'Ah! Viens Fifine'.)

Pepito worked harder than ever before to publicise *Zou-Zou*. One of his ideas was little short of brilliant. He had stickers printed saying "Joséphine Baker is ZOU-ZOU", and sent a team of salesmen out to fruiterers all over Paris to talk them into sticking these on every banana they had for sale and building prominent mounds of these bananas in their shops.

The couturier Marcel Rochas also designed a dress named Zou-Zou, and other products continued to be linked to Joséphine. Her hair preparation, Bakerfix, was still selling steadily, and she publicised other cosmetics as well – a Joséphine Baker shoe, made from brown lizard skin, was on the market all over France. With all of this, and with the success of *Zou-Zou*, her career was continuing to soar. She was reported in a financial magazine as now being the richest black woman in the world.

But her private life remained unsatisfactory. Jacques Pills was now a successful singer in partnership with pianist Georges Tabet, as he would continue to be so for many years. Having been helped on his way by his association with Joséphine, he began to stop calling her, and soon would go out of his way to avoid her. Their affair dwindled, and he went on to become a composer and impresario, marrying first Lucienne Boyer and then Edith Piaf, coming back unexpectedly between the two to ask Joséphine if she would, after all, become his wife. Well over him by that point, she said no.

During the time in which Joséphine was trying to get over him, she had a brief affair with the Maharajah of Kapurthala. He was a slender, cultivated man, then in his 60s, who owned one of the very few houses in the Bois De Boulogne, to which he travelled frequently from his small kingdom in northern India. As well as being cultured, he was also immensely rich, and Joséphine persuaded him to hold a luncheon for her at the Ritz Hotel. This was a political statement for her because in Paris the Ritz was a bastion of rich, white America. It had 500 staff to cater for 200 guests, and there were 60 more rooms in which guests could house their own servants.

As it happened, the luncheon went off without a hitch or a complaint. Those gathered by the Maharajah to fête her were mostly actresses and minor nobility, and Joséphine made a stunning entrance in a tailored black dress, a huge silver fox fur and a close-fitting turban decorated with flowers. The Maharajah was enchanted, telling her: "One must be born a princess to know how to act like one, but you are the exception that proves the rule."

At around this time, in contrast, Joséphine had sad news from St Louis. The man that her mother had married, Arthur Martin, had died. After Joséphine left home, his depressed withdrawals and outbursts of temper had eventually become so severe that Carrie had had no option but to have him committed to the municipal mental hospital. He remained there for several years, until one day in 1934 a policeman came to Carrie's door to tell her: "Your husband is dead. He broke the glass in the window in his cell and ate it." Although Joséphine had continued to keep in touch with her family, writing letters and sending money, it was a tragic reminder to her of the world from which she had escaped.

Zou-Zou having been a success, Aris Nissotti was encouraged to produce another film starring Joséphine, but before that happened she was approached with a proposition that would give her career yet another twist. As her performances were now depending more and more on her singing and less on her dancing, and as her singing had improved so markedly, it occurred to theatre owner Léon Volterra (he who had sold the Casino De Paris to Henri Varna and Oscar Dufresne) to offer her the lead in an operetta.

Volterra had recently taken over the Théâtre De Marigny, off the Champs-Elysées, the theatre at which the composer Offenbach had launched his troupe in 1855. He proposed to Joséphine that for his Christmas 1934 production he should present her in a role for which she might have been born. He suggested that she played the lead in a revival of Offenbach's 1875 operetta *La Créole*. He played her some of the music, and at first she was dubious. It wasn't the sort of music she was used to performing. "Ça ne jazze pas," she told him. She was also uncertain whether Monsieur Offenbach would want her for the part.

It was explained to her that sadly Monsieur Offenbach had been dead since 1890, and once that problem was out of the way she turned her attention again to his music. Gradually, she began to like his melodies, which, to be honest, were well suited to her voice, which Janet Flanner, writing about her performance in the show, accurately described as a "high, airy voice, half child's, half thrush's".

La Créole is not, in truth, one of Offenbach's greatest works. Set in the year in which it was written, it tells the story of how a Jamaican girl, born of an English father and a West Indian mother, is seduced by a French sailor, who then leaves for France, abandoning her. She bravely follows him, finds him and is reconciled with him in a happy comic-opera ending.

Albert Willemetz, co-director of the Théâtre De Marigny, worked with his partner George Delance to improve the piece and tailor it a little more to Joséphine's performing style. They somewhat rewrote the libretto, borrowed a few numbers from another of Offenbach's works – *La Boulangère A Des Écus*, written in 1874 – and added a children's *corps de ballet*, Les Huit Petits Rats De Marigny.

Joséphine became increasingly excited about the project. She was thrilled that for the first time she would be presented in a legitimate theatre, and was delighted to be working with a chorus of children. The children were equally delighted to be working with her, and took to crowding into her dressing room at every opportunity. "It was a happy time," Joséphine said later. "I wore costumes which reminded me of the long dresses with trains and the leg-of-mutton sleeves I had borrowed from my grandmother when I played dress-up. I could laugh in this role, sing, prattle, make faces, dance, cry like a bird, howl, at my pleasure."

It was at around this time, too, that she changed her hairstyle again. She kept it short, but the shiny helmet she had worn since her early days in Paris became fluffed out into soft short waves.

When *La Créole* opened, on 15 December 1934, the critics – while still not quite sure that Offenbach's piece was all that good – were almost unanimous in their praise for Joséphine. *Variety* reported: "The revival of Offenbach's *Créole*, starring Josephine Baker, finally consecrates Miss Baker as a full-fledged French headliner. Opening day of the show clinched its success, and all credit is being given the star, not the operetta." Composer Henri Sauget, meanwhile, wrote: "She is adorable, her singing, acting and dancing are all in pure Offenbach style...each of her appearances is a miracle of fine grace and tact. This is her début in operetta, it is dazzling, there is simply nobody else today who possesses such radiance, spontaneity and unique charm." Again, a couturier named a dress for her, this time Jeanne Beauvois, calling it La Créole.

La Créole ran for months, and was Joséphine's biggest artistic success of the Thirties. By the time its run had finished, Aris Nissotti was ready for her to begin shooting her next film for him. This was to be called *Princess*

Tam-Tam, and this time the whole scenario had been provided by Pepito, who would also be credited on it as artistic director.

The film begins in Tunisia, where the disillusioned French novelist Max de Mirecourt spots a beautiful goat girl (Joséphine). Back in Paris, his wife is having an affair with a maharajah, and Max hatches the plan of taking the goat girl to Paris, dressing her in fashionable clothes and passing her off as an exotic princess he is squiring around. This, he hopes, will teach his wife a lesson.

As things turn out, the goat girl becomes disenchanted with sophisticated Paris life, marries the novelist's servant and returns with him to Tunisia. In Paris, the novelist and his wife are reconciled, and the film ends back in Tunisia, in the now-deserted hut in which the novelist had lived, where a donkey is munching the pages of a book lying on the floor. Its title is *Civilisation*.

This time the film's director was Edmond Gréville, and Joséphine's co-stars were Albert Préjean and Viviane Romance, who played Odette, a Parisian socialite. It turned out to be nowhere near as good as *Zou-Zou*, although Joséphine did perform a couple of entertaining dance numbers: a conga, which Odette encourages the goat girl to dance more and more wildly in order to scandalise the onlookers in a Paris night club, and another, even better routine, in which she dances on the steps of a ruined Roman amphitheatre imitating a chicken.

The Tunisian sequences of the film were actually shot on location in Tunisia, and travelling back from there via Italy, Pepito and Joséphine stopped off briefly in Rome. While they were there they learned that Mussolini was to make a public address. Joséphine, remembering their brief meeting two years before and how impressed by him she had been, went to hear him, and stood crushed uncomfortably among the throng as Il Duce addressed them from an open window. He was in fact justifying the Italian invasion of Ethiopia, which had begun on 7 June 1935, and Joséphine was again bowled over by him. Hearing him, she came to believe that Haile Selassie, the Emperor of Ethiopia, was "an enemy of the negro race, for he maintains slavery, which Mussolini is determined to stamp out. If need be, I am willing to recruit a negro army to help Italy."

The interview from which those words were taken was given by her to a group of reporters back at Le Beau-Chêne. Published first in the French papers, it was taken up by the *Associated Press* and republished in

America, and the Americans – especially blacks – were appalled by her remarks. To many Americans, Haile Selassie was a hero, bravely leading his small country in a forlorn stand against Italy's fascist might. He was fêted as "the lion of Judah", and committees were formed to aid Ethiopia with money and medical supplies.

Joséphine was always naïve and impulsive, and often wrong headed. It was unfortunate for her that she made such a statement at all, but doubly so in light of the fact that in only a few weeks' time she would be setting off to appear at last in her native America.

10 *Citoyenne*

In spite of an increasing physical frailty, Pepito doggedly continued to further Joséphine's career. In 1935 he pulled off another coup: he managed to get her an engagement in New York.

She had been away from America now for ten years. She had been a stunning success all over Europe – in music hall, in cabaret, in films, in operetta – and she was now a singer as well as a dancer, and more and more she longed to be a similar success on Broadway.

And why shouldn't she be? She knew that she was famous in America. A few years previously, in 1933, Ethel Waters had even impersonated her in a Broadway revue, *As Thousands Cheer*, singing a song specially written by Irving Berlin, 'I've Got Harlem On My Mind'. The lyrics, supposed to be sung by Joséphine, told of how, in spite of her success in Paris, her heart still yearned for Harlem. This had a great deal of truth in it. A part of her missed America. She wrote at the time: "I've longed to go back, if only for just one evening, to walk along Broadway and look at the lights."

The engagement Pepito had obtained for her could not have been more appropriate. She was to appear in the Ziegfeld Follies of 1936.

The American impresario Florenz Ziegfeld had attended the Folies Bergère in the early years of the century, and decided to mount a similar series of shows in New York, beginning in 1907. In those days, before Paul Derval began to present the Folies, the nudes there were sexier and less "artistic", and Ziegfeld had made much the same changes for his productions as Derval did later in his, but had carried them even further so as not to offend American respectability.

His girls were stately rather than erotic, and although they wore fewer clothes than any other showgirls on the American stage, they did not bare their breasts. Also, unlike Derval, he had continued to feature comedians as an established part of his shows. He didn't much like comedians, regarding even such performers as WC Fields and Will Rogers as something to fill the stage while his girls got ready for their next number, but the audiences liked them, so he retained them. He presented the Ziegfeld Follies for 25 years, until he died in 1932, leaving in his will an amount that was then a record: $6 million. What made this even more impressive was the fact that he was $6 million in the red.

The Ziegfeld Follies did not die with him. His wife, Billie Burke – best remembered today for playing Glinda, the good witch, in the film *The Wizard Of Oz* – continued to produce the annual shows in association with long-established theatre owners and impresarios The Shubert Brothers. Pepito had approached the Shuberts to find out if they would arrange for Joséphine to tour America. They responded by offering her a place in the Follies of 1936. She would be the first and, as it turned out, the last black woman ever to appear in the Ziegfeld Follies.

The talents involved in this 1936 show were impressive. America's most exciting new stage designer, Vincente Minnelli, then 28 and later to become a famous film director, was in charge of the sets and costumes; David Freedman and Moss Hart provided the dialogue; Ira Gershwin and Vernon Duke (the composer of 'April In Paris') wrote the songs; and Joséphine's ex-teacher, George Balanchine, choreographed the ballet numbers. He had been brought into the production by Vernon Duke, and they had worked together some years previously as composer and choreographer for Diaghilev's Ballets Russes.

The star of the show was to be Ziegfeld's most famous female comic, Fanny Brice, and also featured were the rising young comedian Bob Hope, actress Eve Arden, singer Gertrude Niesen, comedian Ken Murray, come-dienne Judy Canova, ventriloquist Edgar Bergen and tap dancers Harold and Fayard Nicholas.

Pepito did well to negotiate a weekly fee of $1,500 for Joséphine. He also got the Shuberts to agree that she need not start rehearsals until October 1935, while all of the others were to begin rehearsing in August. He also arranged for Joséphine and himself to sail to America on what was then the world's newest and largest liner, the *Normandie*, just back from completing her maiden voyage.

On the day before they left, Joséphine attended a book-signing session to publicise her newly-published set of memoirs, *Une Vie De Toutes Les Couleurs*, co-written with André Rivollet. Some hundred or so of her fans turned out for the signing and, as was usual on such literary occasions, she dressed soberly, in a checked tailored suit and matching hat, looking every inch the gracious author.

But when a friend of hers reached the head of the line and presented a copy of the book to be autographed, and asked her how she felt about going back to the States, Joséphine's poise slipped, and for a moment she looked vulnerable. "I'm so excited," she said. "I'm all puffed up like a frog. Pepito's heard that New York is a wonderful place, all new and friendly, but I'm afraid I'll feel like a stranger. I don't know what will happen."

On the following day, sad at leaving Le Beau-Chêne and apprehensive about what lay ahead, Joséphine had her Vuitton luggage and her two pekinese, Fifi and Bébé, stowed into her new Bugatti, and she and Pepito set off to drive to Le Havre, where she was treated like a star. The police allowed her to park on the pier, and as she walked up the gangplank the ship's captain was waiting at its head to present her with a bouquet.

Once she was *en route*, her mood changed and she couldn't wait to get to New York. Pepito had notified the press and wire services that she was on her way, and she chatted to him excitedly, wondering if she was newsworthy enough for them to show up and meet her. She chatted about her dreams, of becoming a hit on Broadway, of playing not only in musical comedies but also in dramatic roles, and of becoming the first black woman to break the colour bar and become a star in Hollywood.

As the Statue Of Liberty came into sight, she was reminded of watching it disappear when she left in 1925, and she reflected on how much she had changed, how lacking in confidence she had been then and how glad she had been to escape. Looking down at the landing stage as the ship docked, she was at first surprised to see so many black faces. Then she realised that these were the faces of maids and porters. She was also relieved to discover that some 30 reporters had turned up to interview her, and were already calling out the usual sort of questions: "What do you think of Joe Louis? Do you consider him more important than Einstein?" "Do you know the president of France?" "Are you going to see Roosevelt?"

Once on shore she gave them a press conference, and then she and Pepito passed through customs and took a cab to their hotel, the St Moritz, which faced Central Park South. Pepito had chosen this because it was famous for having a continental atmosphere, even to the extent of having a sidewalk restaurant, the Café De La Paix. This, he felt, would remind them of Paris, and thus ease the shock of transition.

The first shock was not long in coming, either. After the hotel manager had welcomed them cordially and arranged for their baggage to be taken up to their suites (a large one for Joséphine and a small one for Pepito), he apologetically told Joséphine, that whereas she was welcome to be a guest in the hotel, he had to insist that she never in the future showed herself in the lobby but entered the hotel through the service entrance at the rear. He could not, he told her, afford to offend his many guests from the southern states. Shrewdly, she made no fuss on receiving this rebuff, swallowing her hurt and anger. As was now her habit when disconcerted, she became *très grande dame*.

In her luxurious suite she continued to receive the press, among a bustle of unpacking maids, her two pekinese and the loyal Pepito. To build up her image as the great star, she ordered him around relentlessly: "Vite! Vite! Pepito. Cherchez les sandwiches pour tout le monde." She had decided to continue speaking French whenever possible while in America, still uncomfortably aware that her English was littered with uneducated errors, and that similar errors would be forgiven her when speaking a foreign tongue.

This was to lead her into trouble on more than one occasion. One such occasion was when the great lyricist Lorenz Hart invited her to dinner. As the cultured company spoke mostly French, that was what Joséphine also spoke, playing her role as sophisticated international lady for all she was worth.

However, this did not go down well with Larry Hart's maid, Mary Campbell, a sharp-tongued black woman notorious for putting up with no nonsense from either her employer or his friends. When Joséphine, having finished her main course, asked "Donnez-moi une tasse de café, s'il vous plait," Mary angrily yanked away her plate and, returning, banged down a cup of coffee.

Joséphine, although startled, graciously managed to say "Merci."

"Honey," shouted Mary, "you is full of shit. Talk the way yo' mouth was born."

Before beginning rehearsals, Joséphine had enough time to go to St Louis and visit her family, whom she had not seen since 1921, although she had kept in touch with them by letter and regularly sent them money. Her sister Willie Mae and her step-father, Arthur Martin, were dead, as was her beloved grandmother, but her mother Carrie was there, and her brother Richard and her sister, Margaret.

Her father, Eddie Carson, was still around as well. When the

Depression had set in at the beginning of the Thirties, many of the clubs in Chestnut Valley had closed down, and work for musicians in the city had become so scarce that he had no longer been able to make a living as a drummer. However, he had found himself a civil service job with the municipal government, and still played drums – as he had for years – with the Pythian Society's band. Joséphine called on him, but remained wary of him, never having really forgiven him for abandoning her as a baby.

Most of her five days she spent with her mother, taking her house hunting in the most up-market black neighbourhood in the city. They managed to find a house that Carrie liked, a large one of white stone, but when Joséphine offered to pay the asking price of $20,000 in cash Carrie immediately became defensive, and told her: "When you come back, we'll talk about it." As her brother Richard later explained: "It was hard for Mama to realise that somebody could have that much money."

Nonetheless, they were impressed with the sophisticated and successful woman she had become. "She was classy," remembered Richard. "More high strung, but very happy."

At around the same time, she made a trip to Chicago to see her husband, Willie Baker, but only to make arrangements to divorce him. Willie had by now left the railroad and was working as a waiter. Interviewed by the press about Joséphine's visit, he was quoted as saying, rather pathetically: "I'll take her back if she'll have me."

Back in New York, her rehearsals for the Follies got under way. The show was to be presented at the Winter Garden Theater, but it had such a large cast and so many scenes that rehearsals were held in four different theatres. This meant that few of the others in the show saw Joséphine rehearsing, and she didn't see them.

Her rehearsal schedule was punishing. Every morning she worked with a dance coach and had singing lessons, and during her lunch break she had costume sessions with Vincente Minnelli. Rehearsals proper started in the afternoons, from two until to six, and then again from nine until midnight. Continually comparing Paris and New York in her mind, she observed: "In Paris, rehearsing is a pleasure. In New York, it is a matter of discipline." She also said that she had never in her life worked so hard or had so little fun doing it.

The director of the show was John Murray Anderson, a famous director of revues and something of an eccentric. He never started work before noon and never put his ideas in writing. It was his habit to soak in his bath for an hour each morning, planning his day's work. It was also his custom, or superstition, to wear the same suit every day during the rehearsal period of a show, and then, just before opening night, ritually burn it.

His original idea for Joséphine had been to have her perform the same kinds of numbers that were then being done by other black singers and dancers, but when he saw and heard her in her early rehearsals he realised that that would never do. Not only had Joséphine successfully developed her performance along French lines but she was also almost completely out of touch with the many developments that had taken place in American music and dance over the past ten years.

In 1925, when she had left for France, jazz was just beginning to reach its first flowering. Since then, many great and influential figures had emerged – Louis Armstrong, Duke Ellington and Fats Waller, to name only three. In the early Thirties, hot music had gone out of fashion with the general public, but only a couple of months before she returned a new phenomenon had burst on the scene: swing. This had a simplified and driving rhythm that needed to be approached differently by singers and dancers alike.

In black dance, tap had become the dominant form, and whereas Joséphine was familiar with tap (Louis Douglas in *La Revue Nègre* had been a tapper), she had never much employed it herself. Certainly she was unable to compete with the likes of The Whitman Sisters – long-time stars of the TOBA circuit – in the sort of dancing now expected from blacks. Nor could she in any way be compared as a singer to two recent arrivals on the scene, Billie Holiday and Ella Fitzgerald. John Murray Anderson wisely decided that the only way to present her in his show was as a sophisticated Parisian songstress. Unfortunately for Joséphine, her other talent, as a goofy comedienne, was also one of the major talents of Fanny Brice, and there was clearly no room for two such acts in the same show.

It was decided that Joséphine's first number in the show should be an exciting conga-style dance, performed in a Caribbean setting. It was introduced by Gertrude Niesen singing 'There's An Island In The West Indies', after which a set of curtains parted and Joséphine danced with a line of chorus boys, knocking them over one by one. For this number, Minnelli's assistant, Raoul Pène Du Bois, devised a costume for her designed to be reminiscent of her famous banana girdle. It was rather an odd outfit, resembling a silver two-piece bathing costume (no naked breasts could be revealed in America), embellished with sturdy, white, four-inch spikes. Intended by Du Bois and Minnelli to represent tusks, they jutted from her rear, her pubic region and her breasts, and the whole effect was more menacing than wittily sexy.

Her other two numbers were built around songs, both of them written by Ira Gershwin and Vernon Duke. The first was called 'Maharanee'. It was supposed to be set at "the midnight races in Paris" (at Longchamps), and for it she was costumed as an Indian princess in a shimmering sari.

The second was called 'Five AM', and showed her as a weary socialite returning at that hour to her Paris room, which was dusky pink and decorated with African sculptures. For this number she both sang and danced, partnered by four shadowy, black-masked men, representing remembered lovers. The choreography was by Balanchine, and Minnelli designed for her one of his most striking costumes. Wanting her to look "as glamorous as possible", he provided her with a clinging dress made of real gold mesh. First he made a mock-up in muslin, and when the fitting was complete he sent it to a factory specialising in manufacturing metal mesh bags. "They wove it exactly to specifications. The dress weighed almost 100 pounds. With it Joséphine wore a plum-colored ostrich cape...her gorgeous figure did [it] more than ample justice."

On the subject of the songs themselves, Vernon Duke recalled that "Mlle Baker was the possessor of a small but quite exquisite coloratura soprano. Ira Gershwin and I wrote two highly-spiced tropical arias with fioriture that would have scared Lily Pons out of her wits; Joséphine mastered the acrobatic intervals and larynx-defying trills like a trouper."

During the rehearsal period, in spite of the hard work, Joséphine set about enjoying New York. One lucky coincidence of timing was that, on Thursday 10 October, she was able to attend the Alvin Theater and see the premiere of a ground-breaking new black show: George Gershwin's *Porgy And Bess*. She adored it, and told several people – including George himself, when he dropped by at rehearsals to see his brother – how much she would like to play the part of Bess, although this was a role emotionally outside her range and for which her small and exquisite soprano voice would have been quite inadequate.

After the première, there was the usual first-night party. This time it was given by the publisher Condé Nast in his huge penthouse apartment on

Fifth Avenue. It was deliberately planned to be the grandest party of the season, and among the host of celebrities invited was Joséphine.

Another celebrity there was the comedienne Beatrice Lillie, who was then at the height of her career. Being the star that she was, she was surrounded by an adoring mob, and was not best pleased when Joséphine made a grand entrance wearing a white mink coat and with white lilies in her hair. Stopping just inside the doorway, she simply let the coat fall off her shoulders to the floor. Under it she was wearing a satin gown in buttercup yellow, slit in the front up to the waist. Every eye in the room was on her as a butler hurried to pick up her coat. All that Miss Lillie could find to say was "Who dat?"

Later, however, she exacted a small revenge. When Joséphine approached her, telling her in a torrent of French how much she adored her and how much she felt that they were kindred spirits, Lillie replied acidly: "Honey chile, yo' mighty good yo'self."

Rehearsals for the Follies ended in December, and were followed by a month of out-of-town tryouts, as was customary for such big shows. These were to be held in Boston and Philadelphia. They opened at the Boston Opera House on 30 December 1935, and whereas everyone else in the show was greeted with high praise Joséphine's reviews were mixed. Several papers commented on the fact that her "long residence in Paris [had] resulted in almost turning her into a French cabaret performer", and for some reason the critics seemed to find this unnerving. They seemed to feel that somehow she was cheating. One referred to her "impersonation of a French songstress".

This French influence apparently bothered the critics more than the audiences. *The New York World-Telegram* reported that the first-night house liked her in all three of her numbers, and a curious sidelight on the situation is that Fanny Brice's most successful and well-loved number, 'My Man', was in fact a Parisian song, a translation of Mistinguett's equally successful 'Mon Homme'.

It was the critic for the *Boston Traveler*, however, who uttered the most telling criticism of Joséphine's performance. He enjoyed her dancing, he wrote, but found her singing inaudible.

This inaudibility was to bedevil her for the whole run of the show, and it's hard to see how it came about. Her voice was not as strong as that of some, but she had no difficulty in making herself heard at the Casino De

Paris. Nonetheless, however, the fact remains that many people did find her hard to hear. Vernon Duke mentions that, in spite of her talent, "she was seldom audible", and Vincente Minnelli wrote in his autobiography: "Critics complained that her thin, reedy voice didn't fill the theatre."

The show had other problems in Boston, too, the main one being that it was far too long. Cuts had to be made and, unfortunately for Ken Murray and Edgar Bergen, they were cancelled.

The show went on to Philadelphia, where its reception by press and public was much the same, and on 31 January 1936 it opened in New York. Here again the critics loved almost all of the show. Fanny Brice played in a sketch that became famous, her 'Sweepstakes Ticket' sketch, and also teamed up with Bob Hope in several other scenes, one a sequence sending up backstage musicals of the Dick Powell/Ruby Keeler type.

Balanchine had devised a surrealist ballet, *Night Flight*, that was danced by Harriet Hoctor, and a running gag in the show was Bob Hope's pursuit of Eve Arden, during which he sang to her a new song by Ira Gershwin and Vernon Duke, 'I Can't Get Started'. This became a real show stopper, mainly due to the presence in the pit band of the great trumpeter Bunny Berigan, just back from the famous tour with Benny Goodman that gave birth to the swing era overnight. At every performance Bunny stood up in the pit and played the number, and it became so identified with him for the rest of his short life that many people believed that it had been written especially for him.

Another aspect of the show that came in for high praise was the spectacular look that Minnelli had devised for the sets and costumes. As one critic wrote: "Veteran observers who have seen every Ziegfeld show, from the first 'Follies', are agreed that this current version...is far and away the most beautiful of all. Mr Minnelli, for one thing, manipulates colours in a way that would bring bravos from a European audience. Perhaps his most striking flair is for using contrasting colours in combination – reds and greens, for instance – with results of rich beauty instead of what you would naturally expect."

Joséphine's performance, in contrast, was slaughtered. In the vast Winter Garden Theater, twice the size of the Folies Bergère, her voice was even less audible than in Boston and Philadelphia. "She sings prettily, if more or less to herself," one member of the audience was reported as saying, and the *New York Post* described her voice as "dwarf-like".

Once again she was criticised for being Frenchified. Brooks Atkinson commented in *The New York Times:* "After her cyclonic career abroad, Joséphine Baker has become a celebrity who offers her presence instead of her talent...Her singing voice is only a squeak in the dark and her dancing is only the pain of an artist. Miss Baker has refined her talent until there is nothing left of it." His obvious disappointment at her not providing what he felt black entertainers were best at is revealed in his next comment, that The Nicholas Brothers, who followed her with some excellent tap dancing, "restore your faith in dusky revelry".

Most savage of all was *Time* magazine: "Josephine Baker is a St Louis washer-woman's daughter who stepped out of a Negro burlesque show into a life of adulation and luxury in Paris during the booming 1920s. In sex appeal to jaded Europeans of the jazz-loving type, a Negro wench always has a head start...But to Manhattan theatre-goers last week she was just a slightly buck-toothed young Negro woman whose figure might be matched in any night-club show, and whose dancing and singing might be topped almost anywhere outside of Paris."

Pepito, aware that her appearances were needing all of the encouragement that they could get, arranged a claque for her on opening night, applauding wildly whenever she appeared or finished a number. But this was rather a naïve stunt to try in Thirties' New York. As columnist Walter Winchell observed: "Critics aren't fooled by noise."

Joséphine, hurt by having to appear night after night in the worst personal failure she had ever had, blamed Pepito. If he'd negotiated top billing for her, she'd have been treated like a star and given better presentation and billing. He knew how to handle things in Paris, but New York was different and be obviously couldn't cope.

Nor was she happy in the Ziegfeld Follies' company. She felt that the rest of the company, and Billie Burke in particular, were cool and distant towards her.

She was also upset by interviewers perpetually asking her what she thought of Ethel Waters. Ethel was then the only major black female star on Broadway, frequently appearing as the only black in an otherwise all-white show, such as the one in which she was appearing at the moment, *At Home Abroad.* But this situation meant that she was limited to always portraying a black, and this was something which Joséphine had fought successfully to avoid. In the film *Zou-Zou* her skin colour had been referred to only once, and then only briefly, while in *La Créole* she might have been a soprano of any race. It disturbed her to be back in a country which thought that her blackness was her most salient characteristic, and which discriminated against blacks.

She found that discrimination in the Thirties was more severe than it had been in 1925. This was partly because black performers and artists were no longer as fashionable as they has been in the mid Twenties, and partly because the Depression had caused a great deal of competition between blacks and whites for the more menial jobs. One night, for instance, she was out on the town with a group that included the fashionable socialite Mrs Potter Palmer of Chicago, and was refused entrance to an East Side club.

Joséphine had two contradictory responses to such rebuffs. One was to insist proudly that she was now French, and should be treated like any Frenchwoman. The other, and rarer, was to say that, all right, if she was black she was black, and she would head for Harlem, where she might feel safe among her own kind. She didn't do that often, although one night she did sing incognito at the Apollo Theater's amateur night, under the name Gracie Walker.

Amateur night, held every Wednesday, could be a forbidding experience. Acts that did not entertain the house were greeted with catcalls, and a clown would dance onto the stage firing blanks from a pistol while the pit band went into a honky-tonk version of the Apollo theme, 'I May Be Wrong (But I Think You're Wonderful)', drowning out the performer. "Gracie Walker" got through her song uninterrupted.

Overall, during the run of the Ziegfeld Follies, Joséphine spent so little time in Harlem that many of its inhabitants took against her. (Her remarks about Mussolini the previous year hadn't helped.) Some, hearing reports of her being barred from hotels or clubs, said "It serves her right. She has no business trying to be white," or "The Negro should know his place and stay in it and avoid the ofay like the plague."

Roi Ottley, a journalist on Harlem's newspaper *The Amsterdam News* rallied to her defence. Campaigning against discrimination, he hailed Joséphine as a heroine, saying: "Harlem, instead of taking up the cudgel of prejudiced whites, should rally to the side of this courageous Negro woman. We should make her insults our insults." He understood that Joséphine was not flattering herself on her social advancement in managing to mix with whites but was simply trying to live as if all races were one.

One of her forays into Harlem, however, was to have tragic consequences. Annoyed with Pepito for letting her down as far the Follies was concerned, as she saw it, and learning that one of her old lovers from Paris was in town, she scooped up the Frenchman and went off with him to spend several nights with him in a rented Harlem apartment.

Pepito was devastated. He was feeling increasingly unwell, and had come to the conclusion that he was suffering from hepatitis. Joséphine was no longer treating him as a lover but more and more as a rather unsatisfactory business partner. (It hadn't helped that he had been unable to negotiate a film contract for her, although he had discussed with various studios the possibility of her co-starring either in a film with Paul Robeson or in a film version of *Porgy And Bess*.) Her nights away with her French lover finally proved too much for him and, after a final row, he sailed off back to Paris alone towards the end of January 1936.

With so much going badly for her, Joséphine roused herself into action. Unsurprisingly, what she did was open a New York version of Chez Joséphine. "Just as in Paree," the adverts said. It was situated at 125 East 54th Street, in a house that had been the residence of one of America's richest and most famous celebutantes, Barbara Hutton, heir to the Woolworth fortune. She had recently married her second husband, the Danish Count Kurt von Haugwitz-Reventlow, and they had gone off to England together to live in their newly-built London mansion.

On Friday 25 February 1936, at 10.30pm, after the evening performance of the Follies closed, the new Chez Joséphine (which during the day functioned as a smart restaurant, Le Mirage) opened. On the first, night Joséphine made a point of greeting all of her guests personally, and entranced them by having a baby pig in a pen brought onto the small stage, picking it up and feeding it from an infant's feeding-bottle.

Here she was in her element. With the small band she had hired, Ray Benson And His Orchestra, she would sing from time to time, maybe two songs in an hour, and in English or French as the mood took her. Here, too, she could dance more wildly than in the Follies. Mocking the colour bar, she developed a *pas de quatre*, accompanied by three white male dancers in Zouave trousers and tarbooshes, a routine that was to remain in her regular repertoire for the rest of the Thirties. Similarly, she hired Alice Delano

Weekes, a cousin of President Roosevelt, as a hip-shaking dancer, pairing her in her dance with a Harlem doorman who wanted to get into show-business and who went by the name of "Truckin'". And as had been her habit in Paris, if she felt that the place needed livening up she would stage a dance competition among her customers.

Those who came on the opening night were mostly the social set, many of them minor European nobility, such as Baron Henry Hennet of Budapest and the Count De Gramont, but as the weeks went by she attracted many famous fellow entertainers, including Rudy Vallee (on whose radio show she would appear, singing a song in both English and French), Simone Simon, Ben Lyon, Lily Pons, Fred Astaire, Paul Robeson, and George and Ira Gershwin. Also, naturally enough, Barbara Hutton attended, back on a visit.

Reviewers, too, appreciated her more as the hostess of her *boîte*. *The New York Herald-Tribune*, for instance, wrote: "To miss hearing her and seeing her in her club is to miss one of the most exciting and entertaining cabaret performers of our day."

But of all of those who came to her New York Chez Joséphine, there was one what she was more pleased to see than any other. This was Paul Derval, who had sailed to America especially to ask her if she would star in his 1936-7 show at the Folies Bergère, bringing the contract with him. He had a specific reason for seeking out Joséphine: during the season of his next show, Paris was to hold another exposition, this one called L'Exposition Internationale, and it was his hope that by having her as his star they would be able to repeat the success of *La Folie Du Jour* ten years before. The exposition was to open on 24 May 1937, and Joséphine signed the contract with delight, pausing only to insist on a clause guaranteeing that she would remain in the show for the duration of the exposition, and that the advance Paul was offering her would be raised from 40,000F to 42,500F. He agreed.

It had been planned that the Ziegfeld Follies would run until September 1936, which would have given Joséphine (and Paul Derval) a tight schedule, as his show at the Folies Bergère was scheduled to open only a few weeks later. As luck would have it, however, Fanny Brice was taken ill, suffering from arthritis and dental problems, and the Follies was forced to close its season for a few weeks while she recovered.

The management gave the members of the cast the option of leaving the show or staying on a retainer until it reopened. Most, of course, stayed.

The only two who did not were Bob Hope – by then an increasingly popular radio star – and Joséphine. She was relieved to find so easy a way of ending her contract with the Shuberts, and so were they. When the show re-opened, her West Indian dance would be taken over by Gypsy Rose Lee, and her two song spots would be dropped completely.

Her return visit to the USA had been an unhappy experience for her, and one of which she rarely spoke in later years, either in the books she co-wrote or in interviews. During it she learned that she would never be as welcome in her home country as she had been in France, and that in America she would always be seen as a coloured girl first and as a person second.

The Ziegfeld Follies had of course been a massive disappointment to her, but her performance was not quite as bad as many critics made out. Audiences were generally pleased with her, and Vincente Minnelli was so taken with her West Indian dance that towards the end of February, when the show was running smoothly, he went there for a few weeks on a recuperative holiday with Ira Gershwin and Ira's wife, Lee.

Joséphine set sail for France in June 1936, but before that she received sad news: Pepito had died. On returning to France he had not gone to Le Beau-Chêne but instead had rented himself an apartment off the Champs-Elysées. Continuing to feel tired and run-down, he had consulted a doctor, who discovered that it wasn't hepatitis that he was suffering from. It was terminal cancer of the kidneys. In the few weeks left to him, he devoted all of his fading energy to tidying up Joséphine's financial affairs as much as he could. He made a will, leaving her everything he owned, saying ruefully (and rightly) to a friend: "She's going to need it."

When he died he was buried in a crypt in Neuilly. Joséphine was stunned by the news of his death, and deeply regretful that their last words had been angry ones. Unsatisfactory though their nine-year relationship had been by conventional standards, she naturally felt isolated without him. But, being the strong character she was, there was a small consolation for her in feeling that now at least she was in command of her own life, free from his controlling influence.

She arrived back in Paris on 2 June 1936, the day before her 30th birthday, and was met from the train by Paul Derval with a small army of fans bearing bouquets of flowers, a small army of photographers and newsreel cameramen, and an accordionist to accompany her singing a snatch of 'J'ai Deux Amours', after being prompted into it by an interviewer.

In 1928, shortly after Joséphine had last appeared at the Folies Bergère, Paul Derval had considerably modified its auditorium and its façade. The new façade featured a bas relief by the designer Pico, depicting the dancer Lila Nicolska. Inside it a painted frieze depicted Joséphine, bejewelled and befeathered, drinking a toast with a top-hatted young man. Also, the auditorium had almost doubled in size, its seating capacity rising from 920 to 1,740. This had largely been achieved by removing the famous promenade at the rear of the stalls, in days gone by a haunt of high-class whores and immortalised by Manet in his painting 'Un Bar Au Folies Bergère'.

Appearing at the Folies Bergère did something to lessen Joséphine's loneliness at this time. In spite of its changes she was back in a familiar theatre, among many familiar faces, and this was reassuring, even if returning to the Folies did represent a slight step backwards in her career, after moving on to the Casino De Paris, her two talkies and La Créole.

The new show, En Super Folies, also represented something of a step back for Paul Derval. For his previous show, La Folie D'Amour, he had experimented with a more witty and intelligent production, including in it satires on Manon Des Sources, La Dame Aux Camelias and Swan Lake, but it had not drawn audiences as well as hoped, so he was firmly returning to light-minded spectacle and nudity.

The designer for En Super Folies was the Hungarian artist Michael Gyarmaty, and among Joséphine's dancing partners was the 22-year-old Frédéric Rey, who was to appear with her often in succeeding years. A handsome young man with silver-blond hair, originally from Austria and originally named Franz, he had been brought to Paris from Vienna five years previously by Mistinguett. This he had instigated by presenting himself backstage at the Ronacher Theater, telling her that he was a dancer crazy about the music hall and begging to be taken with her to Paris. Mistinguett had not needed to be asked twice. In fact, so taken was she with this blond Adonis that she not only offered to help him find work in Paris but also refused to waste time in hanging around while he obtained a visa. Instead, so the story went, she hid him under costume plumes in a wicker wardrobe skip and he didn't stick his head out of it until the Eiffel Tower came into view, when he joyously cried: "Bonjour, la Tour!"

One day, towards the end of the rehearsal period, while onstage running through a dance routine Joséphine was delighted to see at the rear of the stalls the frizzy hair of her old friend Colette. The dance over, Joséphine rushed to embrace her. Colette, having watched the rehearsal, went away and wrote an account of Joséphine's performance, couched in such enthusiastic and closely-observed terms that it almost has the obsessive intensity of a lover:

"As for the nude female dancer, a recent innovation rediscovered from antiquity, if she smirks and smiles she is unacceptable. Her purity depends upon her seriousness. This brings me to my point: to the tableau in the revue at the Folies Bergère which shows us Joséphine Baker miming and dancing in the nude. Other scenes promote her grimacing black-child frenzy, or display to advantage her instinctive gift for comedy. We love her assured, penetrating, emotional voice...and we do not tire of of that gentleness, that affecting desire to please, which in Joséphine is more touching than any coquetry...

"But today I am stopping with the Joséphine who, before revealing herself naked, is covered by a white woollen oriental cape, and swathed in veils. In a décor which depicts, in colours both fiery and pure blue, the delightful entrance to the Oudayas garden in Rabat, this African Joséphine encounters lust in the guise of four handsome young men whose strong arms disrobe her. The veils fall, she steps over the fallen garments as over the parapet of a well, and with one firm step she enters into nudity and gravity.

"The hard work of company rehearsals seems to have made her slimmer, without stripping the flesh from her delicate bone structure. Her oval knees, her ankles flower from the clear, beautiful even-textured brown skin, with which Paris is besotted. The years, and coaching, have perfected and elongated and retained the admirable convexity of her thighs. Joséphine's shoulder-blades are unobtrusive, her shoulders light, she has the belly of a young girl with a high-placed navel. Naked except for three gilt flowers, pursued by her four assailants, she assumes the serious, unsmiling look of a sleep-walker, which ennobles a daring music-hall number. Her huge eyes, outlined in black and blue, gaze forth, her cheeks are flushed, the moist and dazzling sweetness of her teeth shows beneath dark and violet lips – her face shows no response to the quadruple embrace under which her pliant body seems to melt. Paris is going to see, on the stage of the Folies, how Joséphine Baker, in the nude, shows all other nude dancers the meaning of modesty."

For Joséphine, after the disappointment of New York, this was nectar. On reading it, she rushed round to Colette's apartment and left armfuls of flowers there.

The routine which Colette described, which ended with the four male dancers – including Frédéric Rey – lying face down on the stage with Joséphine on top of them, was of course only one of several that she performed in *En Super Folies*, each of them set in a different quarter of the world in honour of the forthcoming Exposition Internationale. There was a jungle scene, 'La Jungle Merveilleuse', for which the stage was dominated by a massive statue of a green elephant, trumpeting up out of green foliage, for which Joséphine wore a delicate white evening dress while the chorus were predominantly in red – red dress suits for the men, short red skirts and red, feathered head-dresses for the girls.

In a dramatic dance sketch, playing a mother whose two-year-old child has been stolen by gypsies, she crept into their camp, rescued her child and set the camp on fire. As 'The Queen Of The Far North' she greeted a polar expedition, riding in a sleigh drawn by huskies and wearing a ten-feet-long ermine cape. It was all very much the mixture as before, and commentators observed that the audiences which the Folies was now attracting was almost entirely composed of foreign visitors.

Feeling directionless without Pepito, and considerably lonely (because, in spite of her huge army of acquaintances, she had miserably few close friends), she entered one of her hectic phases. In March 1937 she went into a recording studio and, aware of how popular songwriting had developed in America since she first left, recorded several new songs she had heard there, with lyrics translated fairly directly into French. This was the custom of the time, and it wasn't always successful. Composing completely fresh lyrics for such translations came later.

The American songs she recorded were 'Vous Faites Partie De Moi' ('I've Got You Under My Skin'), 'C'est Si Facile De Vous Aimer' ('Easy To Love') and 'C'est Un Nid Charmante' ('There's A Small Hotel'). When she occasionally sings the original lyric, her English accent sounds cultivated and assured, without a trace of the uneducated St Louis accent that she feared she still possessed.

To coincide with the opening of the exposition in May 1937, she opened another Chez Joséphine, this time taking over a night club called Le Frontenac on the Rue François I, off the Champs-Elysées. It so happened that at this time Bricktop had moved her activities to Cannes (temporarily, at it turned out), and Joséphine benefited from this. The club was only a couple of minutes' walk from the exposition grounds, where the German pavilion, designed by Hitler's architect Albert Speer, for the first time flew a swastika over the city. Tourists flocked to Chez Joséphine, and Joséphine, as usual, entertained them exuberantly long into the night. This became her favourite of all of the *boîtes* she ever had.

The buildings for the exposition were designed in a streamlined, futurist manner, and couturiers hastened to reflect this modern simplicity in their dresses. These suited Joséphine well, her new softer hairstyle offsetting their harder lines. Although Madame Vionnet was still frequently designing clothes for her, her favourite designer during the Thirties became Jean Dessès, who at around the time she opened her new club opened his first salon just across the road from it, in the Avenue Georges V.

In spite of the persistence of the elegant Paris lifestyle, which was succeeding in riding out the Depression, there were ominous political currents in the air. At the exposition, the most famous and controversial exhibit was in the Spanish pavilion. It was Picasso's angry and bitter painting 'Guernica', which commemorated the destruction of that town in 1937 by German bombers supporting Franco.

On 5 June 1937, the publishers of the magazine *Ce Soir*, Louis Aragon and Jean-Richard Bloch, organised a benefit concert for the children of Spain. The front cover of the programme, reminiscent of 'Guernica', was drawn by Picasso. The back cover was by Jean Cocteau, who was also one of the presenters of the concert.

The cast was star studded. Famous French singers appearing included Fréhel, Georgius, Alice Cocea, Charles Friant and Etcheverry. From Spain had come Raquel Meller, Joan Magrinia and Emil Vendrell, who sang and danced alongside Isadora Duncan's sister, Lisa. The famous actors Michel Simon and Jean-Louis Barrault were also there, and so were both Joséphine and Mistinguett. Mistinguett was accompanied by a band led by bandleader Jo Bouillon, and this was one of the very few occasions on which she and Joséphine ever appeared on the same bill, although it may not have been entirely accidental that they were placed far apart on the bill, with an auction of paintings by the likes of Cocteau, Chagall, Léger and Paul Colin between their acts.

At around the same time, Joséphine drew renewed attention from the Axis powers. Her portrait appeared prominently on the cover of a notorious leaflet produced by the German minister of propaganda Josef Goebbels. Its purpose was to denounce "decadent" artists, and among those named in it as such were Max Reinhardt, Siegfried Arno, Ernst Deutsch and the unfortunate brothers who had presented Joséphine on her ill-fated last appearance in Berlin, the Rotters. As a result of the publication of this pamphlet, Mussolini, who may not have known of her ill-advised public support of him in 1935, announced that she was henceforth banned from appearing in Italy.

For affection at this time Joséphine turned to her dancing partner, Frédéric Rey, and they became lovers. It was not a love affair. As Rey himself recalled in his sixties, "If she needed a certain man around then she felt she had to go to bed with him." Like so many of her lovers, he also noticed her remoteness in bed. "It was like making love to a boy," he said. "She was not soft and cuddly. She was in charge, in the driver's seat. She decided what to do and how to do it." Their affair did not last long, but they remained close, their friendship – as well as their professional relationship – lasting for the rest of her life.

What she desperately sought, now that she was divorced from Willie Baker, was a husband. Still hoping to be married by some respectable and wealthy Frenchman, and taking a succession of them as lovers, she tried hard, by exerting all of her considerable sweetness and charm, to win them (and their families) over into accepting her as a wife. In the case of one of them, a wealthy businessman, she went out of her way to call on his mother, who lived on the highly-respectable if slightly run-down Boulevard Lannes, bearing the gift of three dozen white roses. Presenting these to Madame, who liked her, she formally requested her son's hand in marriage. Madame laughed delightedly. "Mademoiselle," she said, "it is true that there have been some scapegraces in our family, but not for two generations, and certainly nothing like this. No, no. What you want is quite impossible."

Joséphine continued to be the man's mistress for a while but she did not give up her search, and after that it wasn't long before she found a wealthy man who was not only prepared to marry her but was delighted with the idea. His name was Jean Lion. He was 27, good looking and athletic. He had made a large fortune by refining and trading in sugar on a worldwide basis, and he enjoyed making daring and flamboyant gestures, such as marrying Joséphine. He was also Jewish, and somewhat spoiled by his doting parents.

Being athletic, he enjoyed sports such as flying and horse riding, and it was while riding in the Bois De Boulogne that he had become acquainted with Joséphine, who also frequently rode there. (Her horse's name was Tomato.) He took to spending many of his evenings at Chez Joséphine, and they became lovers. He gave her lessons in his private plane, and she took to flying with enthusiasm, soon obtaining her pilot's licence. He arranged for her to ride as a jockey in a two-horse exhibition race at Tremblay, on the outskirts of Paris.

Her delight in his company was such that it even began to imperil her career. One day, out of the blue, Paul Derval received a doctor's certificate at the Folies. It stated that Joséphine was ill, was desperately in need of rest, and was taking indefinite leave of absence from *En Super Folies* and leaving Paris. Derval, furious, had no option but to hire a replacement for her, and he was further disconcerted a few days later to receive a phone call from Joséphine herself. "I'm in Vendée," she told him. (Vendée is a département on the western coast of France.)

"What are you doing there?" Derval demanded.

"I'm hunting with Jean. I shot a fox and I'm going to give the pelt to Madame Derval."

Jean delighted in her company, as she did in his, but his growing love for her was tempered with good business sense. He was naturally aware of her huge popularity in France, and felt that, as a wife, her fame would be an asset to his career, especially as he was considering making a move into politics, possibly by entering the French Senate or running for mayor of Paris.

On 3 June 1937, Joséphine invited him to her 31st birthday party at Le Beau-Chêne. That night much of the talk was about the marriage that day of Mrs Simpson and the Duke Of Windsor, who were now living in France. This prompted Jean to propose to Joséphine, and she accepted.

His respectable Jewish family were outraged when they heard the news ("They almost died," said Bricktop), and his two partners in the firm of Jean Lion & Company were unable to believe that he could be taking his intended wedding seriously. Their names were Albert Ribac and Maurice Sallioux. "Why do you want to marry her?" asked Ribac. "You are already sleeping with her."

"I think you'd be crazy to marry her," Sallioux added. "She's an actress, she's coloured, and she's older than you are."

Feeling that if Jean only took a little time to reflect he would give up his insane idea, Ribac suggested that the three of them went on a short around-the-world cruise. "As a farewell to your bachelorhood," he told them, adding that it would give Jean a chance to enjoy the women of Singapore and Saigon while he was still free.

Jean, with his love of wild romantic adventure, instantly agreed. He was shrewd enough to realise, however, that Joséphine might not react graciously to the idea, and so instead he told her that he had to go away for several months to take care of things in his New York office, and regrettably their marriage would have to be postponed until his return. He told her how sorry he was that her commitment to finishing her run at the Folies would prevent her coming with him.

Furthermore, he wrote a flood of love letters to her, sending them all to a business associate in New York with instructions to post them to Joséphine at weekly intervals until his return. He and his friends thought that the whole thing was a great lark, and off the three of them went.

When he returned, however, rather to his friends' surprise he went ahead with the wedding. His parents resigned themselves to it, and even agreed that it should take place in the little town where they lived, Crèvecour-Le-Grand, about 45 miles north of Paris. It was to be a civil ceremony, the only sort of marriage which is legally recognised in France, conducted on the steps of the town hall by the mayor of the village, Jammy Schmidt. The date agreed was 30 November 1937.

The whole village had been invited, and most of them turned up. Paul Derval was there as a witness. Joséphine arrived wearing a black hat and a full-length sable coat, and standing on the steps made a romantic little speech to the assembled crowd. "Haven't we all got a heart?" she asked them. "Haven't we all got the same ideas about happiness? Please tell me. Isn't it the same for every woman? Isn't it love?"

Jammy Schmidt, revelling in being in such a high-profile situation, spoke next. "Until now," he told the crowd, "the prominence of our village has been confined to a 15th-century château and our famous black chicken hatcheries.

Now it will be known as the place La Belle Baker chose for her wedding." He then read out the marriage ceremony from the *Code Napoléon*, and when he was done the local firemen sounded trumpets and local sportsmen fired shotguns into the air. During the ceremony, Joséphine had been formally asked if she was prepared to give up her American citizenship, and she stated firmly that she was. At last she had become a legal citizen of France.

Her earlier wealthy lover, the man to whose mother she had taken roses, believed that she had only married in order to make him jealous. It wasn't long, however, before he found himself a "suitable" wife.

On the day after the wedding, Joséphine set off for England to tour its music halls and to appear for the Christmas season at the Café De Paris, a fashionable night club on London's Coventry Street. During this tour, she flew back to Paris every week to spend Sunday with her new husband. She was so pleased to be married to Jean that she took to saying her prayers from a Hebrew-French prayer book, and even told some of her friends that she had converted to Judaism.

They had set up house in an apartment on the Rue De Trémoille, off the Champs-Elysées, although they would also spend a lot of time at Le Beau-Chêne, which Joséphine had no intention of giving up. Pleased to be married or not, she knew that marriages had a way of not lasting, and that a house was better security.

She was right to be cautious. Although she adored Jean, and took the marriage seriously, it turned out to have serious practical drawbacks. One was the disparity in their work schedules. "I used to return home at five in the morning," she later wrote. "One hour later Jean was on his way to the factory. I slept until late in the afternoon. I dined early before going on to the theatre, and often Jean had not come back from his office."

Trying to accommodate herself to Jean's lifestyle, Joséphine decided that she would retire. This was something that she even wanted herself. All of her life a large part of her yearned to give up the bright lights of the entertainment world and devote herself to building a home.

When *En Super Folies* finished its run, she made a short farewell tour, taking in the Côte D'Azur and North Africa, but as the end of the tour grew nearer she found herself forced to confront the fact that she was addicted to performing. She could no more give up the stage and the applause than she could stop breathing. When Jean joined her on the tour, they had rows about this.

His parents had become fond of Joséphine, sometimes visiting Le Beau-Chêne, and his mother, reassuring her, told her that she was the only person who could possibly put up with her son.

She loved Jean, and she loved the security of marriage, but having craved respectability, when confronted with it she found that it was not for her. A secure home, yes, but not dull and responsible ordinariness.

Jean, being Jewish, was also to some extent on the outside of respectable French society. Lacking a university education, the things that he had going for him that might help him to be accepted were his success in business, his well-mannered presentability and his charm. In spite of his youthful raffishness, he needed to present to the world a conventional front, which included a conventional wife, and he expected Joséphine to become just that, to supervise his wardrobe, to wind his watch and fill his fountain pen, and to plan meals and arrange a proper seating plan for dinner. A particular ordeal for her was the wifely task of writing thank you letters. As well as she could now speak French, writing it correctly was some way beyond her.

Their rows continued. A particularly dramatic one highlighted the differences in their attitudes. It took place at the famous restaurant Maxim's, identified above all others as the restaurant of the *belle époque* of the 1890s. By the late 1930's it had become considerably more respectable than in those heady days, and with its lingering history of raffishness it was Jean Lion's favourite restaurant, elegant and exclusive. But Joséphine saw it as a stage, a place to display herself in its Grand Salle. Almost as if she was in her own *boîte* she would table hop, wave to acquaintances across the room, talk loudly, laugh, and generally be in her element.

Jean preferred to dine with his business associates in the sumptuous calm of one of the private dining rooms upstairs, and his dissatisfaction with Joséphine's behaviour there rose to boiling anger one evening when the maître d'hôtel, with deliberate condescension, addressed him as "Monsieur Baker". The resulting row took place at Le Beau-Chêne, and ended with Jean removing his possessions while Joséphine stood in her driveway threatening to kill herself, pleading "Please don't leave me. I promise I'll change."

Somehow they patched things up, and it wasn't long afterwards that Joséphine, to her surprise and delight, discovered that she was pregnant. Just as she had done in her first marriage, she began knitting baby clothes. However, the pregnancy didn't last. Soon she miscarried, and again, as in her first marriage, the baby clothes instantly disappeared.

The emotional upset of the miscarriage put additional pressure on the marriage, exaggerating their differences, and it wasn't long afterwards that Joséphine found out that Jean was having an affair with the American wife of a French aristocrat. Desperately hurt by this, and wanting to hurt him in return, she sought revenge by embarking on an affair with another wealthy Frenchman. His name was Claude Meunier, and his fortune derived from his family's business of manufacturing chocolate. In the spring of 1938 he took Joséphine on a holiday to south-central France.

There, in the Dordogne Valley, with its richly-forested hills and spectacular rock formations, Joséphine took Claude to meet an old acquaintance, whom she had met aboard the *Normandie* when sailing to America in 1935. He had been the ship's doctor, and had told her that he owned a 15th-century château near the small town of Castelnaud-Fayrac, not far from the bigger town of Sarlat-La-Canèda. He gave Joséphine and Claude a conducted tour of his château and, although it was somewhat run down, Joséphine was enchanted by it. Called Les Milandes, it was like something out of a fairy tale. Situated on the crest of a low hill, it had round towers topped with slated conical roofs. When the doctor explained that he was trying to rent it out because his wife (who was also American) preferred to live in the States, Joséphine announced on the spot that she would rent it.

The château had 50 rooms, connected by long dark corridors, and its surrounding estate consisted of hundreds of acres of rolling land. Unfortunately, it had no central heating or electricity, so she decided not to occupy it just yet.

She was probably wise. The winter of 1938 in France turned out to be bleak. Sitting in a Montparnasse cinema, Joséphine saw newsreel footage of poverty and malnutrition in the Paris slums. Moved to tears, on the very next day she hired a lorry, filled it with cheap food (tripe, pigs' feet, potatoes and bread) and coal, and with toys for the children, and had her chauffeur drive it slowly through the back streets while she herself stood in the back, heaving out largesse to the surprised but grateful residents as if she was feeding her fowls.

In 1939, with her marriage to Jean Lion tottering, Joséphine devoted much of her time to repairing and furnishing her rented château, moving in some of her paintings, her crystal and her tableware. It was lucky for her that she did so because, by the end of the year, her life would have changed almost beyond recognition, and Les Milandes would come in very handy.

11 *The Honourable Correspondent*

In the summer of 1939, Henri Varna was planning a new revue for the Casino De Paris. It was to be even more spectacular than ever, and its theme was to be Brazil, with music leaning heavily towards the Latin rhythms of South America, and Joséphine was to be its star. As it happened, she had just returned from a short tour of Argentina, and had brought back to Le Beau-Chêne a collection of exotic birds and monkeys. But before rehearsals for Varna's new show could get under way, the Second World War broke out.

The coming of war had been feared all over Europe for months. During 1939, pacts and defensive agreements had been signed all over the place – England with Turkey, Italy with Germany, France with Turkey, England with Poland, France with Poland, and Germany with the Soviet Union (although that one didn't last). As the situation became more ominous, countries began to mobilise – Holland on 28 August, and the British fleet on 31 August.

Germany invaded Poland on 1 September, and Britain and France mobilised on the same day. Two days later, on 3 September, honouring their pact with Poland, both countries formally declared war on Germany.

The advent of war brought about a considerable change in Joséphine's priorities. Always straightforward in her reactions, often to the point of simple-mindedness, she had already identified the Nazi party in Germany with the racists of America. As far as she was concerned, they were one and the same thing.

Late in the previous year, following the appalling *Kristallnacht* of 9 November 1938, the "Night Of Broken Glass" – when Nazis all over Germany and Austria had set light to Jewish homes, shops and synagogues, clubbing Jewish men, women and children to death as they tried to escape – Joséphine, then technically a Jewish wife, had publicly declared her position by joining the International League Against Racism And Anti-

Semitism. For a person who had never felt sure of her own value, to enlist in a great cause – especially one that touched her own life so personally – was empowering. It diluted her desperate need for the love and applause of audiences, and so her performing life took second place as she engaged in a whirlwind of activity in support of the Allied war effort. Almost at once, and not at her own instigation, she was recruited into the ranks of the French military intelligence organisation La Deuxième Bureau. This came about through a theatrical agent of Tunisian birth called Daniel Marouani.

After Pepito's death, needing someone to handle her business affairs, Joséphine had hired an agent. His name was Félix Marouani, and Daniel was his older brother. Daniel knew that La Deuxième Bureau was on the look-out for undercover agents who would be able to move around freely without arousing suspicion, especially near the Front or near military installations, picking up information about enemy spying activities and willing to work without pay.

Joséphine, given the nature of her business, not only could but needed to move around all over the place, and Daniel, knowing of her crusading anti-Nazi attitude, was sure that she would be not only willing but even eager to work without pay. He suggested her name to the head of military counter espionage in Paris, an officer named Jacques Abtey.

Abtey had been in counter espionage since 1936, and he was at first deeply suspicious of Daniel's idea. For a start he was suspicious of women agents, remembering – like most Frenchmen – the supposedly exotic cabaret dancer Mata Hari. In reality a Dutchwoman named Margarete Zelle, she was recruited by France during the First World War as an undercover agent. She turned out to be a double agent, nursing a deep hatred of the English and feeding information to the Germans. In October 1917 she was shot at Vincennes, near Paris, as a traitor.

He also wasn't at all reassured by what he knew of Joséphine's character, regarding her, as he told Daniel Marouani, as "une artiste exceptionelle mais quelque peu excentrique", not to mention "une grande amoureuse". Daniel begged him to at least meet Joséphine, urging him that she was "une femme courageuse." Abtey agreed to a meeting, and Marouani hurried off to see Joséphine, explaining about La Deuxième Bureau and asking her to receive Abtey at Le Beau-Chêne. Joséphine eagerly agreed.

She later admitted that she had not known what sort of a man to expect. Her idea was that an officer for an anti-espionage organisation would be something like Simenon's Inspector Maigret: short, fat and middle aged, with an unattractive moustache and clothes smelling of tobacco. As it turned out, she was agreeably surprised. Jacques Abtey was 33 and handsome, a blue-eyed, blond Alsatian with an actor's ability at role-playing and adept at accents. In fact, when they met at Le Beau-Chêne, Marouani introduced him to her as "Mr Fox", an Englishman, which was his cover at the time.

Jacques for his part was charmed by Joséphine's warmth and naturalness. When he and Marouani arrived, she was walking around her garden wearing a crumpled felt hat, picking up snails and dropping them into a jam jar. She led her two guests into the house, sat them in chairs in front of the fire, and gave them champagne. As they drank, she explained earnestly why she was interested in their proposition, exerting all of her theatrical charm. "France made me what I am," she told them. "I will be grateful forever. The people of Paris have given me everything. They have given me their hearts, and I have given them mine. I am ready, captain, to give them my life. You can use me as you wish."

Jacques was impressed by the intensity of her patriotism. She was co-opted as an agent – or, as her position was officially known, as an "honourable correspondent" – and it was agreed that she should use her social contacts to attend as many embassy cocktail parties as possible, appearing frivolous and irresponsible but keeping her ears open for interesting scraps of information about such things as German troop locations.

This she did. A particularly useful source of information was the Italian embassy, where she was a welcome guest, partly because the Italians remembered her public support of Mussolini four years earlier. Abtey asked her to find out as much as she could about the possibility of Italy entering the war, and within a week of starting work as an agent she had produced what he later cautiously described as "some extremely useful information".

At around the same time, Henri Varna decided that a stately, highly-produced revue set in Brazil was not the sort of show that Paris now needed. With France mobilised for war, materials might become hard to obtain, and many of his work-force might be called up. Besides, he felt that in wartime people would want a light, fast-paced show, something cheering, full of "charm, rhythm and beauty", as he put it. He decided to mount a show starring "the two greatest stars of song and dance",

Maurice Chevalier and Joséphine, featuring them separately in each half of the show.

In Joséphine's half she played in a skit entitled 'Yes, We Have Bananas'. Unusually for her she danced tap, her partner for the number being Ben Tyber. In another routine she was partnered with six black dancers, one of whom, Sam Marshall, had been with her in *La Revue Nègre*.

Her big finish was called 'L'Ile Hereuse'. For it, playing "La Belle De Bahia", she was costumed by Rosevienne in one of the skimpiest costumes she ever wore. It consisted of a skeleton of rhinestone-studded straps, her bare-breasted nipples concealed by curlicues of the same. From each hip spread a fan of long plumes, and from her waist, down the outside of each leg, hung a cascade of flounces of light tulle that swung as she danced. On her head was a small hat, designed by Suzy, made of the same sparkling straps as her costume and crowned by a similar spray of plumes. The song she sang for this scene, 'Mon Coeur Est Un Oiseau Des Iles', was by Vincent Scotto, and it was one of the best that he ever composed for her.

Chevalier and Joséphine had of course known each other slightly for years. They had appeared together at the annual charity ball at L'Opéra, La Bal Des Petits Lits Blancs, in as far back as 1927. He and his wife, Yvonne Vallée, had from time to time visited Joséphine's first *boîte*, the one in the Rue Fontaine, and in only the previous year he and Joséphine had posed together for press photographers as they "christened" a new baby elephant with champagne at the Cirque D'Hiver.

Nonetheless, they did not make the easiest of co-stars. Quite apart from the professional jealousy between them, which made each wary of the other, Chevalier was a great supporter of Mistinguett. Indeed, back in the Twenties he had not only been her lover but the one of all of her lovers whom Mistinguett claimed to remember and regard most fondly. He was therefore not particularly disposed to be sympathetic to her great rival.

Being professionals, however, they got down to work preparing the show, which was to be called *Paris-Londres* in the interests of Allied solidarity, pausing only to bicker over the size of their billing and over whose half of the show should be presented first. Chevalier insisted on appearing last, traditionally the star's privilege, and Joséphine agreed to this with surprisingly little fuss. By this time she had a bigger cause than her own career.

In both France and England, the first months of the Second World War had something of an air of anti-climax. To civilians braced for a blitzkrieg invasion or for the ferocious bombing of cities – which some experts had predicted would be so devastating as to wipe out whole populations in a matter of days – nothing much seemed to happen. In Britain this period was nicknamed "the phoney war", and in France the "drôle de guerre", but to Joséphine it was deadly serious. Using all of her considerable energy, she drove herself mercilessly. Each day she reported for work at the Red Cross relief centre on the Rue De Châteaudun. This was an ancient, run-down alley in the shadow of L'Église De La Trinité, a haunt of the homeless even before the war. At the centre she helped prepare *pot-au-feu* for the new homeless who were beginning to stream into the city, refugees from the borders of Belgium, France and Germany.

Jacques Abtey had asked her, in her capacity as honourable correspondent, to keep her eyes and ears open for possible spies pretending to be refugees, and for a while her enthusiasm ran away with her. Several times she got him to investigate suspected German Nazis who turned out to be harmless blond Belgians.

On her one day a week off from rehearsals, and later from the show, Joséphine used her skill as a pilot to fly Red Cross supplies into Belgium. She wrote hundreds of encouraging letters to French soldiers manning the frontier with Germany, the heavily-fortified Maginot Line, and at Christmas 1939 she sent presents to 1,500 of them, each with a signed photo of herself.

In the December of 1939, she went into a studio and recorded half a dozen songs, of which four were released. One was her new Scotto number from *Paris-Londres*, 'Mon Coeur Est Un Oiseau Des Iles', and the other three were aimed at raising wartime morale, looking especially towards France's ally, England: 'Oh, Tommy', 'London Town' and an 'English Medley' of two songs from the First World War, 'Tipperary' and 'If You Were The Only Girl In The World'. Her recording of these two songs became very popular, and she would frequently sing them in her performances for the rest of the war.

The first performance of *Paris-Londres* was given not at the Casino De Paris but for the bored soldiers manning the Maginot Line, waiting tensely for a German assault that had not yet materialised. As agreed, Joséphine appeared first, but the soldiers were so delighted with her that they demanded encore after encore, and so the first half of the show – Joséphine's half – ran for much longer than planned. Unfortunately for Chevalier, there was a curfew in operation, a time beyond which the show could not run, and his half of the show had to be shortened.

Infuriated, he threatened never to stage another show for soldiers, and Joséphine felt that she had to remind him that it was the soldiers for whom they were performing, not for their own personal gratification. This incident gave her a lifelong contempt for him. "He is a great artist but a small man," she once told Jacques Abtey.

Chevalier, for his part, didn't even feel respect for Joséphine as an artist. Speaking to members of the press at the time, he said dismissively: "All she does is get up there and wiggle her rear end."

When the show opened at the Casino, Chevalier tried to get Henri Varna to move Joséphine to the second half, but Varna refused. However, Chevalier had the satisfaction of closing the show with a song which was to become the Paris anthem through the coming German Occupation, 'Paris Sera Toujours Paris'.

Joséphine's estranged husband, Jean Lion, had also engaged himself in the war from its outset, in his case by enlisting as an army pilot. Sent to the Maginot Line, he was not there long before being unluckily involved in a jeep accident. He sustained serious concussion, and for two weeks was laid up in a hospital near the front line. During those two weeks, among all of her other activities, Joséphine obtained official permission to visit the hospital, and made time to drive there from Paris every day. But these visits only served to make clearer them both how far they had drifted apart. In spite of all that they had done to adapt their unadaptable selves to each other, it became obvious to Joséphine that their marriage was unsalvageable.

Often she was accompanied to the hospital by Jean's business partner, Albert Ribac, and while driving back to Paris after one visit she said to him: "I can't believe it. I've lost him forever." At around the end of January 1940, after 14 months of marriage, she filed for divorce.

At around that time she began work on another film – her last, as it would turn out. It was called *Un Soir D'Alerte*, and again, attempting to build public morale, it was a light, topical drama depicting the petty rivalries and mutual suspicions of bourgeois Parisians in wartime, as they learned to wear gas masks and enter air raid shelters. It was directed by a veteran but rather unexciting director, Jacques de Baroncelli, who had been directing films since 1916, and in it Joséphine performed three songs. Unfortunately, by the time it was completed, France had been occupied by

Germany and had signed an armistice. The French were no longer at war, the film had lost its meaning, and it was shelved. (It was eventually released in 1945, after the war had ended, heavily edited and retitled *Fausse Alerte*.)

The expected attack on the Maginot Line never came. The German army, when it finally invaded France, outflanked it by simply invading Holland, Belgium and Luxembourg, and thus marching around its northern end. This invasion began on 10 May 1940.

Joséphine was still as hard at work as ever. A few days before the German advance began, George Guignery, Joséphine's electrician friend from Le Vésinet, was driving from there into Paris and saw her walking on the road. Naturally he offered her a lift, but she declined, explaining that she was walking the 15 miles into Paris to see how long it would take. "When the Germans take over Paris," she explained, "we won't be able to get petrol any more. I must be able to get into town on my own in order to look after the sick."

Soon enough there were more sick. As the Germans advanced, entering northern France towards the end of May, Paris hospitals began to receive a flood of wounded soldiers. Joséphine not only helped to look after them; she also lifted their morale by singing for them in the wards.

During the second week in June, with the victorious Germans marching south towards Paris after forcing the British Expeditionary Force to flee from the Continent at Dunkirk, Henri Varna assembled the cast and crew of *Paris-Londres*, announced that he was closing the show, and wished them all luck. It seemed obvious that Paris – and probably all of France – would soon be occupied, and no one knew what that might entail.

Parisians, uncertain and afraid, fled their city in droves. For Joséphine, the situation was serious. She was black, she was married to a Jew, she was an outspoken anti-Nazi, and she had been branded by Goebbels as decadent.

It's possible that word had also reached her that one of her near-contemporaries, the singer, dancer and trumpeter Valaida Snow, had been touring in Copenhagen when the Germans invaded Denmark in April, and – although an American citizen, born in Chattanooga, Tennessee – had been sent to a concentration camp on charges of theft and misuse of drugs. (She was released in 1942, returned to America and survived, physically weakened but still performing, until her early death in 1956.)

After consulting with Jacques Abtey, Joséphine reluctantly decided to leave Paris and head for Les Milandes, her rented château in the Dordogne, over 300 miles to the south. There she would be safe, at least for a while, and she could be of more use to the war effort than she would be living and hiding in Paris. (Several did, among them the Jewish-Hungarian designer at the Folies Bergère, Michael Gyarmaty, who allegedly spent the entire Occupation hiding in its basement.)

Leaving Le Beau-Chêne in the care of a skeleton staff, she loaded her Packard with as much personal gear as she could, plus her maid, Paulette (nicknamed "La Libellule" – The Firefly), two Belgian refugees and three of her dogs. Knowing that petrol would be difficult to come by on the road, she took a supply with her, carefully collected in advance in empty champagne bottles. Thus loaded down, the Packard entered the stream of traffic fleeing south from Paris. The roads were jammed with pedestrians and with vehicles of all sorts, swarms of refugees taking as many of their possessions as they could, leaving most behind, in laden cars or vans, using cycles, motorcycles, prams, push carts and whatever they could find.

Shortly after dawn, on 14 June 1940, the Germans captured Paris. By then it was estimated by the police that its population had dropped from five million to 700,000.

It had not been defended. The government of France, in a state of disarray, had decided that it was more sensible not to engage in a defensive battle that might cause untold damage to its many irreplaceable treasures. In any case, they felt that resistance to the mighty German army would be futile. None was offered. Not a shot was fired.

Under the Germans, the 84-year-old Maréchal Henri Philippe Pétain was declared president of France. A national hero since leading the defence of Verdun in 1916, France's greatest success of World War One, he had strong fascist sympathies and instantly signed an armistice. France and Germany were no longer at war.

After the armistice, it was swiftly arranged that France's administration would be divided into two halves: the northern part (occupied by the Germans) would be administered by them, and the southern part (which included the Dordogne) would be administered by President Pétain. His government – eventually known as the Vichy Government because its seat was based in that health resort, in south-central France – was effectively under the control of Hitler, and in these early days of its existence it was located in Bordeaux. On 15 June, Pétain and his government moved there. Among those helping in the move was Jacques Abtey, who was still technically a French army officer and thus answerable to the government. His job was to oversee the safe transportation of important documents.

For a few weeks after the beginning of the Occupation, the remaining Parisians were stunned. However, mentally shrugging their shoulders, they decided to make the best of a bad job and reverted very much to business as usual. It was estimated that by 15 July two thirds of the commercial enterprises in the city were operating fairly normally. Fashion houses held displays, cinemas and music halls re-opened and cafés were thronged, although their menus were now printed in German and they displayed signs explaining that they were "Forbidden to Jews".

Although Joséphine could not safely have stayed in Paris, it does highlight her brave anti-Nazi stance to consider how many French artists, performers and intellectuals contrived to quieten their consciences enough to live on easy terms with their conquerors.

"As long as there's a German in France," she had declared, "Joséphine won't sing." But Jean Cocteau, joining the Nazis sipping Dom Perignon at Maxim's, was heard to cry "Vive la paix honteuse!", and the popular actor, producer and playwright Sacha Guitry fell into such easy friendships with the invaders that it was reported that he had dined with Hitler's second in command, Hermann Goering. (It should be borne in mind, however, that such Frenchmen were unaware at the time of the worst excesses of Nazism. To them their conquerors were simply Germans, France's historic enemies.)

Of course, it wasn't easy for many performers to do anything else but go with the flow, such as Maurice Chevalier and Mistinguett, both of whom were later criticised for being on too-friendly terms with the occupying forces. Their stock in trade was to make themselves likeable to their audiences, and what difference did it make if their audiences were mostly German soldiers? They had to be wooed in the same way.

In the early days of the Occupation, organised resistance to the Germans had hardly begun, but even in June 1940 there were a few faint encouraging signs. After an abortive attempt to marshal his troops and mount some sort of defence of Paris, a young French colonel had fled to England, where, having promoted himself to the rank of général (thus making himself the youngest général in the French army), he was attempting to raise a resistance movement in France, mostly by making morale-raising radio broadcasts from London. His name was Charles de Gaulle. He had declared himself the head of what he called the "Forces Françaises

Libres" (which he would eventually get the British government to sub-sidise), and he appealed to anti-Nazi Frenchmen either to try and get to London to join him or to engage in resistance work in France.

It's hard, in retrospect, to realise what a voice crying in the wilder-ness he seemed to be at that time. France had lost many men in the ter-rible First World War, and even a "paix honteuse" seemed preferable to fighting the Germans again, especially now that they seemed more effi-cient in war than any fighting force the world had ever seen. It was esti-mated that no more than two per cent of France's population ever rose to de Gaulle's support.

Jacques Abtey was one of those two per cent. Having helped the Pétain government to relocate to Bordeaux, he heard one of de Gaulle's broad-casts and decided that he would defect from the French Army, now under the control of Pétain, and do what he could to escape to England, meet de Gaulle and offer to co-ordinate resistance networks in England and France. He had no clear idea how to get to England safely, but he decided that the person who might have the contacts to help him was Joséphine.

There is also the very definite possibility that he was in no way reluc-tant to see her again. Although a happily married man, and in the book he wrote about those days always discreet about the nature of their relation-ship (as was she), it was always obvious to anyone who saw them togeth-er that he worshipped her. Whatever his mixture of motives, he made his way west across southern France from Bordeaux to Les Milandes.

Joséphine was delighted to see him. "Foxy," she said, taking him by the arm, "when are we going to join de Gaulle?"

As it happened, and as he had to explain to her, he was no longer the English Mr Fox. Now that France was occupied, he had changed his nationality and accent, and was now the American Jack Sanders (because America was still a neutral country). He carried a passport in that name.

Over the next weeks, during the summer of 1940, a like-minded group of people began to gather at Les Milandes, some staying and some passing through. As well as "Jack Sanders", Joséphine, her maid Paulette and the two Belgian refugees, there was a Mexican-born French naval officer, an elderly French couple named Laremie, a Breton aviator, and several young airmen and sailors, now in civilian clothes, all anxious to join either de Gaulle's Free French (as it would come to be known) or otherwise to help in the Résistance.

Those there would tune into de Gaulle's crackling broadcasts from London. (It was in one of these that they actually heard the word "Résistance" used for the first time). Hearing them, Joséphine became – and remained for the rest of her life – devoted to "le grand Charles".

Jacques, while trying to involve himself in the Résistance network and possibly to find a route to London, spent enjoyable days hunting, fishing and kayaking. Eventually he managed to make contact with a Colonel Paillole, who was based in Marseille, directing under-cover military intelligence while pretending to run an office of rural works.

Travelling to Marseille, Jacques told him how he wanted to get in touch with de Gaulle, and about Joséphine and her involvement in the Résistance. Paillole was initially as sceptical about Joséphine as Jacques himself had been, partly because of that old Mata Hari connection and partly because he believed that people involved in showbusiness were inclined to be emotionally fragile. But Jacques explained to him how strong Joséphine's character was, and convinced Paillole of her value.

Through one visitor to the château, named La Besnerais, they made contact with a priest on the staff of President Pétain, Father Dillard, who had been a theology lecturer before the war. He was able to pass on much useful information about the activities of Pétain's government. This he would go on doing for the Résistance until 1942, when he was betrayed to the Nazis and sent to the concentration camp at Dachau, where he died.

With such possibilities always in the air, this was an anxious time for Joséphine, who was always aware that anyone claiming to be a sympathiser might in fact be a secret Nazi. There were other dangers as well, and not long after La Besnerais visited Les Milandes five German officers showed up there and demanded to search it. "We are informed, madame, that you are hiding weapons in your château," said the senior officer grimly. "What have you to say to that?"

Joséphine reacted with what Colonel Paillole afterwards described as "sang-froid remarquable", especially bearing in mind that she was housing a number of would-be Résistance fighters at the time. "I think that *monsieur l'officier* cannot be serious," she said. "It is true that I had Red Indian grandparents, but they hung up their tomahawks quite a while ago now, and the only dance I've never taken part in is the war dance."

The Germans left, charmed. Nonetheless, it was obvious that things were hotting up around Les Milandes, and Jacques and Colonel Paillole agreed that it was time that she moved on, perhaps to England. Nothing was certain. In collaboration with the Free French headquarters in London, they agreed on a plan which would make use of her professional reputation. She would go to Lisbon, the capital of the neutral country of Portugal, pretending to be *en route* to a performance in South America. Jacques would accompany her as her secretary and assistant, and they would carry information – supplied by Paillole – to Lisbon, from where it could be transmitted to London. Such information might be about German activity at harbours and airfields, or about German troop movements.

In addition, Jacques hoped to find someone while in Lisbon who worked for the British civil service, and who might help him to make contact with Général de Gaulle in London. To accompany Joséphine, he had to change his identity yet again, becoming Jacques-François Hébert, a Frenchman and former music hall performer. As no man under 40 was now allowed to leave France, it was arranged that his new passport would state his age as older than the 34 he was.

Going to Marseille, Jacques learned from Colonel Paillole that, although he had successfully got hold of a passport for "Jacques-François Hébert", there would be a three-week wait before visas could be obtained from the Portuguese embassy. Moving from place to place in wartime inevitably involves even more paperwork and bureaucracy than in peacetime, and this was to prove a recurrent problem for Joséphine. But this time, as so often, she was able to circumvent it through her wide range of influential contacts.

It happened that she knew someone in the Brazilian consulate in Nice. She and Jacques went there, and she told her contact that she wanted to perform in Rio De Janeiro, asking him to arrange visas that would take her secretary and herself through Spain and Portugal to Brazil.

When the visas arrived, Jacques was impressed and touched that she had arranged to have his visa bear the words "accompagne Mme Joséphine Baker". Not only would this give him added protection by providing him with a clear reason for travelling but, if it should happen that his true identity was unmasked then Joséphine would instantly be implicated in the deception. It was a brave thing to do.

They returned from Nice to Les Milandes, said farewell to those of their comrades who were still there, and late in November 1940 they set off by car to drive the 150-odd miles to the southern French town of Pau, in the

Pyrenees. Joséphine had left her château in the care of the local villagers (who on their own initiative had hidden all of her valuable paintings, crystal and cutlery, safe from looting Germans). This, too, was brave, to set off to who knew where, for God knew how long, without the security of a home. The information that they were carrying, gathered by Colonel Paillole from his growing Résistance network, concerned the disposition of German forces in Western France.

Reaching Pau, they took a train from there into Spain, and from Madrid took a plane to Lisbon. Joséphine checked into the Aviz Hotel and Jacques checked into a less expensive one.

Portugal, although Britain's oldest ally, was at the time governed by a fascist dictatorship not inimical to the Nazis. Therefore, during the Second World War it remained neutral, and financially did quite well out of being so. The whole country – and Lisbon in particular – became a crossroads of international intrigue. Through it passed a constant procession of diplomats, emissaries, spies and intelligence workers of all persuasions. Lisbon was a city full of rumour and counter-rumour.

The Portuguese were so delighted with Joséphine's arrival that she made front-page news. Reporters and photographers descended on her at the Aviz. She told them that she was en route to an engagement in Rio. Yes, she had sung at the Front. Yes, she had seen some horrible things. No, she had not been to Paris since the Occupation. No, she did not like the Germans. (She was not best pleased when some of the resulting articles commented on how "well preserved" she was at the age of 34. "It is terrible to grow old," she told Jacques.)

Her fame enabled her to arrange to attend the usual diplomatic parties at the British, Belgian and French Embassies, at which she kept her ears open for any helpful gossip. Accompanying Joséphine to the British Embassy, Jacques was able to meet the British air attaché. Through him he was able to transmit Colonel Paillole's information to England, and also to get the message through to the Free French in London that he wished to establish contact between them and the growing Résistance movement in France.

A few days later, the message came back that his idea for liaison was approved, and that he and Joséphine could now consider themselves members of the Free French, but it was preferred that they would both remain in France rather than come to England. Joséphine was asked to return immediately to Marseille and liaise with Colonel Paillole, while Jacques was to remain in Lisbon for a few weeks awaiting instructions about where the two of them could most usefully operate.

Joséphine set off back to Marseille on 6 December 1940. Once there, she booked herself into the grandest hotel in town, the Hôtel De Noailles, and went to see Colonel Paillole, who took to her at once, both for the solid reliability which Jacques had insisted that she possessed and for the optimism she expressed about the eventual outcome of the war, an optimism shared at that time by few French. She was certain that sooner or later America would join the Allies, and that when that happened the Allies would win.

Waiting in Marseille, Joséphine was growing short of ready cash, and accordingly booked herself out of the Hôtel De Noailles and into a cheap hotel near the Gare St Charles, "filled to the gills with whores".

The winter of 1940-1 was bitterly cold all over Europe, and her hotel room was unheated. To try and keep warm at night she wore an overcoat in bed but, even so, frequently woke up shivering. She developed a mild case of pneumonia.

Being on the southern coast of France, Marseille was of course in what was termed the "Free Zone", the area governed by Pétain. It was not yet occupied by the Germans, although everybody felt that it would be before long. Because of that, and because it was a seaport, it was crowded with refugees anxious to escape from France for one reason or another.

One of these, whom Joséphine was surprised and delighted to run into, was her old friend and dancing partner Frédéric Rey. He was in trouble because his papers weren't in order, and the reason that they were not in order was that nine years before he had been smuggled into France by Mistinguett. Joséphine vowed to help him. "Il faut!" she said emphatically, jabbing her fist at the air in front of her nose. (Frédéric, recalling their meeting, observed wryly that this was her favourite expression and her characteristic gesture.) "Il faut que tu quittes la France."

It was Frédéric who came up with a solution to her shortage of ready cash. Why not offer to mount a revival of La Créole for the Christmas season at the Théâtre De L'Opéra? he suggested. This would not only earn them money but it would also give them a legitimate excuse for being in Marseille.

Joséphine had sworn never to perform in France as long as there was a German on French soil, but she quietened her conscience with the rationalisation that Marseille was in the Free Zone, and thus outside the Occupation. They approached the management of the Opéra, who gladly agreed to the project, and she and Frédéric set to work.

Even for Joséphine, if she had not been coming down with pneumonia her energy during the next few days was phenomenal. Inside two weeks she had reassembled the score of an operetta she had not performed for six years, chosen a cast, coached them in their parts, scrounged around for costumes and mounted the show. It opened on Christmas Eve 1940.

In contrast, Jacques Abtey was for the moment having an easy time. Waiting for instructions from London, he spent many hours happily walking the beaches of Estoril, just outside Lisbon. If questioned, he told people that he was waiting for a passage to South America in order to organise a tour there for Joséphine. During the last days of 1940, the instructions came through, relayed to Jacques by an Englishman named Bacon. A route for transmitting information from France to London had been worked out, and he and Joséphine would be part of it.

It was expected that the Germans would soon make a move to occupy the whole of France. When that seemed imminent, Jacques and Joséphine would move to one of the French colonies in North Africa and base themselves there. From there they would travel to Lisbon from time to time, carrying information gathered from the Résistance network by Colonel Paillole and bringing back information or instructions from the Free French in London. It was hoped that soon these trips would be made easier for them by the Free French's purchase of a small boat, which would enable them to make the short sea journey from North Africa to Portugal.

At his meeting with Bacon, Jacques insisted on making his position clear. He regarded himself as a soldier of the Free French: he was a military intelligence officer, not a spy. The same was broadly true of Joséphine: she was not to be asked to spy, simply a carrier of information. The difference between them was that he, as a soldier, would receive regular military pay whereas she, as a civilian, would not.

Jacques returned to Marseille and to Joséphine. When she learned that she was to go to North Africa, she immediately despatched someone (possibly Frédéric Rey, on one of his days off) to travel north to Le Beau-Chêne and collect several more of her animals, to wit three monkeys, two white mice, a great dane named Bonzo and a hamster. She explained that she couldn't leave France without them, and she knew that, if their positions were reversed, they wouldn't leave without her. Also, they would be useful cover. Who would expect an intelligence courier to be travelling with such a menagerie?

La Créole was still running when Jacques returned, and Joséphine's magnetic presence had attracted a small group of like-minded people, most of them refugees who, like Frédéric Rey, were attempting to assemble the necessary visas for wartime travel and to obtain passage out of France. One of the group (although not a refugee) was Daniel Marouani, the Tunisian-born theatrical agent who had introduced her to Jacques.

Another was a Jewish film producer, Rodolphe Solmsen. Born in Germany, he had left there in 1933 after the Nazis came to power, their racial laws prohibiting him from marrying his non-Jewish fiancée. They had both moved to France, where he continued to make films, married and had a daughter. When war was imminent, he had shipped his wife, daughter, mother and sister to the safety of Peru, and now he was having endless trouble getting a visa to join them, either one for Peru or one for some other country, such as the USA, which might help him on his way. In Marseille, he was spending much of his time at the Hôtel De Noailles, buying drinks for the Peruvian, Spanish and Portuguese consuls, hoping that one of them might help him.

It was there that he had met Joséphine and Daniel Marouani, both of whom he had known slightly in Paris. Frédéric Rey soon joined the group, as did a friend of Rodolphe Solmsen's called Fritz and as did Jacques Abtey on his return from Lisbon. The group became so close that, when *La Créole* was booked to make a short tour of towns in the south of France in early January 1941, beginning with a week in Nice, Joséphine insisted that they all accompanied her there, telling them that they would all be safe with her and Jacques.

Back in Marseille, later in January, it seemed to the Free French in London that the Germans were about to occupy the remainder of France, and a message came through from them ordering Jacques and Joséphine to leave for North Africa at once. With them was to go Frédéric Rey, who had also been co-opted by Jacques into the Résistance. Jacques immediately went to the management of L'Opéra and requested, on Joséphine's behalf, that they release her from her contract to complete the tour. He explained how urgent it was for her to leave France, especially as she had worked for the Deuxième Bureau. He did not, of course, tell them that she was now a Résistance worker.

The management were understanding. They suggested that her easiest way out would be to produce a doctor's certificate saying she was in ill health, and the contract could then be cancelled without any legal repercussions. This was easily done because in fact Joséphine's health was not good. The mild pneumonia that she had contracted earlier in the winter had not entirely gone away. She was continuing to cough, and X-rays taken during her medical examination revealed that she had shadows on both lungs. The doctor who examined her testified that she should move immediately to a warmer climate. It was arranged that Jacques and Joséphine would fly to Algiers, and that Frédéric Rey would follow them there by boat, bringing Joséphine's monkeys and her great dane. From Algiers they would all travel on to Morocco.

At this point, Joséphine suddenly announced that, just as she would not leave France without her pets, she would not leave unless Rodolphe Solmsen and his friend Fritz were also able to leave. She insisted that Jacques arranged visas and passports for them through his friends in the Deuxième Bureau. She also went with Jacques and Rodolphe to see the port commander and got the names of Rodolphe and Fritz entered on a list of people entitled to leave Marseille immediately on a special boat if the Nazis invaded the Free Zone.

To the amazement of Rodolphe, who had been growing increasingly despondent about his chances of ever getting out of France, the passports and visas were brought to him one morning at his hotel. He gratefully wrote: "Joséphine and Jacques had kept their word. When I almost did not believe in it any more, they had opened the door to liberty and life. I do not know if I could have managed this escape by some other means and I do not even want to know. For me it was Joséphine and Jacques who saved my life."

Joséphine, Jacques, Frédéric, Rodolphe and Fritz soon reassembled in Algiers, at the first-class Hotel Aletti, on the waterfront. They all felt easier at having a stretch of water between themselves and the Nazis, even though technically, with Algeria a French colony, they were still under the rule of Pétain. In fact, Algiers even felt French – the streets and architecture were very similar to cities in the south of France.

From there, as had been arranged, they all moved on to another French colony, Morocco, and Jacques and Joséphine arranged visas for Rodolphe and Fritz. They settled in the port of Casablanca, which felt nothing whatsoever like France. It was definitely Arab, and seemingly unchanged since the Middle Ages. It was a mixture of luxury, poverty, riches, filth and decadence, jointly ruled by officials of the Pétain government and by a corrupt and self-serving Arab aristocracy. Even more than Lisbon, it was a city filled with wartime tension and intrigue.

Jacques, Joséphine and Frédéric waited to begin to ferry information, but it proved to be unexpectedly difficult. They had brought with them some information from Colonel Paillole, to be taken to Lisbon, but the proposed Résistance pipeline showed no sign of coming into being to provide them with more.

Nor was anything more was heard of the small boat that had been promised them, and obtaining visas for Portugal proved to be unexpectedly difficult. Even Joséphine's wiles were insufficient to obtain visas for Jacques or Frédéric from the Portuguese consul. All that she succeeded in doing was getting one for herself.

This, however, was better than nothing, and alone she set off for Lisbon, having arranged a short tour for herself and carrying the information from Colonel Paillole written in invisible ink on the margins of her sheet music. As he said years later to Jacques, "The destiny of our Allies and consequently the Free French was written in part over the pages of 'J'ai Deux Amours'."

She sailed to Portugal from the Moroccan port of Tangiers, and while there contrived to be entertained by wealthy and influential Arabs and Spaniards. They showered her with gifts, including a very useful permanent transit visa for Spain.

Crossing to Portugal, she embarked on her plan of giving performances and passing on information, meanwhile attending parties and making influential friends. She did all that she could to procure a Portuguese visa for "Jacques-François Hébert", but with no success. The most likely reason for her failure was that his real identity was known to the authorities.

Returning to Morocco, she and Jacques entered a period of frustrating, but on the whole enjoyable, inactivity. Because Joséphine was still coughing, her whole entourage moved from the seaport of Casablanca to the drier air of Marrakech. They stayed at first in the luxurious Mamounia Hotel, then moved to a house in the Medina, the ancient walled city within the city. Behind the walls of the house was a secret garden planted with orange trees, where Joséphine's animals had room to run.

Marrakech was even more Arabian in its atmosphere than Casablanca had been, and Joséphine turned out to have a real affinity with the Arab way of life. She liked the simple decor of some of the interiors, which seemed to her deeply spiritual after the brash gaudiness of her showbiz world. She adopted the Arab habit of making mint tea, and around the house she took to wearing a *djellaba*, the all-enveloping hooded cloak worn by Muslim women.

Jacques was becoming increasingly frustrated and uncertain about his future. The Résistance network had failed to materialise properly, and he could get no visa for Portugal. Worse, his English contact there, Bacon, had passed word to him that there would be no more money forthcoming for him from the Free French until he provided more information. This annoyed Jacques, who thought that he had made it clear to Bacon that he regarded himself as an army officer, not a mere peddler of information.

Nonetheless, he and Joséphine continued to do what they could. In the spring of 1941, using the Spanish visa with which she had been presented, she made a short tour of Spain, giving several performances and attending a number of official parties, nipping out to the ladies' when she heard any interesting piece of gossip and noting it down on a small piece of paper, which she then pinned inside her underwear. She travelled back to Morocco with a fair number of these notes pinned there. As she said, "Who would dare search Joséphine Baker to the skin?" On her way to Marrakech she stopped off at a clinic in Casablanca and had her lungs X-rayed. The air of Marrakech had been good for her, and the X-rays confirmed that they had cleared.

Another piece of good news was that, while she had been away, Jacques had succeeded in forging a new link in the information network. He had made contact with the American vice consul in Casablanca, and now had a way of passing information to the Allies without having to go to Lisbon. It was to this man that he passed on the contents of Joséphine's notes.

Joséphine was lucky to have important friends in Marrakech. A few years previously, when she had been starring in *En Super Folies*, the Sultan of Morocco and his entourage had come to see her for 14 nights in a row. In Marrakech she had been able to meet the Sultan's cousin, Moulay Larbi El Alaoui, and his brother-in-law, Si Mohammed Menebhi. He was the son of a former grand vizier, and lived in Marrakech in his father's palace.

Through them, in May 1941, she met possibly the most charismatic and dramatic acquaintance of her entire life, the autocratic Pacha of

Marrakech, Si Thami El Glaoui. A lean, dark, handsome man with intense eyes, he was over 60 when she met him but still fit, alert and passionate, maintaining a large harem. (Some said that his palace had 365 bedrooms, with a concubine in each.) His tribe, the Glaoui, had been relatively unimportant when he had been young, but by exercising the traditions of ambitious Berber chieftains – assaulting their neighbours and laying claim to their lands and women – he and his brother, El Mandani, eventually came to dominate the entire range of the Atlas Mountains, the hills that bisect Morocco.

His brother had died in 1918, and El Glaoui was now sole ruler over 660,000 Berbers, owning vast tracts of land and half of the water rights around Marrakech. To Moroccan liberals and nationalists he was anathema and an anachronism. His tribal way of life, with himself as absolute lord, was in direct opposition to the goal of their crusades.

Nonetheless, he was no backward savage. He had impeccable good manners and was capable of generosity and deep thoughtfulness. Educated in Paris, he had become a fervent supporter of de Gaulle, and was delighted to do anything that he could to help Joséphine and Jacques in their undercover operations, and to outwit the Pétainist administrators of his country. During the war years, guests at his palace would include Archie Roosevelt, the American General Mark Clark and Winston Churchill.

He took to Joséphine and she took to him. Quite apart from his delight in her charm and strength of character, and hers in his, he felt a racial bond between them via his mother, who had been Ethiopian. He invited her to feasts at his palace that far outstripped in lavishness anything she had ever seen. In vast salons on the ground floor, with walls opulently decorated with silk and velvet and with perfumed air, his slaves would serve cocktails from an American bar.

After cocktails, his guests sat Arab-style on the floor eating from intricately-carved tables. Dishes, served by black slaves in richly-embroidered white gowns, might include mutton, vegetables, fish, fowl and pastries, all of which were to be eaten using three fingers of the right hand.

After the meal, his dancers would perform, both boys and girls, decked with rings and bangles. It wasn't just his own dancers that he showed Joséphine; he took her to see Berber dancers from the mountains and black Gennaoua dancers from the Soudan. He also took her to see snake charmers, sword swallowers and fire eaters.

Her friends were welcome at his palace as well. Rodolphe Solmsen, with an old Paris friend he had found staying at the Mamounia Hotel, spent days playing golf on El Glaoui's private golf course, and enjoyed himself so much that he might have spent the whole war there. However, like a good husband and father, he asked Jacques to help him get a visa for Peru. Having that, he was able to obtain a transit visa to take him through the USA, and set off from Rabat, on a banana boat bound for Martinique, working his way back to his wife and daughter.

Meanwhile, Joséphine became pregnant again. It's possible that the father was El Glaoui. Certainly he took an active and solicitous interest in what followed.

One day in June 1941 she and Jacques were enjoying a relaxed walk around the older parts of Marrakech when she suddenly developed crippling pains in her abdomen. Jacques got her home and to bed. She developed a high fever and he arranged for her to be packed in ice in an attempt to bring it down, but after three days it was obvious that she was getting no better and would have to be taken to a hospital. Unable to find an ambulance, Jacques laid her on the back seat of a large car and drove her to Casablanca, 250 miles away. There he had her admitted to the Mers Sultan Clinic, where she miscarried. It was obvious that she had a serious infection, and the director of the clinic, Dr Henri Comte, performed an emergency hysterectomy. In spite of that the infection persisted, and she developed first peritonitis and then septicaemia.

Learning of her illness, the head of the Red Cross in Casablanca sent a newly-qualified young girl over to be her private nurse. The daughter of a French Army officer, her name was Marie Rochas.

In the days before antibiotics, septicaemia usually proved fatal, but Joséphine managed to survive, although she was severely weakened. Time after time she would recover sufficiently to get up from her bed only to relapse. She became so weak that she could barely speak or even raise her hand. She lost weight until she was nearly a skeleton, her skin hanging loosely on her bones. The inflammation caused by her repeated infections built up scar tissue on her abdominal linings, causing intestinal blockages that would require surgery, but she would be in the clinic for a year before she was strong enough to undergo an operation.

She was also desperately unhappy – not from the pain of her operation and her infections but from the fact that she had been given a hysterectomy, thus losing even the slim chance she had of becoming a mother. This reduced her to fits of anguished sobbing.

Jacques was deeply distressed by the severity of her illness. "She was doubled up with her legs up to her head and bust," he later wrote. "Her face was tight. Her skin was waxy, as if she were dead." He took to spending as much time by her side as possible, helping Marie Rochas to change her sheets and bathe her. Frequently he spent the night in a cot by her bedside, and when the pain became so bad that she was unable to sleep he would hold her hand and pray with her.

In the late spring of 1942, Maurice Chevalier passed through Casablanca on tour and, hearing of her illness, called at the clinic and asked to visit her, but she refused to see him. On top of her earlier dislike of him, she now regarded him as a traitor for continuing to perform in occupied Paris, and for attempting to get the French people to accept the Nazi Occupation, as she saw it.

Interviewed shortly afterwards, Chevalier, miffed at not being admitted to see her, described her as a wasting-away has-been. "Poor thing," he said. "She's dying penniless."

The rumour that she was dying spread through the world's press, and soon developed into the story that she had died. In America, her old acquaintance Langston Hughes had recently begun to work for *The Chicago Defender*, and one of his first assignments on the paper was to write her obituary.

Just when things seemed to be at their lowest, Joséphine learned that at last El Glaoui was coming to visit her. She learned this when he arranged to have her room and the terrace alongside it flooded with giant baskets of flowers. This roused her remaining strength; if she was to die, and if this were to be the last time he saw her, she was not going to have him remembering her as a shrivelled hag.

Lining the corridor outside her room were trunks full of her clothes and linen. She asked Marie Rochas to fetch satin sheets from these to replace the hospital bedding and to help her change out of her hospital gown into a see-through peignoir. At Joséphine's direction, Marie brushed her hair away from her face and applied her make-up. Because Joséphine's skin had become badly blotched from her illness, this took two full hours. She had Marie place a yellow orchid above her left ear, and for jewellery she wore only a simple pair of diamond earrings (given to her by the Maharajah of

Kapurthala back in 1934). She also instructed Marie to put on make-up herself and to stand beside the bed, telling her "You are blonde and blue-eyed. I am dark. The Pacha will find the contrast *très drôle*."

Joséphine summoned up reserves of energy as if for a stage performance. When El Glaoui arrived and took her hand in his, the colour returned to her cheeks and, for the first time in a long time, she smiled, looking up at him, as Marie remembered, "as if he were the only man on Earth." Still, it was obvious that she was very weak, and El Glaoui made her promise that as soon as she was strong enough she would come to his palace to recuperate.

Gradually, she began to get a little stronger. By the middle of 1942 she was strong enough to undergo the first of a what would be a series of operations to remove scar tissue blocking her intestines.

It became a time of cautious optimism. Jacques was finding more success in his Résistance work. A new American vice consul had replaced the previous one in Casablanca, and Jacques was acting as an intermediary between him and Colonel Paillole. Since Joséphine was American-born, famous and ill, there was nothing suspicious in the American vice consul paying frequent visits to her hospital room. There he naturally met Jacques, and information was easily exchanged. For example, on one such occasion Jacques was able to pass on details of the German defences at Bordeaux, information he had collected during a quick trip to Marseille to see Paillole.

Things were hotting up. America had entered the war in December 1941, after the bombing of Pearl Harbor, and it was planned that American troops would invade North Africa in November 1942. In preparation for that it was desirable that ties of friendship were forged between American diplomats and influential local rulers. Among the most powerful local rulers was of course El Glaoui. He was also pro de Gaulle and pro American, and a great deal of the exchanging of gifts went on between his retinue and American officials in Casablanca. Several meetings to exchange such gifts took place in Joséphine's room at the clinic.

As her health continued to improve slowly, from time to time she was allowed leaves of absence from the clinic. During these she would stay, as promised, at El Glaoui's palace, where she was allotted a whole wing of a great house adjoining the palace itself. She had an enormous bedroom with walls and floor fashioned from Moroccan tiles and carpeted with Berber rugs. El Glaoui gave her an entourage of servants and the use of a carriage drawn by matching bay horses. But she was still weak, and these leaves of absence were short. She spent most of her time in the clinic, and she was there when, on 8 November 1942, American forces landed near Casablanca.

Hearing that they were entering the city, Joséphine was desperate to go out onto the balcony and see them. Jacques, who was there, tried to dissuade her, partly because he was worried that she had only recently had yet another operation and might re-open the wound, and partly because there was still a battle going on between the American Army and the French, who were now officially on the side of the Germans.

"Let me go," insisted Joséphine. "Nothing more can happen to me. Who can stay in bed at a moment like this?" Wearing only pyjamas, she hopped out of bed and ran out onto the balcony to catch a glimpse of the invading troops. "That's the Americans for you," she told Jacques joyfully. "Europe doesn't know their force or their will. They'll win the war for us."

Jacques, as it happened, was not as happy with the Americans as he might have been. For a start, the American president, Franklin Delano Roosevelt, did not much trust de Gaulle, and did everything he could to avoid recognising him as France's representative.

At the time of the landings there were two French armies in North Africa: the official French Army, fighting for the German cause, and a small force of Free French, fighting under the Croix De Lorraine, which de Gaulle had made both his personal symbol and the symbol of the Free French. After three days of fighting, the collaborationist French Army surrendered, and the Americans signed a truce with them. This had the effect of legitimising them, of declaring them, and not the Free French, to be France's representatives. Jacques was furious.

A month after the landings, Joséphine finally left the Mers Sultan clinic. She had been there, with occasional short breaks, for 19 months. She went to Marrakech to continue her recuperation, booking herself into the Mamounia Hotel, where she came down almost at once with a bad case of paratyphoid.

It so happened that a black American war correspondent, Ollie Steward, was also staying in the hotel. He came down with food poisoning and a waiter, coming to his room to take care of him, said: "I hope you will not be as sick as the woman who sings, Madame Baker." Sick as he was, Ollie located Joséphine's room, where he found her being cared for by a nurse.

Learning that he was a newspaperman, Joséphine's voice suddenly became startlingly urgent. "I cannot locate my mother," she said to him. "She's moved since the war started. She must still be in St Louis, but where? *Where?* If you could trace her through your newspaper I would be eternally grateful." Ollie promised to do what he could, and meanwhile wired the news back to America that Joséphine was still alive.

She was, but only just. The paratyphoid, on top of everything else that she had suffered, had discouraged her greatly. She began to feel that she would never again be really well, and that she would spend the rest of her life having one illness after another. And if she did get well, could she ever perform again? Her legs were now like sticks, her cheeky little bum melted to nothing. And would she even be remembered once the war was over?

At around this time she received a surprise visitor in the shape of Jean Lion. Now her ex-husband, their divorce having eventually been finalised during 1942, he had become alarmed by the increasingly severe anti-Jewish legislation in France, and had joined the stream of refugees. He asked Joséphine if she could help him get hold of a visa that would take him to South America. She could, and did.

Recovered enough to leave the Mamounia, she went to stay at the palace of her old friend Si Mohammed Menebhi, the Sultan's brother-in-law. Concerned for her recovery, he distributed bread to three hundred beggars – the destitute, the blind and the maimed – for them to sit night and day beneath her window chanting loud, soothing prayers to aid her recovery.

The commanding officers of the victorious American Army soon realised that, although they had taken Morocco, they now had a considerable morale problem on their hands. There was simply nothing for their men to do in their free time. It was forbidden in Morocco at that time for men and local girls to socialise. If a respectable woman was seen talking to a man, this could even lead to their deaths. Furthermore, the American Army was segregated, which led to tensions between the races.

To defuse an increasingly tense situation, the Red Cross was asked to open a club in Casablanca where both black and white troops could relax and enjoy themselves. It was to be called the Liberty Club, and the man given the job of organising it was a black American sociologist, Sidney Williams, who was attached to the army as director of Red Cross activities.

Hearing that Joséphine was alive and in Marrakech, he sought her out at Si Mohammed Menebhi's palace and asked her whether she would star at the club's opening show. "It was strictly out of *Arabian Nights*," he said of the palace. "I have never seen such a place. I knew enough to take my shoes off and enjoy the hospitality."

Joséphine was hesitant about agreeing to appear in his show. She was still barely able to stand up, and if she did stand up she saw spots before her eyes. The wound across her stomach from her last operation was still not properly healed and still had stitches in it, and she had not performed at all for two years. Nevertheless she agreed, and again the vitality she drew from the act of performing came triumphantly to her aid. As Sidney Williams recalled it, she made her entrance down a staircase about one storey high, singing 'J'ai Deux Amours', and effectively turned the song into a prayer, ending on her knees with her hands clasped and moving many to tears.

After that, backed by a red-hot band of American Army musicians, she sang several more songs, and was a sensational success. The audience screamed themselves hoarse. Weakened as she was, her magical ability to enthrall an audience was still intact. Encouraged by this, she began to recover her strength, and as she did so she embarked on the second part of her wartime career: the more conventional activity of entertaining the French, American and British troops.

The American and British forces had officially sponsored organisations for troop entertainment. The Americans had USO (United Services Overseas) and the British had ENSA (Entertainments National Services Association). The Free French had no equivalent, and so organising her tours was entirely up to Joséphine and her colleagues. Jacques helped, co-opting a friend of his called Zimmer to accompany them on the road and act as Joséphine's producer-cum-road-manager, and Frédéric Rey went along as a dancer.

Over the next two and a half years she would make many such tours, repeatedly travelling the whole 3,000 miles of the North African coast, from Marrakech in the west to Cairo in the east. Most of the fighting took place in the eastern half of this, a narrow strip stretching from Tripoli to Alexandria. Among the towns she would visit – quite apart from the many army camps out in the desert – were Algiers, Agadir, Fez, Tunis, Benghazi, Alexandria, Cairo, Jerusalem, Haifa, Damascus and Beirut.

She and her colleagues travelled in jeeps, trucks or whatever they could get hold of, putting on four or five shows a day, travelling for miles and sleeping rough, often on the ground beside whatever bumpy ill-made track they were driving along. It was often dangerous to venture off such tracks for fear of land-mines. The landscape became one of wrecked and burned-out tanks, trucks, cars and planes.

The desert was a terrain of dust, scorpions and mosquitoes. The days were scorchingly hot and the nights bitterly cold. Often at night they could hear the sound of jackals savaging the dead, and once, as Frédéric Rey recalled, a pack of them started circling Joséphine and her companions. Sitting upright, she suddenly shouted: "Don't eat us!" What they had to eat themselves was often restricted to what they could carry with them. A lot of the time they lived on tinned tuna.

Joséphine rose to the occasion magnificently and uncomplainingly, as she always did when faced with adversity. Right at the beginning of these touring days she discovered that she had no available money at all, and would have to get along as best as she could from day to day. (Her shows, of course, were given free, and she received no pay.) All that she said, though, was: "Isn't it wonderful?" This was a far cry from the acquisitive girl of her pre-war Paris days, but in those days possessions had been a reassurance to her. During the war, fighting the good fight was all the reassurance she needed.

She found entertaining the troops a moving experience. "Often," she wrote, "I knew the men would be sent into battle before they knew. To see them in front of me so full of life and enthusiasm, and knowing that many of them wouldn't come back alive, was the hardest part of the tour."

She danced for them, everything from ballet to the Samba, and sang them songs of all kinds, cheerful and sentimental. The two First World War songs she had recorded in 1940, 'Tipperary' and 'If You Were The Only Girl In The World', were perennial favourites. She also sang 'My Yiddishe Mama', and 'Darling, Je Vous Aime Beaucoup', and she sang a light-hearted piece of foolishness called 'Gertie From Bizerte', written after a town on the northernmost tip of Tunisia).

And she always sang 'J'ai Deux Amours'. She sang it on one memorable occasion to an audience mostly composed of Free French soldiers. It was on the night after Germany had finally invaded the Free Zone and occupied the whole of France, and again she moved almost the entire audience to tears. To them it almost seemed that she was all that was left of the Paris they loved.

As well as performing, Joséphine also made it part of her war effort to proselytise for Général de Gaulle and the Free French, ending every performance by unfurling a giant Croix De Lorraine. De Gaulle himself became aware of this, and in 1943, when he finally arrived to set up his headquarters in Algiers, at last at the head of a real army, he rewarded her with a small gold Croix De Lorraine. By now the Free French had proudly changed their formal name from Forces Françaises Libres to France Combattante.

On one night Joséphine was staying in the famous Shepheard's Hotel in Cairo at the same time that Egypt's King Farouk was dining there. He asked her if she would sing, and she politely refused, arguing that Egypt had remained neutral, cautiously leaving its attitude to the Free French ambiguous. Immediately afterwards, however, she managed to get word to him that she was to sing at a concert in celebration of the ties between the Free French and Egypt, and would be honoured if he would consent to preside at it. He did consent, and by making such an appearance subtly changed Egypt's public allegiance. Joséphine had engineered a small but definite diplomatic coup, and had come a long way from the young girl who worshipped kings and queens as if they were magical mythical beings.

From May 1943, when she was approached by Basil Dean, the head of ENSA, she also engaged in many activities for that organisation. He assigned one of his personal assistants, Harry Hurford Janes, to take care of her affairs, and the two became lifelong friends. On one occasion she sang in a hospital, and Harry reminded her of it in a letter he sent her in 1949. "One of my most treasured memories," he wrote, "is the night when we dragged a little piano into into the ward of that Canadian hospital and you sang 'I'll Be Seeing You' until you nearly dropped. How even the nurses stood with tears in their eyes and those poor helpless men – many of whom would never recover – lying on their backs unable to move, only their eyes showing the relief and comfort you gave them."

Between tours, Joséphine rested at Si Mohammed Menebhi's palace, her whole life alternating between hardship and luxury. On some trips he came along with her, as a supporter of de Gaulle, acting as an interpreter for Jacques in his attempts to rally support for the Free French among lesser Arab rulers.

As the war progressed, and Allied forces crossed the Mediterranean and invaded Italy, Joséphine began to tour there too. In 1943 and 1944 she performed in Corsica, in Sardinia and in Italy itself. On one occasion, when she was flying in a plane with Jacques towards the Corsican coast, they had a narrow escape. The plane lost power and began to dive towards the sea. In the few frantic seconds before the plane hit the water, they managed to wedge a huge flag bearing the Croix De Lorraine between Joséphine and the front wall of the cabin to give her some protection. Fortunately the crash was not too severe: they all survived uninjured, and they were soon rescued by a nearby patrol boat.

Joséphine was also using her tours to raise funds for the Free French. At one of them she auctioned the gold Croix De Lorraine that de Gaulle had given her and of which she was so proud, which raised 350,000F. By the autumn of 1944 she had raised 3,143,000F, and as a reward for having done so was given the honorary rank of sub-lieutenant in the Ladies' Auxiliary of the French Air Force, Les Filles De L'Air.

While Joséphine and her colleagues were operating in the Mediterranean, off the south coast of France, Allied forces were also massing themselves off her northern coast, in England. On 6 June 1944, D-Day, troops from there invaded Normandy and began to push south, while on 15 August Allied forces, including many Free French, landed in southern France, capturing Marseille. Only ten days later, with Allied troops approaching the city from both sides, Paris was liberated.

However, it was several weeks before Joséphine was able to sort out her affairs and get back there. When she did so it was as part of a detachment of the Ladies' Air Auxiliary. They travelled by train from Algiers to Oran, and then by ship to Marseille. She was back in her beloved France.

One sadness was that over the past years of war and illness she had gradually lost all of her pets, including Bonzo, her great dane. However, to celebrate she had acquired another dog, a small one which she had smuggled in under her coat. She had given him the somewhat military name of Mitraillette, meaning "little machine gun", not because he was noisy or harmful but because that was the way he peed, in six little bursts, *rat-tat-tat-tat-tat-tat*.

The coat that she was wearing was of course the one that was part of her lieutenant's uniform. Despite all of the talented couturiers and designers who had fashioned clothes especially for her, of all of the outfits that she ever wore, onstage or off it, this outfit, in air force blue with gold epaulettes, was the one of which she was the most proud

12 *Civil Rights*

Joséphine arrived back in Paris in October 1944. The war in Europe would grind on for another seven months, but to her this already felt like victory. The Germans no longer governed France, and her hero, Charles de Gaulle, had been declared head of the provisional government.

The Paris to which she returned was still adjusting itself to its regained freedom. With the Germans gone, there was much public feeling against those who had collaborated with them, or who were suspected of having been too friendly towards them. This feeling ran high, both in people who had involved themselves in the Résistance and in those who were now reproaching themselves for not having got involved. Girls who were suspected of having had affairs with Germans had their heads shaved, and suspected collaborators frequently met with unfortunate accidents.

Among entertainers who had remained in France during the war and performed, both Mistinguett and the actress Cécile Sorel came under suspicion, and Cécile was even questioned by a tribunal about her wartime activities. Maurice Chevalier and the opera singer Tino Rossi (the man who was originally to have been the face of Bakerfix) were briefly arrested, Chevalier on suspicion of having given performances in Germany. In a cinema newsreel of the time he made a statement exonerating himself, stating that he had indeed performed in Germany during the war, but only once, and then not for Germans. He had entertained French prisoners of war in a camp at which he himself had been a prisoner during the First World War.

Joséphine, of course, was regarded as a heroine. Praised and fêted, she was delighted at being back in her beloved France and delighted with herself. Shortly after her return, in her first show back in Paris, she of course sang 'J'ai Deux Amours', and received a standing ovation, but afterwards she remarked that the song was no longer true. From then on there was only one country that she loved: France.

Columbia records welcomed her back into their recording studios, where she recorded several songs, including 'Brazil' and 'Besame Mucho'. When they released them in early 1945, a caption in their catalogue read: "Thank you, charming officer, for having been heroic and for singing once again for us."

In her excitement at being back, and with all of the adulation she was getting, she sometimes overdid her enthusiasm. Alain Romains, the musician who had composed the score for her film *La Sirène Des Tropiques* and who had also worked for the Free French in Africa, winning the Légion D'Honneur, commented: "She came back to France more French than Louis XVI. I said to her 'It was very nice of you to save France for us, Joséphine.'"

Her first show back in Paris was a charity gala in aid of the French Air Force. It was in three sections, and the last third was hers. Many of the songs she sang were written by her old friend Vincent Scotto. Some were new, but most were from his early days, in a portion of her programme called 'Pot-Pourri 1900'. She sang 'Je T'ai Rencontre Simplement', 'Frou-Frou', and 'Viens Poupoule', a song which had been a favourite of Marcel Proust years earlier. For these she wore an elegant, long, high-waisted dress with elaborate ruched shoulders, based on the style of the 1900s.

The middle part of the show, immediately preceding Joséphine's spot, consisted of instrumental numbers by a band, which also accompanied Joséphine for her part of the show. Its leader was a 41-year-old Frenchman named Jo Bouillon, and his band had a light and lively feel, with the ability to play powerfully when required. Joséphine had known him on the Paris entertainment scene for years, and several members of his band had worked for her, either at one of her various Chez Joséphines or as a member of her Baker Boys.

Jo Bouillon and his band began to accompany her on the tours she went on during the last months of the war, and for some months afterwards. She performed at hospitals and army posts all over France, as well as in other countries as they were liberated, and she was the first performer to appear in the city of Mulhouse, near the eastern border of France, after it was recaptured from the Germans.

On 29 April 1945, she appeared at the Adelphi Theatre in London, at a victory show in aid of the Allied forces. Nine days later, Germany surrendered and the war in Europe was over.

Back in Paris, she appeared in a gala celebration at the Théâtre Des Champs-Elysées, where she had appeared 20 years before in *La Revue*

Nègre. She also attended, as an honoured guest, the victory dinner of a unit of the Résistance, men who had been involved in fierce fighting and were celebrating not only their victory but their survival. The main dish was roast suckling pig. Joséphine, outraged, tore into their commanding officer for his lack of feeling towards animals.

Shortly after that, she visited Germany itself. She performed at a gala in Berlin, and she sang to the liberated but dying inmates of Büchenwald, who were too frail to be moved. Like many who visited the newly-liberated concentration camps, it was an experience about which she was never able to speak in later life.

It was at around this time, too, that Jean Lion returned to Paris, now that the war was over. Seeking out Joséphine, he asked her would she consider remarrying him. Joséphine refused, repeating to him the words of the judge who had put through their divorce, "they were two people who never really had the chance to get to know one another," which is not really a good argument against having another go. However, by this time there was another man in her life: Jo Bouillon.

During the engagements at which they had performed together, she and Jo had grown to know each other well. There was a natural sympathy between them, and quite soon they genuinely fell in love, although it seemed to those who knew them to be a love based on warmth and mutual devotion rather than on wild passion.

Jo was known to be shy with women. Although over 40, he had never married. Nonetheless, he was a handsome man with a cheerful, boyish manner, his boyishness emphasised by his being slightly under middle height, and it was clear that with Joséphine his shyness vanished. He delighted in her company.

He came from a musical family. He and his two brothers, Gabriel and Georges, were all violinists. They had all been taught initially by their father, and all had graduated from the Conservatoire. In the early Thirties, Jo had played in dance bands and in pit bands at the music hall before forming a band of his own. By 1945, this had become extremely popular and well known, making nightly broadcasts on French Radio.

From a practical point of view, he and Joséphine were well matched. At the time when it became obvious that they were now a couple, she told her friend at Le Vésinet, George Guignery, "I need work. He has an orchestra. We can travel together and he can get bookings."

Her reputation as a Résistance heroine was of some help to Jo, protecting him from any criticism he might have attracted for continuing to lead his band in Paris through the Occupation. In return, he was able to allay her fear that, once the post-war euphoria had died down, the public would find her *passé*.

Jo was practical, responsible and down to earth. He also had a genuine love of the countryside. This was extremely handy because Joséphine, after the turmoil of war, now wanted a settled home, and the place in which she had decided to settle was her rented château in the Dordogne, Le Milandes. Gradually a plan began to form in her mind. She would buy Les Milandes and turn it into a tourist centre, selling both Le Beau-Chêne and an apartment house on the Rue Bugeaud (bought for her by Pepito) to finance the purchase and the conversion.

She would also need to earn money by performing, but for the moment she continued to give concerts mostly to members of the forces and to the wounded. These she did for nothing, of course, a practise which, while praiseworthy, caused considerable financial hardship to both herself and to Jo, who did likewise.

At Christmas 1945 she had a reunion at Les Milandes with Jacques Abtey and several of their wartime comrades. She planned that, when she re-organised the château, she would set aside a house in its grounds for his use.

She naturally felt a sentimental attachment to her comrades of the war and to those places in which she had spent it. In early 1946, she and Jo engaged on a tour of North Africa and Italy, playing for the troops still stationed there.

But it wasn't only memories that lingered with her from the war years. She still had severe abdominal problems from her internal scarring, which was prone to become inflamed. A few months after her 40th birthday, in June 1946, she was taken into the Ambrose Pare clinic at Neuilly to be operated on for the fifth time. "They should put a zipper in my stomach," she joked. Jo stayed in constant attendance.

As during her wartime illness, rumours began to circulate that she was dying, and this prompted the government to send a delegation to her bedside to award her the Medaille De La Résistance, Avec Rosette. The delegation was led by Colonel de Boissoudy, and the other members of it were General de Gaulle's daughter, her husband Commander Boissieu and a representative from the League Against Racism And Anti-Semitism, Jean-Pierre Bloch.

Several of Joséphine's friends were also present, among them Henri Varna. Because she was still recovering from her operation, the ceremony took place in her room. She lay in her bed as Colonel de Boissoudy pinned the medal on the elegant red-and-white gown she was wearing, and as was usual in such situations Joséphine managed to appear radiant.

A few days later, on 14 October 1946, she was further delighted to receive a handwritten letter from Général de Gaulle, sending congratulations from his wife and himself on her receiving her medal, and hoping to have to honour of seeing her again.

This operation had at last been successful. Her abdominal ailments were now cured and, although weak, she had recovered sufficiently by the end of the year to go with Jo on a trip to Brazil. This was intended to be simply to convalesce, but while she was there she managed to give a few performances.

Back in France, during the early months of 1947, her performances grew fewer. She continued to make public appearances – judging a jitterbugging contest in Stockholm, and attending the première of a film scripted by Henri Jeanson, who had admired her since she appeared in *La Revue Nègre* – and she sometimes sang on Jo Bouillon's radio show, but mostly she devoted herself to Les Milandes.

It was there that she and Jo married, on 3 June 1947, her 41st birthday. They were married in a civil ceremony, as French law required, and then a Catholic ceremony was staged at the church on the estate. This surprised some of her friends somewhat. Most knew that she had been raised a Baptist, and a few believed that when she had married Jean Lion she had converted to Judaism, but at no time had she been a Catholic. Jo understood her, though, and later he wrote: "For Joséphine, God was in everything. I have seen her enter a cathedral, a synagogue, a mosque, a temple, and show the same respect...for her it wasn't one religion or another but simply the idea of God that was everywhere." In other words, if one's got you they've all got you.

For the ceremony Joséphine wore a two-piece suit and a large pink hat of woven straw, topped with a cloud of densely-curled plumes. The entire village of Les Milandes was invited to the celebration, and in a local ceremony she was served a plate of highly-spiced, "tongue-searing" soup by the local blacksmith. This was supposed to bring the marriage good luck.

Also invited were almost all of Jo's family (his brother Georges played the organ for the ceremony), and as the nearest thing to a family Joséphine could produce she invited Pepito's sister, Christina, who came over from Italy, bringing her husband, parents-in-law and children.

In many ways, Pepito would always be the man who was closest to Joséphine's heart. All of her life she kept a photograph of him on her desk, and not long after her wedding to Jo she had Pepito's body disinterred from the crypt in which he had been buried at Neuilly and reburied at Les Milandes.

Her plans for the development of Les Milandes as a tourist centre had continued to grow, and with Jo by her side she began to put them into effect. Like many such château estates, it was a small community. The farms and cottages that stood on it formed a small village over which the château owner ruled. Joséphine planned to employ the farmers and cottagers to help improve the estate, adding new buildings and tilling the soil, and later to help to run it.

The Dordogne valley had – and still has – many such estates, and many neighbouring owners looked with some disdain on Joséphine's plans, which to them were nakedly commercial. Nonetheless, her energy and the money that she poured into the estate were a shot in the arm for its economy.

Shortly after work got under way, she and Jo had to leave for a short while. It was November 1947, and Jo had obtained a joint booking for them to appear in Mexico. They were a great success there, making both live appearances and twice-weekly broadcasts. These broadcasts were picked up in the United States, and as a result they were approached to appear in a show at the Majestic Theater in Boston, and so Joséphine was once more to appear in her native America, unexpectedly and with little preparation.

Little preparation was the problem. The show, *Paris Sings Again*, was thrown together far too quickly and with too little thought, because the organisers wanted it to catch the Christmas trade. It opened on 25 December 1947, and appearing in it along with Joséphine and Jo were Hurtado de Cordoba, Roland Berbeau and Pierre Guillerman. There was also a 30-piece orchestra, billed as coming from Paris.

The opening number was 'Sous Les Ponts De Paris', which went over fairly well, but immediately after it came a completely un-Parisian version (according to the critics) of 'Jingle Bells', which killed whatever Parisian atmosphere had been built up stone dead.

As the show staggered on, Joséphine sang 'Mama', 'Mon Triste Coeur', 'Hortensia', 'Zoubida' and her medley of numbers from Paris of the 1900s. The critics, however, were lukewarm; most of them commented more favourably on her costumes than on her singing.

This is interesting because it shows the way in which her performances were developing after the war. Feeling that, at the age of 40, it was neither advisable nor seemly to appear onstage half naked (or indeed, she once said, in front of one's lover), Joséphine opted instead for dazzling her audiences with the variety and elegance of her costumes – some the high Paris fashion of the day, and some out-and-out cabaret glamour.

Paris Sings Again closed after three weeks, and as she was in America Joséphine decided to travel south to St Louis and visit her family.

Racially, America was as bad as ever. From Boston they first went to New York, where they had great difficulty in finding a room because Jo was white and she was black. (Later, Jo claimed that they were refused reservations at 36 hotels.) They finally found a room in the Hotel Gladstone at 14 East 52nd Street.

52nd Street then was probably as racially tolerant as any street in America, because in those days it was known as "The Street", and any New York taxi driver knew the name. It was crammed with tiny clubs where famous jazz musicians, both black and white, either had paid jobs or sat in with each other, excitedly developing the jazz of the Twenties and Thirties into the startling new sounds of be-bop.

Joséphine was so upset by the treatment which she and Jo received that she phoned the editor of *France Soir*, Roger Féral, and arranged to write a series of articles for him on the subject of segregation in the United States. In her mind, the idea was becoming ever stronger that the war she had recently been through was only an episode in the ongoing battle against racism. Having been active in a cause, and having found it empowering, she decided that she had to openly continue the fight.

Accordingly, when heading for St Louis, she left Jo behind in New York and for a while travelled incognito through the South as "Mrs Brown". The further south she travelled, the more entrenched she found that racist attitudes were. There were, for instance, still signs all over the place saying: "No dogs, no Jews, no niggers."

There were still several years to go before the anti-racist protests of the late Fifties would seriously get under way, and Joséphine was both brave and ahead of her time. As the black producer Jack Jordan – who would frequently work with her in America in later years – once pointed out: "She was much tougher than all those sit-in cats you see on TV. She used the drinking fountains, the lunch counters and the ladies' rooms. They threw her ass out in the street and she walked right back in."

In St Louis, she found her family – her mother Carrie, her brother Richard and her sister Margaret – and urged them all to come and live with her in France at Les Milandes. There they would be able to share in her success, and there they would experience how good it felt to be treated as free and equal.

Carrie was reluctant. Since Joséphine had last visited her, she had remarried, and her husband didn't want to live in a country whose language he didn't speak. But Joséphine insisted, yearning to have her mother with her, and eventually Carrie agreed to go. Her husband later said bitterly to a friend, "We loved each other dearly and her daughter came along and took her away just like that," which says something about the strain of coldness in Carrie's character that Joséphine had suffered from so much in her childhood.

Margaret, too, had married, but her husband, Elmo Wallace, was quite prepared to move, and so they agreed to accompany Carrie. However, brother Richard was not so sure. He had a life in St Louis and a small trucking company, and for the moment simply said that he would think about it.

Before leaving America, Joséphine had one more engagement, which for her was a new sort of job: she was invited to give a talk at the all-black Fisk University in Nashville, Tennessee, her subject being "France, North Africa And The Equality Of The Races In France". She not only spoke well, but she also discovered that she enjoyed making public speeches, that she was comfortably able to cope with questions from the floor, and that young blacks in America were interested in what she had to say. Telling her audience that this was the first time that she had felt at home since she had arrived in America, she went on to advise them all to visit North Africa or France in order to feel what it was like to live somewhere free from racial prejudice. She returned to France more determined than ever to come back to America one day and continue her crusade.

At Les Milandes, work on constructing the tourist centre was proceeding. When it had begun, not only the château itself but the whole estate had been neglected, partly because of the war. Joséphine saw to it that not only the château but all of the cottages and farmhouses were also supplied with electricity and given modern plumbing. This was naturally well received by the inhabitants, and the atmosphere on the estate was good. The tourist centre grew, until eventually there would be two hotels, three restaurants, a miniature golf course, a soccer pitch, tennis, volleyball and basketball courts, a patisserie, a *foie gras* factory (a delicacy for which the Dordogne is famous), a post office, and a wax museum which displayed scenes from the life of Joséphine Baker.

The château's home farm was provided with livestock on a more lavish scale than Joséphine had ever attempted before. There were cows, pigs and dogs, 600 chickens, and peacocks. Why peacocks? she was once asked. "They're the only things around here that remind me of my music hall days," she said.

Not that her music hall days were over yet. In spite of her crusading ambitions, at heart she was still a star. Performing gave her pride, and applause gave her warmth like nothing else.

Shortly after she and Jo returned to France, in around February 1948, she attended a production in Paris that both excited her and made her feel challenged. It was called *Rhapsodie Caraibe*, it was performed by the Katherine Dunham Company, and it was a stunning success.

Katherine Dunham, six years younger than Joséphine and born in Chicago, became not only a highly talented dancer and choreographer but also an anthropologist. Carrying out comparative studies of dance in Jamaica, Martinique, Trinidad and Haiti, she developed a deep understanding of the history and nature of black dance, and went on to explore its influence (and the influence of black music) on 20th-century American culture.

Joséphine went to see *Rhapsodie Caraibe* four nights running. It spurred her into action, and it wasn't long before she and Jo opened at a new cabaret, the Club Des Champs-Elysées. The first night was on 8 April 1948, and among the attending celebrities were Jean Marais, Jean-Louis Barrault, Madeleine Renaud, Gérard Philipe, François Perrier, Martine Carol and Katherine Dunham.

From the diplomatic world there were ambassadors from Egypt, China, Argentina and Venezuela. The great Joe Louis, whom Joséphine had met in New York back in 1936, made a special trip from Brussels to be there, and while Joséphine was onstage singing she saw entering the room the small perky figure of Mistinguett, who was now around 75 but still dancing. On seeing her, without stopping singing or even missing a beat, Joséphine came down off the stage, crossed the room to Mistinguett, took her by the arm and guided her to her reserved table at the front of the room.

Mistinguett, she felt, was no longer competition, but Katherine Dunham was, although their relationship would always be one of friendly rivalry. Years later, Dunham said: "As we got to know each other, we became friends. Every time we performed in the same town, we made certain to make time to see each other. She called me her sister. I think we had a very good relationship – whatever jealousy existed, I'm sure, must have been mine as well as hers."

With her renewed enthusiasm for performing, she made several other appearances. One was at Bordeaux, only 50 miles or so from Les Milandes, and she seized the opportunity to invite her mother to come and see her, but once again she was disappointed by her mother's reaction. Now deeply religious, Carrie was appalled by the amount of leg and bosom Joséphine displayed onstage. Coming to her dressing room after the show, she fell on her knees in front of her daughter and wept. "Tumpie," she wailed, "you never told me you were one of those painted women!"

In the next year, 1949, Joséphine was again invited by producers Paul Derval and Michael Gyarmaty to star at the Folies Bergère. The show was to be called *Féeries Et Folies* (a departure from their traditional 13-letter titles), and some of the numbers in it reflected the influence of Katherine Dunham.

The whole show was based on fairy tales. In an opening prelude, Veronica Bell appeared as Cinderella, and then Joséphine appeared, first in a comedy skit, playing herself, supposedly on a train bringing her to Paris. Later she appeared as an Arabian carpet seller, then as "la danseuse Zubida", and the first-half finale was called 'Scottish Parade'. In it the chorus girls were dressed in kilts and sporrans, and Joséphine, in a sort of Ruritanian costume, wore a tall white feathered busby.

The second half was introduced by Snow White, and Joséphine then appeared in a series of dances representing 'Love Through The Ages'. First she was Eve, and for this – in a departure from historical accuracy – she wore a leopard skin rather than a fig leaf. She then appeared in a vigorous 'Beauty And The Beast' number wearing a costume reminiscent of the heroine of a courtly romance, with a tall pointed mediaeval hat and a flowing white gown. She was partnered in this by an almost nude Frédéric Rey. In other scenes she played an princess from the *Arabian Nights* and

Napoléon's Joséphine, and danced an 1890s Can-Can in homage to Mademoiselle Raphaëlla, a star of the Bal Mabille.

The most Dunham-esque act in the show was called 'Nuit Perverse', in which she appeared almost nude but in fact wore thin tights and a matching backless top that came up to cover her breasts. For this one number she was hatless, and by this time was habitually wearing her hair longer, pulling it up tightly and coiling it into a round pile on top of her head, a style that she would retain for the rest of her life.

The big finale to the show again had a Scottish theme. In it she played Mary, Queen of Scots, appearing in a wide, pleated satin dress and an elaborate veiled head-dress. It had four movements: 'Prisons Des Femmes', 'Sonate Pathétique', 'L'Exécution' and 'Ave Maria'. In this last, after the axe fell, the lighting changed to turn the backdrop of the stage into stained glass windows. As Gounod's music swelled, dancers costumed as figures from the windows detached themselves from the background and formed a guard of honour around Joséphine. Wrapped in a cape so as to appear headless, representing Mary's departing spirit, she ascended vertically into the clear air, singing 'Ave Maria' as she went. It was a *coup de théâtre*.

As was usual at the Folies, a number of new songs had been written for the show, this time mostly by Jo and by Georges Tabet, and Joséphine returned to the Columbia recording studios after five years' absence and recorded a number of them. In the war years she had begun to use a microphone during her performances, and as a result she was learning to use (if only occasionally) the ability a microphone gives a singer to sing softly and intimately. As the years went by, her voice was beginning to drop, becoming more mezzo than soprano, and her songs were selling better and better.

At Les Milandes, slight cracks were starting to appear in its organisation. For a start, Joséphine had no better an idea than she had had at Le Beau-Chêne of handling her staff. Her unpredictable moods and her outbursts of temper frequently meant that staff either left or were fired, and some of the initial goodwill that her tenants felt towards her began to dissipate.

There were also slight differences between herself and Jo. She and he were turning out to have radically different approaches to running the home farm. Jo, while fond of the country, realised that he had no experience of farm management. Being a practical man, he took to spending long hours in the municipal library of the nearby region of Périgord, mugging up on the subject and trying to become at least adequately knowledgeable.

Joséphine, on the other hand, attempted to farm by instinct – not through an instinctive understanding of the nature of crops and creatures, of course, but instead acting on whatever she felt was the right thing to do on any particular day. For instance, she had the idea of planting tomatoes in October in order to provide a crop for Christmas, "when nobody else has them". Naturally, they were undersized and died on the vine.

Not wanting her 600 hens to be imprisoned in a coop or a run, she let them go loose, insisting that "they must be free", and so they laid their eggs in her vegetable garden, where they could not easily be found. The uncollected eggs attracted vermin, and these attacked her lettuces and cabbages.

She regularly hosed down her pigs "so they will look all pink and pretty", but didn't see to it that they were fed regularly, although this might have worked out all right if she had been able to keep regular staff to look after them.

At one time, the farmer whose job it was to milk the cows quit after some disagreement. It happened on the day when Les Milandes was to have its official opening as a tourist centre, and Joséphine had invited Michael Gyarmaty of the Folies Bergère to be present. When he arrived from Paris she asked him if he would lend a hand with the milking. Michael, whose tastes were totally urban, recoiled at the idea, and so instead Joséphine talked him into installing neon lettering in the cowshed which spelled out the name of each cow above its stall: Jeannette, Rosette, Pervenche, Julie and Honorine. "Quelle merveille!" she exclaimed, clasping her hands with joy at the sight of the finished job. "This is absolutely the model farm!"

When *Féeries Et Folies* finished its run in the summer of 1950, she and Jo set off on tour, going first to Italy, where she had an audience with Pope Pius XII, and then on to a night club engagement in Havana, Cuba.

With her increasing use of striking dress in her performances, she went well provided with *haute couture*. When clothing restrictions had eased after the war, and the new look had come in with its long full skirts and tight waists, Joséphine had taken to it eagerly. By the late Forties most of the time her couturier was Jean Dessès, but her wardrobe also included dresses by Balenciaga, Balmain and Christian Dior.

Her tour was successful in Italy and even more so in Havana, with the result that news of it reached the 180 or so miles across the straits of Florida to Miami. The management of a night club there, the Copa City, had the idea of booking her, and the next thing she knew she had received a phone call in Havana from New York agent Willard Alexander. She told him that she was agreeable to playing at the Copa City, and its manager, Ned Schuyler, came to Havana to discuss terms. Here was her chance to start striking blows for racial equality. She told Schuyler that, although she would be willing to appear, there might be a problem: as Miami was in the southern state of Florida, she assumed that his club would have a policy of segregation, and that no blacks would be admitted.

Schuyler admitted that indeed no blacks had ever been among his patrons, but pointed out in mitigation that none had ever applied to enter his club. Joséphine said positively that she would not play there unless there were some blacks in her audience. Schuyler tried offering her a larger fee, but she firmly refused. Eventually she was refusing a fee of $10,000 per week, and at last Schuyler, who in his heart was on her side, gave in. He even supported her when she insisted on being booked into a Miami Beach hotel that had never previously admitted a black guest.

One other thing bothered her before signing the contract. She was worried about the influential gossip columnist and broadcaster Walter Winchell. Would he attack her for having given up her American nationality to become French?

This was not a foolish worry. Since the Twenties, Winchell had been the most influential voice in the American media. Based around Broadway, he was the doyen of gossip columnists. In fact, it was he who had invented the gossip column, recording and commenting on the doings of celebrities, mainly in the worlds of entertainment and of café society. Most of his stuff was trivial, but on occasion he would take it into his head to attack somebody, and in attack he could be lethal. Schuyler wrote to him to find out his position regarding Joséphine's citizenship. Laconically, Winchell simply wrote back "How's her act???"

In January 1951, Schuyler made Joséphine's opening night a gala occasion. He flew in celebrities from New York, both black and white, to be in the audience. Winchell was among them, seated between the former heavyweight champion Joe Louis and the great cabaret artist Sophie Tucker, "the last of the red-hot mommas", who introduced Joséphine to the audience at the start of the show.

Joséphine was a smash. Sumptuously dressed and singing in a procession of languages – in English, in French, in Spanish, in Portuguese – she danced, mugged, joked and reminisced, filling the place with a torrent of warmth and cosmopolitanism. "This is the happiest moment of my life," she told them at the end of the show, passing among the tables, microphone in hand. "I have waited 27 years for this night. Here I am in this city where I can perform for my people, where I can shake your hands. This is a very significant occasion for us, and by 'us' I mean the entire human race."

Her well-publicised stand on racial equality brought her hundreds of telegrams of support from blacks all over America, and with her growing propensity for engaging in correspondence with leading world figures she sent a telegram herself to President Truman, writing: "My husband and I thank the American people through you for our magnificent reception here and for the opportunity to advance the cause of civil rights which I know is so important to you."

Copa City, which seated 750, was sold out every night for the whole time of her run there. Winchell, in his column in the *New York Mirror* for 17 January, wrote: "Josephine Baker's applause is the most deafening, pro-longed, and sincere we ever heard in 40 years of showbiz. A one-gal show, with exquisite gowns, charm, magic and big-time zing. In two words: a star. PS And her legs are as lovely as Sugar Ray Robinson's. Gets $1,000 a day after a 27-year absence abroad. She won't appear anywhere if members of her race are not admitted." *Variety*, the showbiz bible, reported: "Miss Baker adds up to one of the most solid acts to have played as demanding a room as this since the plushery was opened two years ago...She's money in the bank for any top spot that gets her."

It didn't take long for the top spots to bite. Ned Schuyler had offered to act as her agent, and he negotiated a deal with Warner Brothers for her to appear as a live act between film shows in a chain of their cinemas in major cities right across America. As she set off on it, Joséphine headed back to look after their affairs in France.

The playing of live acts between films was a sort of revival from the days of vaudeville, and it had been brought in by some big cinemas at the beginning of the Fifties to try and compete with the new threat of television. Joséphine's shows were each to last an hour, with six or seven changes of costume, and as in vaudeville she was to play four shows a day. The first cinema at which she was to appear was the Strand Theater in New York, where she would be paid $7,500 per week. She would be back on Broadway for the first time since her disastrous experience in the Ziegfeld Follies.

This engagement made up for a lot. Once again Joséphine was a smash. She had 43 costumes with her, allegedly worth $250,000 and much publicity was garnered from the lavishness of her wardrobe. As usual, she sang in a medley of languages, this time ending each performance with an Italian number, "because Italy is the language of love".

Variety again reviewed her: "The showmanship that is Josephine Baker's, as currently demonstrated at the Strand, is something that doesn't happen synthetically, or overnight. It's of the same tradition that accounts for the durability of almost every showbiz standard still on top, after many years...She 'fractures' all lingos with a sinuous terping temp style that is understandable in any language...Miss Baker is unquestionably a socko new face back on the American scene...Her Broadway comeback is a signal click and her personal performance a payoff satisfaction that comes to few performers. None deserves it more richly."

Why was she such a smashing success in America in 1951 when she had failed before? She can hardly be blamed for the failure of *Paris Sings Again* in 1947 because the show itself had been thrown together too hurriedly, but what was different between 1951 and the Ziegfeld Follies of 1936?

One criticism of her performance then was that her thin voice could barely be heard. Her voice was now fuller, and she was now able to work onstage with a microphone. The other main criticism had been that she was not performing as expected of a black girl but instead aped Parisian mannerisms. Here there was definitely a change in her audience. Also, by 1951 there was no longer a bag of stock black characterisations that made audiences uneasy with something different. It was still there to some extent, but not as rigid as it had been, and now that so many Americans had fought in Europe during the war the public was more aware of all things European, and so her performances felt less alien to them.

There was a change in Joséphine, too. Before the war there was still something about her of the little girl anxious to please. Now she was a secure, mature woman, able to play her audiences like fish, and such confidence in a performer makes audiences themselves feel secure.

Excited by her success, on top of her four shows a day she accepted a booking to appear each night at Monte Prosser's Café Theater at 1619 Broadway, but after making one appearance there she withdrew after a doctor advised her not to take on any more performances than she was doing at the Strand.

It wasn't only the top spots that had become interested in her. Towards the end of January 1951, it had been announced that a musical by José Ferrer and Richard Condon was being planned for her, based on Haitian culture, and that Ernest Hemingway was working on its outline.

As her tour took her across America, she crusaded loudly for what would a few years later be called civil rights. At every cinema at which she appeared, she insisted that there had to be some black musicians in the house band and that no racial discrimination should be shown in the sale of tickets. One city felt unable to guarantee this, and she duly refused a fee of $12,000 per week to play there. Ironically, this was St Louis.

One of her biggest civil rights triumphs occurred when she was booked to appear in Las Vegas, then one of the most segregated cities in America. Blacks were constrained to living in a down-trodden district known as Westside. Its streets were unpaved, without even wooden sidewalks, and the housing consisted of run-down shacks, many of them without electricity or indoor plumbing. Even highly-paid entertainers like Sammy Davis Jr were forbidden to stay in the city's glamorous and expensive venues when they were appearing at them, and couldn't even dine in them or play the tables, having to cross town and stay in lodgings in Westside.

Joséphine exerted all the clout she could, succeeding in getting her whole troupe housed in the hotel at which they were working. She also went even further than her usual insistence on playing to integrated audiences – her contract stipulated that a table for six was reserved every evening for black patrons, which would be provided by the NAACP (the National Association For The Advancement Of Coloured People). On the first night of her show's run, the management admitted the six blacks booked to sit at that table but refused to admit others waiting to get in. Joséphine insisted that her contract specified an integrated audience and forced them to back down.

On later evenings she went further, regularly succeeding in filling tables with mixed-race groups (again with the help of the NAACP). *Variety* reported: "This was the first manifestation of protest by a minority group that has achieved any semblance of success in Las Vegas."

Scheduled to appear at an NAACP convention in Atlanta, Georgia, she refused to attend after being denied accommodation at three of its main hotels: the Biltmore, the Henry Grady and the Georgian Terrace. Publicising her refusal, she drew national attention to the fact that a law in

Georgia explicitly laid down that any white hotel granting accommodation to blacks would be liable to lose its license.

After this incident, she began to receive threatening phone calls from the Ku Klux Klan. Her response was to call a press conference and declare "I am not afraid of the Ku Klux Klan or any other group of hooded mobsters. I'll meet them in the South or anywhere else they like, but I will not go to Atlanta because I have not been assured that they will give me the rights they grant to any other citizen of this country of my birth."

By now she was receiving an enormous amount of fan mail, so much in fact that she had to hire two secretaries to deal with it.

In Chicago, where she was receiving $11,000 per week to perform, she called on the heads of the First National Bank, International Harvester, the National Association Of Television Broadcasters and the Chicago Association Of Commerce And Industry, vehemently urging each of them to employ more blacks. She also called on the president of the Illinois Central Railroad, demanding to know why the carriages of the company's trains serving the South were still segregated.

In San Francisco, where she was appearing at the Golden Gate Theater, this time accompanied by officials of the NAACP, she made similar calls to the heads of the Chamber Of Commerce, the City Of Paris department store and Oakland's Key System Transit Company, although with this last she didn't make out so well. Its president, Frank Teasdale, after being lectured by her about not employing black bus drivers, launched into a counter-tirade of his own about how his buses were worth millions of dollars and that in the wrong hands they might also become a danger to lives and property.

"How can so many negroes qualify to drive trucks in the army but not drive your buses?" Joséphine shot back at him.

Teasdale replied that the decision not to employ blacks was the policy of less senior members of the firm, and it was his policy never to interfere with their decisions. Joséphine, frustrated, walked out on him.

Her reputation as a crusader grew to such an extent that the NAACP had Sunday 20 May 1951 declared Joséphine Baker Day. The celebrations were to be held in Harlem, and Jo Bouillon flew over from France for the occasion, bringing Joséphine two new Dior dresses to wear. Even though the day turned out wet and gloomy, 100,000 people turned out to honour her, travelling from all over America and dressed in their Sunday finery.

The celebrations began with a 27-car motorcade travelling slowly up Seventh Avenue. Joséphine, wearing a tailored suit and a black straw hat, sat perched high in the back of a cream-coloured Cadillac convertible, waving to the crowds thronging the pavements, windows and fire escapes. She blew kisses to them and shouted: "I love you, I love you, I love you."

In front of the Hotel Theresa on Seventh Avenue and 125th Street, where there was to be a luncheon, she was presented with a bouquet of roses by a contingent of 1,500 Girl Scouts. In the afternoon there was a cocktail party in her honour at the Park Palace Ballroom given by the mayor of New York, Vincent Impelliteri, and the day climaxed with a show at the Golden Gate Ballroom on Harlem's Lenox Avenue.

5,000 people crammed in to attend it. Onstage, Joséphine was presented with life membership of the NAACP by Nobel Peace Prize winner Dr Ralphe Bunche, later to become under-secretary general of the United Nations and already the most influential black in America. Among those who later paid tribute to her were Frederic March, Gypsy Rose Lee, Billy Daniels, Buddy Rogers, Duke Ellington and the head of the NAACP, Walter White. By midnight, Joséphine was so moved that she was close to tears. "Mama should be here," she said.

In support of the occasion, the radio station WLIB presented a week-long "salute to Joséphine Baker". The guests appearing on it, as well as Dr Bunche, included Florence Eldridge, Jean Hersholt, Peggy Lee, Josh White, Ella Fitzgerald, Lionel Hampton and Noble Sissle.

The honour that Joséphine Baker Day had paid to her spurred Joséphine to further crusading efforts, and she identified herself publicly with two civil rights issues of the time. One was the crusade to free Willie McGee, a 38-year-old black truck driver who had been sentenced to be electrocuted for raping a white woman while she lay in bed beside her small daughter. Many people, including Albert Einstein, felt that he had been framed and campaigned for his acquittal. His execution had been postponed three times pending an appeal, but at last a fourth date had been set.

Joséphine had first heard of his case when she was playing the Strand, in New York. A "Save Willie McGee" rally had been held at the Golden Gate Ballroom, and she had been asked to be one of the principal speakers. At first, naturally, she agreed, but later she was told that the event was being organised by Communist groups. In those witch-hunting days of the Cold War it wasn't a good thing for any cause to be perceived as having links with Communism, and with unusual prudence Joséphine declined to speak at the rally, merely sending the organisers a statement of support.

Nonetheless, she had kept up with the case. She had learned that Willie's wife, Rosaleen, lived in Detroit, and in June 1951, when her tour reached there, she sought out Rosaleen and spent much time with her, doing what she could to offer consolation. She even paid return air fare for Rosaleen so that she could visit Willie in prison.

She was still appearing in Detroit when Willie was executed, and that night at the Fox Theatre, where she was appearing, on her first appearance she walked to the footlights and announced to the audience that she would perform, but that her heart wasn't in it. "They have killed Willie McGee, one of my people," she told them. With tears in her eyes, she related the facts of the case, explaining that it was not just Willie McGee who had died. "A part of every American negro died with him," she said.

She paid for his funeral and spent much of her remaining time in Detroit with Rosaleen, speaking about the injustice of the case whenever she had the chance. On one occasion, when she was attending a reception being given in her honour and Rosaleen was with her, photographers refused to photograph the two of them together. Joséphine made no fuss; she simply left, which was a good story for the press in itself.

The other case had begun back in the summer of 1948, when the 73-year-old owner of a furniture shop in Trenton, New Jersey, had been beaten to death in its back room with a soda bottle. The police had swept through the black neighbourhoods of the city and arrested six men, who became known as the Trenton Six. The evidence against them was not strong, being mostly circumstantial, and their defending lawyers claimed that they had been arrested mainly because they were black, and that they had been forced to sign confessions after a brutal five-night-long interrogation, in the course of which they had been drugged and repeatedly threatened with violence.

During the time of their trial, Joséphine was making a five-day appearance in nearby Philadelphia, and one day she showed up in the courtroom, unannounced, and sent a note to defence lawyer Raymond Pace Alexander, asking if he could get permission for her to speak to the defendants. Somewhat surprisingly, the presiding judge, Ralph Smalley, granted her request. He adjourned the court for ten minutes so that she could talk to them in their cells. There she did her best to reassure them, telling them to "keep their chins up and have full confidence that justice would prevail".

It turned out that one of the six, John MacKenzie, had served overseas, been wounded and, while in hospital at Le Mans, seen her perform. Seeing her again in such different circumstances caused him to burst into tears.

The six were all convicted of murder and sentenced to the electric chair, but later in the year, on appeal, four were acquitted. Only two, Collis English and Ralph Cooper, remained under sentence of death. Two years later, Cooper turned state's evidence and made a statement incriminating both himself and English. For making this statement, he was freed. English died in prison of a heart attack before he could be executed.

In July 1951, in Los Angeles, where Joséphine was making her last appearance of the tour, she was dining one evening at the Biltmore Hotel and wearing her Air Force uniform, which she often wore as a symbol of her continuing fight against racism. Suddenly, she heard a Texan, sitting at a table next to her, announce: "I won't stay in the same room with niggers."

It was rather similar to the remark that had so mortified her 24 years before in Paris, on the day when Lindbergh had landed, but she was a stronger, tougher Joséphine now. She went to a phone at once, called the police, and demanded that the man be arrested. The police explained that they could not arrest him because no policeman had heard the remark. However, they explained that there was a law in California empowering her to carry out a citizen's arrest in such circumstances. Joséphine told them to send an officer around because she was going to do just that. Putting down the phone, she went and told the man that he was under arrest. He turned out to be a 45-year-old salesman from Dallas, and was shortly sentenced by a municipal judge to ten days in jail or a $100 fine for disturbing the peace. He paid the fine. Joséphine, interviewed by the press about the occurrence, explained that it had been easy for her because her father had been a policeman.

The tour over, she returned to Les Milandes in France, where her mother, sister Margaret and Margaret's husband, Elmo, were staying, and spent the rest of the summer there with them and with Jo. Then, at the beginning of October, it was back to the USA to fulfil the crammed list of engagements which her success there during the first half of the year had prompted. Ned Schuyler acted as her manager.

She began by playing a two-week engagement at the Roxy, in New York, and by now her fee had risen to $20,000 per week. Coincidentally, at around the same time, Mistinguett opened at the Martinique Club on

West 57th Street, and her dismal failure only served to highlight Joséphine's renewed success.

Again, a huge feature of her shows was her wardrobe. Filling six trunks and 48 suitcases, and reputed to have cost $150,000, it included original creations by Christian Dior, Balenciaga, Pierre Balmain and Jacques Griffe, all designed especially for her. New York designers came to the Roxy to sit in the audience sketching them, and in a television poll conducted at the Stork Club she was voted Best-Dressed Woman of 1951.

The Stork Club, on East 53rd Street, had begun life elsewhere in the early Twenties as a speakeasy during the days of Prohibition. It was then, and continued to be, run by Sherman Billingsley, who in spite of his rather elegant name had been raised in a clapboard farmhouse in the town of Enid, Oklahoma, his father being a police chief. As the years went by, the Stork Club gradually became more and more exclusive, until by the early Thirties it was the most fashionable of the three classiest eateries in New York, the other two being El Morocco and the Colony.

It was helped in reaching this pinnacle of success by Billingsley's friend, Walter Winchell. He gathered gossip for his newspaper column and radio show mainly by hanging out in the most exclusive night spots. It was known to every press agent in New York that, if you sought out Winchell and gave him a hot item of gossip, in return he would give a plug to whatever client or show or venue you were hired to publicise. In around 1930, realising that it would make it easier for such people to find him if he were regularly in one spot, and liking Billingsley and the ambience of the Stork Club, he made that establishment his nightly port of call, publicising it heavily.

As well as a main dining room, the Stork Club had a smaller room which catered to the *crème de la crème* of showbiz and society, and this was named the Cub Room. There, table 50 was permanently reserved for Winchell, and a phone was beside it. It was over to this table that Grace Kelly would come a few years later to tell Winchell the news of her engagement to Prince Rainier.

One thing about Sherman Billingsley, as well as his determination to cater only to "carriage trade", was his unspoken policy of discouraging black patrons. It wasn't exactly that he was a racist; his brother Logan, explaining that Sherman's attitude was simply one of appreciating good breeding, said: "You know, he cares only for the finest people and it wouldn't do him any good to let all the niggers in there."

The great middleweight boxing champion Sugar Ray Robinson was on good terms with Winchell, and indeed had been appointed by Winchell to the board of the Damon Runyon Cancer Fund, set up by Winchell in the Forties in memory of his late friend. Sugar Ray once suggested that they met at the Stork Club. "I wish you wouldn't, Champ," said Winchell. "Sherman Billingsley doesn't like negroes and he doesn't want them in the place, and if he came down there and he insulted you I'd have to break with him, although I've known him for 23 years."

It was only a few days after Joséphine had been given the Best-Dressed Woman award in a TV broadcast from the club that she turned up there herself. It was Tuesday 16 October 1951, and on this occasion she wasn't out to make any sort of political point.

The hottest musical on Broadway at that time was *South Pacific*, and the stars who made it such a hit were Ezio Pinza and Mary Martin. It so happened that Ezio Pinza needed a rest, and for a while his role, which was that of a Frenchman, was taken over by an old acquaintance of Joséphine's from Paris, Roger Rico. She had got in touch with him, and on this night Rico suggested that she accompanied him and his wife to the Cub Room for a late snack. They arrived there at 11.15pm. Among those there that night was a young woman who was just the sort of customer that Sherman Billingsley wanted to attract, Grace Kelly, who had then just begun her career in movies. Winchell was there, too, at table 50. He waved to Joséphine and she smiled back.

She and the Rico's were seated, and they ordered drinks. Joséphine alone of the party wanted food, and she ordered crab salad, steak and a bottle of French wine. She later recalled: "The looks that the headwaiter gave and his assistants were giving me made me suspect that something was going to happen, but in fact the exact opposite occurred. Nothing happened at all...nothing, by which I mean that my friends received their orders but mine did not appear."

Service in the Stork Club was notoriously slow – Billingsley's attitude was that his celebrity customers were more interested in looking at each other than in eating – but nonetheless it does seem that this was a deliberate snub. Billingsley, who on Roger Rico's previous visits had courteously stopped by his table to greet him, as was his practise with all of his customers, on this occasion came nowhere near.

After almost an hour's wait, Rico managed to summoned a waiter and demanded that he serve Joséphine her meal at once. The waiter went away and returned empty-handed to explain that the kitchen had run out of both crab salad and steak.

Joséphine felt humiliated and Roger Rico was furious. Together they got up and went to the Cub Room phone booth, where Joséphine made two phone calls, one to black deputy police commissioner William Rowe and one to Walter White, the head of the NAACP. To both she complained that the Stork Club had refused to serve her because of her colour, and demanded that the affair be investigated.

Walter Winchell, sitting a few tables away from their party, noticed Roger and Joséphine get up and cross the room, but later claimed to be unaware that they were upset. "That's nice," he said to those at his table. "They're going dancing."

Sherman Billingsley, however, was aware that Joséphine was upset, and, knowing her reputation as an activist, was furious at the possibility that she might be imperilling his club. If her charge of discrimination stuck, he would be proved to be violating both the State Civil Rights Act and the State Alcoholic Beverage Control Law. When she and Roger returned to their table a waiter at once hurried over and, as she later put it, "A pathetic little steak finally appeared on a platter." But by now she was too upset to eat, and Rico, "his superb voice shaking with anger", asked for the bill and they left. By this time, Winchell, who rarely spent his whole night at the club, had gone too, so he didn't see their final exit. Nonetheless, the whole situation continued to involve him, getting wildly out of hand.

On the following day, Joséphine attended a meeting with Ned Schuyler and his attorney, Henry Lee Moon of the NAACP, deputy police commissioner William Rowe, New York Post reporter Ted Posten, and several others. They discussed the possibility of having the NAACP picket the Stork Club, and debated what else they could do to publicise the affair. In the ensuing publicity, Joséphine rather ill-advisedly laid into Winchell, blaming him for not standing up for her in her public humiliation.

Winchell was outraged. Jewish himself, and an opponent of racial injustice, he had long and often fought for the rights of blacks. In fact, over the years, dozens of ordinary black citizens had written to him as a last resort, pleading for help, and they had rarely been disappointed by his response. He was outraged not only at being dragged into a dispute of which he felt that he wasn't a part but also at being accused of lacking a virtue he prided himself on possessing. Furthermore, he felt that Joséphine and the NAACP were being unfair in putting pressure on him to now denounce the Stork Club's racist policy, which he felt would make him look ungrateful towards his friend Billingsley. He grumbled about the whole affair in his column, defending his past record, swearing his innocence, blaming the NAACP for being influenced by Communists, and eventually, his temper boiling over, he went for Joséphine, whom he felt had instigated the whole mess.

For all of his working life he had boasted of having a "drop dead list" of people he was out to get and some day would, even if years had gone by, and now she was most definitely on it. In his columns and on the air he accused her of having aided the Nazi-installed Pétain government in France during the war, of being anti-Semitic, of herself refusing to patronise black-owned clubs and businesses, and of deliberately fomenting racial incidents in order to get attention. He started referring to her husband dismissively as "Joe Soup", and dug out her 1935 statement praising Mussolini, writing: "While our boys were over there stopping bullets, Josey-Phoney Baker was living it up, making oodles of dough in Paris, wining and dining the Nazis' and Mussolini's bigwig generals."

As it turned out, these attacks signalled the beginning of the end of Winchell's power. They became so hysterical that in the public eye the issue shifted from being Baker v Billingsley to being Baker v Winchell, and so he became the villain. He was more and more perceived as a has-been whose profession of crusading for the underdog in the past had been no more than window dressing, and began a long slide into obscurity.

Joséphine fared little better. The affair made her into a controversial figure, and the theatres that had booked her for her tour backed out of their contracts one by one. The case against the Stork Club finally petered out towards the end of December 1951, and at around the same time Joséphine announced to the NAACP that she was instituting suit against Winchell for $400,000, charging him with having embarked on a "public campaign to vilify, libel and damage" her reputation and professional standing. (However, she never followed up this case, which was dismissed a few years later due to lack of further action.)

She also appeared for two nights running on the radio show of a young disc jockey, Barry Gray, defending herself against Winchell's attacks. Gray had tried to get Winchell to appear on the shows as well but failed to reach him, and the incident also put him on Winchell's drop dead list.

As Joséphine became increasingly regarded as controversial, even many blacks began to shun her, fearing that her reputation would hurt their cause. Sometimes, when she sat down at a table in a Harlem restaurant, people sitting nearby would change tables to distance themselves. This hurt her and bewildered her more than anything.

One booking she had that she did not lose was at the famous Apollo Theater in Harlem. She opened there for a nine-day booking on 19 December 1951 and soon won over the initially suspicious audience.

Jack Schiffman, the son of the Apollo's owner, Frank Schiffman, was then acting as manager of the theatre, and he found her one of the most difficult and temperamental stars with whom he had ever had to deal. As years ago, during the filming of *La Sirène Des Tropiques*, when Joséphine was seriously unhappy she took it out on everyone.

First she insisted on having three dressing-rooms – one for her gowns, one in the wings for quick changes, and one for socialising. Then she objected that the first show each day began too early. (Usually it began at 12.30pm.) For Joséphine they had put it back half an hour, but still she objected. "I'm simply too old to be at the theatre that early," she said, but reluctantly agreed to open each day at one.

All through the run she was trouble. Once she walked offstage in the middle of a matinee and strode out of the stage door to a waiting cab, calling over her shoulder as she got into it "I've got a meeting and I'm not sure when I'll be back," leaving Jack Shiffman the task of explaining her absence to the audience. He also had to worry about whether she would make it for the next show, which of course was sold out. She did make it, but only at the very last minute.

Nonetheless, she was a huge success. Schiffman later wrote:

"Josephine was glamour personified, and temperamental as she was, I could only stand in awe at her masterful performances. She covered the stage with all the agility of a cat and the ease of a seal in water. The audiences adored her as she brought children up onto the stage to dance with her, adults up to talk to her. She appealed to young and old alike. Not once, but six or eight times per performance, she swirled offstage while the orchestra vamped, returning in various outrageous costumes: enormous hats with fruit and flowers on them, gowns that ranged from Arabian striped affairs to furling, sequinned gowns sparkling under the spots…She sang in French, she sang in Italian; she could have sung in Hindustani and that Harlem crowd would have stood up and cheered."

With the rest of her American bookings having dried up, including a $250,000 film contract that Ned Schuyler had managed to get for her, on 28 January 1952 Joséphine set off to Cuba, travelling with her secretary, Carolyn Carruthers. The Castro revolution was still seven years off, and Cuba was then a police state. In Havana, Joséphine was arrested on suspicion of having Communist sympathies, but was released after "full questioning". She said later: "Everyone who believes in brotherhood has been accused of Communism."

Next she and Carolyn went to Mexico, where the performances she gave included one for the inmates of a jail in Mexico City. She sang them two French songs and three Spanish ones, and announced that she wanted to form a world league against racial discrimination.

Then they moved south, to Argentina, which at that time was a country in mourning. Only two months before, the beloved heroine of (most of) the country, the beautiful Eva Perón, had died at the early age of 34. Joséphine found the legend of Eva Perón fascinating. This girl who had risen from poverty to become the most powerful woman in the most powerful country in South America captured her imagination. She wasn't interested in knowing that Evita, adored by many as the the Saint Of The Working Class and the Protector Of The Forsaken, had used her position to recklessly pillage the public purse, spending $40,000 a year on Paris fashions and amassing one of the most valuable collections of jewellery in the world.

When Joséphine made her first appearance, at the Ciné-Opéra Theatre in Buenos Aires, Evita's widower, President Juan Perón, was in the audience. After the show, one of his aides came backstage and said to her: "The general wants to meet you. Be ready tomorrow morning at 11.30."

"We must go," Joséphine said excitedly to Carolyn. "It would be rude if we didn't."

On the following morning, a car was sent to fetch them and they were driven to La Casa Rosada, the pink government house on the Plaza De Mayo, where Perón conducted his business. Ushered into his presence, Joséphine found him to be a handsome man, straight backed and a little above middle height. On the left upper arm of his well-cut suit he was wearing a black band in mourning for his late wife.

Just as Joséphine was fascinated by the legend of Evita, Juan Perón was fascinated by Joséphine. A weak man, in spite of his statesman-like bearing, he was attracted to powerful personalities. Eva had been one, and in Joséphine he recognised another. "My wife followed your career through the newspapers," he told her. "She admired you very much."

He himself had also admired Mussolini, and had built his country into a fascist-inspired police state, a refuge for Nazi war criminals. America was not sympathetic to the Perón regime, and as well as admiring Joséphine he saw in her a useful propaganda tool. He fussed over her, showering her with gifts, and invited her to address a group of workers at an Eva Perón memorial rally. Speaking with burning conviction, Joséphine described Argentina as an "enlightened democracy", praising God for being wise enough to create men like Juan Perón, "a sincere and understanding person" and "an extraordinary man".

Perón's Government Press Office helped to provide her with a platform from which to express her anger and frustration at the way in which she felt that America had treated her. She felt like a saviour rejected. Three articles by her appeared in the newspaper *Critica*, and articles about her appeared in many others. In all of these she railed against the United States, calling it a "barbarous land living in a false, Nazi-style democracy". "As the entire world knows," she said in one piece, "in the Yanqui democracy the negro has no rights whatever," and in another she declared "I have personally seen many lynchings and men and women killed like animals." Referring to Eisenhower, who had just come into office as President, she said "Black people will suffer as they have never suffered...May God have pity on them."

Her remarks were of course reported widely in America, and caused dismay in its black community. The black congressman Adam Clayton Powell, Jr, had no option but to call a press conference to try and repair some of the damage she had done to the cause of civil rights. He castigated her for "deliberate distortion and misrepresentation" of America's racial situation, and stated that she had "completely abolished...any good she may have accomplished in previous years".

In reaction to her remarks, the US Immigration Department issued a public statement saying that if she ever wished to re-enter the country she "would have to prove her right and worth". Joséphine responded to this with a remark that would take her years to live down. "To be barred from the United States," she said, "is an honour." It was a remark that rang around the world.

If Perón was using Joséphine, she was also attempting to use him. More and more her feeling that all races should be treated alike was crystallising into a gospel of world brotherhood. She persuaded Perón to set up the World Cultural Association, which aimed to combat prejudice, with herself as its president.

Still mourning Evita, Perón saw in Joséphine many of the same qualities that he had seen in his wife, not just their rising from poverty and their showbusiness background (although Joséphine was immeasurably more successful in that than Evita had been) but also in their vocabulary. Both constantly spoke of the warm generalities of human concern – freedom, dignity, liberty, love and the heart – words dear to simple kindly folk and to fascist dictators.

Evita's official title had been First Samaritan, and Perón asked Joséphine to take over some of the duties that she had carried out in that position, specifically those associated with the Eva Perón Foundation, which had been set up to build schools, hostels and hospitals. He wanted Joséphine to tour these, especially the hospitals. The tours would be widely publicised, drawing attention to his regime's munificence.

Joséphine agreed enthusiastically, but the tours did not work out as either of them had expected. Unknown to Joséphine, the country had very few first-class hospitals. These were reserved for favoured supporters of the regime and paraded as show places, and it was Perón's intention that she should visit only these. However, the majority of hospitals were old, run down and filthy, poorly staffed and poorly equipped. Some were desperately short of drugs, and even of food. Joséphine, planning her own itinerary, visited many of these and was appalled by the conditions that she found.

She began to realise that the Perón regime was not all that it had seemed. She became increasingly aware of the underlying fear in the community, and of the severe repressiveness exerted by the government. She heard tales of midnight arrests, tortures and disappearances.

Her final disillusionment came when a friend of Jo Bouillon's, living in Buenos Aires, suggested that she made one of her official visits to a particular insane asylum. She went, and Carolyn Carruthers, who went with her, recalled the scene: "The people were treated like animals. They were rolling around the lawn in rags, eating their own filth." Joséphine was sickened and appalled. Suddenly she had had enough of the Americas, both North and South, and headed home to her husband, family and château.

13 *Les Milandes*

Over the next few years, Joséphine worked to turn Les Milandes into not just her home, or simply a tourist centre, but into a little world of her own, where all races would be received as equal. As it developed, it began to take on the air of a small Ruritanian kingdom. Les Milandes had its own flags, and even printed its own postage stamps. These were not accepted as valid by the French postal authorities but they gave visiting tourists (and Joséphine herself) a faint illusion of being in a separate realm.

Its sovereign was, of course, Joséphine. Her image was everywhere. There was the Jorama, of course, with its waxen images recreating key scenes of her life, albeit somewhat fictionalised, with Joséphine as a child, performing in fancy dress for other St Louis children in a cellar; Joséphine dancing the charleston in the banana skirt; Joséphine at the audience she had had with Pope Pius XII in 1950.

Above the door of the theatre was her silhouette in glowing neon. There was a J-shaped swimming pool. Even the wrought-iron grilles over the basement windows bore the initials JB, and in the gardens was a marble sculpture of her, surrounded by children and wearing biblical robes that gave her a passing resemblance to St Francis of Assisi.

The most luxurious room in her hotel, La Chartreuse Des Milandes, was called the Joséphine Room, but she was quick to assure visitors that this referred not to herself but to Napoleon's Joséphine. All of the first-floor rooms in the hotel were named after famous Frenchwomen of fact and fiction – La Pompadour, Du Barry, Camille, Agnès Sorel, Madame de Montespan, Madame Sans-Gàne – just as the second-floor rooms were named after countries, each of which was decorated in the style of the country concerned. The America room, for instance, had a red, white and blue décor and a set of swinging double doors like those from a Western saloon concealing the bidet. The first-floor rooms were naturally more feminine, their décor running more to swathes of pastel chintz and organdie.

It took a little while to establish Les Milandes as a tourist attraction. This was partly because it was ill served by public transport, and during the first years of its existence few people in France had cars, so the majority of its visitors came from the Dordogne neighbourhood. As the prices Joséphine charged at her hotels and restaurants and her theatre were Paris prices, the locals found them a bit steep, and so fewer came than she might have hoped. Then, as the Forties moved into the Fifties and more people bought cars, visitors began to come from further afield, even from abroad. By around 1953, the centre had become well patronised and popular.

During the previous two years, Joséphine had almost entirely given up performing, devoting her attention to Les Milandes. She found jobs on it for her relations. Her sister Margaret helped on the farm, and Margaret's husband, Elmo, maintained and rented out paddle boats on the stretch of the River Dordogne which ran past the estate.

In 1952, Joséphine's brother, Richard, finally decided to come there too, selling his trucking business in St Louis and leaving his wife and son, who was also named Richard. As he was good with vehicles, at first Joséphine employed him as her chauffeur. He was efficient and reliable, and it wasn't long before Joséphine built him something he'd always wanted as a reward: a petrol station of his very own. She had it built on the main road running into the estate, with two Esso pumps and a small garage.

She also had a small house built for him at the foot of the hill on which her château stood. At night he was able to stand in his front yard and look up at its bright lights. Somehow he never felt comfortable about going there. It was Joséphine's place, not his, and he rarely set foot in it except for the family gathering each Christmas.

The one member of the family whom Joséphine did not employ (except for odd tasks here and there) was Carrie, whom she regarded as retired after a lifetime of labour. Carrie lived with Margaret and Elmo in a farmhouse on the estate, and spent her days there quietly. She never learned to speak French, which naturally made her somewhat isolated in the community, but she was contented enough, later admitting that her years at Les Milandes were the happiest of her life. On warm summer days she liked to sit in a rocking chair in the shade of an elm tree that grew beside the château, lost in her own private world. Sometimes tourists would take photographs of her, and if they spoke English she would reply to questions.

One American remembered her telling him that she didn't think that Joséphine had a beautiful body: "Her legs are too long."

In 1953, with Les Milandes now running fairly well, Joséphine once again began to make the odd public appearance. That May she went to Paris and, as so often over the years, appeared at the annual charity evening, Le Bal Des Petits Lits Blancs, this time given at the Moulin Rouge, where she hadn't appeared for years. She wore a flounced, five-tiered, lace-edged skirt which was slashed to the waist to reveal her "too-long" legs. She sang and danced and threw bunches of violets to the crowd, among them Bing Crosby, Gary Cooper, the Aga Khan, Lily Pons and Charlie Chaplin, who in the previous year had found America hostile to him, like Joséphine, and left it after working there for almost 40 years.

At the end of 1953, on 30 December, Joséphine made another trip to Paris to give a speech at the Palais De La Mutualité. It was a simple speech on the theme of racism, entitled "Humilier L'Homme Est Vexer Dieu", and in it she related some of the experiences of her own life.

By now she felt that both she and Les Milandes were ready for the plan that had been growing in her mind for years, by which she hoped to demonstrate to the world – and especially to the USA – that people of all races could live together in harmony. This was a plan that would at the same time assuage her desperate need for children of her own. She and Jo would adopt four children of four different races and religions – one black, one white, one yellow and one red – and raise them together. She even already had a name for this proposed family: it was to be called the Rainbow Tribe.

Jo was agreeable to the plan. Discussing the matter further, they agreed to adopt only boys so that they would avoid any problems in later adolescent years. In the spring of 1954, they arranged for Joséphine to make a tour of Japan, where she would try to adopt a yellow child.

Being Joséphine, she came back with two. Visiting a Tokyo orphanage, she had chosen Akio, a baby approaching two years old who had been abandoned by his Korean mother. (His father had probably been an American soldier of the post-war Occupation.) That was fair enough, but she wasn't even out of the orphanage when she saw another boy, this time half Japanese and half American, and she couldn't resist adopting him too. His name was Tenuya, but she soon changed that to the more easily pronounceable Janot.

This were just the beginning. She embarked on a programme of touring and of collecting orphans, no longer showing any interest in collecting pets. Making a foray to Scandinavia in search of a white child, she found Jari – also almost two – in an orphanage in Helsinki. Going to South America, to Bogotá, she let it be known that she was searching for a black child to adopt. One poor village woman was prepared to let her have one of hers, but when Joséphine took it away many of the villagers seemed upset and later made angry demonstrations. A lawyer advised her to return the child, and explained to her that many members of the village believed that white people stole native babies to drink their blood. Joséphine, astonished, pointed out to him that not only had she no such intention but that she was also not white. He explained to her that to the natives she was. She had money, and only white people have money. Therefore she had to be white.

Shortly afterwards, she was approached by a woman from the nearby town of Homiguero who had eight children. This woman and her husband were finding their large family hard to support, and were prepared to let Joséphine adopt the eighth and youngest.

Even then there was resistance to Joséphine taking him away, again because of fears that she would drink his blood, but eventually it was ruled that she could take him – partly because his mother had offered the child herself, and partly because Joséphine had bought the family a small house and garden in return.

The boy's name was Gustavio Valencia, and in addition Joséphine promised his parents that she would stay in touch with them and bring Gustavio back to visit them from time to time.

Of course, she did no such thing. Any child she adopted was hers and only hers. She changed Gustavio's name to Luis, never let him know his real name and, as his real father later told the Paris *Herald Tribune*, "We never received so much as a phone call or a letter."

She now had four children: two yellow, one white, one black. Akio was Buddhist, Janot was Shintoist, Jari was a Protestant and Luis was Catholic. Racially, all that she still needed to complete the mix was an American Indian, and Jo was slightly disconcerted when one day she came back to Les Milandes from a visit to Paris with a French orphan, Jean-Claude. Jo protested that Jean-Claude was white like Jari and a Catholic like Luis, and not an American Indian, but Joséphine pointed out how unreasonable he was being. "Those are very hard to find," she told him. "You'll just have to be patient."

To lessen Jo's disappointment at Jean-Claude not being an Amerindian, she suggested that they made up for the deficiency by adopting a Jewish boy. After all, the Jewish faith was missing from among their collection of major religions, and what race had suffered more from racism than the Jews?

After some discussion, Jo agreed that they should adopt a Jewish boy, and Joséphine shortly set off to Israel to find one. However, for once she was thwarted. The Israeli government felt that Israel needed every male child it could muster and forbade her to take one out of the country.

This was a setback, but after further discussion with Jo she set off to Paris and, helped by the organisation Legal Aid, was soon back at Les Milandes with a Jewish orphan. She named him Moïse, the Hebrew form of Moses. At ten months old he was the youngest of their adoptees, of whom they now had six.

To obtain money to adopt the children and support them, Joséphine was forced to perform more than she really wanted to at the time. On 10 April 1956, at the Olympia Theatre, she gave what she announced to be her farewell performance in Paris. The first half of the show took the form of a tribute to her on behalf of the major Paris theatres. Singers, dancers and actors from the Folies Bergère, the Casino De Paris, L'Opéra, La Comédie Française, Le Marigny and Le Lido appeared, in each case portraying a scene relating to some aspect of her past career. Among former colleagues of hers who appeared were Paul Colin (who made a sketch of her on-stage), Sidney Bechet (who in 1951 had settled permanently in France, after many years back in the USA) and Henri Varna.

Joséphine, now nearly 50, had rarely looked more regal. Wearing a glittering gold-and-blue strapless dress, and swathed in a floor-length red velvet cloak lined with aquamarine satin, she sang a selection of songs from her past. Of course, these included 'J'ai Deux Amours', but by now she had a second theme song, the melody of which was that of of an old folk song that she had sung from time to time for years. One performance of this song was given to the inmates of Büchenwald, but now it had new words and a new title, 'Dans Mon Village'. In it she sang of Les Milandes, and in it she described each of her children one by one.

Almost every show she would give for the rest of her life resembled this performance. She would sing the songs for which she was famous and reminisce about her life and her performing career while publicising her Rainbow Tribe and crusading for international brotherhood.

A little later in 1956, on 3 June, her brother, Richard, married the post-mistress at Les Milandes, Marie-Louise Dazinière, a woman then in her 50s. It was also Joséphine's own 50th birthday, and the whole family celebrated both events at once.

By now, Les Milandes was at the height of its success as a tourist centre, receiving almost 500,000 visitors a year. Performances by well-known orchestras and dance troupes were presented there, and a lavish procession of fêtes, firework displays and other celebrations were mounted. There was a night club with a dance floor in the château itself.

Having managed to save some money, Joséphine's sister Margaret decided that she wanted to open a tea room on the estate. Joséphine, somewhat resentful of this show of independence, gave her the additional money that she needed but only because she felt sure that the tea room would fail. As things turned out, however, it was a great success. The fare that Margaret provided was of better quality than that supplied by Joséphine's nearby café. She sold homemade pies and American-style ice cream that was richer than French ice cream, and Joséphine began to pressure her into closing down, protesting: "You're stealing my customers." Margaret strong-mindedly refused.

In the advertising for Les Milandes – in brochures, in newspapers and on the radio – there was constant reference to "the Joséphine Baker Children's Camp, a bold experiment in human relations", but Joséphine resisted having her children on display too much, saying that she didn't want them to be regarded as "bêtes curieuses".

She continued to adopt, although at a slightly slower pace. Touring North Africa late in 1956, she returned with two children who had been found hidden under rubble, sole survivors of an air raid during the Algerian War. They weren't related. Brahim was a Berber, and Joséphine would raise him as a Moslem. The other, obviously having French blood, was a girl. Naming her Marianne, Joséphine decided to raise her as a Catholic. Jo wasn't happy about these two new arrivals. He repeatedly tried to explain to Joséphine that she was spending money faster than she was earning it, and that he also felt that six children had been quite enough to cope with.

However, there was no stopping her. During the next year, on another African tour, she visited a hospital and found a black infant there, a boy whose mother had died and who had no known father. His name was Koffi, and she brought him home with her.

At around this time, she also came back from a Belgian tour with a little girl of Hindu blood named Rama. Perhaps in order to avoid another scene with Jo, this time she announced that the child was to be adopted by Margaret and her husband, Elmo, who were childless. Margaret and Elmo were taken aback by this sudden addition to their family, but things turned out well. They quickly came to love Rama, and grew devoted to her.

It wasn't just the growing collection of adopted children that was upsetting Jo at this time. Being the reigning monarch of Les Milandes was causing Joséphine to become more and more autocratic. Demanding more and more control over her domain, she attempted to buy up every house in the village of Milandes. Only two farmers held out against her.

She continually criticised her brother Richard for the way he was running his petrol station, and her increasing high-handedness even upset her mother, who once said to Richard: "I don't think Tumpie loves us any more." She also became more severe with her staff, berating maids or nurses or farm workers in front of others, and more and more she began to treat Jo with something resembling contempt, as she had done with Pepito.

Richard, still occasionally employed as her chauffeur, was sometimes able to see their behaviour together. "She was head over heels in love with Jo," he recalled, "but she was also cruel to him. She talked to him like he was a little kid. She made him miserable. He'd stay in his bedroom for two or three days. He'd hardly eat. And when he came out, he looked like death warmed over."

Being always around at Les Milandes, Jo was in many ways closer to the children than Joséphine was, and this rankled with her. When Akio, the oldest and brightest of their children, was around seven, Jo, who had himself learned the violin young, decided to teach him to play. He bought him a small violin and began giving him lessons. Joséphine resented the two of them sharing something of which she could not be part. Seeing them practice together, she grabbed Akio's violin and cracked it across her thigh.

It began to dawn on Jo that sooner or later he might find her so difficult to live with that he would have to leave. Not strong enough to confront or dominate her directly, he became devious. In collusion with a childhood friend of his who had been appointed manager of one of her hotels, he began to siphon off its profits. Although Jo's motive for doing this was at least partly to provide some financial security for the children, he wasn't the only one stealing from the estate. As the morale of Les Milandes began to slip, many of the staff began to rob it blind. By this time many of them felt that they owed nothing to Joséphine, who would fire people on a whim and was frequently slipshod about paying wages on time.

The general lack of supervision made it easy for them. In Richard's words, "The workers came on motorcycles and left in cars." On one occasion one of her farmworkers came to her and reported that all of her sheep had died of a disease. The odd thing was that nobody could exactly explain what had become of their corpses.

Local shopkeepers shamelessly inflated their prices for her, to such an extent that, when she visited Paris, she would load up her car with groceries, knowing that they were cheaper there, even though the prices were inflated.

In 1957, Joséphine and Jo had yet another blazing row on the subject of her reckless expenditure. Feeling that he was trying to frustrate her crusade, she ordered him to leave. He returned to Paris, and in an interview at the time said: "I abandoned my career as a bandleader to give all my energy to Joséphine's idealism. For ten years I have been a decorator and farmer at Les Milandes. Now I must take up music again. When I am working I shall be able to assure the future of the children myself, but I do not want to divorce because I refuse to destroy, just because of a whim of Joséphine's, the stability of our children's lives."

From Paris, Jo sent five emissaries in succession to Joséphine to plead with Joséphine for a reconciliation, one of them the priest of Castelnaud, a town near Les Milandes. She remained adamant, however, declaring: "I am only doing what I feel is for the best. I have to choose between my husband and my ideals, and it is the ideals I choose. For the first ten years of our marriage Jo and I were mostly apart. The last year spent together has shown me how much we have grown apart. For me, only the spirit is important. Money doesn't count. If Milandes has to go, I shall take the children and sleep in a tent."

She thought of divorcing Jo, but Carrie, still the only person who had any influence at all over her, dissuaded her. At around this time, Joséphine also learned that her previous husband, Jean Lion, had died of the Russian flu at the age of only 47.

The children were now her life, and by now had their own separate dwelling in a converted stable block covered with Virginia creeper. Visitors could come and watch them at play for a small fee, although naturally the children were not keen on being watched and became adept at hiding. With Joséphine so often away, and their lives having been mainly organised by nannies (and Jo, until he left), the atmosphere was more that of a boarding school than of a family home.

All in all, however, their lives weren't too bad. They lived in an amusement park, and were playmates for each other. They also had plenty of countryside to explore, as well as the rooms of the rambling château, and in spite of Joséphine's frequent disappearances, and her consequent slight remoteness, she left them all in no doubt that she loved them, and tended to spoil them when she was there. Returning from each trip away, she brought them such lavish presents that they took to referring to her as "Maman Cadeau". She often frequently took several of them with her on trips, when they would stay in luxurious hotels, which both Carrie and Margaret thought was unsuitable for young children. As with the orphans years before at Le Beau-Chêne, she found herself incapable of telling them off, and always delegated that unpleasant chore to others, unable to face doing anything that might cause them to dislike her.

Their first taste of the world outside their artificial life at Les Milandes came when they attended the village school as day pupils. When the first members of the Rainbow Tribe went there, Joséphine gave them a lavish amount of pocket money. So much, in fact, that the headmaster was moved to protest to her that it was too much. Impulsively, she stopped giving them any at all, with the result that they had to scrounge money from their fellow pupils, which was not at all easy because their fellow pupils were disbelieving: "You, the children of Joséphine Baker, have no money?"

As all of the families living in the neighbourhood were white, naturally the black and oriental members of the Tribe attracted comments from the other pupils. "Not really racist remarks," Jean-Claude later recalled. "It was just what you'd expect from children. But our mother took them as racist and removed us from the school because of that." For the next few years, while they prepared for the exams that would admit them to the *lycée*, they were taught at home by tutors.

In spite of her determination that her Tribe should be of as many religions as possible, the only one of her children to whose religious upbringing she paid much attention was Moïse. While he attended the village school she tried to get him to wear a *yarmulke* (a skullcap worn by orthodox Jewish males). As he was the only Jew in the school, most of whose pupils were, of course, Catholics. Moïse felt odd and ridiculous, and he rebelled. Joséphine spared him the *yarmulke* but insisted that once a week he visited a young Jewish couple in nearby Périgeux, André and Jacqueline Barasche, for proper instruction in the Jewish faith. She told them that her own father had been a Jewish tailor of Polish descent.

When she was on tour in early 1959, while travelling from Rome to Istanbul, she received word that her mother had died. Carrie had been almost 73. On being told, Joséphine recited a saying she remembered hearing as a girl, at funerals back in St Louis: Mama fought the good fight; the battle is over, the victory won.

A little later that year, while touring in Venezuela in around April and still trying to adopt an Amerindian boy, she was arrested in Caracas for attempted kidnap. It turned out to be the result of a misunderstanding. A mother from a nearby village had given her infant to Joséphine for adoption without realising that Joséphine proposed to take him out of the country. When she did understand, she protested to the police. The case was soon dismissed, and the publicity surrounding it caused another mother to come forward and offer Joséphine her baby son to adopt, as she was too poor to feed him herself. The boy's name was Mara, and he was so severely under-nourished that he required careful nursing, but at last Joséphine had her Amerindian child.

On her return to France, she announced that, in order to raise money for her Tribe (which by this time numbered ten), she was making a comeback on the Paris stage. She would star in a show at the Olympia, to be called *Paris Mes Amours*.

She was tireless in rehearsals, working as if possessed, and frequently kept the company at work until well after midnight. So many dancers began turning up late for work from sheer exhaustion that the Olympia's director, Bruno Coquatrix, at one stage gave the entire company two days off on full pay to recover.

The show opened in May 1959, and from it Joséphine acquired several new songs for her repertoire. As well as the title song, there was the wicked calypso '(Don't Touch Me) Tomato', during which she tossed all manner of fruit and vegetables to the audience while dressed in a full-skirted, flounced West Indian costume. There was also a fortune-telling number, 'Donnez-Moi La Main', for which she wore an elaborately-decorated gypsy costume, and there was also a delightful number called 'Avec', which she would frequently use as entrance music in shows for the rest of her career.

But the most dramatic number in the show, the number with which she closed, on many nights moving the audience (and herself) to tears, was again 'Dans Mon Village'. According to Janet Flanner, *The New Yorker*'s Paris correspondent who had been reviewing her shows since 1925, her voice was now "better trained…richer and truer than ever before".

The show ran for the rest of 1959, and it was so enormously successful that, when word of it reached America, there was discussion of her being given a role in her old friend Langston Hughes' play *Tambourines To Glory*. Unfortunately nothing came of this, but she did receive another offer from America, which was to make a short tour in a show of her own, opening at the Huntingdon Hartford Theater in San Francisco in April 1960.

While she was appearing in *Paris Mes Amours*, back at Les Milandes her brother Richard left his wife, Marie-Louise. She had turned out to be something of a gold digger, whose main concern seemed to be the small fortune she expected that he would eventually inherit from his sister. Their marriage turned sour, and Richard – impelled, as he later admitted, by despair as well as desire – left her and moved in with a woman from the village, "a wild-eyed peasant" by the name of Yvonne. At once they set about producing a family of their own in the conventional manner.

It was also at around this time that Richard decided to take no more guff from Joséphine about how he was running the petrol station. From now on, he decided, he would run it his own way, and that was that.

Joséphine and Jo, in spite of their separation, had remained on fairly good terms. He had formed a new band in Paris, and during the run of *Paris Mes Amours* she teamed up with the cast in a recording studio and they laid down an album.

Shortly afterwards, out of concern for the children's welfare, she and Jo agreed that he should return to Les Milandes, and they would try once again to make a go of their marriage. Unfortunately, it didn't work out; their relationship turned out to have been damaged beyond repair.

While they were still in this trial period, at Christmas 1959 a baby boy was found by a tramp in a Paris dustbin. The story was widely reported, and Joséphine heard about it. At once she turned up at the Paris hospital where the baby was being cared for and arranged for him to be transferred to Les Milandes. Naturally she named him Noël.

Jo's heart must have sunk, but whether the arrival of an eleventh child was the last straw or not, soon afterwards he moved back to Paris. Still they did not divorce, and he continued to keep in touch with the children, whose surname, after all, was Bouillon. Before long he emigrated to

Buenos Aires and opened a French restaurant, but even while there he would continue to keep in touch with the family. Members of the Tribe would make trips to Argentina to visit him, and eventually four of them would move there permanently.

It was at around this time that, while she was staying in the Hôtel Scribe in Paris, Joséphine met the boy who would become a sort of unofficially adopted child to her. A few years older than the members of the Rainbow Tribe, being 14 when she met him, he was another Jean-Claude: Jean-Claude Rouzaud. A handsome, dark-haired boy, he had been born in the small village of Saint-Symphorien, near Lyon. His father, a restaurateur, had gambled away all of his money and then deserted Jean-Claude and his mother, who lapsed into broken-hearted despair. Desperately hard up, they became dependent on the charity of friends and neighbours until Jean-Claude eventually escaped from their poverty and headed for Paris to find work. He was working at the Hôtel Scribe as a *chasseur* (something between a commissionaire and a porter), helping guests through the revolving doors and carrying their luggage.

One day he ran an errand for Joséphine. With her quick perception of people, she at once spotted that he was feeling somewhat lost. "Where's your father?" she asked him. "Where's your mother? What are you doing in Paris all alone?" He told her his story, and she impulsively put her arm around him, kissed him, and said: "You'll never be alone again. I'm your mother now."

It was the beginning of one of the more satisfactory relationships in her life. Jean-Claude adored her without reserve, both for the glamour that surrounded her and for her strength of character, which was so different from the weaknesses of his own mother.

Joséphine, for her part, fed from the unqualified admiration of the handsome young man, and whole-heartedly adopted the role of his guide and mentor in the world of glamour and high living. Over the years she would pay for him to attend a hotel school in England, both to learn a trade and to learn English. They would frequently travel together, often to exotic places like Acapulco and Rio De Janeiro, and he would become a kind of wise older brother to the Rainbow Tribe.

On 26 April 1960, as arranged, Joséphine opened her show in San Francisco. Her troubles in America in 1951 seemed to have been forgotten, and she easily obtained a visa to travel there. The show was a success, taking

$10,700 during its first three days, although *Variety* commented: "Some of her confidences to spectators are inclined to be drawn out and tiresome, including constant references to 'being allowed in'."

She had obviously not forgotten her previous troubles, and it turned out that neither had many Americans. When she opened at her next venue, in Chicago, some papers began to rake over the ashes of the old conflagration. The New York publication *Journal America*, for instance, wrote: "Any honest reporter or clap-trap columnist could find material in any fairly good newspaper morgue showing why she should be banned."

At this time in her life, it was noticeable that Joséphine was becoming increasingly devious about money. This arose partly from concern about her increasingly rocky financial situation, and partly from her enjoyment of making a splash no matter what the cost. She reverted more and more to her old habit of cheating people as a sort of revenge on the world for the rough deal which she felt that she was being handed in life.

Her tour had been organised by the promoter William C Taub, and her shows were staged by an ex-pupil of Katherine Dunham's, Stephen Papich. Papich later recalled one example of her behaviour. "I was aware at the time that Joséphine was nearly broke," he wrote. "In order for her to come to America at all, I knew that Bill would have to advance substantial amounts of money to her. She needed a new wardrobe. She had the most pressing obligations to meet before she could come over, and then there were the transportation expenses – particularly for her vast amount of personal and theatrical baggage, which had to come by air – so there is no doubt that Bill did advance her a considerable sum of money. Much later Joséphine denied that he had done so. I let it go at that."

Bill Taub, it appears, was not the only one who felt that Joséphine owed them money. Towards the end of May, shortly before she was due to open in New York, he and four others got together and sued her in the Federal Court for the sum of $157,000.

There was a brief gap in Joséphine's schedule before her proposed appearance in New York appearance, and she used it to cross the border into Canada and perform a show in Montreal. While she was there, Bill Taub succeeded in having her arrested on the somewhat contrived charge that she had stolen her own musical arrangements, some men's straw hats and some furs. All of the cases were eventually either dropped or dismissed, but Joséphine's New York booking was cancelled. She returned to the

Olympia in Paris, where she almost immediately appeared in a revival of *Paris Mes Amours*.

Now that Jo was no longer at Les Milandes to keep some sort of control of its affairs, Joséphines financial situation grew worse and worse. She did what she could to help by asking local businesses for credit and then putting off paying for as long as possible. The effect of this was that the attitude of the locals to her, which had already shifted from enthusiasm and interest to suspicion and greed, now moved to near hostility.

In 1961, however, Les Milandes was the scene of one happy event. There Joséphine was publicly awarded the Légion D'Honneur by General de Gaulle, president of the Fifth Republic since 1959, and while he didn't come to Les Milandes to present it to her personally he once again sent her a personal letter of congratulations, expressing good wishes from himself and from Madame de Gaulle.

Joséphine continued to publicise Les Milandes, her Rainbow Tribe and her ideas of world brotherhood whenever and wherever she could, turning her life into an ongoing soap opera that was avidly followed by her many fans. She continued to tour doggedly in order to raise money, taking on any advertising work that she could (she and the Tribe appeared in a series of ads for the soft drinks firm Pschitt, in which the Tribe appeared somewhat ill at ease) and presenting attractions at Les Milandes. In the early summer of 1962 she mounted a "Festival Of Jazz And Twist" there, and a little later, in August, enjoyed considerable personal success there in fulfilling a long-held ambition by appearing in an out-and-out dramatic role.

The piece was *L'Arlésienne* by Alphonse Daudet, with music by Bizet, and Joséphine presented it as a single open-air performance in the courtyard of her château, installing seating to accommodate an audience of 1,500. She played the heroine, Rose Mamaï, a mother who loves her son more than herself but is unable to save his life. As insurance, in case her acting was insufficient to carry the show, Joséphine made it as spectacular as possible. She wore a genuine 19th-century Arlesian lace dress, and she imported twelve tambourine players and 21 Farandole dancers from Provence. There were flambeaux and elaborate lighting effects, and the voices of the actors and Bizet's music were all pre-recorded, giving the presentation a feeling of *son et lumière*.

The production was a considerable success. The critic of *L'Aurore* wrote: "She has unquestionably made her mark on the character, a rough, human performance full of guts. At the end, as she leans over the corpse of Frédéric, she lets out a piercing cry that will stay in the memory of all who beheld it." Her personal triumph in the piece, with that wrenching last cry, encouraged her so much that on the following day she wrote to Jo, telling him that she felt as if it represented a new beginning for her. She arranged with Bruno Coquatrix for the production to be transferred to the Olympia in Paris, where, lacking the flambeaux and the outdoor setting and with the cast's lines no longer pre-recorded, it flopped badly and quickly closed.

Also in 1962 she adopted her final child. Encouraged by her daughter Marianne, who felt somewhat isolated at being the only girl among a horde of brothers, she adopted a sister for her. Born in France of a Moroccan mother, Joséphine named the new arrival Stellina, in memory of a little girl she had once tried to adopt from an Italian orphanage but whose mother had reclaimed her first. Although Joséphine and Jo were now living apart, they were still married, and he also signed the papers as Stellina's adoptive father, so now they had twelve children: Akio, Janot, Jari, Luis, Jean-Claude, Moïse, Brahim, Marianne, Koffi, Mara, Noël and Stellina.

Between 1953 and 1963, it was estimated that Joséphine had lost 7F and a half million at Les Milandes, and by the end of that time was some 2F million in debt. In her efforts to raise cash she went to Paris and began to sell off her jewels, including the diamond-studded choker she had bought years ago for Chiquita. This caused her surprisingly little grief – Les Milandes was now more important to her than all the jewels in the world, and she would save it at any cost.

Another possible source of income was always her life story. One person who hoped to write it was the poet Langston Hughes. On 8 January 1963, an American friend of his, Arna Bontemps, wrote to him on hearing that he was considering this project. "You are the ideal person to do the Joséphine Baker book. I hope you waste no time getting to it. Her differences with the US press (or a section of it) may hurt her personal appearances here, but I can't imagine this harming the book; it should help. The warm element of controversy combined with the warm element of sex and no strings and the French flavour! This could be your first best-seller as well as a solid possibility for serialisation, etc. So I urge again, let no grass grow, etc."

In 1964, once more in America, Joséphine was still trying to involve Langston Hughes in writing about her life, but now as part of a team of three authors. Her idea was that Langston should write about her childhood, that another author – possibly herself – should write about her professional career, and that the more crusading black writer James Baldwin should write about what she called her "revolutionary side" (her war service, her work for civil rights and the Rainbow Tribe). "Three Negros writing about a Negro woman's life" was the way she put it to an interviewer, adding: "There will be three books because my life is so full." This project fell through, though, for reasons that were never made clear. A possible explanation is that Joséphine had already become notorious in the American publishing world.

Also in 1964, in America, she entered into discussions with yet another author, Gerold Frank, about his writing her life. These discussions led to the pair of them signing a letter of agreement, which his agent, Helen Straus, sent to various publishing houses. Their reactions came as a shock to Gerold Frank. None of them was interested because Joséphine had apparently been taking advances from publishers for years, promising them biographies that always failed to materialise.

By June 1963, her creditors threatened her with the compulsory sale of her château and its contents, but in spite of her financial problems Joséphine continued to have moments of wonderful optimism. It occurred to her that her situation at Les Milandes did not represent a defeat, but was instead a God-given chance for a new beginning. If she was to teach the world about international brotherhood, why stop at a dozen children living in harmony? Why not hundreds? They wouldn't live there permanently as adoptees but would come to Les Milandes as students of all races, and then leave to spread its message across the world.

The students would be in their mid to late teens, and Les Milandes would become an International College Of Brotherhood. "We'll have a series of professors from different countries," she told a reporter, "of all colours and religions and all standards of life to teach the essentials of brotherhood...The students must be able to have board and education without having to worry about the cost...The future of the village will depend on the world's heartbeats."

Soon she was presented with a good opportunity to raise some money for this project, as well as bringing it publicity. She was approached by a black American producer, Jack Jordan, who had been involved in presenting her shows in America in 1960 and now asked her to appear at a demonstration planned to take place in Washington, DC, on 28 August 1963.

Since John F Kennedy had become president in 1960, there had been a new feeling of change and optimism in America, and this had encouraged a new optimism in the civil rights movement. The planned demonstration would show the politicians in Washington the growing power and determination of black pressure groups, and with it they would campaign for a bill ensuring jobs and freedom for blacks. During the same visit, Joséphine would star in four benefit concerts at Carnegie Hall, and the proceeds would be divided between the NAACP, three other civil rights charities and what was described as "Miss Baker's international children's camp".

Jack Jordan had found a backer to put up $15,000 to mount these concerts, but he then ran into a couple of problems. The first was that, on this occasion, Joséphine had trouble in obtaining a US visa. Whether this was because someone had become uneasy at the prospect of her attending a civil rights rally or not, her application was refused. It was only by applying directly to the attorney general, Bobby Kennedy, that the problem was solved. He ruled that she should be admitted, and she was touched and grateful.

The other problem was finding someone to handle Joséphine's publicity. Bill Taub was not the only one who had had unfortunate financial dealings with Joséphine. She had a long history of weaseling such people as promoters, managers and publicity agents out of their commissions, usually by retreating into a sort of fog of vagueness. "He wasn't really my manager. He claimed he worked for me...I'm not a *femme d'affaires*; I'm a humanitarian." As a result, Jack Jordan had difficulty in finding anyone to take on the job.

At last, through the NAACP, a man was found. His name was Henri Ghent and he had come from a dirt-poor black family in Georgia, the youngest of eleven children. Strong and handsome, he had been blessed with a good singing voice, and after training at the New England Conservatory Of Music he had eventually enjoyed a successful 15-year career as a classical singer, most of it spent in France, where he developed an urbane continental *savoir-faire*. Now back in America, he wrote promotional material for Columbia Records, and when John Morsell of the NAACP approached him he agreed to handle Joséphine's publicity as a favour to the movement. "No top PR person in New York will touch her," Morsell had told him.

He had once been introduced to Joséphine in Paris, but when he walked into her suite at the New York Hilton he failed to recognise her. What he saw as he entered was a plain black woman, huddled in an Indian shawl, talking on the telephone. Beneath the shawl she was wearing a knee-length white flannel nightshirt, and her legs were swathed in pink elastic bandages to keep them warm. She was also almost bald, her skull covered only with a thin layer of pure white fuzz. A black wig rested on a table beside her. "At first I though this must be some relative from St Louis," he recalled later. "Then I realised it was Joséphine. Later she told me that she used lye to 'conk' her hair and it had destroyed the follicles."

When she put down the phone and rose to greet him, she was aware that he was shocked by her appearance. Stretching out her arms and thrusting her hips forward she said: "Showbusiness is all illusion...all illusion."

In spite of her bravado, Henri sensed fear and uncertainty in her, along with a desperation to win back her American public. He shrewdly decided that the way to sell her to the public for her Carnegie Hall appearances was as an artiste rather than as a music hall performer. He arranged a press conference, and advised her to speak only French at it, telling her: "You sound so refined *en Français*." He arranged that he would translate for her (and in that way he would be able to edit out any unguarded comments that she might make).

The press conference went well, and that night the two of them took a cab uptown to dine with friends. As they sped up Seventh Avenue towards Harlem, Joséphine put her hand on his knee. "Oh, Henri," she said, "it's so good to be home."

"Down deep in her heart," Henri remembered, "she was never anything but a black American."

The demonstration, later famous as the March On Washington, became the largest civil rights demonstration in American history. Black and white protesters flooded into Washington. At 4.30 that morning, 450 chartered buses set off for there from Harlem. Fourteen special trains were dispatched from New York's Pennsylvania Station. People flew in from Los Angeles, from Seattle, from all over America. By eleven in the morning, 90,000 people were assembled in front of the Lincoln Memorial. By early afternoon, when the proceedings began, there were 200,000.

The proceedings began with a series of singers, all there to demonstrate their solidarity with the cause. Odetta, Josh White, Bobby Darin, Bob Dylan, Joan Baez and Peter, Paul And Mary all performed.

Joséphine was on the platform among the group of performers and principal speakers, proudly wearing her Air Force uniform and deeply moved, as she later said, by the sight of all those thousands of people, "united as in a common dream".

Asked to speak herself, she told the crowd: "You are on the eve of a complete victory. You can't go wrong. The world is behind you." Looking at the throng of faces of all shades, she said happily: "Salt and pepper. Just what it should be."

It was noted at the time that, among the speakers, two were the most hopeful. Joséphine was one, and the other was of course Martin Luther King. This was the day on which he delivered the most famous speech of his life, which included the words:

"I have a dream that one day on the red hills of Georgia the sons of former slaves and the sons of former slave owners will be able to sit down together at the table of brotherhood...I have a dream that my four little children will one day live in a nation where they will not be judged by the colour of their skin but by the content of their character."

Joséphine, almost alone among the crowd, was not entirely happy with this speech. She told her nephew Richard (the son of her brother, Richard): "He wasn't strong enough. He should have put his foot down and demanded rights for black people. I could have done it better."

Nonetheless, she was delighted with the progress that America was making in the field of civil rights, and proud to have been part of it. Of course she also continued to be part of it, although those leading the fight were not so sure of her. The older members remembered her foolish and harmful remarks when visiting Juan Perón in 1951, and the younger members – ignorant of the good work she had done back then – were not entirely sure who she was. Some militant young blacks blamed her for coming back to America when the hard part of the battle was over, branding her "a beneficiary of others' pain and blood".

Her Carnegie Hall concerts helped to restore her image. The first took place on 12 October 1963, and they were all a huge success, probably the biggest shows she ever had – or ever would have – in America.

This was the era when the styles of fashion were heavily influenced by the president's wife, Jackie Kennedy, who favoured clean, simple, almost severe lines. Joséphine's show costumes were defiantly different. They were exuberantly feminine, exaggerating her hips and bust and narrowing her waist, a riot of sequins and curves and feathers. To conceal the effects of age in her face, the wrinkled forehead and the bags under the eyes, she wore a dusting of glitter under her eyes, across the bridge of her nose and even on her lips. "Not bad for 60, huh?" was her opening line. (She was actually 57.)

On reviewing her performance for *The New York Times*, John S Wilson wrote: "Every phrase she sang, every word she spoke, was delivered with an unfailing sense of theatrical values...She brought the hall alive with excitement the moment she stepped on the stage and that excitement never diminished until she finally retired after receiving a roaring tribute of approval that brought the entire audience to its feet and led many to rush to the footlights to shake her hand."

On the streets of New York, people stopped her to ask for her autograph. Bruno Coquatrix contacted her from Paris to tell her that he was planning a production based on the book *La Dame Aux Camélias* by Alexandre Dumas, Fils, and asked her if she would star in it, performing in French in Paris and in English in New York. Jack Jordan was also able to set up a string of further American bookings for her.

She was still in America on 22 November 1963, the day on which John F Kennedy was shot, and like most Americans she was numbed, especially in the light of her grateful feelings towards his brother, Bobby. She sent a brief cable to Jo Bouillon, who by then had emigrated to Buenos Aires. It simply said: "Our world is toppling. Affectionately yours."

Like others before him, Henri Ghent was having difficulty in getting Joséphine to pay him his fee and was finding her increasingly elusive. He finally managed to confront her in the lobby of the Essex Hotel. "She had just moved over from the Hilton," he recalled. "She skipped out of there without paying her bill." When he asked her to pay him, she simply pretended that he didn't exist. Not by ignoring him, he explained later, but by regally dismissing him. "When she put on her prima donna act," he said, "she diminished the other person. You weren't aware that your legs had been cut from under you until you started to walk."

With Henri, however, this tactic failed to work. Growing furious, he shook his fist in her face, yelling: "I don't go for this star shit. Two weeks ago you were hungry. I gave you back the American public and I'll take 'em right back." She still didn't pay, and so he phoned *The Amsterdam News* and persuaded them to publish an article in which it was written that he was about to sue Joséphine. That at last did the trick, and she paid him.

She also replaced him early in 1964 with a successful theatrical publicist who had worked for the film and Broadway star Rosalind Russell. Her name was Shirley Hertz, and while she was aware of Joséphine's penchant for financial misdealing she also had a great admiration for her talent. "I've known many stars with a glow," she once said, "but Joséphine had a fire the likes of which I have never seen." With Shirley Hertz handling her publicity, Joséphine played the Strand and Brooks Atkinson Theaters in New York, and went on to tour other cities in both America and Canada.

Shirley managed to keep getting paid, but outwitting the people to whom Joséphine owed money was a constant feature of the tour. In Philadelphia, after having failed to get their money, a group of her creditors planned to seize her expensive wardrobe. Shirley and Joséphine, getting wind of this, fled through the revolving doors of their hotel while the marshal was coming in through another entrance. "We had to get them out of Pennsylvania," remembered Shirley, "so we took the costumes to the 30th Street station and gave them to a porter on the train. We didn't have a claim check. Nothing. Then we called a friend in New York and asked her to run over to Penn Station and meet the train."

With Joséphine in her shows were a couple of talented black dancers, Geoffrey Holder and his wife, Carmen de Lavallade. Geoffrey had grown up in Trinidad, and he was one of those blacks to whom Joséphine had been an idol and an inspiration for years. He couldn't believe how lucky he was to work with her, and was amazed and delighted by how little she played the prima donna while working. He found her easy to get on with, and was further impressed by her professional discipline. At the end of her finale, for instance, she never moved from her position onstage until the orchestra had finished playing her theme, even after the curtain had fallen. Nor, on one occasion, would she leave the stage after the show without apologising to the conductor for having been off key.

Joséphine, for her part, was impressed by Geoffrey's and his wife's dancing. Describing his approach to dance, Geoffrey once said: "I don't study. I understand dance, I understand music. I suppose I have learned from observation, from theatrical analysis...I want a performance. I want a dancer to be like a child playing games in the park." His approach was therefore remarkably similar to Joséphine's. During the shows, Geoffrey would take turns dancing with Carmen and with Joséphine, each woman attempting to top what the other had done in a spirit of friendly rivalry, spurring each other on like musicians in a jam session.

Joséphine enjoyed working with them both so much that, when she returned to France in the late spring of 1964, she took them with her, having arranged with Bruno Coquatrix for them to appear in her new show at the Olympia.

Arriving back at Orly Airport on a Monday at 10.30pm, Joséphine took an overnight train to Les Milandes at once, arriving there at 7.30 the following morning. She spent a day assessing the situation – her creditors were still attempting to force her to sell her château and its contents – before travelling back to Paris to begin rehearsals with Geoffrey and Carmen.

She saw Carmen as being her natural successor. "Paris is going to love you like they loved me 40 years ago," she told Carmen on the opening night. "I can't go on like this. I need somebody to take my place."

While nothing like the sensation Joséphine had been in the Twenties, the Holders were received rapturously, the newspapers calling them "a royal gift" from Joséphine to the French public. They also observed how generous and self-effacing it was of Joséphine to bring onstage with her someone as young, lovely and talented as Carmen de Lavallade.

While the show was running, things at Les Milandes continued to deteriorate. Not only were Joséphine's creditors pressing her for 2F million; in June 1964 it was further reported that her electricity, gas and water had been cut off. Thus, in the height of the summer season, she had been forced to close her restaurants and bars.

She invited a group of bankers, philanthropists and old friends to attend a meeting at Les Milandes in order to discuss strategy, and one result of this was that Brigitte Bardot – who was then at the height of her fame – appeared in a television appeal asking for donations to help pay off Joséphine's debts. Dozens of letters from France and from abroad began to arrive at Les Milandes, most containing small contributions but some with sizeable sums. One such came from Empress Farah Dibah of Iran.

In addition to this, a benefit performance was held at the Théâtre Des Champs-Elysées, starring Yvette Cahuviré, Marcel Marceau, Rosella

Hightower and André Prokowski, and this raised her a considerable sum. Some friends set up a committee in order to try and handle her affairs, headed by the well-known author André Maurois, and armed with the amount that had been raised she was able to arrange for a Swiss bank to lend her enough money to stave off the threatened auction. On the committee's advice, she also set a sizeable sum aside in a fund to protect her children's future.

However, the strain and worry had at last taken their toll. On 25 July 1964, she had a heart attack. Although not too serious, it put her in hospital for a couple of weeks, and when she was released she went with her family to Juan-Les-Pins, on the Côte D'Azur, for a few extra days of rest.

Her life continued to be hard, however, and became a constant round of engagements, performing where she could (often in Scandinavia, where she had become popular in the late Twenties and never stopped being so), attending conferences to campaign for racial tolerance and to publicise the College Of Brotherhood which she still hoped to found, juggling her finances, and trying to manage her Tribe, who as they moved into their teens naturally provided the usual teenage problems. Had one of the boys been stealing? Was one of the girls sleeping with someone?

On one occasion she was shocked to hear Jean-Claude boasting to Moïse that, being white, he was superior to blacks, who were dirty, lazy and stupid. One of her children a racist? What had gone wrong? After much thought she decided that Jean-Claude must have suffered from outside influences, but for a time it worried her deeply. Had she been wrong in assembling her Rainbow Tribe?

The raciness of her own past worried her at times, too. At one time a television programme showed a clip of film of her dancing the banana dance, and at once she rushed over to switch it off. She wasn't even quite sure about the suitability of her performances in the Sixties for children. In 1966, it was briefly suggested that she should appear in Franz Lehar's *The Merry Widow* in Paris, and although nothing came of the suggestion she was attracted to the idea because for once she would have been in something that her children could watch.

In early November 1965, she was again threatened by her creditors, who demanded 25,000F on pain of her château and its contents being forcibly auctioned. Desperate, she made a quick trip to Fez, Morocco, to beg the help of King Hassan II. He came through like the monarch he was, giving her a cheque for 30,000F and promising her an annual donation of 100,000F per year.

In July 1966 she was invited to Cuba by Fidel Castro, who in 1959 had succeeded in seizing power in the country. He wanted her to visit there and appear at the seventh anniversary celebrations of his revolution. He offered to pay for her travel expenses and to provide accommodation for her and some of her children. Joséphine went with several children, and they were duly housed in a beautiful villa by the sea, about ten miles from Havana. The trip was idyllic. Joséphine gave a speech in Havana, and sang for some workers in the sugar cane fields.

After leaving Cuba, she and her children made a short visit to Mexico City, then to Bogotá, and then on to Buenos Aires, where they had a reunion with Jo. Now that he and Joséphine were separated, even though they were still married, the ferocious arguments that had sprung up during the latter part of their marriage did not recur, and the visit was peaceful. He would even return to the château for a visit at the end of 1966, in order to spend Christmas with Joséphine and the Tribe.

In spite of having such a restful and enjoyable trip, almost immediately after returning to France Joséphine was hospitalised with a recurrence of her old intestinal problems. The hospital was in the Paris suburb of Neuilly, and there she underwent a five-hour operation in which, as a friend said, "They took out everything but her heart and liver."

While recovering, and still concerned about her finances, it occurred to her that Castro – who had been so generous with the expenses for her trip to Cuba – might be disposed to help. She wrote him a long, plaintive letter, illustrating her desperate situation and hinting (only hinting) that a cheque would be much appreciated.

He replied at once, writing: "I'm going to send you a present." He did. Some days later, the postman, whom she had eagerly been looking out for every day, delivered two dozen oranges and six grapefruit.

Les Milandes became increasingly run down, and although it still continued to attract a trickle of visitors, Joséphine was forced to lay off more and more staff. Several times these cutbacks included nannies, and some of the children found this upsetting, especially the younger ones. With Jo gone and Joséphine often away, their nannies were the nearest thing to dependable adults that they had in their world.

She could have helped her situation somewhat by selling off some of her land, but this she doggedly refused to do, partly because it was hers and partly because she still intended to transform Les Milandes into an international college. In 1967, she even invited a group of Danish architects to stay there for a month and develop a feasible plan for the transformation. It was understood from the start that preparing this plan would be done for a fee, not as a work of charity, but although she wined and dined them for the duration of their stay, during which they did a great deal of expensive design work, Joséphine succeeded in avoiding to pay them a penny.

Early in 1968, her creditors actually succeeded in getting Les Milandes sold, but the director of the Olympia, Bruno Coquatrix (who was by now strongly active on Joséphine's behalf), managed to have the sale annulled. Her creditors agreed to give her until May to come up with a sum of somewhere around 2,500,000F. To help her, Bruno went out of his way to allow her to star in a show at Olympia, although personally he felt that she would do far better by getting rid of her estate. As far as he could see, it was a bottomless pit.

The show didn't help her enough. The estate was sold again in May, fetching considerably less than it was worth. Many locals around Les Milandes were bitterly anti-Joséphine by this time, and her eldest son, Akio, who was 16 at the time, attended the sale and felt that her creditors went after her property like "ferocious animals". Bruno tried to have this sale annulled as well, but this time he failed. Joséphine had lost her château, although there was still the faint hope that, if she made enough money from her show, she might be able to bid to buy it back.

1968 was the big year of student unrest in Paris, the year in which students all around the world returned from the placid attitudes of hippiedom to a new and more heated political activism. Riots on the Parisian streets in that same May caused the Olympia to close down Joséphine's show for a few weeks, and while it was closed she bravely took the risk of alienating some of her public by taking part in a march down the Champs-Elysées in support of her old hero, President Charles de Gaulle, whose nationalist and right-wing views were anathema to the rioting students.

It was only a few days after she took part in this march that another of her heroes, Bobby Kennedy, was assassinated on 6 June 1968. She decided at once that she absolutely had to fly to the States to attend his funeral, taking five of her sons with her. This decision – which to him simply meant squandering the money that she was earning from his show – made Bruno Coquatrix almost despair of her. (Curiously, the assasination of Martin Luther King in the previous April had seemed to affect her little.)

Returning to Paris after Bobby Kennedy's funeral, she resumed the run of her show. In July she had a mild stroke but managed to carry on a few weeks to the end of the run before collapsing. She was then taken to hospital, and after she had sufficiently recovered she went with her whole family for a short holiday in Algeria to recuperate.

She was still technically living at Les Milandes, although now under the threat of eviction by the new owners. On 22 September, she was actually served with an eviction notice, but managed to persuade a local court to postpone the date until December. Because French law forbade evictions during the colder days between 15 October and 15 March, this meant that in effect she would be able to stay there until the spring.

She continued to live there for a while, with all of her children. It was reported that the new owners had had the electricity and water supplies turned off, and so for heating the children gathered fallen branches and they all huddled around a single fireplace. The new owners insisted indignantly that they had done no such thing, and that, as they had not taken possession, they had no way of turning off the electricity and water, and if Joséphine was having trouble with the heating and washing facilities it was because she had removed all of the fixtures – the sinks, taps and radiators – and sold them. They also accused her of keeping the children in such primitive conditions entirely for show, when she and they could quite easily have gone to live in relative comfort with her sister, Margaret, who still owned her house in the village.

Her brother, Richard, had long since packed up and moved away, unable to stand his sister's domineering ways any longer. The way he saw it, "She was always talkin' 'bout liberty, equality and fraternity, but she'd tell everybody what to do."

At last, in early 1969, Joséphine left Les Milandes without a fuss and moved with her children into a cramped two-bedroom apartment in Paris which had been lent to her by her friend Marie Spiers, the wife of her then accompanist and arranger. Her eldest boys were already boarding at a Paris *lycée*. It was a severely Catholic one, and they didn't like it much – nothing but prayers, complained Brahim.

Joséphine began preparations to open in cabaret at a restaurant called La Gouloue, which had recently been bought by the film actor Jean-Claude Brialy. He didn't know Joséphine well, but he had generously taken over the premises in order to give her a venue. Before she could open there, however, she received word that the new owners of Les Milandes were proposing to actually take possession, even though 15 March had not yet arrived.

Immediately returning to her château, she barricaded herself into its kitchen. Still vainly hoping to have the sale declared illegal, she gave interviews to the papers about her miserable situation, having herself photographed clambering in through the kitchen window and claiming that the new owners refused to speak to her. They replied that the miserable situation was all her own fault, that had been her decision to barricade herself in the kitchen rather than remain in a comfortable flat in Paris.

On Wednesday 12 March 1969, three days before she was legally required to leave, they suddenly took drastic action. At seven am, eight sturdy men sent by them forced their way into the house and, although Joséphine fought bitterly, manhandled her out of it, picking her up by her arms and legs, wrenching her shoulder and banging her head against the stove. She was still in her dressing gown, and had a plastic shower cap on her head. Dressed like this, barefoot and with a rug around her knees, she sat on the front steps of her château all day, surrounded by a pitiful collection of tins and bottles and cardboard boxes, numb with misery.

Someone concerned for her, and feeling that a wrong had been done to her, sought out a judge from the local tribunal, and towards the end of the day the judge decided against the new owners and ruled that Joséphine should be allowed to re-enter the château and could remain there for another three days.

By this time, however, she had collapsed on the steps from sheer exhaustion. An ambulance was summoned and she was taken to the hospital in nearby Périgueux.

14 *Here I Go Again*

In spite of having lost the estate that she had fought so long and hard to save, and in spite of having collapsed from exhaustion, Joséphine's formidable resilience again came to her aid. Two weeks after her collapse, on Thursday 27 March 1969, she gave the opening performance of her planned season at La Gouloue, renamed Chez Joséphine for the duration of her stay. On that opening night many famous performers showed up to give her moral support, some of whom she was only barely acquainted with. Among them were Anna Magnani, Catherine Deneuve, Françoise Sagan, Marc Bohan and Ludmilla Tcherina. She appeared there for 57 performances, playing every night of the week except Monday (when the restaurant was closed) and letting it be known that on Mondays she was available for bookings elsewhere.

She also continued to find money in any way she could. Returning to Paris from a brief trip away, she landed at Orly airport. While waiting at the carousel to collect her luggage she spied two English friends also waiting for their luggage a few carousels away. Their names were Jack Hockett and Peter Barrett and they were partners in a ticket agency in London's Shaftesbury Avenue. They had known Joséphine since 1959, when, having been to see her perform at the Olympia, they had made themselves known to her at the stage door. Always delighted to meet people who spoke English, and pleased that they were connected with the theatre, she had greeted them warmly and declared that from now on they would be "her little English boys".

She had remained friendly with them over the years until, about six months before her arrival at Orly, Jack Hockett, hearing that she had been appearing in Copenhagen, had gone there to spend a few days with her. He didn't get to spend a few days there. Within 36 hours he was back in London, spluttering: "That woman!" His partner, Peter Barrett, never exactly found out what had happened, although his guess was that she had done something like sticking Jack with the restaurant bill for a party she had hosted.

Whatever the reason, Jack was furious with her, and had remained furious for six months. Joséphine being Joséphine, her presence at Orly naturally caused a stir, and Peter Barrett, noticing the commotion, said to Jack: "You'll never believe it, but look who's over there."

Jack replied: "I know. I saw her. Don't look. Take no notice."

Peter said: "Jack, what a perfect opportunity to make up." But Jack insisted that they turned their backs. Then Jack felt a tap on his shoulder and there was Joséphine. "Jack, you naughty, naughty boy."

It turned out that she was staying with her sister, Margaret, who was then living in an outer suburb of Paris, and she urged Jack and Peter to come with her and meet her. They weren't all that keen, being anxious to get to their hotel, but she insisted, and so they all piled into a taxi and drove the half hour or so to Margaret's house.

"Keep the taxi waiting," said Joséphine, "then you can use it to take you back into the centre of Paris." They helped her unload her luggage, briefly met Margaret, and then got back into the waiting taxi. As it drove back into town, Jack suddenly realised that she had landed them with the taxi fare. "That woman!" he howled. "She's done it again!"

In June, when the school year ended, Joséphine took all of her children away from their cramped Parisian flat to stay in Spain with friends. From there she made a trip to Monaco to make a one-day appearance at a charity gala in aid of the Monacan Red Cross. This gala was an annual event, organised by the Sporting Club Of Monte Carlo, and in 1969 it took place on 25 July. Joséphine was backed in the show by a highly-professional team of dancers and musicians, and by her friend and recent employer Jean-Claude Brialy, who had helped to assemble it.

The president of the local chapter of the Red Cross was Grace Kelly, Princess Grace of Monaco since 1956. Eighteen years earlier, at the beginning of her career as a film star, she had been in the Cub Room of the Stork Club on the night that Joséphine had had trouble with the service there. She had been impressed with Joséphine's fighting spirit then, and with the courageous way in which she had confronted the then-powerful Walter Winchell in the press (wrong-headed though that might have been), and had remained aware of Joséphine's continued campaigning through the long years – her battle to keep Les Milandes, her attempts to found the International College Of Brotherhood, and the raising of her Rainbow Tribe.

Meeting Joséphine while she was rehearsing for the gala, and discovering that Joséphine and the Tribe were now effectively homeless, Grace arranged for the Red Cross to give her a down payment on a villa in Roquebrune-Cap-Martin, a French coastal town about three miles east of Monte Carlo, close to the Italian border. She also arranged for the mortgage to be guaranteed by Arys Nisotti, who had produced Joséphine's films *Zou-Zou* and *Princesse Tam-Tam* years earlier, and who was now living in Monaco.

Roquebrune is a pretty town, with many gardens and hibiscus trees, set on the cliffs of the Côte D'Azur and overlooking the Mediterranean. Joséphine's villa – which she named "Maryvonne" – was not large but it was large enough, and its setting was beautiful. It had four bedrooms, two bathrooms, a large living/dining room and an adequate kitchen. From the picture window in the living room, Joséphine had a commanding view of Cap Martin, and along the coast, on a promontory, she could see the Grimaldi castle in Monaco, where Princess Grace lived with her husband, Prince Rainier. "I'm not very far from paradise," she once said, and she was endlessly grateful to the Rainiers for having rescued her Rainbow Tribe, as she saw it. "If Prince Rainier asked me to go jump in the water, I'd do it in a second."

In September, her Tribe came back from their holiday in Spain and joined her in Maryvonne, and soon her sister Margaret moved to live nearby in order to help look after them. Margaret's husband, Elmo, came too, of course, and helped Joséphine to look after her garden.

This was period of relative stability for Joséphine. At last, now that she was reaching her mid 60s, her formidable energy and drive were beginning to ebb slightly, although when she was onstage and performing she was as compelling as ever. This slight quietening made her easier company.

She patronised the local shops, dressed simply – often in a skirt and cardigan – and at first often went unrecognised. A local stationer, Pierre Cazenave, remembered her coming into his shop with her children around her, all addressing her as "Maman". Looking at their dissimilar faces, his reaction was: "Mon Dieu. This woman has certainly been around."

One cause of sadness in her life was that, as her children grew older, they increasingly grew away from her. Having had too much of a procession of maids, nannies and teachers coming and going, they had evolved a fierce closeness with each other, a closeness from which she was largely excluded. Their behaviour towards her became more and more remote and offhand.

They enjoyed life in Roquebrune, which was freer for them and more normal than anything that they had previously known. As they adopted the teen fashions of the early Seventies, Joséphine often disapproved, trying to exert her authority as she had at Les Milandes, but now they were more rebellious. Once she disapproved of the boys growing their hair long, complaining that it made them look like a bunch of homosexuals, only to have them ask why she should object to that when so many of her friends were gay.

Sometimes she blamed their unruliness on their not having a father, and often felt guilty about having caused Jo's departure. On the wall of the first-floor landing at Maryvonne she had hung a photograph of herself and the Tribe in their younger days, and would often stand for a long time staring at it. She once said ruefully to her friend Marie Spiers, who had lent her the small flat in Paris, "Soon I'm going to be alone again."

She would have liked to have been able to spend most of her time at Maryvonne, and to try and nourish her relationship with the children, but she also had to keep on working. In spite of now having a stable home, she needed money to feed her family and to pay off her mortgage, and in addition by this time she was heavily in debt to the French tax authorities, who were pressing her for payment of income tax.

Once, on a visit to Paris, dress manufacturer Jacques Anselm observed her trying to deal with this problem in a manner that was wholly Joséphine. They were walking down a street when she suddenly announced that she had to make a phone call. Finding a pay phone, she told the operator who she was and asked to put her through to Giscard D'Estaing, who was then secretary of the treasury. "Allo, Giscard," she said. "Mon cher. How can you bother me about taxes when I have so many children? Stop sending me these collection notices. I have no intention of paying. *Au revoir.*"

During the early Seventies, the jobs she got were no longer the big, glamorous shows. She was even beginning to believe that her performing career was coming to an end. "I'm too old to play Joséphine Baker," she said to several friends.

She may have been getting old, but she could still make the transformation into a glamorous star – a transformation that, as the years went by, became more and more astonishing.

In 1970, in Paris, Joséphine's protégé, the dancer Geoffrey Holder, took the American writer and sculptor Barbara Chase Ribaud backstage to meet Joséphine. Barbara later described what she saw.

"I thought, 'Anybody's aunt from St Louis. What is all the fuss about?' The bright but melancholy eyes, the extravagant eyelashes behind bifocals, the aging jowls, the slight dowager's hump, the small, rather dumpy figure looked ridiculous in the chorus-girl costume cut high on the hip. Yet in the midst of a rather grandmotherly conversation La Joséphine, then 64, received her cue to go onstage. And before my unbelieving eyes, the superstar emerged from the frump and folds of age.

"She appeared to shed pounds. The line of her back straightened, her upper thighs tensed and lengthened, her stomach flattened, her jowls disappeared. Her eyeglasses were hurriedly exchanged for a rhinestone microphone, her chin lifted, her head went back, and the Joséphine of Parisian dreams suddenly appeared as if by magic onstage. A huge and collective sexual sigh seemed to rise from the audience upon her entrance, the smooth siren voice slid out over the audience. I turned to Geoffrey in amazement. He just shrugged his shoulders and said, 'I told you she was something else.'"

She played mostly in hotels and clubs and at charity galas, and in 1970 she appeared again at the annual Red Cross gala in Monte Carlo. "I would like to say goodbye to the stage," she said in October that year, "but I see that I won't have time to retire. My strength must not let me down. I have to earn a lot of money. Sometimes I look at myself and say: 'Perhaps you are just a slave.'" Mellowing with the years, she found herself admiring Mistinguett – who had died in 1956, at the age of 83 – for the tenacity with which she had gone on performing into her 80s.

Even though she was not as huge a star as she had been, Joséphine was by no means out of the public eye. At the beginning of that same year, a distinguished committee had assembled, proposing to lobby for her to be awarded the Nobel Peace Prize. When they approached her, however, she dissuaded them, saying in an interview at the time: "I don't deserve this great honour. It should be shared by each man and each woman on this Earth who struggles to love and live in peace with his neighbour and himself. We're all created in God's image, and we're all each other's redemption, resurrection and miracle. I believe in redemption. I believe in resurrection. I believe in miracles."

The one "child" she had with whom she continued to be close was her extra, unadopted son, Jean-Claude Rouzaud. He was proving to be a bright and ambitious young man, and was still her devoted admirer. Early in the Seventies she helped set him up as the owner of a Berlin cabaret similar to those that she had known there in the Twenties. It was called Pimm's, and from time to time, she would appear there when she had no other work, sitting at the tables like a hostess and urging customers to buy more drinks.

"If Joséphine wasn't getting work, her self-confidence evaporated," Jean-Claude once explained. "When she got in those states, she'd take anything." Once, when she was in such a low state, a Berlin theatre approached her about performing there. "We must find a woman singer to be the headliner," she said to Jean-Claude, fearing that her name alone would be an insufficient draw to fill the house.

Jean-Claude also came to Maryvonne from time to time. As he was older than the other children, at mealtimes he would sit at the head of the table, as if he were the man of the house, with Joséphine at the other end. While he was there he observed how hard she worked at trying to be a good mother. As her greatest talent in life was helping people to enjoy themselves, to enjoy life, she tried to do the same for her children, wanting them to see her as bringing joy rather than perpetually nagging. "She would take all of us out to a restaurant together to eat and dance," he remembered. "Of course, it was always at the expense of someone else, but it was fabulous. Mostly she liked to go for walks, or to an amusement park or the theatre. Her favourite outing was the zoo. She loved to see the animals through the eyes of the children."

She could nag as well, however. On one occasion, while the whole family was sitting round the dinner table, she announced to the Tribe that Jean-Claude was going to read out a letter from her doctor to them. She then put her head in her hands as Jean-Claude read out the note she had given him.

"Dear boys and girls," he read. "You are being very mean to your mother. You are killing her. If you don't start being nice soon, she will die."

As he finished, Joséphine rose to her feet. She paused for a moment (as if, he recalled, she was expecting applause), then ran off into her bedroom, which adjoined the dining room.

All of the children were startled, but the younger ones were actually frightened, and the youngest, Stellina, started to cry. "Don't be silly," one of the older boys told her. "It's an act. She's nutty. Leave her alone."

Early in 1972, her career received a welcome shot in the arm. The promoter Jack Jordan, who had been involved in presenting her in America in 1960 and 1963, approached her with the proposition that he present her again at Carnegie Hall, again for four performances. This time the show would be in aid of UNICEF, and it would also celebrate 50 years since she first appeared in the road company of *Shuffle Along*. He came to Roquebrune to discuss the matter.

Joséphine, talking to him in her living room, was dubious about making another appearance in the States. "Nobody wants me," she said. "They've forgotten me."

Her sister Margaret, overhearing, butted into the conversation. "I don't know what you're horsing around about," she said. "Go to New York and make some money."

Joséphine decided to give it a go, and Jack Jordan stayed on for a few days while they discussed details. While he was there, Joséphine took him sightseeing. In Nice, she deliberately led him past a jeweller's shop window that was displaying a pair of gold earrings which she fancied. Jack, who was a considerable hustler himself, was somewhat bemused to find himself inside the shop writing out a traveller's cheque to pay for them. Wryly he complimented her on her ability as a courtesan. She laughed cheerfully. "You know, Jack," she said, "I'm old now, but don't think I didn't know what to do with a man in bed."

It was arranged that her Carnegie Hall appearance should take place in the following year, in June 1973. Meanwhile, among all of her other activities, from time to time she still talked about founding her International College Of Brotherhood. Somewhat surprisingly, word of this project reached the ears of Marshal Tito, president of Yugoslavia. He invited Joséphine to visit him and his wife to see if he could help with the project. She went in February 1973.

Tito was a flamboyant character. Of peasant stock, during the Second World War he had organised partisan forces to successfully repel Axis invaders from his country, had been elected its first communist prime minister in 1945, and in 1953 he had become its president. His wartime record made him popular in the West, which helped him to remain allied to the

Soviet Union while remaining surprisingly independent of it. At the same, time he held together the mutually hostile assortment of nations that made up Yugoslavia simply by the strength of his personality. After he died in 1980, it soon disintegrated.

As president, he lived royally, having sumptuous palaces and a private island. In fact, he was just the sort of man that appealed to Joséphine. They got on well, and he prevailed on the Croatian town of Sibenik to offer her the use of one of the many small islands that were dotted along its Adriatic coast. The island was called Brioni, and it had a mediaeval fortress called Saint Nicholas which he thought would make an ideal setting for her college. Joséphine was pleased by his offer, but was coming to realise that such an exhausting enterprise would be now beyond her, and nothing ever came of it.

Jack Jordan's partner was a successful advertising agent whose name was Howard Saunders. He specialised in black promotions, and in preparation for Joséphine's return to Carnegie Hall he set about publicising her. Shrewdly, he targeted two main groups: blacks and gays, and gays in particular. "Josephine's greatest fans were the gays," he recalled. "They love to watch artists like Marlene Dietrich, Judy Garland or Jo Baker camp it up, with their exaggerated gestures and their clothes. To a gay, they represent theatre pushed to its fullest expression."

He advertised in gay bars and paid gays to spread the word about the forthcoming show. For the black public, "I got models from the Black Beauty Agency and dressed them in flesh-coloured outfits and Nefertiti wigs. They walked up and down Madison Avenue, Park, Lexington, Third and all over Harlem. They passed out flyers, 'Black Legend Returns'. Five days I did that. It worked. It turned the town on."

On her opening night, she was introduced by Bricktop, who had just turned 80. Reminiscing to the audience about their days in Paris almost 50 years previously, she told them "she was a simple little girl – she's still a simple little girl," at which point the band struck up with 'The Last Time I Saw Paris' and Joséphine entered in a skin-tight net body stocking, glittering with beads and sequins, and wearing a four-feet-high head-dress of bright orange plumes and clutching a rhinestone-studded microphone.

Throughout the show, all of her outfits were similarly extravagant, culminating in a stunning floor-length white fur cape that she let fall to the stage, revealing her in a simple black frock, in which she sang 'J'ai Deux Amours'.

The whole show was a compendium of old and new songs. She sang 'Bill', from *Show Boat*, Bob Dylan's 'The Times They Are A-Changing', and she also sang 'My Way', at the climax of which she almost shouted: "I did it! I did it my way because I so profoundly believe in humanity in general!"

The show was a huge success. Among its reviewers, John Wilson of *The New York Times* wrote: "There is about her, one eventually realised, something of the aura that Duke Ellington projects. It is not simply that they both have style and wit and a confident knowledge of who they are. It stems from basics – Miss Baker moves the way Ellington plays."

While in New York she also gave one performance at the Victoria Theater in Harlem, in aid of the Harlem Police Athletic League for children. Another reviewer for *The New York Times* compared it to her performances at Carnegie Hall, writing: "The single Harlem performance produced a different, more intimate communication between star and audience. Though some 60 per cent of those who attended the downtown performance were black, her appearance in Harlem served to underscore Miss Baker's triumph in blazing her way through international barriers...The audience's feeling was that the woman on the stage was as much heroine as artist."

Heroine she may have been to a new generation of blacks, but she was increasingly out of sympathy with the new crusading attitudes evolving in that American era of "black power". As she said in an interview printed in *The Chicago Sunday Times* in September 1970, "Don't talk to me about black power. All power is power. I don't like discrimination. I'm shocked when I hear our own people saying 'black people this', 'black people that'. It just shows you we haven't come very far. They're so frightened of everything in America." Her own attitude was that race should be ignored, not asserted, and she missed the fact that this new rhetoric was simply the emergence of a new self-confidence which was then going through the period of overstatement common in all new movements.

Her four Carnegie Hall performances earned her $120,000, and with that amount of money in her purse she felt solvent for a while, and her priority became to get back home to Roquebrune. This, however, was tough on Howard Saunders and Jack Jordan. In the wake of her success at Carnegie Hall, they had managed to line up a tour of major American cities for her, which was scheduled to take place a couple of months later. But as they sat discussing this with her, going over the terms of her contract, the old wilful Joséphine suddenly resurfaced and she announced: "I don't understand what you are talking about because my English isn't very good. But you know something? I listen when I hear the money. And it doesn't sound like the right money. Now, gentlemen, you keep on talking and when you get finished you let me know what the outcome is. *Goooood night!*" And back to Roquebrune she went.

There she found that she had a new problem. Her daughter Marianne had run away. She duly came back, but meanwhile the worry of her being missing caused Joséphine's heart to develop a severely irregular rhythm. In fact, it was so irregular that she was admitted to the American Hospital in Paris, where it was stopped and restarted.

Her heartbeat now steady, she insisted on fulfilling a singing engagement in Denmark. In July, in Copenhagen, she suffered a combined heart attack and stroke which left her semi-conscious for days. Her face was partially paralysed for a time, and when three of her sons – Brahim, Koffi and Noël – came to visit her in hospital, she failed to recognise them.

While she was beginning to recover there, she had a phone call from an American friend, the artist Robert Brady. Then in his 40s, he lived in the Mexican town of Cuernavaca, and Joséphine had met him in 1967 while appearing in Mexico City. Wealthy and successful, he made his money from designing tapestries, which local craftsmen would weave for him in wool. He was also an international jet setter, a handsome man – dark, lean and moustachioed – who enjoyed the company of successful women. Among his friends were heiress and art collector Peggy Guggenheim and actresses Helen Hayes and Dolores del Rio. However, he was a man with a vein of coldness and remoteness in his character, a man who felt contempt for the general run of people and did not always bother to hide it. Once he had remarked to a woman sitting next to him at a dinner table: "Nothing you could possibly say would have the slightest interest to me."

Joséphine's natural openness seemed to bring out a warmth in him, though, and they had kept in touch, mostly by phone and letter. Perhaps this long-distance communication had made it easier for Robert to express his feelings, and their friendship had developed. Hearing of her illness, he phoned her to cheer her up and, as they spoke, he suddenly told her that he loved her. Feeling devastated and helpless from her illness, she was bowled over.

He followed up his call with a letter proposing that they married – not in the conventional sense of setting up a home together, or even of making love, but married in spirit, each continuing to live a separate life, but each knowing that the other was there to lean on and share thoughts and feelings.

Joséphine was delighted with this suggestion, and worried only that she hadn't properly understood what he was suggesting. "Did I rightly understand...that you want us to be married?" she wrote back. "If so I am so happy, because you are the only man I can trust with my ideas and life etc but we will do it with the understanding that nothing changes your life, that it will be a pure marriage without sex etc etc because sex spoils everything – that we stay free – that we be married by God and not by man."

When she left the hospital, her doctors recommended that she should have at least four months of complete rest and then take things easy for a year, but Joséphine would have none of it. Not only did she have to carry on supporting her family but she also couldn't afford to let anyone know how ill she had been. If word got out, bookings would dry up.

In just over a week she was back to working twelve hours a day. She did take the precaution of making a trip to Lourdes, however, the town in south-west France where, in 1858, the Virgin Mary had appeared to a peasant girl, Bernadette Soubirous, and told her to dig up roots and eat them. Where she dug, a spring appeared, reputed to cause miraculous cures, and the grotto around it attracts thousands of believers each year.

Joséphine knelt there and prayed for strength. "God," she prayed, "please don't take me now. I have too many things to accomplish. You can't take me away. Not now. Give me some more time. I have to survive."

Telling a New York friend, Florence Dixon, about the occasion, she said: "All of a sudden there was a fire under my feet. The fire rose and came through all my limbs, all over my body. I felt it in my hair and in my fingers. It only lasted for a few minutes. When I walked out of there I felt like the most beautiful well person."

She and Robert Brady continued to exchange letters, planning their spiritual marriage. "It makes me so happy," she wrote to him, "and stupidly like a young girl in love for the first time. I can't stop thinking about you and see you in my dreams continuously." They both felt that not seeing each other all the time would make the marriage all the stronger. They would combine the reassuring stability of a relationship with the lives of free spirits.

Saunders and Jordan had meanwhile managed to come up with the right money, and in September 1973 she returned to America to make the

17-city tour that they had arranged for her. *En route* she went to Mexico to spend a few days with Robert, and there – in a church in Acapulco, without an officiating priest – they swore a solemn, private oath that they belonged to each other. Robert gave her a ring and a gold chain. Eccentric or not, they were both devout, and both felt themselves to be Catholics. So much so, in fact, that they felt nervous about taking Holy Communion after their secret ceremony, and refrained from doing so. Afterwards, both felt guilty at the omission.

During her subsequent American tour, as companion and master of ceremonies, she took along her "13th child", Jean-Claude Rouzaud, who was now calling himself "Jean-Claude Baker", with her blessing. He introduced her during her shows, and his French accent and sophistication charmed the American audiences. He then reappeared from time to time as she chatted between songs, and helped her with onstage costume changes. "And now my son Jean-Claude will help unbutton my dress for me so I can do a strip tease to help feed my children."

Getting her from one city to another was a nightmare, though. "She'd miss the plane," he later recalled. "There would be a second one and then one after that. If she met a woman with a baby at the airline counter, she'd say: 'You take my seat, I'll get on the next flight.'"

Learning that there was a four-day break in her schedule before she was scheduled to appear in San Francisco, she was appalled. "Four days!" she said to Jack Jordan. "What am I going to do for four days?" He advised her to rest, but that night she flew back to France, went to Maryvonne and collected her youngest child, Stellina, and with her flew on to Israel, where she had been invited by Prime Minister Golda Meir to celebrate 25 years of the country's existence. She was one of 450 notable guests who had been invited, and with them she attended the festivities that had been arranged. In Jerusalem she ate stuffed vine leaves under the stars at an outdoor feast, she went to see Nureyev dance, and she took part in a torchlight parade through the Citadel.

At the Jerusalem International Hotel, she befriended the Arab porter whose job it was to clean her room. She accepted his invitation to visit his home in the West Bank village of Bethany, drank coffee there with him and his family for two hours, and while there noticed that they were using a block of ice to chill their food. On her return to Jerusalem, she bought and sent them an electric refrigerator that they (and she) could not afford.

When the press reported this generous gesture, she at once became the most popular celebrity attending the celebrations.

She got back to San Francisco too late to make her first scheduled appearance there. The house had been packed, and Saunders and Jordan – forced to refund all of the admission money – had lost thousands of dollars. Furious, they announced that they were docking Joséphine's pay. Joséphine, furious in return, quit the tour cold, first taking the precaution of getting Jean-Claude to fly all of her costumes back to France and suggesting that he used his original surname, Rouzaud, to do so.

Her relationship with Jean-Claude was deteriorating, too, mainly because of her urge to dominate. For instance, she started trying to control his sex life. He was bisexual, and whereas she didn't mind him sleeping with men she became bitterly jealous if he slept with women, even though her relationship with him was not a sexual one. (They did often share a bed, but that was because of her lifelong dislike of being alone at night, made worse now by a growing fear that she might die in the night). He recalled: "She used to cruise for me just so I'd be with boys. One day I slept with a black girl in the suite next to her room. She almost killed me."

Being in America didn't help their relationship, either. While they were there, Jean-Claude realised that America was where he wanted to live and make his mark. Attempting to establish himself, he began to talk more freely to the press, and his growing assertiveness roused Joséphine's hostility. She wanted him to remain dependent. She wanted to continue being his guide in the world.

In one interview, he was quoted as saying that Joséphine was thinking of marrying Robert Brady. He later vehemently denied having said any such thing, but its appearance did nothing to help things between him and Joséphine. On their return to France she dumped him, leaving him hurt and confused. "I saw her use everybody," he said, "but I never thought she would do it to me. I said to myself: 'But I am her son!'" It made no difference.

However, her dumping him gave him the impetus he needed to establish himself in New York. Continuing to call himself Jean-Claude Baker, and realising $60,000 from the sale of Pimm's in Berlin, he launched a successful French-language cable television programme, *Téléfrance USA*, and went on to produce documentaries, news programmes and dramas. He also opened a restaurant, Chez Joséphine, on West 42nd Street, which always retained her favourite dish on its menu: spaghetti with red peppers.

"I would have been a success anyway," he says of her, "but I would have been a bourgeois. I would have seen life through a small window. She taught me to see life through a big window."

Before he fell out with Joséphine, he had arranged for her to appear during Christmas week at the famous Palace Theater in New York, the most prestigious theatre in America in the days of vaudeville. The Palace did not seem to be over-enthusiastic at presenting Joséphine, and when she arrived there, its frontage was still dominated by a ten-storey-high advert for Bette Midler, who had appeared in the previous week. Joséphine's name appeared simply in small aluminium letters on the marquee. To reduce the warmth of her welcome still further, there was a picket line outside the theatre who had been hired by Saunders and Jordan and were protesting that her appearance there was a breach of the contract she had made with them.

Inside, things weren't much better. The band with whom she was to rehearse seemed bored and unhelpful, the theatre was cold and the stage had not been swept. The young journalist Dotson Rader, who was there on assignment to write a piece about her for *Esquire* magazine, heard her remark to "no one in particular": "You could not even wash the floor for Joséphine? You could not even do that?"

Dotson himself, initially somewhat bored and sceptical about her (and a little taken aback when she called him "child"), found his admiration for her growing as he saw her dominating her rehearsals, gradually triumphing over the cold, the dirt and the band.

However, he found her first-night performance painful. With her advancing years, and with exhaustion, her memory was becoming unreliable. Sometimes she had trouble remembering the words of her songs, and her speeches between them tended to ramble. "…Then I came back to New York and Billie Brice, no, not Billie…at the Follies in New York before the war, Bob Hope and…Brice…" He found her songs corny when she remembered the words, "corny – but eerie and deeply moving", and he noted that, although she had fewer people in her whole audience than Bette Midler had had in the aisles, the few that there were had given her a standing ovation. Many of the young people among them, seeing her for the first time, were bowled over by her still-magnificent star presence.

Overall, though, seeing her backstage as well as onstage, he sensed her tiredness. He thought: "She wants to stop now. She wants to throw it over…Time for your travellin' shoes, sweet Josephine."

Now that Jean-Claude was gone, Joséphine had with her as companion and errand-boy her nephew Richard from St Louis, and when the reviews for the show came in – which were almost unanimously hostile and referred frequently to her lapses of memory – she dumped them in the wastebasket of her suite at the Waldorf Astoria Hotel and said: "I'm going to go to one of those youth doctors in Switzerland and get shots for my brain."

Buckling down to the task of generating more work, she began to take Richard on the rounds of New York, turning up at galas and receptions and generally letting the world know that she was in town. On one occasion she invited 20 people to a dinner of her own at the Waldorf, serving them steak and champagne. Richard was horrified. "Auntie," he begged, "where are you going to get the money?"

"Richard," she explained, "I have an image to maintain and I'm going to maintain it."

During this period, in January 1974, she made a trip south to Mexico to stay with Robert Brady in his house in Cuernavaca. His house, the Casa Del Torre, was elegantly furnished, and crammed with African and Pacific sculpture, with Spanish colonial sculpture, textiles and paintings. With many servants to attend her needs, it was an oasis of ease and calm, and was just what Joséphine needed.

The trouble was that Robert wanted to show her off. Not only that but he also wanted to shock some of his more staid neighbours by bringing his black guest to swim in their pools. Joséphine would rather have swum in their own pool. She wanted to be quietly at home with him, not going out every night to dine. Eventually they had a blazing row. Robert insisted that her desperate need for love was weighing too heavily on him, and Joséphine, broken hearted, decided that she would leave the next day. She stayed up all night and wrote him an anguished letter of goodbye. "*Je suis une pur sang*," she wrote. "*Pour moi*, to be or not to be. I who love freedom it is torture to me to be here where all eyes are on me judging my every moment or move. Why can't I have a moment of freedom with you? I don't want anything else."

She left, leaving the ring and chain that he had given her. Their marriage was over, but in spite of this rift they continued to keep in touch, their friendship going back to what it had been before. She would often write him letters four or five pages long, pouring out her thoughts on world brotherhood or asking his advice on practical matters.

Back in New York, her campaign of self-publicity had paid off in a small way. A small private club in the Sherry-Netherland Hotel catered to an elegant and wealthy clientèle and called itself Raffles, and the owners wanted a hostess who possessed a strong nostalgic attraction. They hired Joséphine for a month during January and February 1974.

The opening night was, as so often, attended by celebrities. Anita Loos, Debbie Reynolds and Janet Flanner were among them, as were Andy Warhol, escorting Paulette Goddard, "who shone like klieg lights in a white dress, sequin cardigan and frankly diamond necklace. 'It's not the one made of my engagement rings, but just the leftovers,' she explained." But in spite of the glamorous milieu, Joséphine was still so tired that there was something missing from her performance. Anita Loos, who had seen her perform as far back as her days at the Plantation Club, noted: "The crunch was gone. She sounded like a second-rate singer from St Louis."

To keep her expenses down during her run at the Raffles Club, Joséphine got Richard to book them both into a cheaper hotel, the Navarro on Central Park South. In their suite there she cooked meals for them both, sometimes soul food – greens and pork ribs – and sometimes Chinese. Richard, growing bored with endless economy meals, took to sneaking out from time to time to Rumpelmayer's Café for roast beef and a glass of wine.

Despite her below-par performances, reviewers were kinder about her appearances at the Raffles Club than they had been about her appearances at the Palace, and she went on to perform in several other American night spots, but her exhaustion grew worse. By April, when she was appearing at the Beverly Hilton in Los Angeles, it was obvious that she was ailing, and after that engagement she headed home to Roquebrune.

There at last she could rest for a time, although money continued to be tight. One particular aggravation to her was her telephone bill, which – with all of the many calls she made, many of them international – was always astronomical. On many occasions she was unable to pay it and was cut off.

The children frequently obtained items from the local shops on credit, which left Joséphine unsure how much she owed. She kept the shopkeepers happy as far as she could by paying them a bit here and a bit there whenever she had any spare cash, explaining to the children: "If you pay everybody a little bit, they don't mind."

She was certainly not afraid to sponge. Aware that her memory was failing, she hired a secretary to help with her correspondence. The girl's name was Marie-Joli Gomi, and she showed up for work on her first day driving a white Fiat. Joséphine found it enchanting, and Marie-Joli's first job was to write a letter to Italy, to the president of Fiat, Gianni Agnelli. "Dear Gianni," it began, "the Fiat is marvellous. Be a darling and send me one." He did, free of charge.

But life was becoming a strain. Once, getting a bill from the local school, she misread it as being ten times what it was. Her eldest son, Akio, attempted to set her right, but she this only bewildered her further until at last she burst into tears, sobbing: "What's going to become of us?"

Help was at hand, however. In the middle of 1974, André Levasseur, a close colleague who had designed sets and costumes for Joséphine for more than ten years, suggested to her that for that year's Monacan Red Cross Gala they should mount a special revue celebrating the forthcoming anniversary of her 50 years in French showbusiness. Jean-Claude Brialy had agreed that he would act as the show's MC.

To be called simply *Joséphine*, it would be a heightened version of the sort of nostalgic shows she had been already staging for some years, and would use song, dance and spectacle to tell the story of her life. It would tell of her childhood in Louisiana (or so the programme said), her arrival in Paris and her time in *La Revue Nègre*. It would also cover her dancing the banana dance at the Folies, her war service, her life at her château and her arrival in Monte Carlo. She would be onstage for almost the entire show, although young dancers would portray her during her early years in such numbers as the banana dance.

Joséphine put everything she had into this show (not that she ever did anything else), well aware that her audience for the gala night would be more sophisticated than they had been at, say, Carnegie Hall, where she was able to get by to some extent by camping it up. She was also delighted that all of her children would at last be able to see her give a proper performance.

Henri Astric, the theatrical director of the Sporting Club of Monte Carlo, where the gala took place, thought Joséphine by far the most compelling star he had ever seen. "In her style," he once said, "as the leading lady for a spectacular show, she is the number one who ever lived. She had fantastic appeal. In French we say *elle dépasse la rampe*. She went over the footlights. Pow! Did she ever. You had the feeling she was singing for you and only you. For everyone in the audience she was sitting in each one's lap."

The revue was a stunning success, so much so that the producers decided to transfer it to Paris as soon as possible. This was a tonic for Joséphine, who hadn't appeared on a Parisian stage since 1968. (Part of the reason for this, she thought, was that, in that year, she had been a little too outspoken in her unfashionable support of de Gaulle.) What a marvellous thing it would be to conquer Paris all over again 50 years after doing so the first time!

Naturally, the producers thought first of the big theatres in which she had enjoyed stunning successes in the past – the Folies Bergère, the Casino De Paris, the Olympia – but none of these were prepared to book the show. Not because they felt she would not be a draw, but because they were aware of her frail health. No insurance company would give her cover, and if she was forced to cancel performances because of ill health or, worse, to abandon the run, it could cost them a fortune.

The dancer and choreographer Roland Petit, who was then director of the Casino De Paris, agreed to stage the show, but only on the condition that a young, up-and-coming black dancer, Lisette Malidor, would be employed to rehearse the show alongside Joséphine so that, if necessary, she could appear as her double. Joséphine dismissed the idea at once. "Nobody can take my place."

The Paris theatre that was eventually found for the show was a small one, the Bobino, on the Rue De La Gaieté in Montparnasse. It was a former music hall and it was built like one, with an old-fashioned promenade at the rear of the stalls where people could stand and watch the show or simply stand and drink.

While plans for the Paris presentation of Joséphine were proceeding, Joséphine continued to tour. In the August of 1974 she appeared for a week at the London Palladium, performing twice nightly as the second half of the bill. She brought her youngest child, Stellina, with her, and as usual stayed at the Savoy Hotel. Peter Barrett – whose partner, Jack, was now back on speaking terms with her – often baby-sat Stellina while Joséphine was rehearsing or performing. At the Palladium she was on good form, and was such a success that she was invited to return there later in the year to star in the annual *Royal Variety Show*.

She also made a less happy tour of South Africa. As always, she tried to insist that her audiences weren't segregated, but in that country, at that time, this was simply impossible. No matter how she tried to insist, apartheid ruled. Angry and upset, she performed poorly, and the tour became a procession of disputes and hostile reviews. In Capetown, the Three Arts Theatre even received bomb threats, but she refused to leave the theatre while it was searched. In an angry telephone interview to London, printed in the *Radio Times*, she said: "They are all sick here. The place reminds me of a stagnant pool, never changing, breeding malaria. But why should I run away? There are many people here who can see what is happening, but who are not running away from it. Then why should I?"

In November 1974, she returned to the Palladium to appear in the *Royal Variety Show*, co-starring with Perry Como. She was in London for only one weekend's rehearsal and for the show to be performed and recorded on the Monday, and was due to fly out again on the Tuesday afternoon.

Again, as Jean-Claude had noted was her habit, she gave herself trouble catching her plane. On the Tuesday morning she insisted that Peter Barrett drove her down into the wilds of Kent to visit her old friend Harry Hurford Janes, who had been with her during the war when he was working for ENSA. As with so many people in her life, she had kept in touch with him, even sending groups of her children to holiday from time to time at his Kent farmhouse.

She and Peter Barrett and Jack Hockett had lunch at the farmhouse with Harry and his wife, after which it proved impossible to get her to leave. Peter became increasingly anxious about the cross-country run from Kent to Heathrow which he had to make in a small car that he was still running in. Eventually, at about ten to three, he and Jack managed to persuade Joséphine to leave, but by now they had no hope of catching the plane to take her to Israel to meet Golda Meir, which was scheduled to leave at six. Then Joséphine had an inspiration: Peter should phone the airline, El Al, and explain to them that they were to hold the plane for Joséphine Baker, who was flying to meet President Meir.

From a village phone box, he found the number of El Al at Heathrow, phoned them, explained the situation, and his explanation worked: they held the plane. Anxious airline officials were waiting at Heathrow to escort Joséphine to the plane, but even then she was in no hurry, insisting on saying a long and affectionate goodbye to her friends Peter and Jack.

Rehearsals for the Paris run of *Joséphine* took place all through the early months of 1975. Joséphine was so delighted at opening again in her beloved city that she was filled with energy. François Rosset, the technical director of the show, observed that she seemed to have more energy than the young showgirls with whom she was dancing, and at times seemed younger than them. She had gone back to being the vital person she had been before losing Les Milandes. Even her memory seemed improved, although the management took the precaution of concealing large cue cards around the stage with key phrases written on them to help her out.

Only one thing bothered her. Observing her softy weeping in the wings at one moment during the dress rehearsal, Rosset asked her what was wrong. "I wish my children could be here," she said.

Joséphine was given a number of try-out performances before its official opening, and the audience reaction was so enthusiastic that it became obvious that the show was going to be a massive hit. It was soon booked out for weeks ahead. It opened on Tuesday 8 April 1975, and Jean-Claude Brialy was again her MC. For her opening scene, depicting her arrival in Monte Carlo, she wore a long, sumptuous Cecil Beaton-esque white dress and a flounced cartwheel hat in the style of the 1900s. The twelve changes of costumes that followed it were no less stunning.

She appeared in a Brazilian carnival dress complete with feathered headdress, in a short white pleated Twenties' dress in which she danced the charleston, in a white motorcycling costume with a peaked hat for a New York/Broadway/Chicago scene in which she roared on atop a Harley-Davidson, in leggy black tights for a scene that was supposed to depict life at her château, in an air force uniform, and finally in a skin-tight, sequinned body stocking that showed how attractive her figure still was at the age of nearly 69.

The songs she sang were the songs of her life. She sang 'I'm Just Wild About Harry' from *Shuffle Along*. She sang songs from *Paris Qui Remue*, from *Féeries Et Folies*, and from *Paris Mes Amours*. There had been a rumour that she would re-enact the 'Ave Maria' scene from *Féeries Et Folies*, but that didn't happen.

At the end, half singing and half whispering, she sang a new song for Paris that had been especially written for her, 'Paris-Paname', and she finished by saying to her audience: "Good night, ladies and gentlemen, *buona sera, buenos noches, shalom, shalom, ciao, ciao.*" The reviewer for the weekly news magazine *L'Express* commented: "Ce n'est plus un comeback. C'est l'éternal retour."

In the audience that first night were many of her friends and colleagues, as well as other celebrities, including Prince Rainier and Princess Grace (who was the guest of honour), Sophia Loren, Jeanne Moreau, Alain Delon, Mick Jagger, Mireille Darc, Tino Rossi, Madame Sukarno and Pierre Balmain. Giscard D'Estaing, now president of the republic, sent a telegram, which Jean-Claude Brialy read aloud to the audience: "In tribute to your limitless talent, and in the name of a grateful France, whose heart has so often beaten with yours, I send you fond wishes, dear Joséphine, on this golden anniversary. Paris is celebrating with you."

After the performance, 250 members of the celebrity audience adjourned to dinner at the Bristol Hotel, where the centrepiece of the meal was a huge, seven-tiered cake, iced and covered with spun sugar. As she left the hotel after the feast, Joséphine waved goodnight, saying to everyone: "Next stop London, my friends, and then...New York!"

On the next night, after the second performance, there was a smaller celebration, a party for just Joséphine, her three co-stars in the show – Jean-Marie Proslier, Laurence Badie and Annie Siraglia – and the show's director, Jean-Claude Dauzonne. It was held at a café across the road from the theatre, La Barate, and Joséphine ate her favourite meal, spaghetti. By now she was almost delirious with joy at her success. After the waiters cleared the table, she climbed up onto it and began chanting: "I'm 17. I'm 17." Jean-Louis Preslier had difficulty in getting her back to *terra firma*. At last, exasperated, he said to her: "All right, Joséphine. We believe you are 17. But let's not go all the way back to infancy."

By three in the morning, with the others flagging, Joséphine was still fizzing with excitement and vainly tried to persuade someone to go on with her to a cabaret called Chez Michou, where she had heard that a beautiful black boy was giving an impersonation of her in her Paris youth, wearing a bone through his hair like a cannibal. "I'm the youngest of you all," she told her exhausted co-stars.

Nonetheless she eventually went home, to an apartment she had rented on the Avenue Paul Doumer with her companion, a niece of Pepito's called Lélia. There she slept. On the following day she woke up, made some phone calls, had a mid-day bite to eat and lay down for an afternoon nap. She was due to be interviewed by a journalist at five o'clock, but when he arrived she appeared to be sleeping so soundly that Lélia was reluctant to wake her. She let Joséphine sleep on for almost an hour, and then, feeling that it would be rude to make the journalist wait any longer, attempted to rouse her.

It proved impossible. She had had a stroke, probably at about the time that the journalist had arrived, and was now in a coma. Lélia phoned director Jean-Claude Dauzonne and he arrived with a doctor, who at once realised that the only thing to do was to get Joséphine to a hospital. An ambulance was summoned and she was taken to La Salpétrière.

Lélia then phoned Joséphine's sister Margaret in Roquebrune. Years before, the two sisters had made an agreement with each other that, if anything happened to either one of them, the other would come no matter what. Margaret immediately caught a plane to Paris, arriving at the hospital at about the same moment as Princess Grace, who had also learned the news. Squeezing her unconscious sister's hand, Margaret said: "Tumpie, I made it." At five o'clock on the morning of Saturday 12 April, Joséphine died without regaining consciousness.

Margaret washed her body and laid her out, dressing her in the same dress that she had worn for her first-night dinner. She put no make-up on her, feeling that Joséphine looked better with her face naked, and as soon as she was in her coffin Margaret insisted that the lid was screwed down. "Nobody's takin' pictures of my dead sister," she told the waiting paparazzi.

As a decorated war hero, Joséphine was accorded a full-scale military funeral at the Madeleine, with a flag-draped coffin and a 21-gun salute. Thousands lined the route as the hearse would its way through the Paris streets, passing the Théâtre Bobino as it went. It was estimated that outside the church there were 20,000 standing, and the congregation inside included many who had been at her gala first night only a few days before.

She was not buried in Paris. After the funeral, her body was taken to Monaco, where it stayed in a mausoleum for six months until a suitable last resting place was found for her in the crowded cemetery. She had fought the good fight. The battle was over, the victory won.

And what was the battle? She fought bravely for so many things over so many years: for her success as an entertainer, for blacks (by which she meant anyone who was oppressed or slighted), for the Allied cause in the war, for her animals, and for her children, who – in spite of the oddness of their upbringing – turned out well and remember her with affection.

Back in the early Sixties, her friend Langston Hughes wrote the couplet "Look at that black girl shake that thing. We can't all be Martin Luther King." He didn't write it about Joséphine, but she might well have crossed his mind. Tremendous at shaking that thing, she came surprisingly close to also being as much of an inspiration in the world as Dr King himself.

As her wartime friend Harry Hurford Janes wrote after her death, she was a "dear, mystical, magical, unpredictable, idealistic, foolish, generous and warm woman". She brought a lot of joy and excitement to a lot of people. She was a Star.

Bibliography

Jacques Abtey: *La Guerre Secrète De Joséphine Baker* (Éditions Siboney [France], 1948)

James Agate: *Around Theatres* (Jonathan Cape [UK], 1945)

Joséphine Baker and Marcel Sauvage: *Les Memoires De Joséphine Baker* (Éditions Kra [France], 1927)

Joséphine Baker and Marcel Sauvage: *Voyages Et Aventures De Joséphine Baker* (Éditions Marcel Sheur [France], 1931)

Joséphine Baker and André Rivollet: *Joséphine Baker: Une Vie De Toutes Les Couleurs* (B Arthaud [France], 1935)

Joséphine Baker and Marcel Sauvage: *Les Mémoirs De Joséphine Baker* (Corréa [France], 1949)

Joséphine Baker and Jo Bouillon: *Joséphine* (Laffont [France], 1976)

Patrick Beaver: *The Spice Of Life: Pleasures Of The Victorian Age* (Elm Tree Books [UK], 1979)

Sidney Bechet: Treat It Gentle (Hill & Wang [USA], 1960)

Laurence Bergreen: *Louis Armstrong: An Extravagant Life* (HarperCollins [UK], 1998)

Rudi Blesh: *Combo: USA* (Chilton Book Company [USA], 1971)

Jean Claude Bonnal: *Joséphine Baker Et Le Village Des Enfants Du Monde En Perigord* (publisher unkown [France], 1992)

Ezra Bowen (editor): *This Fabulous Century, Volume Three, 1920-1930* (Time-Life Books [USA], 1971)

Bricktop, with James Haskins: *Bricktop* (Atheneum [USA], 1983)

André Brunelin: *Gabin* (Editions Robert Lafont [France], 1987)

Luis Buñuel: *My Last Breath* (Flamingo [UK], 1985)

James Lincoln Collier: *Duke Ellington* (Pan Books [UK], 1989)

Paul Derval: *Folies Bergère* (Dutton [USA], 1955)

Rudolph Dunbar: *Triumph And Tragedy* (Bayou Press [UK], [unpublished],)

Janet Flanner: *Paris Was Yesterday: 1925-39* (Viking [USA], 1972)

Neal Gabler: *Walter Winchell* (Papermac [UK], 1996)

Douglas Gilbert: *American Vaudeville* (Whittesley House [USA], 1940)

Lyn Haney: *Naked At The Feast* (Robson Books [UK], 1986)

Rex Harris: *Jazz* (Penguin [UK], 1956)

Jim Haskins: *The Cotton Club* (Robson Books [UK], 1985)

Langston Hughes: *The Big Sea: An Autobiography* (Knopf [USA], 1940)

Randi Hultin: *Born Under The Sign Of Jazz* (Sanctuary Publishing [UK], 1998)

Bryan Hammond & Patrick O'Connor: *Josephine Baker* (Jonathan Cape [UK], 1988)

Barry Kernfeld (editor): *The New Grove Dictionary Of Jazz* (Macmillan [UK], 1988)

Isabel Leighton (editor): *The Aspirin Age: 1919-1941* (Bodley Head [UK], 1950)

Walter Lord: *The Good Years* (Longmans [UK], 1960)

Vincente Minnelli: *I Remember It Well* (Angus & Robertson [UK], 1975)

Charles Panati: *Panati's Parade of Fads, Follies And Manias* (HarperPerennial [USA], 1991)

Stephen Papich: *Remembering Joséphine* (Bobbs-Merrill [USA], 1976)

Roland Penrose: *Man Ray* (Thames & Hudson [UK], 1975)

Phyllis Rose: *Jazz Cleopatra: Josephine Baker In Her Time* (Chatto & Windus [UK], 1990)

Brian Rust & Allen G Debus: *The Complete Entertainment Discography* (Da Capo Press [USA], 1989)

Jack Schiffman: *Harlem Heyday* (Prometheus Books [USA], 1984)

Robert Short: *Dada And Surrealism* (Octopus Books [UK], 1980)

Cornelia Otis Skinner: *Elegant Wits And Grand Horizontals* (The Riverside Press [USA], 1962)

Marshall and Jean Stearns: *Jazz Dance: The Story Of American Vernacular Dance* (Macmillan [UK], 1970)

David Thomson: *A Biographical Dictionary Of Film* (Andre Deutsch [UK], 1995)

Mark Twain: *Life On The Mississippi* (Airmont [USA], 1965)

Harriet Welchel (editor): *Josephine Baker And* La Revue Nègre (Harry N Abrams, Inc [USA], 1998)

Ean Wood: *Born To Swing* (Sanctuary [UK], 1996)

Ean Wood: *George Gershwin – His Life And Music* (Sanctuary [UK], 1996)

Index

also available from sanctuary publishing

JAMAICAN WARRIORS – REGGAE, ROOTS & CULTURE
Stephen Foehr ● £15 ● 1-86074-314-5

HIGH ART – A HISTORY OF THE PSYCHEDELIC POSTER
Ted Owen ● £20 ● 1-86074-236-X

COUNTRY ROADS – HOW COUNTRY CAME TO NASHVILLE
Brian Hinton ● £12.99 ● 1-86074-293-9

VISTA – THE PHOTOGRAPHY OF ANDY EARL
Andy Earl ● £27.50 ● 1-86074-296-3

THE UNCLOSED EYE – THE MUSIC PHOTOGRAPHY OF DAVID REDFERN
David Redfern ● £20 ● 1-86074-240-8

MAJOR TO MINOR – THE RISE AND FALL OF THE SONGWRITER
Mike Read ● £15 ● 1-86074-316-1

SNIFFIN' GLUE – THE ESSENTIAL PUNK ACCESSORY
Mark Perry ● £20 ● 1-86074-275-0

JONI MITCHELL – BOTH SIDES NOW
Brian Hinton ● £12.99 ● 1-86074-311-0

THE WAGNER LEGACY
Gottfried Wagner ● £12.99 ● 1-86074-251-3

EYE OF THE STORM – ALBUM GRAPHICS OF STORM THORGERSON
Storm Thorgerson ● £20 ● 1-86074-258-0

LET THEM ALL TALK – THE MUSIC OF ELVIS COSTELLO
Brian Hinton ● £12.99 ● 1-86074-196-7

NEIL FINN ONCE REMOVED
Neil Finn & Mark Smith ● £20 ● 1-86074-297-1

BORN UNDER THE SIGN OF JAZZ
Randi Hultin ● £12.99 ● 1-86074-252-1

MIND OVER MATTER – THE IMAGES OF PINK FLOYD
Storm Thorgerson ● £20 ● 1-86074-268-8

FOR MORE INFORMATION on titles from Sanctuary Publishing Limited visit our website at www.sanctuarypublishing.com or contact Sanctuary Publishing Limited, 32-36 Telford Way, London W3 7XS. Tel: +44 (0)20 8749 9171 Fax: +44 (0)20 8749 9685.

To order a title direct call our credit card hotline on **0800 731 0284** (UK only) or write to Sanctuary Direct, PO Box 2616, Great Dunmow, Essex CM6 1DH. International callers please ring +44 (0)20 8749 9171 or fax +44 (0)20 8749 9685. You can also order from our website www.sanctuarypublishing.com